FAREWELL SERMONS

OTHER PURITAN TITLES
FROM SOLID GROUND BOOKS

In addition to *Farewell Sermons* printed here, Solid Ground has reprinted the following Puritan titles:

THE WORKS OF THOMAS MANTON - 22 Volumes
The Baptist Confession of Faith and Catechism - Leather Bound
A Body of Divinity by James Ussher
A Christian's Present for All Seasons: Thoughts of Eminent Divines
The Christian Warfare by John Downame
Classic Puritan NT Commentary by John Trapp
Commentary on Hebrews by William Gouge, 2 Volumes
Commentary on Second Peter by Thomas Adams
The Communicant's Companion by Matthew Henry
Exposition of the Baptist Catechism by Benjamin Beddome
Exposition of the Epistle of Jude by William Jenkyn
Exposition of the Ten Commandments by Ezekiel Hopkins
Gospel Sonnets by Ralph Erskine
The Harmony of the Divine Attributes by William Bates
Heaven Upon Earth: Jesus, Best Friend in Worst Times by Janeway
The Marrow of True Justification by Benjamin Keach
The Redeemer's Tears Wept Over the Lost by John Howe
The Secret of Communion with God by Matthew Henry
A Short Explanation of Hebrews by David Dickson
The Travels of True Godliness by Benjamin Keach

Call us at 205-443-0311
Visit our web site at soild-ground-books.com

FAREWELL SERMONS

OF SOME OF

T<small>HE</small> M<small>OST</small> E<small>MINENT</small>

OF THE

NONC0NFORMIST MINISTERS

DELIVERED

AT THE PERIOD OF THEIR EJECTION
BY THE ACT OF UNIFORMITY IN AUGUST 1662

TO WHICH IS PREFIXED

A HISTORICAL AND BIOGRAPHICAL PREFACE

Then Peter and the other apostles answered and said,
"We ought to obey God rather than men."
Acts 5:29

S<small>OLID</small> G<small>ROUND</small> C<small>HRISTIAN</small> B<small>OOKS</small>
B<small>IRMINGHAM</small>, A<small>LABAMA</small> USA

Solid Ground Christian Books
6749 Remington Circle
Pelham AL 35124
205-443-0311
mike.sgcb@gmail.com
www.solid-ground-books.com

FAREWELL SERMONS
Of Some of the Most Eminent of the Non-Conformist Ministers Delivered at the Period of Their Ejection by the Act of Uniformity in August of 1662.

Taken from the 1992 edition by *Soli Deo Gloria* Publications, Ligonier, PA

Farewell Sermons was first published in 2 volumes in London in 1662. It was reprinted by Gale and Fenner, London in 1816.

First Solid Ground edition in June 2011

Cover design by Borgo Design
Contact them at borgogirl@bellsouth.net

ISBN- 978-159925-256-8

HISTORICAL

AND

BIOGRAPHICAL PREFACE.

THE season of religious intolerance is, we trust, passing away. The increase of knowledge has been marked by the diminution of bigotry; and the mighty convulsions which have for a series of sanguinary years shook the foundation of thrones, and led every man to examine by what principles his life was governed, and how far they were capable of sustaining him in the prospect of future, perhaps of greater calamities—have resulted not only in universal peace, but in general improvement. Institutions have of late sprung up which have produced the effect of making christians of different persuasions better acquainted with each other, and the stiffness of jealousy has relaxed into the interchanges of mutual friendship and conciliation. One great lesson at least we may venture to pronounce has been learned in Britain; namely, that different denominations may and ought to maintain their respective peculiarities of sentiment without cherishing a persecuting hostility against each other; and that no man is to be burnt as a heretic, because he aims to be a christian. This opinion indeed is held with some exceptions, for some fiery spirits are always to be found who imagine that their ecclesiastical pretensions can only be sustained by violence, and proved by the sword; but we speak of the *general feeling*. The wise and good attached to the hierarchy are disposed to censure those parts of their own public creed which display the essence of persecution, and shrink with pious abhorrence from antichristian anathemas. How far they are justified in still adhering to a system so manifestly corrupt in all its principal parts, must be left to the determination of their own consciences.

The satisfaction we feel, however, in the present anti-persecuting state of society, should not prevent our sympathizing recollections of ages past, nor render us the less disposed to do honor to those who suffered for righteousness' sake. The light they beamed amidst surrounding darkness cannot be too gratefully acknowledged, nor can their holy firmness in maintaining truth, by which they obtained the charter of our religious liberties, be too closely imitated. Although we do not expect another Bartholomew-day, or fresh edicts of proscription and banishment, let us remember the days of our forefathers, and study their principles.

Most of the sermons contained in this collection were delivered on the twenty-fourth of August, in the year 1662. On that day the act requiring a perfect conformity to the book of Common Prayer, and to the rites and ceremonies of the church took place: the effect of which enactment was the silencing of nearly *two thousand five hundred* ministers, the death of *three thousand* nonconformists, and the ruin of *sixty thousand* families. Such was the result of the restoration of Charles the Second of infamous memory.

To ascertain the spirit which actuated the ejected ministers, it is sufficient to refer to the following selection of their farewell sermons, which were delivered at the very moment they were agonizing under the fangs of persecution, but which discover nothing but a combination of christian graces. Bishop Burnet admits that " many of them were distinguished by their abilities and their zeal ;" and the celebrated Locke has remarked, " Bartholomew-day was fatal to our church and religion, by throwing out a very great number of worthy, learned, pious and orthodox divines."

Brief notices of those amongst them whose last discourses are preserved in this volume, will not be unacceptable to the pious reader.

EDMUND CALAMY, B. D. of Pembroke Hall, Cambridge, was born in February, 1600, and admitted to the university at the age of fifteen. He was well read in the different controversies; but especially in the holy scriptures, which he studied daily. He first held the living of St. Mary's, Swaffham, Norfolk, where he was very useful, then resided ten years at Bury St. Edmunds, Suffolk, then at Rochford in Essex, and finally removed to Aldermanbury in 1639. In 1659, he united with those who encouraged General Monk to restore the king, preached before parliament on the day previous to their voting his return, and was appointed with the other divines, who were sent over to him to Holland. After the restoration, he was made one of the chaplains in ordinary, and was often with his majesty. He refused a bishopric, because he could not have it on the terms of the king's declaration.

Mr. Calamy united with others of his brethren in presenting a petition for indulgence, and on that occasion made a speech intimating their fidelity to the king, but their deep sense of the treatment they had received. Soon afterwards he was imprisoned for an occasional sermon, which was alleged, but without evidence, to be seditious. The circumstance was a singular one: Mr. Calamy going to the church of Aldermanbury, with an intention to be a hearer only, the person expected to preach happened to fail. To prevent a disappointment, and through the importunity of the people present, he went up and preached on the subject of Eli's concern for the ark of God. For this he was committed to Newgate by a warrant from the Lord Mayor, as having violated the act of uniformity; but his majesty being informed of the numerous visitors who rushed to see him, and the great dissatisfaction this proceeding had excited, gave express orders soon afterwards for his release. Mr. Calamy's death was occasioned by his extreme grief at the fire of London.

THOMAS MANTON, D. D. of Wadham College, Oxford, was born in 1620, at Lawrence-Lydiard, Somersetshire. He was ordained at the age of twenty by Bishop Hall. His first settlement was at Stoke-Newington, about the year 1643, where he continued seven years, till he was presented with a living in Covent Garden. He was far from courting the favor of government; but the Protector made him one of his chaplains, and he belonged to the committee for trying ministers.

He was one of the commissioners to Charles II. at Breda, and instrumental in his restoration. He afterwards was imprisoned for his nonconformity. Dr. William Harris relates the following anecdote, in his memoirs. "Being to preach before the Lord Mayor, the court of Aldermen, &c. at St. Paul's, the Doctor chose a subject in which he had an opportunity of displaying his judgment and learning. He was heard with admiration and applause by the more intelligent part of the audience; but as he was returning from dinner with the Lord Mayor in the evening, a poor man following him, pulled him by the sleeve of his gown, and asked him if he were the gentleman that preached before the Lord Mayor. He replied, he was. "Sir," says he, "I came with hopes of getting some good to my soul, but I was greatly disappointed, for I could not understand a great deal of what you said; you were quite above me." The Doctor replied with tears, " Friend, if I did not give *you* a sermon, you have given *me* one, and by the grace of God, I will never play the fool to preach before my Lord Mayor in such a manner again." Dr. Manton took great pains with his sermons, so as sometimes to transcribe them more than once, and if one he had composed did not please him, he would sit up all Saturday night to make another. If a good thought came into his mind in the night, he would light his candle and sometimes write for an hour. He died Oct. 18th, 1677.

PREFACE. ix

Joseph Caryl, A. M. of Exeter College, Oxford, was born in London in 1602. He was preacher to the Honorable Society of Lincoln's Inn. In 1653, he was appointed one of the *triers* for ministers. He was sent by parliament to attend the king at Holmby-house, and was one of the commissioners in the treaty of the Isle of Wight. After his ejectment he raised a church near London-bridge, which at his death, Feb. 7th, 1673, consisted of one hundred and thirty-six communicants.

Thomas Case, A. M. of Christ-church, Oxford, was the son of Mr. Geo. Case, minister of Bockley, in Kent. He was the first that set up the *morning-exercise,* which proved a very useful lecture for many years. In 1660, he was one of the ministers deputed to wait on the king at the Hague, and in 1661, one of the commissioners at the Savoy. He died May 30, 1682.

William Jenkyn, A. M. of St. John's College, Cambridge, was born at Sudbury, 1612. Not satisfied to desist from the ministry, which he exercised in London, he preached after the act of uniformity in private, and upon the Oxford-act retired to his own house, at Langley, in Hertfordshire. Upon the indulgence in 1671, he returned to London, where he raised a numerous congregation in Jewin-street. He continued in his work till 1682, when the storm of persecution raged afresh; but he continued to preach whenever he could do it with sufficient secresy in various places. He was taken by a soldier on Sept. 2d, 1684, while spending a day in prayer with some eminent ministers who escaped, and was committed to Newgate, where he died Jan. 19th, 1685. A nobleman having heard of it, said to the king, " May it please your majesty Jenkyn has got his liberty."—" Aye!" he replied eagerly; " who gave it him?" The nobleman replied, " a greater than your majesty, the King of kings," with which the king seemed much struck.

RICHARD BAXTER was born Nov. 12th, 1615, and was pious from early childhood. He first preached at Dudley, then at Bridgenorth, afterwards at Kidderminster. " When he first came thither," says the Nonconformist's Memorial, " there might perhaps be a family in a street that worshipped God; but when he came away, there was not above a family on the side of a street, that did not do it. He had six hundred communicants; and there were but few families in the whole town, but what submitted to his private catechising, and personal conference."

PREFACE. xi

During the war he retired two years to Coventry, where he preached to the garrison and inhabitants. After the battle of Naseby, he became chaplain in Col. Whalley's regiment, but was separated from them on the very day in Feb. 1647, when they commenced their conspiracy against the parliament, and just before the battle of Triploe Heath. He once made a speech before Cromwell, in which he had the fortitude to say, " that the honest people of the land thought their ancient monarchy to be a blessing, and desired to know how and to whom they had forfeited it." When the king was restored he was made one of the chaplains in ordinary. He assisted at the conference at the Savoy, and drew up a reformed Liturgy. He was offered the bishopric of Hereford, but refused it. In 1665, he went during the plague into Buckinghamshire, when it was over, and returned to Acton, where he remained while the act against conventicles continued in force. Then he preached publicly, but was apprehended and committed to prison for six months. After the indulgence of 1672 he returned into the city. He was again apprehended, but preached in various places in London. In 1682, he was seized in his house—but through the interference of Dr. Cox, a physician, released, though his goods and even his bed were distrained upon. In

1684, he was seized again when scarcely able to stand. In the reign of James II. he was committed prisoner to the King's Bench for some passages in his paraphrase on the New Testament reflecting on the prelates of the church. He met with much insult on his trial. He lay in prison two years, but at length was pardoned. He lived to witness the glorious revolution by King William; and died Dec. 8th, 1691. During his last illness, his usual reply to any question respecting his health was, " almost well"—and sometimes " better than I deserve to be, but not so well as I hope to be."

THOMAS JACOMB, D. D. of Magdalen Hall, Oxford, was born at Melton Mowbray, Leicestershire. He came to London in 1647, and was received into the family of the Countess Dowager of Exeter as her chaplain, by whom he with other nonconformist ministers was supported after his ejectment. He possessed an amiable disposition, was of moderate principles, and eminently pious. His sermons were clear and solid. March 27th, 1687, he died in peace at the house of his patroness.

WILLIAM BATES, D. D. was the son of a physician, and born in November, 1625. At the return of Charles II. he might have been a dean, and afterwards been preferred to any bishopric in the kingdom upon condition of deserting his principles. He was an elegant preacher. Mr. Howe says of him, " I never knew any one more frequent or affectionate in the admiration of divine grace, upon all occasions, than he was, as none had a deeper sense of the impotence and depravity of human nature. Into what transports of admiration of the love of God, have I seen him break forth, when some things not immediately relating to practical godliness, had taken up great part of our time. How easy a step did he make it from earth to heaven! With what high flights of thought and affection was he wont to speak of the heavenly state! Even like a man much more akin to the other world than this. Let those who other visited him say, whether he did not usually send them away with somewhat that tended to better their spirits and quicken them in their way heavenwards." He died July 14th, 1699. In the latter part of his life, he exercised his ministry at *Hackney* with great success.

THOMAS WATSON, A. M. of Emanuel College, Cambridge, was a man of learning and a popular preacher. He had an eminent gift in prayer, and died suddenly in his closet in that engagement.

THOMAS LYE, A. M. of Wadham College, Oxford, was remarkable for his excellent method of catechising and instructing children. He died June 7th, 1684.

MATTHEW MEAD was appointed by Oliver Cromwell, to the care of the New Chapel, Shadwell, Jan. 22d, 1658, whence he was ejected for nonconformity in 1662. In the year 1674, the large meeting-house in Stepney was erected for him, the four pillars of which were presented to him by the states of Holland. He was the father of Richard Mead, the eminent physician.

MATTHEW NEWCOMEN, A. M. of St. John's College, Cambridge, was a member of the Westminster assembly, and one of the commissioners at the Savoy. He was fixed at Dedham till ejected in 1662, when he was invited to a church at Leyden which he accepted. He died of an epidemical fever in 1668 or 1669. Dr. Collinges says, " that he had had thirty years acquaintance with him, and never knew any that excelled him, as a minister in the pulpit, a disputant in the schools, or as a desirable companion."

THOMAS BROOKS was a very affecting and

useful preacher. He was for some time at St. Thomas Apostle, and about the year 1657, was chosen by the parishioners of St. Mary Magdalene. There he gathered a church of the congregational order. He died Sept. 27th, 1680.

John Collins was the son of a deacon of the church at Cambridge in New-England. When the act of uniformity took place, he was chaplain to General Monk, and afterwards became pastor of a church in London, where he was an eminent preacher. His death took place in 1687.

John Galpine was for some time a student in Exeter College, Oxford, during the reign of Cromwell, and afterwards at New-Inn. After the liberty by act of parliament he settled at Totness, where he died in Sept. 1698.

Lazarus Seaman, D. D. of Emanuel College, Cambridge, was born at Leicester, of mean extraction. He was soon obliged to leave college and seek subsistence by keeping a school. But he became master of Peter-house and vice-chancellor in 1653. In 1642, he was presented by Bishop Laud to Bread-street parish by order of parliament. He was a great divine and a very learned man.

He was one of the commissioners sent to Charles I. to the Isle of Wight. In Sept. 1675, he died.

GEORGE EVANKE appears from his Farewell Sermon to have been a man of ability. All the account we have of him is comprised in the title of that discourse, where he is stated to have been chaplain to Sir George Norwood, at Cleveland.

CONTENTS.

SERMON by Mr. CALAMY	- - - - -	page 1
——— Dr. MANTON	- - - - -	- 13
——— Mr. CARYL	- - - - -	- 29
——— Mr. CASE	- - - - - -	- 43
——— Mr. JENKIN	- - -	- 61
——— Mr. BAXTER	- - - - -	- 103
——— Dr. JACOMB	- - - - -	- 134
——— Dr. BATES	- - - - - -	- 156
——— Mr. WATSON	- - - - -	- 182
——— Mr. LYE	- - - - - -	- 223
——— Mr. MEDE	- - - - -	- 253
——— Mr. NEWCOMEN	- - - -	- 272
——— Mr. BROOKES	- - - - -	- 294
——— Mr. COLLINS	- - - - -	- 309
——— Mr. CALAMY	- - - - -	- 332
——— Mr. GASPINE	- - - - -	- 348
——— Dr. SEAMAN	- - - - -	- 397
——— Mr. EVANKE	- - - - -	- 412

SERMONS.

MR. CALAMY'S SERMON.

Preached August 17, 1662.

2 SAM. XXIV. 14.

And David said unto Gad, I am in a great strait; let us fall now into the hand of the Lord, (for his mercies are great) and let me not fall into the hand of man.

IN which words we have three parts:
I. David's great perplexity and distress, " I am in a great strait."
II. David's resolution.
1. Affirmative, " Let us fall into the hand of the Lord."
2. Negative, " Let me not fall into the hand of man."
III. We have the reasons of David's choice, " for the mercies of God are great." The mercies of wicked men are cruel; " therefore let me not fall into the hand of men:" but the mercies of God are many, and great; therefore " let us now fall into the hand of God."
1. For the first, that is, David's great distress, wherein we must speak—
1. To the distress itself: Then
2. To the person thus perplexed: " I am in a great strait;"
David a great man, David a godly man.

1. In the perplexity itself we shall consider,
1. The reality of this perplexity.
2. The greatness of it.

1. For the reality of it. After David had sinned in numbering the people, God sends the prophet Gad to him, and puts three things to his choice, as you may read in verse 12. God was determined to make David smart for numbering the people, but leaves it to David's liberty, whether he would have seven years famine, or three months to flee before his enemies, or three days pestilence. This was a posing question, and David had cause to be in a great strait, for these objects are not amiable in their own nature, they are objects to be avoided and declined; in the first view of them they seem to be equally miserable, therefore David had cause to say he was in a strait.

2. This perplexity was not only real, but exceeding great; "I am in a great strait;" and there were two things made this so great.

1. The greatness of the punishments proposed, famine, sword, and plague; these are the three besoms with which God sweeps mankind from off the earth; these are God's three iron whips, by which he chastiseth sinful man; these are the three arrows shot out of the quiver of God's wrath, for the punishment of man; they are, as one calleth them, *tonsuræ humani generis*. In Rev. vi. you shall read of four horses, when the four first seals were opened, a white horse, a red horse, a black horse, and a pale horse. After Christ had ridden on the white horse, propagating the gospel, then follows the red horse, a type of war; then the black horse, an hieroglyphic of famine; then the pale horse, the emblem of pestilence. Now God was resolved to ride on one of these horses, and David must chuse upon which God should ride: this is a great strait. Let me present David's lifting up his eyes to Heaven, and speaking to God thus, "O my God, what is this message thou hast sent me? thou offerest me three things: I am in a strait, I know

which to refuse, but which to chuse I know not. Shall the land of Canaan, a land flowing with milk and honey, shall this land endure seven years' famine, and be turned into a wilderness, and dispeopled? and shall I whose hands thou hast taught to fight, and whose fingers to war, shall I that have subdued all mine enemies, shall I in my old age, and all my captains, fly three months before our enemies, and be driven to caves and rocks to hide ourselves? O thou my God, who art my refuge, shall I and my people be a prey to the pestilence, that walketh in darkness and destruction, that walketh at noon-day? O my God, I know not what to do, I am in a great strait."

2. The second reason why this strait was so great, was, because of the guilt of sin that lay on David's spirit; for David knew that this severe message was the fruit of the sin he committed in numbering the people. But you will say, Why was it a sin in David to number the people? Moses had often numbered the people, three times, and it was not counted sin. Josephus answereth, the sin of David was, because he did not require the half shekel, which he was to have had from all that were numbered. Exod. xxx. 12, 13.

Others say he sinned in numbering all ages, whereas he was to number but from twenty years: but these are conjectural reasons. I conceive the sin of David was, because he did it without a lawful call, and for an unlawful end: *Sine causa legitima:* he sinned in the manner rather than in the matter; for there was no cause for him to number the people but curiosity, and no end but vain glory. "Go through all the tribes of Israel, and number the people, that I may know the number of my people," v. 2. David's heart was lifted up with pride, and creature-confidence: he begins to boast of the multitude of his people, and to trust in an arm of flesh: therefore God sends the prophet to David, to prick the bladder of his pride; as if God should say, I will teach you to number the people by lessening the number of your people.

Now the burthen of his sin did add much to the burthen of this heavy message: verse 13. "After David had numbered the people, his heart smote him:" the message smites him, and his heart smites him; "and he said, I have sinned greatly in that which I have done: now I beseech thee take away the iniquity of thy servant, for I have done very foolishly." If David had been to suffer this great punishment out of love to God, or for a good conscience, he would not have been so distracted. There are two sorts of straits in scripture; some suffer for God and a good conscience, and there are straits suffered for sin.

1. There are straits suffered for God and a good conscience, Heb. xi. 36, 37. Those martyrs there were driven to great straits; but these were straits for God and a good conscience, and these straits were the saints' greatest enlargements, they were so sweetened to them by the consolations and supportations of God's spirit, a prison was a paradise to them, Heb. x. 34. they look joyful at the spoiling of their goods, Acts v. 41. "They departed from the presence of the council, rejoicing, that they were counted worthy to suffer shame for his name." Straits for a good conscience are greatest enlargements, therefore St. Paul glorieth in his strait; "Paul a prisoner, &c."

2. There are straits suffered for sin, and these are envenomed by the guilt of sin: sin puts poison into all our distresses and perplexities. Now such was the strait into which David was now driven; it was a strait caused by sin, and that made it so unwelcome and uncomfortable: so that from hence I gather this observation:

> *Doctrine.* "That sin and iniquity brings persons and nations into marvellous labyrinths and perplexities; into true, real, and great molestations; and a man free from sin, is free in the midst of straits; a man guilty of sin, is in a strait in the midst of freedom."

After Adam had sinned in eating the forbidden fruit, the whole world was a prison to him; Paradise itself was an hell to him, he knew not where to hide himself from the presence of God. After that Cain had murdered his brother Abel, he was brought into such a strait, that he was afraid that every one that met him would slay him. Alas, poor Cain! how many was there then in the world? We read, but his father and mother, yet such was his distress, that he crieth out, every one that met him would slay him, Gen. iv. 14. Into what a strait did sin bring the old world? the deluge of sin, brought a deluge of water to drown them. Into what a strait did sin bring Sodom and Gomorrah? the fire of lust reigning in Sodom and Gomorrah, brought down fire from heaven to destroy them. Sin brings external, internal, and eternal straits upon persons and nations.

1. Sin brings external straits; sin brings famine, sword, and plague; sin brings agues and fevers, gout and stone, and all manner of diseases: yea, sin brings death itself, which is the wages of sin. Read Lev. xxvi. and Deut. xxiii. and you will see a black roll of curses, which were the fruit of sin. Sin brought Sion into Babylon; and when the Jews had murdered Christ, forty years after they were brought into that distress, when the city was besieged by Titus Vespasian, that they did eat one another, the mother did eat her child, that whereas David had a choice which of the three he would have, either famine, plague, or sword, the poor Jews had all three concatenated together in the siege. Sin brings all manner of external plagues.

2. Sin brings persons and nations into internal straits: sin brings soul-plagues, which are worse than bodily plagues: sin brings hardness of heart, blindness of mind, a spirit of slumber, a reprobate sense: sin brings a spiritual famine upon a land, it brings a famine of the word, Amos viii. 11. Sin causes God to take away the gospel from a people; sins brings internal plagues: sin awakens conscience, and fills it full of perplexities. Into what a state did sin drive Judas after he had betrayed Christ? Into what a state did sin drive Spira? St.

Paul gloried in his tribulations for God; but when he speaks of his sin, he crieth out, "O wretched man that I am, who shall deliver me from the body of this death?" David, a valiant man, when he speaks of sin, saith, "they are too heavy a burden for him to bear." "A wounded conscience who can bear?" saith the wise man.

3. Sin bringeth eternal straits. O the strait that a wicked man shall be brought into at the great and dreadful day of judgment, when all the world shall be on fire about him! when he shall call to the mountains to hide him, and to the rocks to cover him from the wrath of God; then will he cry out with David, "I am, O Lord, in a great strait." And when the wicked shall be condemned to hell, who can express the straits they then shall be in? "Bind them hand and foot, and cast them into everlasting darkness," Mat. xxv. When a wicked man shall be bound with everlasting chains of darkness, then he will cry out, "I am in a great strait." Consider what Dives said to Abraham; he desires that Lazarus might but dip the tip of his finger in water, and that he might cool his tongue, not his whole body, but his tongue; but that would not be granted.

It is impossible the tongue of man should set out the great straits the damned suffer in hell, both in regard of the greatness and everlastingness of them.

This is all I shall say for the explication.

Use 1. I chiefly aim at the application. Doth sin bring nations and persons into external, internal, and eternal straits? Then this sadly reproves those that chuse to commit sin to avoid perplexity. There are thousands in England guilty of this, that to avoid poverty, will lye, cheat, and cozen, and to gain an estate will sell God and a good conscience; and to avoid the loss of estate and imprisonment, will do any thing; they will be sure to be of that religion which is uppermost, be it what it will. Now give me leave this morning to speak three things to these sort of men, and O that my words might prevail with them!

1. Consider it is sin only that makes trouble deserve the name of trouble; for when we suffer for God's sake, or a good conscience, these troubles are so sweetened by the consolations of heaven, that they are no troubles at all: therefore in Queen Mary's days the martyrs wrote to their friends out of prison, " If you knew the comforts we have in prison, you would wish to be with us." " I am in prison before I am in prison," saith Mr. Sanders.

Famous is the story of the three children: they were in a great strait when cast into the fiery furnace: " Bind them hand and foot, and cast them into the furnace;" but when they were there, they were unbound, Dan. iii. 25. Saith Nebuchadnezzar, " Did we not cast three men bound into the midst of the fire? and lo I see four men loose, walking in the midst of the fire, and the form of the fourth is like the Son of God." I have often told you, when three are cast into the fire for a good conscience, God will make the fourth: therefore, I say, straits and sufferings for God are not worth the name of straits. David was often driven into straits, 1 Sam. xxx. 6. he was sore distressed when his town was burnt, and his wives and children taken captives by the Amalekites: aye, but that was a distress of danger, not of sin; therefore he encouraged himself in the Lord his God. Jehoshaphat was in a great strait, 2 Chron. xx. 12. " We know not what to do," saith he; this was a strait of danger, not caused by his sin: and God quickly delivered him: but the strait that David was in, was caused by his sin, and that made it so bitter. I am loth to enlarge here: St. Paul was in a great strait, Phil. iii. 23. but this was a blessed strait, an evangelical strait. Saith St. Chrysostome, " He knew not whether to die for his own sake, or to live for the church's sake, were best:" he was willing to adjourn his going to heaven for the good of the people of God. Nay, Christ was in a strait, Luke xii. 15. " I have a baptism to be baptized withal, and how am I straitened till it be accomplished ?" I am to shed my blood for my elect; this is the baptism he speaks of.

This was a strait of dear affection to the elect of God: all these were blessed straits: but now straits caused by sin, these are imbittered and envenomed by the guilt of sin, and sense of God's wrath. It is sin that maketh straits deserve the name of straits; therefore you are spiritually mad that commit sin to avoid straits.

2. There is more evil in the least sin, than in the greatest outward calamity whatsoever: this the world will not believe; therefore St. Austin saith, "That a man ought not to tell a lie, though he might save all the world from hell: for there is more evil in one lie, than there is good in the salvation of all the world." I have often told you the story of St. Austin: saith he, " If hell were on one side, and sin on the other, and I must chuse one, I would chuse hell rather than sin: for God is the author of hell, but it is blasphemy to say he is the author of sin." There is a famous story of Charles the Ninth, king of France, he sent a message to the prince of Conde, a zealous protestant: gives him three things to chuse, either to go to mass, or to be put to death, or to suffer banishment all his life long: saith he, *Primum, Deo juvante, nunquam eligo :* " The first (God helping) I will never chuse: I abhor the idolatry of the mass; but for the two others, I leave it to the choice of the king to do as he pleases: there is more evil in the least sin, than the greatest misery."

3. The third thing I would have you consider, that whosoever goeth out of God's way to avoid danger, shall certainly meet with greater danger. Balaam went out of God's way, Numb. xxii. 22. and God sent an angel with a drawn sword, and he riding upon an ass, verse 26. the angel stood in a narrow place, where was no way to go from the right hand or from the left: if his ass had not fallen under him, he had been run through by the sword of the angel. Jonah, for fear of the king of Nineveh,

went out of God's way, but he met with a mighty tempest, he met with a whale. What do you do when you commit sin? you make way to be cast into the eternal prison of hell; you destroy your precious souls, to save your perishing bodies.

Use 2. If sin be the father and mother of all perplexity and distresses, then I beseech you, let us above all things in the world abhor sin: all the curses of the Bible are all due only to a sinner; and all the curses not named in the Bible: for that is observable, Deut. xxviii. 36. every plague that is not written in the book shall light upon him: there are strange punishments to the workers of iniquity, Job xxxi. 3. Is not destruction to the wicked, a strange punishment to the workers of iniquity? since it bringeth the sinner to little ease: little ease at death, little ease at the day of judgment, and little ease in hell, tribulation and anguish: the word in the Greek is ἀπαλλοτρίωσις, little ease to every soul that doth iniquity. O my beloved, will you promise me to look upon sin, and consider it in all its woeful consequence, as the father, mother, and womb, out of which come external, eternal, and internal straits? more particularly there are twelve sins I especially command you to take heed of and avoid.

1. Take heed of covetousness: the love of the world will pierce you through with many sorrows? the love of money is the root of all evil; the love of the world drowns men in perdition.

2. Take heed of the sin of pride; into what a woeful strait did pride bring Haman! God crossed him in what he most desired; God made him hold the stirrup, while Mordecai rode in triumph; and God hanged him on the gallows which he had made for Mordecai.

3. Take heed of drunkenness; look not on the wine when it gives its colour in the cup, &c. Drunkenness will bring you into snares, it will bite like a serpent, and sting like an adder.

4. Take heed of disobedience and rebellion against the

commandments of God; it brought Jonah to the three nights and three days in the whale's belly.

5. Take heed of fornication and adultery, and all uncleanness; this brought Samson to a woeful strait; this brought David and Solomon into great perplexity.

6. Take heed of oppression, and all acts of injustice; this brought Ahab into great straits, insomuch that the dogs licked his blood.

7. Take heed of unnecessary familiarity with wicked men: this brought Jehoshaphat into a great strait.

8. Take heed of mis-using the prophets of God; this made God destroy the children of Israel without remedy. 2 Chron. xxxvi. 15, 16.

9. Take heed of coming profanely to the Lord's table: this brought the church of Corinth into great distress, insomuch as the apostle saith, "For this cause many among you are sick, and many weak, and many fallen asleep."

10. Take heed of loathing the manna of your souls; this brought the children of Israel into woeful misery, that God destroyed all their carcases in the wilderness, save Joshua and Caleb.

Take heed of slighting the gospel; this brought Queen Mary's persecution, and many godly and learned men fled for religion's sake out of the land; and unfruitfulness under the gospel in King Edward the Sixth's time, brought the persecution in Queen Mary's time.

11. Take heed of losing your first love; that makes God threaten to take away his candlestick.

12. Take heed of profaning the Christian sabbath, which is much profaned every where; a day that Christ by his resurrection from the dead hath consecrated to be kept holy to God. Certainly if the Jews were so severely punished for breaking the sabbath, which was set apart in memory of the creation, surely God will severely punish those that break the sabbath, set apart in

memory of Christ's resurrection. May be some will say, I have committed many of these sins, but am not brought into any strait. Remember, it was nine months after David had numbered the people before he was in this strait; but as sure as God is in heaven, sin will bring straits sooner or later; though one sin a hundred years, yet shall he be accursed; may be thy prosperity makes way for thy damnation; and this is thy greatest distress, that thou goest on in sin and prosperity.

Use 3. If sin bringeth a nation into marvellous labyrinths, learn what great cause we have to fear that God shall bring this nation into great distress, because of the great abominations that are committed in the midst of it. Our king and sovereign was in a great strait in the days of his banishment, but God hath delivered him. God hath delivered this nation out of great straits; but alas, we requite God evil for good, and instead of repenting of old sins, we commit new sins. I am told there are new oaths invented, oaths not fit to be named in any place, much less here. Certainly the drunkenness and adultery, the oppression and injustice, the bribery and sabbath-breaking, the vain and wicked swearing and forswearing, this nation is guilty of, must of necessity provoke God to say of us, as he did of them in Jer. xv. 29. "Shall I not visit for these things, saith the Lord? Shall not my soul be avenged on such a nation as this?" God will not only punish us, but be avenged on us. There is no way to avoid a national desolation but by a national reformation.

Lastly, Learn what cause you of this congregation and parish, have to expect that God should bring you into great straits, because of your great unthankfulness and unfruitfulness under the means of grace, you that have so long enjoyed the gospel; you have had the gospel in this place in great abundance; Dr. Taylor he served an apprenticeship in this place; Dr. Stoughton served another apprenticeship, and I through divine mercy, have served three apprenticeships and half another amongst you; you have had the spirit of God seven and thirty years in the faithful ministry of the word, knocking at the door of your hearts, but many of you have hardened your hearts. Are there not some of you, I only put the question, that begin to loath the manna of your souls, and to look back towards Egypt again? Are there not some of you have itching ears, and would fain have preachers that would feed you with dainty phrases, and begin not to care for a minister that unrips your consciences, speaks to your hearts and souls, and would force you into heaven by frighting you out of your sins? Are there not some of you, that by often hearing sermons, are become sermon-proof, that know how to sleep and scoff away sermons? I should be glad to say, there are but few such; but the Lord knoweth there are too many that by long preaching, get little good by preaching, insomuch that I have often said it, and say it now again, there is hardly any way to raise the price of the gospel-ministry, but by the want of it: And that I may not flatter you, you have not profited under the means you have enjoyed, therefore you may justly expect God may bring you into a strait, and take away the gospel from you: God may justly take away your ministers by death, or other ways. Have you not lost your first love? Why did God take away the gospel from the church of Ephesus, but because they lost their first love? Are you not like the church of Laodicea, that was neither hot nor cold? therefore God may justly spew you out of his mouth. What God will do with you I know not; a few weeks will determine: God can make a great change in a little time; we leave all to God; but in the mean time let me commend one text of scripture to you, Jer. xiii. 16; "Give glory to the Lord your God, before he cause darkness, and before your feet stumble upon the dark mountains, and while ye look for light, he turn it into the shadow of death, and make it gross darkness." Verse 17. "But if you will not hear it, my soul shall weep in secret places for your pride, and mine eyes shall weep sore, and run down with tears, because the Lord's flock is carried away captive" Give glory to God by confessing and repenting of your sins, by humbling your souls before the Lord, before darkness come, and who knoweth but this may prevent darkness?

DR. MANTON's SERMON.
Preached August 17, 1662.

HEBREWS XII. 1.

Wherefore, seeing we are compassed about with so great a cloud of witnesses, let us lay aside every weight, and the sin which doth so easily beset us; and let us run with patience the race that is set before us.

IN the former chapter you have a spiritual chronicle, or a catalogue of the Lord's worthies, and all the eminent effects of their faith; and now the apostle comes to make use of this history, that he had produced through so many successions of ages of all the holy men of God that excelled in faith. "Wherefore seeing we are compassed about with so great a cloud of witnesses, &c."

The text is wholly horatory. In it observe,

I. The premises, or principle the apostle worketh upon, " Seeing we are compassed about with, &c."

II. The practical inferences which are deduced from thence, and they are two—

1. One concerning the private part of our duty, " let us lay aside every weight, &c." There is something external and without, like to clog us in our way to heaven, " every weight;" and something within that will hinder and trouble us within; therefore he saith, "and the sin which doth so easily beset us."

2. Here is the positive part, " let us run with patience the race that is set before us." There's motion, (run)

the manner (with patience) the stage or way (the race that is set before us.)

My purpose is to give you some brief thoughts upon this useful and practical inference of the apostle, from the history of the faithful before recorded, therefore I will sum up the whole text in this point.

Doct. "The people of God that have such a multitude of examples of holy men and women set before them, should prepare themselves to run the spiritual race with more patience and cheerfulness."

There are two things in this doctrine, the encouragement and the duty. I shall open both with respect to the circumstances of the text.

First, the encouragement, a multitude of examples, or, as in the text, " seeing we are compassed about with so great a cloud of witnesses," mark here are "witnesses, a great cloud of witnesses," and these "compassing us round about."

First, Here are " witnesses." By that term we are to understand those worthy saints mentioned and reckoned up in the former chapter, Abel, Enoch, Noah, Abraham, Moses, &c. All the saints of God that have had experience of the goodness of his providence to them, and the fulfilling of his promises, they are called " witnesses;" why? because they depose a testimony for God, and speak to future generations to be constant, as they were, that they might receive the like reward. This witness was partly in their faith, and partly in the fruit of their faith.

1. They witnessed by their faith, John iii. 33. " He that hath received his testimony, hath set to his seal that God is true." A man that hath soundly digested the promises, that expresses his faith by cheerfulness and patience under all difficulties, troubles, delays, and those sundry trials that he meets with, he gives it under hand and seal, proclaims it to the world that he hath to do with the true God. And

2. They witnessed in the fruits of their faith, as they

give us an instance of God's fidelity towards them that faithfully adhere to, and firmly believe in his promises; so it is said, Heb. vi. 12. "Be not slothful, but followers of them who through faith and patience inherit the promises." Let faith but set patience a work, do but hold out a little while with God, and you may learn by the example of all those holy men; we shall inherit the promises, they shall be made good to a tittle, and not one thing fail of all that the Lord hath spoken, as those holy men were exercised and tossed to and fro, but it succeeded well with them at the last. O then let us hearken to the deposition of these worthy witnesses that are recorded in the scripture, and with such an invincible resolution as theirs was, let us hold out our course towards true happiness. If we do not, they that are now propounded as witnesses to us, will at the day of judgment be produced as witnesses against us. And pray also let us remember that we are to continue and keep afoot that testimony to succeeding generations: for not only the prophets and holy men of God, were God's witnesses, but all God's people also are his witnesses, Isai. xliii. 10. by their faith, patience, diligence, constancy and cheerfulness under afflictions, they are to give it under hand and seal to the world, that God is a true and faithful God. But now, if we either by our sinful walking, or by our drooping discouragements, discredit Christ and his profession, then we are witnesses against him, we deny that religion which we would seem to profess and cry up. Tit. i. 16. "They profess they know God, but in works they deny him;" and the more dangerous, because deeds are more deliberate than words, and so a greater evidence of what we think in our hearts. If we by drooping discouragements and sinful walking discredit religion, we deny it, and do in effect put the lie upon Christ. Therefore let us remember they were witnesses, and so must we.

Secondly, By a figurative speech they are called a "cloud, having a cloud of witnesses;" why so? I might trouble you with many conceits interpreters have had of this word " cloud ;" say some, because of the raisedness of their spirits, because clouds fly aloft: " clouds," for the fruitfulness of their doctrine, as clouds send down fruitful showers upon the earth ; and " clouds," because they cool and cover us from the heat; so some would gloss for our comfort: others with more judgment say, a " cloud," with allusion to the " pillar of cloud" which conducted the Israelites to Canaan ; yet neither doth this come up fully to the scope of the apostle; for the apostle speaks not of a cloud that goes before us, but of a " cloud that compasseth us round about," and therefore a cloud; the reason why it is called so, is the number and multitude of those witnesses, as a cloud is made up of a multitude of vapours gathered together, and condensed into one body : and so the expression is often used, Ezek. xxxviii. 9. " Thou shalt be like a cloud to cover the land," &c. noting the increase of the people when God would restore them, the multitude of converts; and so in profane authors, Livy hath such an expression, an army of men is called a cloud. But this is enough to shew the intent of this expression, that there are a multitude, a very great number: though the godly comparatively, and with respect to the wicked, are a few, yet considered in themselves, they are a great number; for, if the martyrs, and those glorious instances of heroic faith, and that under the Old Testament, when God's interest was more confined to one people, if there were such a church then, of so great a number, what will the whole church of the Old and New Testament be, when we shall meet together in Heaven? We are often discouraged with the paucity of professors, and are apt to think ourselves to be " left alone," 1 Kings xix. 10. But let us remember " there is a cloud of witnesses," we are not solitary now, and certainly we shall not want company when we come to heaven, " To the innumerable company," &c.

Again, it meets with an ordinary and strong temptation which Satan suggests to the heart of the godly, that they are singular and matchless in their afflictions, that none of the people of God have ever undergone such difficulties as they are exposed unto; and this makes them question their father's affections, and put themselves out of the number of his children. If but all these things are accomplished in the saints of God before you, here is a " cloud of witnesses" that have been exercised and tried to purpose, 1 Pet. iv. 9. They are troubled with a busy devil, a naughty world, a corrupt heart, all have had their trial from God's correcting hand. The same afflictions are accomplished in your brethren, that are in the world. So that we have many fellows, our lot is no harder than the saints of God that have gone before us, for there is a cloud of witnesses.

3. Observe, the apostle calls it a "cloud that compasses us round about," i. e. We have instances for every trial, temptation, duty, that we are put upon. Here we have examples of those that have fulfilled the commands of Christ on this side with an undaunted courage, and the examples of those that have borne the cross of Christ with an invincible patience. Here we have examples of those that have conquered right-hand temptations, that have despised the delights of the world; and there are those that have conquered left-hand temptations, that have not been broken and affrighted with the terrors of the world. All the saints of God have trodden that way; the same paths wherein we are to walk after them. We cannot look this way or that way, but we have instances of faith, confidence in God, and patience; "we are compassed about," &c. In short, here lies the encouragement that Christians should propound to themselves:

1. That there are examples. Christians of latter times have more to answer for their infidelity, than those of former ages. They that first believed the promises, believed without such a cloud of witnesses, or multitude of examples. Many have gone before us that have bro-

ken the ice, and that found good success from their own experience; they have commended God to us, as a true and faithful God, and will not you go on? When Jonathan and his armour-bearer climbed up the rocks of the Philistines, then the people were encouraged to go up after: so here are some that have gone before you, and it hath succeeded well with them.

2. These examples are many. Not one or two that might be supposed to be singularly assisted, and to have eminent prerogatives above the rest of their brethren, but many in every age; a whole cloud of them.

3. There are examples of many rare and excellent men, the best that ever lived under heaven. Take, my brethren, the prophets for an example, &c. Jam. v. 10.

4. They are propounded to us, not for their words only, and for their profession, but for their deeds, for their bitter sufferings; and they abundantly manifest to us, that there is nothing impossible in our duty, nor any thing so difficult but may be overcome, through Christ's strength enabling us. They all had the same nature we have; they were of the like passion with us, flesh and blood as we are, of the same relations and concernments; and then on the other side we have the same cause with them, the same recompence of reward to encourage us, the same God and Saviour to recompence us. He suffered for us as well as for them; therefore we should follow in their steps, and hold fast our confidence to the end, for they have shewed us, that poverty, reproaches, death itself, and all those things that would look harsh, and with a ghastly aspect upon the eyes of the world, are not such evils but that a believer may rejoice in them, and triumph over them. I say, they have shewed the blandishments of the world have not such a charm, but they may be renounced without any loss of considerable joy and contentment, and that the duties of christianity are not so hard, but that a little waiting upon God will bring in grace enough to perform them; therefore, saith the apostle, " Seeing we have a cloud of wit-

nesses, let us lay aside," &c. And so I come to the encouragement, to the

Second thing, and that is the duty here pressed. 1. Here is the privative. 2. The positive part of our duty: here is mortification and vivification. Mortification, " Let us lay aside," &c. Vivification, " Let us run with patience," &c. In both the branches he alludes to terms proper to races. In a race you know men strip themselves of their clothes, and whatever is burdensome and heavy, that they may be the more light of foot; and so the apostle bids us lay aside every weight; and they do withal diet themselves, that they might have no clog from within, 1 Cor. ix. 25. " Every man that striveth for the mastery, is temperate in all things;" i. e. They took care that they did not clog and indispose themselves for the race they were to run: but they verily run only for a corruptible crown, we for a crown that is incorruptible and glorious. So according to this double practice of races, we are to cast aside every weight from without, &c. So here's a double object, laying aside every weight, and of sin, there's *onus externum*, the weight without, that presses us down, and hinders our speed; and then there's *impedimentum internum*, there's sin, that which weakens within. By reason of the former we make little speed; by reason of the latter we are often interrupted; and therefore we must do as they, that they might be swift and expedite, " lay aside every weight," and be more " temperate in all things." Herein a runner in a race differs from a traveller. A traveller strengthens himself for his journey as well as he can, his clothes on, sometimes carries a great burden with him; but a runner of a race makes himself as light as he can. But to come more particularly to the words.

First, " Lay aside every weight." By weight is meant those things that burden the soul, and make our heavenly progress more tedious and cumbersome: and by weight is meant, I think, the delights and cares of the world, the multitude of secular business, all our earthly contentment and affairs, so far as they are a burden to us, hinder us in our way to heaven; these must all be put off, Luke xxi. 3, 4, saith Christ: "Take heed to yourselves, lest at any time your hearts be overcharged with surfeiting and drunkenness, and cares of this life," &c. The heart that is depressed cannot be so free for God, and the offices of our heavenly calling, when we give way to "surfeiting, drunkenness, and cares of this world."

1. The heart may be overcharged with the delights of the world; surfeiting and drunkenness must not be taken in the gross notion; you must not think of reeling, vomiting, as if to avoid these were a full compliance with Christ's direction; the heart may be overcharged when the stomach is not. There is a dry drunkenness, and a more refined surfeiting, and that is when the heart grows weary, unfit for prayer, relishes not the things of the Spirit, when the delights of the flesh clog the wheel, abate that vigour and cheerfulness that we should shew forth in the worship of God and holy actions, when the delights of the flesh withdraw us from that watchfulness and diligence that is necessary in taking care of our souls, then the heart is overcharged. Voluptous living is a great sin, it choaks the seed of piety so soon as planted in the heart, so that they can bring nothing to perfection; it brings a brawn and a deadness upon the conscience and affections; there is nothing hardens the heart as much as the softness of carnal pleasure, Jude xix. "Sensual, having not the spirit." Sensuality quenches our natural bravery and briskness of spirit that becomes a man; much more doth it hinder the sublime operations of the spirit of God. Well, then, remember Christians, you are not only travellers by the way, but runners in a race: if we were to speak to you only under the notion of travellers in a way, this were enough to wean you from the delights of the flesh, 1 Pet. ii. 11, "As strangers and pilgrims, abstain from fleshly lusts which war against the soul." The more you indulge these fleshly lusts, the more you hearten and strengthen the great enemy of your souls, and starve

the better parts; but you are as runners in a race: by this metaphor the duty is more bound upon you, much more should you beat down the body, and keep it in subjection. The Apostle hath a notable word, 1 Cor. ix. 27, "I keep under my body, and bring it in subjection," &c. I beat down my body; you must either keep under pleasures, or pleasures will keep you under; for a man is soon brought under the power, dominion, and tyranny of evil customs, and some brutish pleasure, by indulging the lusts of the flesh, 1 Cor. vi. 12. Be but a little addicted to any one thing, and you are brought under the power of it; the flesh waxes wanton and imperious, and a slavery grows upon you by degrees: the more you cocker carnal affections, the more they increase upon you; and therefore you must hold the reins hard; exercise a powerful restraint. Solomon, in his Penitentials, gives us an account of his own folly; and how fearfully he was corrupted this way, Eccles. ii. 20, "Whatsoever mine eyes desired, I kept not from them, I withheld not my heart from any joy," &c. This was that which brought him to such a lawless excess, and at length to fall off from God. When we give nature the full swing, and use pleasure with too free a license, the heart is insensibly corrupted, and the necessities of life are turned into diseases, and all that you do, it is but in compliance with your lusts; your eating and drinking is but a meat-offering and drink-offering to lusts and carnal appetites. I remember Solomon saith, Prov. xxix. 21, "He that delicately bringeth up his servant from a child, shall have him become his son at length;" *i. e.* allow a servant too much liberty, and he will no more know his condition, but grow contemptuous, bold, and troublesome: so it is here, we are all the worse for license; natural desires, unless they feel fetters and prudent restraints, grow unruly and excessive. And therefore it is good to abate the liberty of the flesh, that the body may be a servant, and not a master. When you deny yourselves in nothing, but satisfy every vain appetite, a custom grows upon the soul, and intemperance proves a trade, and an habitual distemper, so that you cannot when you would, upon prudent and pious respects, refrain and command your desires; and therefore it is good sometimes to thwart and vex the flesh, as David poured out the water of Bethlehem that he longed for, 2 Sam. xxiii. 17. Not to deny ourselves in what we affect and cover, lust grows into a wanton, and bold, and imperious, and so prescribes upon us, " and we are brought under the power of these things."

2. The business and cares of this world; for these immoderately followed, and not in obedience to God, are a sore burden, and make the soul heavy, and allow no time and strength for God and his service, and those happy opportunities of private communion with him, when we are incumbered with much service, we neglect that " one thing necessary," Luke x. 42. And therefore Christians must take heed that the lean kine do not devour the fat; that Sarah be not thrown out of doors, instead of Hagar; that religion be not thrust to the walls, which should be our prime and chief business, while every business hath its time and course. The Scriptures, knowing the proneness of our hearts to temporal things, deal with us as we do with a crooked stick, we bend it so much the other way, and therefore sometimes they forbid necessary labour, John vi. 28, " Labour not for the meat which perisheth," &c. the meaning is, not chiefly; but it bends the stick another way, " set not your affections on the things of the earth:" a man must have some kind of affection to his work here below; but we had need to be bent the other way: We may gather this from this precept, it is better encroach upon the world, than the world should encroach upon godliness. In short, things are a burden and clog to us, according as our delight and scope is, if the pomp and increase of the world be our end and scope, then religion will be looked upon as a burden, that will be a weight, and all duties of godliness as a melancholy interruption, as they, Amos ii. 8, " When

will the Sabbath be over?" The exercise of godliness will be a troublesome thing, and we shall go about the work of religion as if we went about it not. But, on the other side, if heaven and heavenly things be our scope, then the world is a burthen, and then we shall use it in the way, but not abusing, as taking up our rest here, 1 Cor. vi. 31, 32. Man hath a body and soul, and he doth provide for both, but for one in subordination; the soul is the chief, and therefore we must not look after the interests and concernments of the bodily life as to forget the interests of the soul, or to neglect them. Many will not so grossly idolize present things as to renounce things to come; aye, but they so often follow the things of the world, that they neglect their eternal concernments. The happiness of a people is in communion with God, and therefore that must be looked after; we must take heed that the cares of the world have not such a hand and power over us as either to divert us from, or unfit us for these higher and nobler pursuits, the enjoyments of God in Christ. This is the first thing the apostle speaks to these spiritual racers, to lay aside every weight, that is the delights of the flesh and the cares of the world.

Secondly, The next thing to be laid aside is sin, which doth so easily beset us. As we must guard against things without, so we must mortify our corrupt inclinations within: or else, it will soon make us weary of our heavenly race, or faint in it. Sin, you know, is two-fold, original and actual. Actual sin is not meant primarily, for that is not *peccatum agens*, the sin that easily besets us, but *peccatum transiens*, the sin that passes from us; and original sin is that which is emphatically called sin, Rom. vii. 8. Now this original corruption may be considered as merely native, or as acquired and improved into evil customs and habits: for according to men's tempers and constitutions, as they are severally disposed, so by the corruption of nature they are inclined to one sin more than another; as the channel is cut, so corrupt nature finds a vent and issue: in every man there is some predominant sin, and in every regenerate person some relics of that sin, from whence is the greatest danger of his soul: thus David speaks of his iniquity, Psal. xviii. 23. Well then, this is that sin that doth easily beset us: original sin improved into some tyranny or evil custom, which doth increase and prevail upon us more and more. Now this is said (easily beset us) for three reasons: partly because it hath a great power and restraint over us, and implies the whole man, the members, the body, the faculties of the soul; so great an interest hath it acquired in our affections, it doth easily beset us, it hath great power and command over us. Partly, because it sticks so close, that we cannot by our own strength lay it aside, Jer. xiii. 23. " Can the Ethiopian change his skin, or the leopard his spots?" &c. A man can as soon change his skin as lay aside his customs, that are so deeply engraven as the blackness of an Ethiopian, or the spots of a leopard. And partly because it mingles itself with all our motions and actions, Rom. vii. 21, &c. It easily besets us; it is present with us, it impels us, and solicits us, and draws us to sin further and further, and doth make us negligent in what is God's. We cannot do or speak any thing, but it will infest us in all our duties of piety, charity, justice; on every side it is interposing, vexing, thwarting the motions of the Spirit, and so abates our strength, vigour, and agility, and retards our course towards heaven and glory; therefore lay aside, as every weight, so every sin, &c.

Quest. Now what is it to lay aside? or how can we lay aside, since sin sticks so close to us, and is engraven in our natures?

Answ. Certainly, something may be done by us; for this is every where pressed as our duty, Eph. iv. 22: " Put off the old man;" and 1 Pet. ii. 11, we may put it off more and more, though we cannot lay it aside. Then we are said " to lay aside the sin that so easily besets us," when we prevent and break the dominion of it, that it shall not " reign over us," Rom. vi. 12. " Let not sin reign," &c. Though it dwells in us, lives in us, and works in us, yet it should not overcome us, and bring us into bondage, and so it will not be imputed to our condemnation; and at length when the soul shall be separated from the body, we shall be wholly free from it.

Quest. Aye, but what must we do that we may so repress it? (the question returns,) that we may break the dominion of it?

Answ. I answer, this is the work of the Spirit of God. But we must know, the Spirit of God doth work the work of mortification two ways: by regeneration, and after regeneration. By regeneration; and so he doth immediately, without any co-operation of ours, mortify the deeds of sin, gives sin its death-wound; that which is left, is a thing mortified, is broken. The Scripture often speaks of this first work of regeneration, Rom. vi. 6; Colos. ii. 11. First, when we are planted into Christ, then we put off the body of sin; and though it doth not presently die, yet it is weakend, that it cannot reign, though it be not destroyed.

2. After regeneration, the Spirit doth more and more destroy sin, the relics of sin, this crucified body of sin, till it dieth wholly away. This he doth in us, but not without us, Rom. viii. 13: "Through the Spirit mortify the deeds of the body." Not the Spirit without us, nor we without the Spirit; but "ye through the Spirit." -- What is then required of us?

1. Seriously purpose not to sin, and promise to God to yield him unfeigned obedience. Especially should we make this promise in the use of those solemn rites by which the covenant between God and us is confirmed. Take up a solemn purpose not to grieve the Spirit, nor to break his law, Psal. cxix. 106: "I have sworn, and I will perform it, that I will keep thy righteous judgments." This purpose of heart is the root of all good actions; therefore, in the confidence of God's help, in the sense of thy own weakness, Psal. cxix. 32, we cannot lay wagers upon our own strength, yet it is our duty

to engage our hearts to God. To sin against the light of our own conscience and illumination of the Spirit, and the chastening and instruction of our own reins, that aggravates our sin: but to sin against, and besides our fixed purpose of not sinning, that lightens sin, for then it is a sin of weakness and infirmity, not of wilfulness and malice; and then we can say, as Paul, Rom. vii. 19, when the heart is fixedly bent towards God, "The evil which I would not, that do I." Two ways may we be said to sin against purpose; either when we are overborne besides our purpose, or our purpose still remains to please God: as, when the water breaks over the bank, the bank remaining, in such a case the fault is not in the bank, but in the violence of the flood. Or, 2, when we break off our purpose, or consent to do evil, as when we cut through the band, the water may easily make through. There's a great deal of difference between sin dwelling in us, and sin entertained by us; between sin remaining, and sin reserved. When you have a firm purpose against all sin, there is sin remaining; but it is not reserved, it is not kept and allowed.

2. Watch over thyself with a holy suspicion, because thou hast sin within thee, that doth easily beset thee; therefore "consider thy ways," Psalm cix. 59; "Guard thy senses," Job xxxi. 1; but above all, "keep thy heart," Prov. iv. 23. Conscience must stand porter at the door, and examine what comes in and what goes out. Watch over the stratagems of Satan, and seducing motions of thy own heart.

3. Resist and oppose strongly against the first risings of the flesh, and the tickling and pleasing motions of sin that doth easily beset us, when it doth entice us away from God, or do any thing that is unseemly, and contrary unto the duties of our heavenly calling. O remember we are not debtors to the flesh. Rom. viii. 20. Thou art tied to the Lord by all obligations and indulgences, therefore break the force of sin by a serious resistance; check it, and let thy soul rise up in indignation against it. My business is not to pleasure the flesh, but to please the Lord.

4. Bewail thy involuntary lapses and falls with penitential tears, as "Peter went out and wept bitterly," Matt. xxvi. 57. Godly sorrow is of great use for laying aside of sin, as salt potions kill worms. When children are troubled with worms, we give them salt potions; so these bitter penitential tears are the means God hath appointed to mortify sin. That is the reason the Apostle saith, 2 Cor. vii. 10, "Godly sorrow worketh repentance to salvation, not to be repented of." It is not only a part of repentance, but worketh preserving, durable resolutions, a walking closely with God. It is a means God hath blessed to this end and purpose.

5. Recover from thy falls, renew thy combat, as Israel, when they were overcome in battle, they would try it again and again, Judg. xx. 28. Take heed of ceasing for the present, for though thy enemy seems to prevail, though the flesh seems to prevail against the spirit in the battle, yet thou shalt have the best of it in the war; by the power of grace thou shalt have the victory.

Thus I have gone over the privative part of our duty, "Let us lay aside every weight, and the sin that doth so easily beset us." I should have come to the positive, "Let us run with patience the race that is set before us:" there is the duty, "Let us run the race that is set before us;" and there is the manner of the duty, "Let us run with patience." I should have shown you, that a Christian's life is like a race from earth to heaven, in a way of holiness and exercise of grace. This race it continues as long as we continue in the world, from our nativity to our death; after death the strife is ended. Now in this race we must run, and "so run that we may obtain the crown," 1 Cor. ix. 24. Running is a motion, and a speedy motion; there is lying, sitting, or standing, out still there must be running : we must make a further progress in the way to heaven, "forgetting those things which are behind, and reaching forth unto those things which are before." Phil. ii. 13.

The runner was not to enquire how much of the way already was past, but to strain himself to overcome what was yet behind. And so should we consider what sins are yet to be mortified, what duties yet untouched, almost untouched; what hard conflicts are yet to be undergone, and still to hold on our way, without wining aside, or halting, because of difficulties, discouragements, stumbling blocks. And there are fellows and copartners with us, that run this race, with whom we may strive in a holy emulation, who should go forwardest, who should be most forward in the course of pleasing God. O Christians, there are many contentions amongst us, but when shall we have this holy contention? Heb. x. 24. In a race there is the Agonetheta, the judge of the sports; so here God observes all. No matter what the standers-by say, the judge of the sports must decide who must have the crown, 1 Cor. xiv. 3, 4. And then at the end of the race there is the crown, 2 Tim. iv. 7, 8. "I have fought a good fight, I have finished my course, I have kept the faith, henceforth there is laid up for me a crown of righteousness," &c. In a race there are spectators; so there are here, God, angels, and men, 1 Cor. iv. 9: "We are a spectacle to the world, to angels, and to men," &c.

Thus for the similitude of our race, in our way to heaven. Now wherein it differs.

This is a race not undertaken out of wantonness, but out of necessity. God hath called us to this course, and if we run not in this race, we are undone for ever. And in other races, but one had the crown, here all are crowned, 2 Tim. iv. 8, though they be not so eminent as the apostle; here all are crowned that run in the manner God hath required: "Henceforth is laid up for me a crown of righteousness, which the Lord, the righteous Judge shall give me at that day; and not to me only, but unto them that love his appearing."

For the manner, (with patience,) "Let us run with patience:" patience is necessary.

1. Partly because of the length of the race, and the distance between us and the promised reward. Our race cannot be ended, but after some degrees of time; long waiting is troublesome to the flesh, and therefore we have need of patience.

2. Because we meet with many impediments, troubles, and temptations by the way. There are spiritual adversaries with whom we must fight; for we go on, we not only run, but fight; therefore, " Run with patience," &c.

3. Because the spectators will be ready to discourage us. We are set forth not only as a spectacle to God and angels, but to the world, and they will be ready to deride, scorn, and oppose us for our zeal to God, and our forwardness in the ways of God, to discourage us by bitter mockings, &c. Therefore, " Let us run with patience the race that is set before us."

MR. CARYL'S SERMON.

Preached August 17, 1662.

REV. III. latter part of ver. 4.

And they shall walk with me in white, for they are worthy.

IN the former part of this verse, you heard the commendation of those few names in Sardis. It was this: " They had not defiled their garments." In this latter part you have their encouragement in their reward: " They shall walk with me in white." In which encouragement I told you we might consider two things, or take it into two parts.

First, " That they should walk with Christ."

Secondly, " They should walk in white."

I have spoken to the former of these, " They shall walk with Christ," and that the scripture holds forth under a two-fold notion:

First, as matter of duty. It is a duty to walk with Christ.

Secondly, it is matter of promise. That they keep their garments undefiled, and live in high favour with Christ, they shall walk with Christ. We favour those that walk with us.

Walking with Christ notes to us three things.

1. That we have peace with him.
2. That we have intimacy with him.
3. That his being so much above us, we should have this favour from him.

And hence I noted the great privilege of the people of God, that they shall walk with Christ.

1. It notes the great satisfaction of the saints to walk with Christ; they shall be filled with his company.
2. How safe it is, and what safety there is to walk with Christ: he hath a wing to spread over them.
3. What opportunities such have as walk with Christ.
4. What liberty such have as walk with Christ.
5. Such as walk with Christ, may be sure he will communicate his secrets to them, he will show them what they have to do.

2. We shewed you the great goodness of Jesus Christ, that he should take such creatures to walk with him, such defiled creatures.

3. Then let us take heed of keeping our garments undefiled, lest Jesus Christ cast us out of his company, and we can no longer walk with Christ any more. Oh take heed of walking blameless in the ways of Christ.

These things were spoken from the first point. Now I come to the walking with Christ in white.

In opening the text, I told you white might be considered two ways.

1. As it respects our state, and so that by way of justi-

fication, and thus they shall walk with Christ; but this is not the " walking in white" the text means.

2. Here is a further " walking in white," and that is matter of reward to the people of God.

1. To walk with Christ in white, it is matter of honour, " white garments" are matter of honour. Princes, great kings " walk in white garments," so the saints of God shall " walk in white," Christ will honour them, and give them honour among them, because they have kept their garments undefiled. They shall " walk in white" like great princes, and honoured persons. " A good name is better than precious ointment:" they that are good indeed, they shall have a good name, they shall " walk in white." To keep the conscience clean, is to keep the credit clean; and they who are careful not to blot their conversation, Christ will take care of their reputation, that they be not blotted, that they walk with men in honour.

It was worthily spoken in the 11th of the Hebrews, " they kept their garments undefiled;" and it was by the power of faith, and they obtained a good report by faith, keeping themselves from the pollutions of the world, they kept to themselves a good report. This honour and good report which we get by keeping our garments " undefiled" is sure. Abraham had an honourable title, " Abraham my friend, and a man after mine own heart." Isa. xlv. 4, " Since thou wast precious in my sight, thou wast honourable." And not only so that the people of God are honourable in his eyes, but they also sometimes " walk in white," in the eyes of the men of the world: he can give his people room in the opinions of men, he moves their hearts to think well of them, and he opens their mouths to speak well of them; though, indeed, the honour which they, who keep their garments undefiled, have in this world, it is most usually from good men, from godly men, and, indeed, honour of them is most honourable.

It is not much to us what others say or think of us,

what the wicked world judge of us, yet I say, God can and doth sometimes raise a testimony of honour for his people amongst carnal men of the world. Joseph would not defile his garments, he " walked in white" amongst men: true, he was cast into prison, what of that? he was respected by the keepers of the prison, afterwards he " walked in white."

In the whole Chaldean court, Daniel was one that " walked in white" with common men of the world; first with the prince of the Eunuchs, he had tender favour with him; he told him, he would not disobey God, to please men; yet he did not rail against him, and call him a stubborn fellow, because he would not bow to Baal: and afterwards Daniel was as great a man as any in all that province, he " walked in white." God hath created testimonies of honour for his people from some men of the world; yea, they many times put white garments upon them. So it was with Christ, in Matt. xxvii. and verse 4: common men put a good report upon Christ, a white garment; " Truly," saith the Centurion, " this was the Son of God. Truly, this was a righteous man," saith he. When he saw how he carried himself at his death, he gave him a good report. Thus it doth come to pass, God doth sometimes keep up their honour in the world, who will not defile their garments, nor touch the sacrifice of Baal; and it follows so with them, that the Lord shall clear up their credit and reputation, and they shall walk in white, in honour before the men of the world, Rev. vi. 11; where the souls under the altar are spoken of, who were miserably used in this world, white robes were given them, to every one of them, that is, their evidences were cleared.

This may teach us the readiest way to the white robe, to the robe of honour; it is to keep us from being defiled with sinful practices. Certainly they who please God, he can make the world to honour them; if God approves us, he can make the world approve us too; yet we must not think to have all speak well of us. Yet this we may say, if we keep our garments undefiled, we shall walk in white in the eyes of men; if God see our garments in the dirt, and spotted with the filth of the world, it will spoil the honour we should have in the world. As it was said of Arius, when his garments were defiled, they called him Satanarius, that is to say, devilish. Thus it may be, for the Lord hath a time to take our good name from us, to cause our light of honour to be taken from us.

And as he hath caused us to walk in the white of honour in the world, so he doth sometimes cause us to walk in reproach with the world. They who defile their garments, lose their honour with men, and they lose their joy they should have hereafter, Mal. ii. 9: " You have departed from my law, therefore will I make you contemptible in the eyes of all men." It is a design of the spirit of wickedness to draw men to sin, that they may upbraid them; that I conceive is the sense of the apostle, Gal. vi. 13. " For neither they themselves who are circumcised keep the law, but desire to have you circumcised, that they might glory in your flesh," saith he. Oh, there are some of this wicked spirit, that would draw men to such and such wickedness, not that they joy in their returning, but that they might glory in their flesh; when as they who stand fast, do even force a good testimony from their enemies: so it was the unhappy chance of Cranmer, the Pope did persuade him to subscribe, and did he get any honour by it? No, truly, they did upbraid him, and reproach him, and so he had died in a raving condition, had not the Lord been merciful to him. I remember a speech of St. Austin, about drinking of healths: "Oh," say they, " it is upon the king's birth-day, and we cannot avoid it; if we deny it," say they, " we shall be reproached and scorned of all men." He gives them many answers to it, one of which (as I remember) was this: " God will so work, that if you will not comply with them, they in their hearts will honour you; and whereas, if you did comply with them, they would dishonour you, and say you are base spirited." That is one thing of this point, that keeping close to Jesus Christ will get you this reward; you shall walk with him in the white of honour with his people, and it may be with the world too.

2. " They shall walk in white," in the white of peace and joy, and inward comfort.

I shewed you in the opening of the text, how the Scripture calls that walking in white, then the point is this : whatever becomes of the other white of honour in the world, they shall be sure of this, that abundance of peace, and joy, and comfort, shall possess their souls that keep their garments white; they shall walk in the inward white of joy and peace with Jesus Christ, and this is a blessed reward.

Indeed now this joy, this white of joy, arises in the soul three ways.

1. From the testimony of their own consciences. O they who have a good testimony from their own consciences, walk in white, 2 Cor. i. 12. " We have this for our rejoicing, the testimony of our consciences, that in all simplicity, and godly sincerity, we have our conversation in heaven :" that is, walking in white. This is our rejoicing, our conscience speaks well of us, and kindly to us ; and who is able to express the sweetness of this thing ? None can know what this is, but they that have it, as it is said of the " new name written upon the white stone," Rev. ii. 17. It is a thing beyond expression, what the joy and peace of a good conscience is ! Now this I say, that our white garments, and our walking in white, ariseth from the testimony of our consciences.

2. As from the testimony of our consciences, so from that testimony which is greater than our consciences, the Spirit shedding abroad of divine love. Thus it is with those that do not defile their garments, but endure any thing, rather than defile their garments, Rom. v. 3, 4, 5.

And not only so, but we glory in tribulations, knowing tribulations worketh patience, and patience experience, and experience hope, and hope maketh not ashamed; and whence was all this? because of the Holy Ghost which was given to us; this causeth joy unspeakable, "The Spirit itself beareth witness with our spirits, that we are the children of God." This witness doth cause wonderful joy; much more than the witness of our own consciences.

3. This joy doth arise from a well-grounded hope, which that soul hath that keeps himself clean; hope of enjoying heaven at last, hope of future glory, is our present joy, Rom. v. 2: "By whom also we have access by faith into this grace wherein we stand, and rejoice in hope of the glory of God."

Now they who keep their garments white, have good ground of hope of the love of God; therefore this must needs cause them to walk comfortably, as they who have this hope purify themselves; so they who purify themselves have good ground of their hope, and therein great cause to rejoice, 1 Pet. i. 5, 6: "Who are kept by the power of God through faith unto salvation, ready to be revealed in the last times, wherein ye greatly rejoice, though now for a season (if need be) ye are in heaviness through many temptations."

We walk in white, in hope we have of that inheritance. Now lay these three things together: if they who keep their garments undefiled, have the testimony of their own consciences, and the testimony of the Spirit shedding the love of God in their hearts, and a well-grounded hope of future glory, how can it be but these must walk in white with Jesus Christ? that is, in comfort and joy of the Spirit, and of their own spirits.

Thus David walked; he had abundance of joy upon his conscience of his own integrity, and of keeping his heart and hands clean from those iniquities his enemies charged him with, Psal. iii.: "The Lord shall judge his people. Judge me, O Lord, according to my righteousness, and according to mine integrity that is in me."— He appeals to the Lord,—" The Lord shall judge his people. Judge me, O Lord, according to my righteousness." Thus he appeals to God himself; he had so much confidence, that his heart gave him, he kept himself from those sins.

So Job walked in white; though his friends blacked him exceedingly, yet he walked in white in his conscience, Job xvi. 10: " Behold, my witness is in heaven, and my record is on high." I have not only a witness in my conscience, but my witness is above. He walked in white, notwithstanding all his afflictions from God and his friends. Hezekiah walked in this white, when death looked him in the face: " Lord, thou knowest I have walked uprightly with thee."

I need not stay in the proof of the thing; let me make some use and improvement of it.

Use. Is this blessed reward to those who keep their garments white, to walk in the white of peace and joy? Then here we see the happiness of all those who are true to Christ and his ways, Psal. cxix. 1. " Blessed are the undefiled in the way, who walk in the law of the Lord." It is just in the language of the text; they indeed shall walk in white. It is a great part of our blessedness to have peace of conscience, and inward joy. Oh how much better is it, than the peace and joy of this world, and the comforts of this world? Prov. xv. 13. "A merry heart," or as another translation saith, " A good conscience," and indeed a merry heart and a good conscience do but one explain the other: " A merry heart," or, "a good conscience, is a continual feast." Here is no surfeiting in this feast, but a continual music, continual joy and comfort; Oh how blessed are they who are undefiled in the way!

That which Christ said of the lily, " Solomon in all his glory was not arrayed like one of these," so may I say of the lily-white soul that keeps himself white in the world, who keeps himself white in matter of practice and worship, " Solomon in all his glory was not arrayed like one of these lily-white ones." Oh the rivers of consolations that flow to them that keep themselves out of the puddles of the world! If you keep yourselves from the puddles of the world, from the dung of the world, ye shall have rivers of joy flowing into your souls. I may say to all such, as Solomon saith, Eccles. xi. 9. " Go thy way:" it is a familiar speaking to them: Go thy way, blessed soul, eat thy bread with joy, though the world feed thee with the bread of adversity, and though the world give thee nothing but the water of affliction, yet let thy garments be always white; though the world clothe thee in mourning, and cause thee to prophesy in sackcloth with the witnesses, yet be of good comfort, O lily-white soul, for God now accepteth thy works; now drink thy wine with a merry heart, thy labour, thy ambitious labour is that, whether present or absent, thou mayest be accepted of him, thou hast the fruits of thy labour, the Lord accepts thy works, therefore rejoice in it. Here is the happiness of those who keep themselves clean from a defiled, and a defiling world.

2. This point gives us an account why the servants of Christ stand so strictly upon their terms with the world, even while some call it peevishness, others ignorance, others wilful stubbornness.

What is the reason? the reason is, because they understand in some measure, and have had experience in some measure what it is to walk in some measure with Christ in white, and it hath left such a relish upon their souls, that they would not lose it for all the dainty morsels of this world: they had rather indeed walk with Christ in white, than walk with the world in scarlet; therefore they must stand upon their terms, Prov. x. 32. " The lips of the righteous know what is acceptable:" the lips are instruments of speech, not faculties of knowledge.— Aye, but there is a great deal of commerce and converse between the speech and the understanding, and a righteous man will speak nothing with his lips, but what he understands; therefore he is said to understand. The lips of the righteous know what is acceptable: to whom? "The lips of the righteous know what is acceptable to God," for they are acquainted with his rule, and God hath shown them his covenant, he hath shewed them the pattern of his house, and the way of his worship. Now because they are pretty well skilled, and know what is acceptable to God, therefore they will run any hazard, undergo any affliction, rather than do any thing that will not please God, or be hurtful to their own consciences; they are afraid of losing their peace, and comfort, and joy with God, therefore they will not let go the ways of God, as Job saith, Job xxvi. 6. "I hold fast my integrity, and my heart shall not reproach me so long as I live:" as if he had said, You my friends have reproached me, but I am resolved my heart shall not reproach me so long as I live.

The heart or conscience is a busy faculty, and hath many offices, it records what we do, and comes as a witness. The conscience is judge of what we do, and accordingly reproves what we do amiss; therefore saith Job, "I will take care of this:" I am more afraid of the reproach of conscience, than of any man whatsoever; therefore I will not do any thing that may cause my conscience to reproach me as long as I live. This is upon the heart of God's people, they are resolved, let men reproach and rail against them as much as they will, their hearts shall not reproach them.

3. In the third place, let it be a word of caution and admonition to all at this day, to take heed of defiling their garments: if you defile your garments, Christ will pronounce another sentence, he will pronounce a sentence against you; he hath threatenings for those who defile their garments, in the place of rewards, for those who keep them clean; they who defile garments, shall walk in **garments** of black, in the black of dishonour, as Job saith, "I walk all day mourning without the sun:" the sun of righteousness shall not shine upon them. Oh what bitter and sore things have many tasted for defiling their garments, when for favour of men, or to please men, they have stained their

own garments! What sad bitter things have been upon them, how hath conscience risen up against them! O take heed of the after-claps of conscience, I may say, take heed of the thunder-claps of conscience; for they will come upon you one time or other, if you defile your garments. As they who to please men defile their garments, often fall into their displeasure, whose favour they sought: so oftentimes such fall into displeasure with themselves, or to be sure they shall at last. There is many a one lives under the disfavour of his own conscience, many a one that his conscience will not give him a good word, or a good look, whence hath it been? they have defiled their garments. They who venture to do things displeasing to God, shall not long be pleasing to themselves.

The story speaks of Francis Spira, that to please men, to save an estate, he defiled his garments; and he presently fell into rebuke of himself, and lived under the rebuke of his conscience a long time.

Job viii. 15. speaking of the hypocrite, " his hope shall be cut off;" the word signifies to loath, so some translate, " his hope shall be a loathing to him, he shall loath his hope." There is a two-fold loathing: first, a loathing to repentance; that is, a gracious loathing, a loathing ourselves for our sins against God. And there is a loathing of despair, and that is the loathing there meant: the hypocrite shall loath his own hope; that is, he shall loath it despairingly. It is an affliction to be loathed by men, but it is a dreadful judgment to be loathed of ourselves despairingly; this is the suburbs of hell, for this will be the portion of the damned for ever, for their vanity, for their madness, it is next to the regions of hell, for their worm dieth not; and that is the worm of conscience. Oh therefore take heed, conscience may be silent, yea it may flatter for a time, but when conscience is provoked it will speak, yea thunder.

There is no such thundering preacher in the world as conscience is, the thundering of Mount Sinai is not like the thundering of our conscience.

Fourthly and lastly, let it be for exhortation and encouragement, for Christ here makes it an encouragement, so let this be an encouragement to keep our garments undefiled, the remembrance that we shall walk with him in white, in the white of peace and joy in this world. Who would not walk in this white? Who would not be among those who keep their garments white in the midst of a defiled and defiling world?

Let me give you but a three-fold consideration to stir you up to an exceeding exactness and carefulness not to defile your garments, seeing there is such a reward promised, such a habit of white promised as this white, wherein we shall walk with Jesus Christ. It is an angelical happiness, so much Heaven is come down upon ye while ye have this white. It is Heaven before Heaven, Mat. xxviii. 3. The angel that came down to the sepulchre of Christ, his raiment was white as the light. The martyrs, when they had angelical apparitions, they always appeared to them in white; as one upon the rack thought he felt an angel supplying him, while his enemies tormented him.

Christ calls the Pharisees " whited sepulchres;" they are whited, but whited sepulchres; that is a woful condition to be whited like a sepulchre. Thus it is with those who defile themselves, they are whited walls and whited sepulchres. They that keep themselves white shall walk in white, shall have angelical glory.

Secondly, Consider this white, or walking in white, is such as conquers all the blackness of this world. It is not possible for the world to alter the colour of this white, how much dirt soever they put upon it; this white will be white still, they cannot turn it to be black; they cannot take away this peace, this joy from us; they cannot strip us of this habit; they may pull off your fine garments, but you cannot be stript of this white. " Your joy shall no man take from you," 2 Cor. vi. 20.—" As sorrowful, yet always rejoicing; as poor, yet making many rich; as having nothing, yet freely possessing all things." The world may put us into a sad estate as to the world, yet we are not out of our white garments, always rejoicing, Heb. iii. 13. Although the fig-tree shall not blossom, neither shall fruit be in the vines, the labour of the olive shall fail, and the fields shall yield no meat, and the flock shall be cut off from the fold, and there shall be no herd in the stalls, this cannot take away the white garments; no, saith the prophet, " yet will I rejoice in the Lord, and joy in the God of my salvation." It is a conquering joy, turns all sorrow into joy, and blackness to white, therefore keep clean.

Thirdly, Consider this: this white of peace and joy, as it is a joy unconquerable, so it is that will be with us most when we most need it, when worldly joys are farthest from us then this joy will be near to us. That is a marvellous comfort to have comfort in its season. The martyrs who have kept themselves white, have had this white, and walked in this white; but when they had most need of it, and come actually to suffering, then they have had most of it. This is a blessed thing! this the martyrs of Jesus Christ hath given witness of, although they have had peace and joy in their consciences at other times, yet never so much as in the hour of temptation. When they have been cast into the coal-house, they have had white garments; when they have been cast into prisons and dungeons, how have they rejoiced! It is said of Paul and Silas, they were men that kept their garments undefiled, and they had a great deal of peace and joy; when they were put in the stocks and dungeon, then they sung at midnight: what an enlargement of heart had they at that time!

So in the stories of ancient and latter times, how have they rejoiced, and gone triumphing to the gibbet! for then Christ gives most of this white. It hath been the use of persecutors to put filthy garments upon the martyrs, drawing pictures of devils upon them; and as their malice hath risen to the height (that in the time of sufferings) to make them look like devils, then the love of Christ hath risen to the height, and they have been full of peace and joy at that time; therefore be encouraged to walk with Christ in this white. This white is an angelical habit, it is an unconquerable habit, and it is that will be with us most when we have most need of it. I should have added a third, that walking with Christ is an honour, and it is walking in the white of peace and joy.

So, thirdly, it is a truth of walking with Christ in the white of glory, as in the transfiguration, which was a type of Heaven, " his raiment was white, so as no fuller on earth was able to whiten it;" and that is it which I might have spoken of to you, that they who keep their garments undefiled here, shall be sure of that, to walk with Christ in glory hereafter. If we should miss of the white of honour, and have not much of the white of joy, yet be sure we shall walk with Christ in the white of glory.

I would only say this to you, that as I have from this text, and many more, laboured to bring poor souls into a white state, to a state of justification, to a state of holiness; and as I have been pressing you to keep your garments white, that you may be in the habit of white as your reward; so it shall be the desire and prayers of my heart, that if I should have no more opportunities among you, that as you have been stirred up to get into this white of grace, that you and I may meet in the white of glory, where we shall never part.

Here are three whites: the white of honour is good, the white of peace and joy is very good, the white of glory is best of all; that is the answer of all our prayers, and that is the issue of all our working; then we shall have as much as we can hold for ever.

MR. CASE'S SERMON.

Preached August 17, 1662.

REV. ii. 5.

Remember therefore from whence thou art fallen, and repent, and do thy first works; or else I will come unto thee quickly, and will remove the candlestick out of his place, except thou repent.

CHRIST here prescribes precious physic for the healing of this languishing church of Ephesus; it is compounded of a threefold ingredient:—

    1. Self-reflection, " Remember from," &c.
    2. Holy contrition and humiliation before the Lord, " Repent."
    3. Thorough reformation, " Do thy first works."

I left the last time upon the second of these, namely, " Repentance;" and that which I did upon this part of Christ's advice was, not so much to open to you the nature of repentance (which is not so proper for this place), as to give in a catalogue or list of such special sins, as Christ doth expect that all his people in these three nations should lay to heart, and repent of before the Lord. I gave you in a list of eleven special sins that we should repent of, and humble ourselves for before the Lord.— As,

    1. Omission of duty, prayer, reading the word, meditation, &c.: any thing will be for excuse to lay by duties, and we are secretly glad of an excuse.

    2. Remissness of duty. In things of the world we are all in all, and all in every part; a man cannot thrust another thought into us; but in prayer, how many things are we doing!

3. Hypocrisy. How unlike are we at home to what abroad? and in company to what in secret?

4. Pride. In apparel, houses, parts, blood, birth-right, yea of grace itself, of humility, ministers, ordinances, &c.

5. Covetousness. Never did covetousness invade the professing party as now: the more goods men get, the less good they do.

6. Sensuality. Voluptuousness, wantonness, Christians let themselves loose to the creature; lay out their affections on things below, as if part in the serpent's curse as well as their own.

7. Animosities and divisions among Christians. Many have been active to kindle, but few to quench divisions.

8. Uncharitable censuring one another.

9. Formality in duty. Witness, 1. Unprepared coming. 2. Unsuitableness of spirit to, and 3. Want of reflection after, duty; how we have sped, what we have got; Sabbaths, sacraments, come and go; Monday morning finds us the same as before.

10. Mis-spent Sabbaths, some profane, others idle away the sabbath, &c.

11. Neglect of our Bibles in our families and closets. I pray God it forego not some great evil coming upon you, as before the massacre in Germany it was observed, &c. I proceed.

12. That want of mutual forbearance among Christians. Alas! Christians know not how to bear one with another in the least kind of measure. Oh the short-spiritedness among Christians! they cannot bear one another's burdens, they cannot bear with one another. It is very sad that we that stand in need of so much forbearance, should express so little to our brother. It is an argument " we know not of what spirit we are of," as Christ told his disciples. Oh, how unlike to that God whom we profess to be our God! he is long-suffering, patient, full of goodness, gentleness, mercy, &c. We can bear nothing, we can suffer nothing one from another.

13. Our great murmuring against reformation and re-

formers. " God hath heard the voice of our murmuring,"
Exod. ii. 6. As if there had been nothing that would
have undone us but reformation; and truly God seems
to speak such a word as that was, (Num. vii. 5.) in displeasure and anger, " I will make your murmuring to cease;"
I will take away the cause of your murmuring; I would
have reformed you, and you would not be reformed. As
Christ to Jerusalem, " I would, but you would not,"
Mat. xxiii. The time may come when we would, and God
will not; when we shall cry, "Other lords have had dominion over us," &c. Isa. xxvi. 13. but thou, Lord, set up
thou thy government; rule thou over us; and God may
say, No, it is too late; " I would have healed you, and
you would not be healed."

14. The great neglect of the care of our families.
Truly it is not the least sin that threatens the removal of
our candlestick. How generally have the duties of religion been let fall in our families, reading the word, singing psalms, &c. Time was, when one could not have come
through the streets of London on an evening in the weekday, but we might hear the praises of God, singing of
psalms; now it is a stranger in the city, even upon the
Lord's own day. Oh! how have governors of families
cast off the care of the souls that God hath committed to
them? How careless are they of the souls of their yokefellows that lie in their bosom, of their children, the
fruit of their loins, masters of their servants, &c. And
in the mean time are ready to stand up and justify themselves with the boldness of Cain, to say to God, " Am I
my brother's keeper?" Am I the keeper of my yokefellows', children's, servants' souls? Yes, thou art the
keeper, &c. God hath put them into thy trust, and if
they perish through thy fault, " they may die in their
sins, but their blood shall be required at thy hand."
God will say to thee as he did to Cain, " Thy brother's
blood crieth in my ear."

15. Our "indifference as to matter of faith and doctrine:" that we have not been more zealous for the

truth of Christ, that great trust and depositum which hath been committed to us. We have accounted it no matter of what opinion or judgment men be in these latter times. It is an universal saying, "No matter what judgment men be of, so they be saints:" as if "truth in the judgment," did not go to the making up of a saint, as well as holiness in the will and affections: as if Christ had not come into the world to bear witness of the truth, which was his great design: as if it were no matter, if God have the heart, so the devil be in the head: as if no matter that be full of darkness, so the heart be for God.

16. The "unsuitableness of our conversation to the gospel of Christ:" It is the only thing the apostle puts the Philippians in mind of, and commits to their care, Phil. i. 27. and truly in these unhappy days it hath been the only thing men have neglected and despised: how little care that our conversations should honour the gospel, &c.

17. "Our living by sense, and not by faith." Surely (my brethren) among all the sins in England that the people of God have cause to be humbled for, there is not any whereby we have more provoked God than by that sin of our unbelief. Murmuring and infidelity have been our two great sins, for which, it is the wonder of God's mercy that he hath not caused our carcases to fall in the wilderness: he may take up that complaint of us that he did of Israel, Num. xiv. 22. "Because all those men which have seen my glory and my miracles which I did in Egypt and in the wilderness, and have tempted me now these ten times, and have not hearkened to my voice, surely they shall not see the land, &c. And this is the lamentation we may take up, that truly to this very day we have not faith enough to carry us from one miracle to another, from one deliverance to another, from one salvation to another: let one deliverance pass over our head, and no sooner one wave rises higher than another, but we are ready to cry out with Peter, " Lord, save me, I perish :"

And well were it if our fears did issue into tears, and cries after Christ: we rather are ready to cry out, as those in Ezek. xxxvii. 11. " Our bones are dried, and our hope is lost, we are cut off for our parts." We are a people that never knew how to honour God in any distress God hath brought us into; never learnt to glorify God by believing: if we cannot see him, we cannot believe him. Surely that which God hath done for us in such a succession of miracles, it might well at least have been found for our faith, during our sojourning. In our pilgrimage we might have learned by all that we have seen, to believe God: we might have made experience to be the food of our faith: and upon all the providences of divine power, wisdom, and goodness, we might have discoursed ourselves into belief, as David, 1 Sam. xvii. 37. " The Lord hath delivered me out of the paw of the lion, and of the bear, he will deliver me out of the hand of this Philistine." So Paul, " He hath delivered, and doth deliver, we trust he will also deliver."

Oh, my brethren, we dishonour God, and starve our faith, by forgetting our experience, while we proclaim by our own unbelief, that we have a God that we dare not trust. If we perish we may thank ourselves for it; surely if we miscarry, that account may be given for it, that we find, Mat. xiii. 58. " Because of our unbelief." There is a rest of God before us: if we do not enter in it is because of our unbelief.

18. " Want of sympathy with the bleeding, gasping, groaning, dying, churches of Jesus Christ." They have been in great afflictions round about; have called to us, pity me! Oh pity me my friends! for the hand of God is gone out against me. We cannot look any way but we see cause of bitter mourning; but we have not laid the blood of Germany, Lithuania, Piedmont, &c. to heart; therefore God may justly lay it to our charge. Want of fellow-feeling, with our brethren in their afflictions, it is a kind of persecution, a kind of being accessary to their sufferings. That we have not mourned, wept,

bled with them; that we have not lien in the dust, smote on our thighs, &c. God may justly say to us, as Amos vi. 6, 7, "They shall go captive with the first that go captive, because they are not grieved for the afflictions of Joseph." The word in the Hebrew signifies, none of them have been sick for the afflictions of Joseph. Oh, my brethren! When did we go to bed sick for the afflictions of God's people abroad? When did their miseries cost us an hour's sleep? or a meal's meat? When did we lie in the dust, and cry out, Ah Lord! their glory! Because we have not shed tears for their blood, God may justly say, The next turn of persecution shall be yours, because you have not been afflicted in the afflictions of my people, &c.

19. "Our grievous unsensibleness of God's dishonour." Religion never suffered the like as it hath done these latter days, by the pride and hypocrisy of some pretenders to it. God's name hath been thereby blasphemed by an evil and hypocritical generation, the people of God have lien under the greatest reproaches and contempt that ever any did under the heavens; and yet all this while we have not been concerned in it, carried ourselves as if unconcerned in the reproaches of religion: blasphemously reflected upon the name of God, who in these times of blasphemy, have gone in secret, lien in the dust, and cried with holy Joshua, "What wilt thou do unto thy great name?" Josh. vii. 9. We have not laboured to preserve in our own souls, or stir up our brethren, to a holy sense of God's name, as those primitive saints, Mal. iii. 16. Where are they that have been affected with, and afflicted for the sufferings of the name of God? O consider how little is God and religion beholden to us for our tears, sighs, or groans? What is become of that child-like spirit that was wont to possess the spirits of God's people? It is perished, and with it, without special timely repentance, we shall perish also.

20. "That epidemical sin of self-seeking, and self-pleasing." Oh, my brethren, we may revive that complaint of the apostle, "all seek their own, not the things

which are Jesus Christ's," Phil. ii. 21. This, this hath been the source of all our miseries. While some had power in their hands to have done great things for God, what did they do, but neglect the interest and trust in their hands, and fell a feathering their own nest, and building to themselves house and names, that they thought would continue for ever: and to divide the spoil among themselves, as if their own game they hunted, and others in inferior station began to divide, and every one began to snatch, as if the dust of the earth would not serve every one for a handful: and in the mean time a sea of error hath been ready to over-turn us. Yea, all men seeking to be pleased, not to please: whereas our duty is to study to please, not to be pleased, &c.

You see in all this I have not mentioned one of those gross profanenesses, that stare heaven in the face, as drunkenness, filthy and abominable whoredom, fornication poured out in every place, horrible blasphemy, contempt of God and religion, profanation of God's sabbath, &c. because I speak now to those that are professors. I have given in a catalogue of the sins of those that profess the name of Christ, that relate to Christ by a special engagement and relation: these have been the sins of God's family. And if we would have God repent of the evil of punishment, we had need to make haste to repent of the evil of sin. We have been a long time in sinning, we had need be a long time in repenting. I tell you, Christians, we have been these late twenty years doing nothing else but sinning against God; and should God let us live twenty years more, it would be too little to weep for the procreation thereof. Learn to lay these and other sins to heart, that God may never lay them to your charge.

The third advice Christ gives here for the prevention of the removal of her candlestick, is reformation, "do thy first works." Reformation indeed is a fruit and evidence of such repentance: repentance is nothing else but the breaking of the heart for and from sin.

I have spoken of it merely as it is the contrition of the soul for sin : I come to speak a word of the other part, as it consists in " turning to God, and doing our first works."

This is the method God prescribes his people, Lam. iii. 39. " Wherefore doth a living man complain, &c." under God's afflicting hand? Instead of reforming, men are prone to fall a complaining; not only naturally as irrational creatures may, under some pinching extremity; but sinfully, *i. e.* when their natural grief is let out in a distempered and inordinate manner; when natural groans are accompanied with unscriptural affections, which vents itself,

I. Sometimes upon the affliction, as if but one intolerable burden in the world, and God must needs lay that upon them. Lam. i. 12. and iii. 1. and v. 10.

II. Sometimes of instruments. Thus Esau complains of his brother; "is he not rightly called Jacob, a supplanter?" of his father, " hast thou but one blessing, &c. ?" Gen. xxvii. 3, 4. of any thing rather than of himself. He doth not say, " Am not I rightly called Esau ? What a wretch am I that have despised and sold my blessing ?" Mostly we complain of that which deserves no blame, the guilty of the innocent, 1 Kings xviii. 7. Isa. x. 5. Jer. viii. or we pore too much upon second causes, or complain of instruments, not of ourselves, or of wicked men, not of wickedness; of their cruelty, more than of their blasphemy; of their injuries against us, more than as God's enemies; or more of revenge in our complaints than murmuring : our complaints concerning their afflicting us, not accompanied with our prayers for their conversion, &c.

III. Sometimes of God himself, not as one of his children, who complains

1. To God, not of God : thus " Christ, my God, my God, &c."

2. With a holy confidence, " my God, my God," two words of faith, for one word of fear, &c.

3. In his complaints, is very tender of God's glory, afraid to think or speak a hard or uncomely thought or word of God.

4. Carefully distinguishes between what God doth, and what man doth; observes and separates the unrighteousness of men from the righteousness of God.

5. With humble enquiry what cause may be of his dispensation, Job x. 2. and xxxiv. 31.

6. With a disposition to bring up his will to God, not that God should bring down his will to him; if it be possible let this cup pass; however glorify thy name, provide for thy own glory, and do with me as thou pleasest, but as a sinful creature, sometimes ready to call Providence in question, Ezek. viii. 12. or to break forth and to charge God foolishly, either of too much severity, Ezek. xviii. 2. 25. or of too long delay, Isa. xlix. 14. or their mournings are turned into murmurings, Num. xiv. 27. or their complaints are mixed with unbelief: Psal. lxxviii. 19. or of their punishment, not of their sin; and nothing will satisfy them but deliverance.

Now this is not the way; for this way of complaining is,

1. Fruitless, a house on fire is not quenched with tears. Murmuring will not scatter the clouds.

2. Causeless: Thou hast thy life for a prey, Jer. iv. 5, 6. What, a living man, and complain, and that when it is for the punishment of his sins? This kind of complaining is causeless: if you compare sin and punishment together, there is no proportion: for sin is a transgression against an infinite God; punishment but an affliction upon the finite creature: Sin is an evil against God; punishment an evil against the creature: Or if you consider what sin is in its nature, it is a contrariety to God's nature (God is holy, sin impurity.) A contradiction to God's will: God saith, "Do this;" the sinner saith, "I will not." God saith, "Do not this abominable thing which I hate:" The sinner saith, "I will:" It is the transgression of God's pure and holy law: Nay it is a

practical blaspheming against all the names of God, the rape of God's mercy, and the dare of God's justice, the challenge of God's power. Sin gives the lie to God's truth and the fool to God's wisdom; and what can sin do more, than to take away God's good name? God's being? and that sin would do. Or, it is causeless if you consider against whom sin is, *i. e.* God himself, who is a jealous God. Now a sinner takes another lover into his bosom before his eyes; yea, he is a holy, righteous, omnipotent, almighty, living God. Thoughts of this may well keep us from complaining. Indeed, whatever our affliction be, we have as much cause to give thanks, as to mourn; if you consider, whatever the punishment be, it might be worse; or do but look well into it, you will see more mercy than affliction, Psal. cxix. 75.

3. Sinful. There is in it, 1. Unthankfulness; while we complain of one affliction, we over-look a thousand mercies: whereas true grace is ingenuous, and can see a little kindness mingled with a great deal of severity. The church of God in captivity comparing her afflictions with her mercies, breaks forth, " It is of the Lord's mercy that we are not consumed," Lam. iii. 22. Blessed be God, it is not yet so bad, but it might be worse, 2 Cor. iv. 8. " We are troubled on every side, yet not distressed;" though laid wait for, beset on every side, put to strive and struggle, yet we escape; God gives an issue in the temptation. " We are perplexed but not in despair:" we are not so helpless that we know not how to turn us: we have a God to go to as bad as things are, the Lord's name is a strong tower: " persecuted, but not forsaken," we are shaken out, but not to shivers; persecuted, but not conquered, our God hath not quite forsaken us: " Cast down, but not destroyed," Psal. cxviii. 13. we are cast down, but not cast off. So Luther, " they may thrust me back, but they cannot thrust me down: they may crush me, but they cannot kill me, or, they may kill me, but they cannot hurt me: they may shew their teeth, but they cannot devour." Is it a fever? It might have been eter-

nal flames: Is it scarcity? it might be universal famine. Is it the danger of losing the gospel? it is the mercy of God it is not done already. Are we in captivity? We might have been in hell. Are we in prison? It might have been Tophet. "The Lord hath chastened me sore, but he hath not given me over unto death," Psal. cxviii. 18. Though men have lost their bowels, God's compassions fail not; God is as faithful as ever; he hath taken away some of our mercies, but he hath not taken away all; he hath left us more than he hath taken: They are new, they are renewed every morning. When old mercies are spent, God sends us new; he is the Father of Mercies, begets new mercies every moment. Who can number or measure his mercies of one day? Whatever our fears are, O blessed be God, he loads us with mercies.

Now the complainer overlooks all these, there is much unthankfulness in it, and that is a kind of atheism. "She knew not that I gave her corn and wine," &c. Hos. ii. 8.

2. Pride—only by pride comes contention. Men never quarrel with God about their condition, but it is out of the pride of their heart. Proud man would feign sin, and not hear from God; would take liberty to sin, but would not have God take liberty to punish, Isa. viii. 3. God must take notice of our duties, not of our sins. God shall hear of it, if he take not notice of our prayers; but it shall be by complaining if he take notice of our sins. A proud man, whatever he hath, it is no more than his due, and whatever he wants, God is his debtor, Hos. vi. 14.

The want of a compliment undoeth him in the midst of honor. If we want but one thing our hearts would have, surely nature is proud and ready to pick quarrels with God on the least occasion: nay, if he will not give that mercy we would take all, &c.

3. Rebellion—God strikes him for sin, he strikes against God, Jer. xxxi. 18. God draws one way, and he another, &c.

4. Unbelief—He that complains of his punishment,

never believed sin to be so great an evil, or God to be such a one as revealed in the word.

5. Interpretative blasphemy.

1. While we dispute our afflictions, and wrangle with the present dispensation, what is it but to make ourselves wiser than God? We seem to tell God how it might have been better, and so we do, as it were, give God counsel. When he calls for obedience, is not that blasphemy to set up our wisdom against God's?

2. While we complain of punishment, we take sin's part against God ; we do, as it were, justify sin, and judge God. God is unrighteous to punish such a sin as this with such grievous afflictions.

3. By complaining, we do, as it were, summon God to our bar, to come and give an account of his actions at our tribunal. What poor miserable creatures are we, that in our afflictions are so far from helping ourselves, that we commonly add to our own misery!

No affliction is intolerable till sin come in it.

The yoke God hath made easy, we make intolerable ; and make God to be our enemy, while he by affliction would become our friend.

Now this being found not to be the way: that which God counsels and advises is—

1. Self-examination — " Let us search and try our ways ;"—Sin and hypocrisy lies close and deep ; therefore, we must take pains, dig to the bottom, set up a tribunal in our own conscience, summon, try, judge ourselves over and over in God's presence. He stands at our closet doors, to hear what we will say, Jer. viii. 6. before execution : what indictment we will bring in against ourselves.

We can tell what such a drunkard, such an unclean person, &c. hath done; but no man saith, what have I done? my pride, my unthankfulness, my unfruitfulness, &c.

2. Reformation—" And turn again unto the Lord." Sin is *aversio a Deo, & conversio ad creaturam* ; reformation is a turning again from the creature to God.

3. Frequent and fervent prayer,—"Let us lift up;" there is the frequency, let us do nothing else but pray; let us be continually lifting up our prayers; make our houses houses of prayer. Thus David "Thou foughtest against me without a cause: (Did he take counsel against princes to be disloyal? to take up arms? No) but I gave myself unto prayer," Psal. cix. 4. Therefore if you prayed before, now do nothing else; it notes habitual and constant prayer (our hearts with our hands) to crave, and, as it were, to pull down mercy, as if we would wrestle with God, and say, Nay, nay, "I will not let thee go until thou bless me," Gen. xxxii. 26. It notes our fervency. And for our encouragement it is (unto God in the Heavens) which expresses his sovereignty, omnisciency, omnipotency, everlastingness, &c.

4. Judging ourselves, or confessing of sin,—"We have transgressed."

5. Aggravating our sins,—" and have rebelled," i. e. we have turned sin into rebellion; rebellion hath been the aggravation of our sin. We have sinned against the clearest light, dearest love, &c. Neh. ix. Ezek. ix. Dan. vi.

6. Justifying God,—"thou hast not pardoned." A word not of murmuring, complaining, or accusing God of hard dealing, but by way of justifying God: we have transgressed, therefore thou hast not pardoned. Why shouldst thou repent of the evil of punishment, when we have not repented of the evil of sin? Thou hast punished us less than our iniquities deserve.

So in the text, "Do thy first works." Sin is a departure from God, repentance a coming back again to God. Turn thou to him from whom the children of Israel have deeply revolted. The soul hath many turnings and windings, but there is the best motion of all, when the soul (with the dove) returns to God, from whom it came.

Apostacy is the loss of our first love. Repentance is the recovery of it, and reformation is the doing of our first works. I have not time to enlarge as I desire: I shall only offer a few things, that might help to quicken you to this great duty.

My brethren, we have no great cause to boast of England's first love. Never so good as it should be, yet many can remember when England hath been much better than it is.

Time was, when doctrines have been more sound, discipline more exercised for the suppressing of sin and profaneness; ordinances kept more pure from sinful mixtures; when London kept sabbaths better than now, loved their godly ministers more than now, honoured them that were set over her for their works' sake, would have thought nothing too good for a faithful minister; when Christians loved one another with a dear, hearty, fervent love; when there was less compliment, but more real love and affection among Christians; when Christians improved their meetings, converse, Christian conference, and other soul duties to better purpose than now; not to foolish disputations, or wanton sensual excess, but to their mutual edification; when they improved their times for comparing their evidences, communicating their experiences, and building up one another in their most holy faith; when there was more industry in professors than now, to bring in converts; when private Christians thought it their duty to be subservient to the works of their ministers, to bring in others to Christ, especially their family.

Time was, when more care of young converts than now, when none could have looked out after religion, but some or other ready to lend them their hand, and shew them the way, explaining it clearly to them; but now young converts may be snapt into separation and error, and none look after them.

Time was, when more care of the truly godly poor; when error was more odious; when popery was more hated than now: when the name of a toleration would have made Christians to have trembled; when Christians were better acquainted with their bibles; when more time spent in secret prayer; when more tender of one another's names and honours, would heal one another's reputations, and would spread the lap of charity over those mis-reports and scandals that might be cast upon them; when Christians rejoiced more in one another's good, and mourned in one another's sufferings: when Christians did more earnestly contend for the faith once delivered to the saints, &c.

Oh do you not only your first works, but our forefathers first works be as zealous for God and his truths, as tender, mutually careful of one another as they.

Our fears be very great, and truly our provocations be greater: our dangers are great, but our sins greater: yet here is a word, here is matter of encouragement, that yet there is balm in Gilead, physic of Christ's own composition, for the reviving and healing of a back-sliding people. Christians, Christ Jesus is become your physician, he hath prescribed you a potion made up of these three ingredients, self-reflection, holy contrition, thorough reformation. Christians, now take this receipt. Christ advises you, if you will not, there is no way but one, " Or else I will come unto thee quickly, and will remove thy candlestick."

There is yet a means or two I find in scripture for the preventing of threatened ruin that hath been very near, that God hath prescribed for a people or person in great danger, when ready to be cut off and destroyed.

Now that which I would commend to you in reference to what you would beg of God for England, is,

First, in your addressing yourself to God for that mercy your souls are set upon, and you wrestle with God for, that you would make some special vow to God. I find the saints have done so, when reduced to great straits, not knowing what to do. Thus Jacob vowed a vow, saying, " If God will be with me, and will keep me in this way that I go, and will give me bread to eat, and raiment to put on, so that I come again to my father's house in peace, then shall the Lord be my God. And this stone which I here set for a pillar, shall be God's house," Gen. xxviii. 20, 21, 22. The special thing Jacob vows, is, that he would continue in the pure worship of his forefathers, that he would still honour God as his God, in that way he would be worshipped; the special thing is, that he would build a house for the worship of God; here he would erect a place of public worship. And thus " Israel vowed a vow unto the Lord, and said, If thou wilt indeed deliver this people into my hand, then will I utterly destroy their cities," Num. xxi. 2. They vowed they would not spare any of the enemies of God, if he would deliver them into their hands. Thus Jeptha, Hannah, David, &c. Judg. xi. 31. 1 Sam. i. 11. Psal. cxxxii. 1, 2. Certainly in times of great distress, it is not improper or uncomely, but that which God may expect and take well, that you make some special vow, if God would prevent your fears, if God would continue forfeited mercies, dearer to you than your lives, you would set apart some special thing for God, something for the propagation of the gospel abroad, for the maintenance of a godly ministry at home, for setting up the preaching of the gospel in the dark corners of the kingdom, &c. This must have some cautions with it: As,

1. We must be sure our vow be of what is in our own power, we must not make vows of that which is none of our own. " I hate robbery for burnt-offerings."

We must not make a vow to God of that which hath been unjustly or unrighteously taken away, or with-held from any. It is Sacrilege instead of a Sacrifice.

2. It must be of things warrantable and justifiable by the word.

3. It must be of such things that we are not bound to do, before vows, by the standing obligation of religion, and of our profession: but of something that is in our own choice, that we will voluntarily make a free-will offering of it to God.

4. We must take heed that we do not entertain a superstitious thought of our own vows, as if we had merited a mercy at God's hands by our vows. God looks for some special vow at our hands, that we may shew how much we prize and value the mercy we would have, that

we would be content to part with any thing, though to the half of our estate for it.

2. Another thing I find, is, that in the mean time we should do something by way of extraordinary bounty and charity to the relief of God's indigent servants. Thus the prophet Daniel: Wherefore, "O king, let my counsel be acceptable to thee; break off thy sins by righteousness, and thine iniquities by shewing mercy to the poor, if it may be a lengthening of thy tranquillity," Dan. iv. 27.

The prophet advises him to break off his sins by righteousness, there is reformation: and besides reformation, that he would do something in an extraordinary way to the relief of the poor. "Mercy to the poor," what is that?

Interpreters conceive, by the poor, here he understands God's poor, i. e. the poor Jews that were now in the Babylonian captivity: he advises, he would do something by way of sympathy to the Jews, to ease their yokes and oppressions. Break off thine iniquities by pitying and shewing mercy to thy poor captives, under thy power now at this time; take off their yoke, ease their burdens, and restore them to their liberties again. Thus do you, and those that have been the instruments of your conversion, or edification, set apart something extraordinary for their relief and supply. The prophet Daniel seems to advise this to the king, as it were by way of satisfaction.

There be two things in repentance; in wrongs we have done, there must be confession, and satisfaction, or restoration. He seems to advise this to make up compleat repentance, namely, to make restoration and retribution of what he had injuriously taken from the Jews. O then! let me say, without breach of charity, that whatsoever, except it be in this case of extraordinary supplies for his poor, it will be found but making restitution and satisfaction. It may be upon a twofold ground.

1. With some it may be truly restitution and restoration of what he hath taken away by unjust means. God

knows how, that is between God and their own souls, what unlawful means have been used to augment the heap, and swell their estate.

If there be any that hear me this day, whose consciences shall tell them that they have increased their estate by undue and unwarrantable means, O "restore, restore, break off your iniquities by shewing mercy," &c. by making reparation as you can. It will be but like Zaccheus giving half his goods to the poor, and restoring four-fold, &c. in a liberal contribution to the poor.

2. It will be restitution in another sense, in reference to an unjust withholding. Some have injuriously, and I am afraid too many have kept injuriously. Have we not robbed the poor by an unjust denying of what God hath commanded us to distribute to their necessities? "there is that withholdeth more than is meet," &c. Prov. iii. 17. and xi. 24. It may be God hath given you so much: there is God's share, there is the minister's portion, &c. Now all that you have with-held beyond the rule of scripture, is all stolen goods, and is like a wheat-sheaf on fire, will burn down the whole barn of corn.

That which I would exhort you to, is, for every one to set apart some considerable part of your estate, and account it as a solemn thing, dedicated to God, as a thing, which to touch, were sacrilege; that you may be ready on all occasions, in all regular and due ways, to bring out for the relief of the poor. You know objects abounding in every place, and you may expect warrantable means for dispensing of what God shall put into your hearts in this matter.

MR. JENKIN'S FORENOON SERMON.

Preached August 17, 1662.

Heb. xi. 38. The former part of that verse.
Of whom the world was not worthy.

THE apostle in this excellent chapter, (that by some is deservedly called a little book of martyrs) discovers the triumph of faith, or victory against all difficulty we meet with.

I. Faith assents to truths be they never so improbable.

II. It puts men upon duties, be they never so irrational, or against carnal interest.

III. It enables to sufferings, be they never so afflictive. These worthies went through all by the victory that overcame the world, the bitterness as well as the sweetness thereof.

In these verses the apostle doth two things: 1. He sets down the greatness and smartness of their sufferings, which are by some learned men reduced to three heads.

First, those sufferings that were to tempt them, and draw them from God, by those pains and tortures they were to undergo.

Secondly, those sufferings they underwent in dying.

Thirdly, their sufferings in regard of wandering, and leaving their comforts, rather than they would lose God.

There were all kinds of persecutions laid upon these saints, through all which they waded, and never would be brought to forsake God and his truth for any of them.

2. We have here the excellency of the sufferers, and that is in that expression: these men, or these persons, when they were under all these distresses from the world, yet they were such of whom the world was not worthy.

Brethren, the excellency of these saints and servants of God is considerable two ways, that we may proceed distinctly and clearly.

First, in reference to the wicked; their excellency was so great that the wicked world was not worthy of them.

Secondly, their excellency is discovered from the estimate or judgment that the apostle passes upon them, who tells us, that he accounted them to be such; though they were under such distresses, and troubles, yet they were a people of whom the world was not worthy.

I shall fall upon the due estimation the blessed apostle raises upon these persecuted saints, who was enlightened by the spirit of God, and so was able to pass a right sentence upon these persecuted saints. From this I raise this ensuing observation.

> Observe. "That a godly man doth see a very great worth and excellency in the people of God, in the midst of all their troubles and distresses; or, that a godly man, a gracious heart, one that hath spiritual spectacles, does see an excellency and worth in the people of God, in the midst of all trouble and persecution that can befall them."

Here I shall handle it first doctrinally, according to my constant method, then come to improve it by way of application. For the doctrinal handling of it, there are two things must be discovered.

First, wherein the high estimation of a gracious heart does appear, wherein it doth discover itself, wherein they shew they have such an high estimation.

Secondly, whence it is, and how it comes to pass, that godly men have this high and honourable esteem of the saints and people of God in their troubles and distresses which befall them.

For the first, wherein the high estimation of a gracious heart does appear, I shall shew it in five or six following particulars.

First, it appears in this, in that they are not ashamed

of owning their persons and faith, that they profess in their troubles and distresses. The society of the people of God, and the fellowship of the faith and profession, is highly respected by a gracious heart, let the saints lie under never so great distresses. This is manifested in Moses, in the 25th and 26th verses of this chapter; "He chose rather to suffer affliction with the people of God, than to enjoy all the pleasures and preferments of Pharaoh's court." The Israelites' religion, the profession of the truth of God, and owning the faith and those truths the Israelites stood up for, this was that which Moses would not desert: and thence it was he did not desert their company and society, but went and visited them when they lay under those burthens under which they lay.

Secondly, the second thing wherein is discovered so high an estimation of the saints and people of God in suffering, is, their sympathizing and fellow-feeling with them in their suffering. If it goes ill with the church and people of God, all the rest sympathize with them; if one member suffers, all the rest suffers: instance Nehemiah (who had the greatest favour of the greatest prince then on the earth) he looks with a sad countenance, because of the sufferings of the saints and people of God, Nehem. ii. 2. "Wherefore, the king said unto me, why is thy countenance sad, seeing thou art not sick? This is nothing else but sorrow of heart. Then I was very sore afraid, and answered the king, because of the distresses the people of God lie under." The pleasure of music should never be with him, says David, Psal. cxxxvii. 5. "If I do not remember thee, let my tongue cleave to the roof of my mouth, if I prefer not Jerusalem above my chief joy." As it is with two strings in an instrument rightly tuned, if one be touched, the other trembles, if one servant of Christ be in a suffering condition, the rest suffers with him. This is the damp of all worldly delight, if it be ill with any of the people of God, the rest suffers in the way of compassion.

Thirdly, in that they can plead for them, and take their parts, when they are never so much out of favour, when they are never so much despised and abused. This was in the case of Jonathan, how he pleaded for poor David before his cruel father Saul, though Saul called him a cursed son, and fell foul on his mother because of him. See this in the case of Esther, though it was death to go into the king to plead for the Jews, yet for all this she says, " If I perish, I perish:" resolved I am, come what will come of it, in I will go, I can die, but I cannot be silent.

Fourthly, in that they will relieve them, and help and supply them with all needful good things they can, if they cannot do what they would, they will do for them what they can. See this in the case of Jeremiah, chap. xxviii. v. 8, 11, 12, 13. Ebedmelech went forth of the king's house and spake to the king——" So Ebedmelech took the man with him, and went into the house of the king under the treasury, and took thence old clouts, and old rotten rags, and let them down by cords into the dungeon to Jeremiah. And Ebedmelech the Ethiopian said unto Jeremiah, put now these old cast clouts, and rotten rags under thine arm-holes, under the cords. And Jeremiah did so, so they drew up Jeremiah with cords, and took him out of the dungeon, &c. Jeremiah remained in the court of the prison." He would never be quiet till he got the prophet out of the dungeon, and though the cords were lined with rags, yet more with love and this favour of Ebedmelech, God remembered. 1 Kings xviii. 4. Obadiah's master was not only an oppressor of the saints and prophets of God, but a very great persecutor. This good man Obadiah " took and hid four hundred prophets of the Lord, and fed them with bread and water." (I will not undertake to prophesy to you this day, yet time may come when bread and water may be good food for a faithful prophet.) Here note the gracious disposition of good Obadiah, as well as the providence of God in this act, 2 Tim. i. 16, 17, 18. " The Lord give mercy unto the house of Onesiphorus, for he oft refreshed me, and was not ashamed of my chain. But when he was in Rome, he sought me out very diligently, and found me. The Lord grant unto him, that he may find mercy of the Lord in that day: and in how many things he ministered unto me at Ephesus, thou knowest very well." A most admirable scripture to this purpose: blessed Paul being thrown into prison, being in bonds, Onesiphorus often refreshed him, and was not ashamed of his chains. How did he shew this? When he was in Rome, he sought him out diligently. By the way note, that Rome was the place where the cruel Nero was emperor, it was the place where much blood of the martyrs was spilt, yet there this good man sought out Paul diligently. Mark what follows, which is the prayer of Paul, " The Lord grant to him that he may find mercy of the Lord in that day." I profess, sirs, I had rather have the prayer of Paul, than the preferments of the greatest court on earth. Christians, it is the greatest treasure in your house, to have the prayers of good men to God for you, you that have shewn your great and abundant love to the saints and servants of God in distress, I do from my soul, beg mercy for you, that whatever you have done for his, may be ten thousand times made up by him, that you may find mercy in that day; and truly, sirs, in that day mercy will be worth receiving.

Fifthly, They supplicate to God for them; they do not go to the throne of grace for themselves, but Sion is in their thoughts. I am confident it is so with some, and am persuaded it is so with all; they never beg daily bread for themselves, but they remember Sion. In the 51st Psalm, David was under trouble of conscience, soul-trouble, which is the soul of trouble; yet, at the latter end of the 51st Psalm, he breaks out into this earnest supplication to God, " Do good in thy good pleasure unto Sion, build thou up the walls of Jerusalem." So long as it is ill with the people of God, so long they are earnest with God; and though they cannot overcome men with their prayers (which by the way they are to endeavour) yet they will never leave supplicating the Almighty, till they have overcome. As the sufferings of God's people are precious in the sight of God, so they are in the sight of the people of God.

I come now to shew whence it is, that there is such an high esteem in the people of God, of the people of God, when under trouble and distress: for this take two heads of reasons.

First, In regard of those people of God that do behold their sufferings.

Secondly, In regard of those people of God that are in sufferings.

First, In regard of those people of God that do behold their sufferings, troubles, and distresses, in three regards.

First, Those of the people of God that look upon others in trouble, though they are such as may differ from them in regard of outward estate. One may be in honour, the other in dishonour, yet they have an interest in the same head, and do belong to the same body that they do, they are not wooden legs, nor glass eyes; therefore Christ is called the common Saviour, and the Saviour of the body, the whole church. Faith is called, the " like precious faith," 2d Pet. ch. i. in the beginning. The faith of one believer does as truly lay hold of Christ, as the faith of another. This salvation is called common salvation; my meaning is, this outward disproportion as the birth and education, puts no difference at all in a spiritual respect between believer and believer: a king and a beggar are all one in Christ; a Jew, or a Greek, a great scholar, or a poor ignorant man, as to the spiritual state, all are made happy the same way.

Secondly, Because these look at spiritual excellency, and are able to discern spiritual excellency. They have a renewed judgment, as they look upon their old courses and sins with a new eye, so they look upon their company with a new eye. Those that before they highly esteemed, they now dis-esteem. Those persons that before they esteemed a damp to their mirth, they now look upon them as the excellent ones of the earth, Prov. xii. 26. " The righteous is more excellent than his neighbour." In the 16th Psalm, says David, " My goodness extends not to thee, but to the saints, the excellent ones, in whom is all my delight." Here was a renewed estimation; David saw excellency in those which worldlings despised. A carnal eye sees no glory but in carnal objects. Worldlings bless the covetous, whom the Lord abhors. A gracious heart sees a spiritual worth in a man divested of worldly enjoyments, as a curious eye may, and does see a great deal of art and curiosity in a picture, though in a broken frame. A beast can see the shining of a diamond, but knows not the worth of it. A beast would rather lick up a lock of hay than a diamond, though of never so great value. A wicked man wants a spirit of discerning. The people of God are the workmanship of God, which a godly man is very much taken withal, not with the greatness, but with the goodness that is in them. The four monarchs of the earth is expressed by four beasts, which shews their cruelty, not their curiosity, in observing that of God which may be observed. A child is taken with the gay, but a learned man is taken with the learning and art of a lesson.

Thirdly, A child of God is one that highly esteems the people of God, judging of them as God judges. The child esteems as the father esteems. If the father cannot love any one, the ingenuous child cannot endure that he should come into the house. The courtier follows the favourite of the king; whom the king honors, they cringe to. But to be sure it is true as to spirituals. God judges not by the gold ring, or silken suit. A sinner is a vile person in God's account, and so he is in a godly man's account. God is more taken with a broken-hearted sigh than with all the gaudery in Solomon's temple. He did not chuse the eagle or lion for sacrifice, but the lamb and the dove: not many noble, not many rich, but the poor hath God chosen; he that hath the choice of God hath the life of God.

The second reason is from the people of God that are beheld. And this will appear in five or six particulars.

First, The people of God, those that are truly such, let their present condition be what it will, their end shall be happy. Men are not regarded in reference to what they have in possession, but what they shall have in reversion; the poor here are rich in faith, and shall be rich in glory. 1 Pet. iii. The people of God are heirs of glory, co-heirs with Christ; when he shall appear, they shall appear with him in glory. They are not possessors here, but they are heirs, and are to be looked upon as what they shall be hereafter. Here they are princes going to their crown, hereafter they shall be possessed of it. Here they may be oppressed, banished, disgraced, libelled, hereafter they shall shine as the sun in glory.

Secondly, They are not only such as shall be happy, but they are very useful and beneficial in the world; they are those, for whose sake the world was made, they are the great common blessings of the world, like fire and water, they are those for whose sake God spares the world. If God would have spared the city for ten righteous persons' sakes, surely for many tens God spares the world. Those that are pulled down by the world, are those for whose sake God doth not pull down the world; they are the soul of the world, as I may so say. If God hath gathered in all his elect, the world would not continue one hour longer.

Thirdly, The excellency of their performances is highly esteemed, there is a worth in every holy work that worldlings are not able to discern; every heavenly prayer, and sincerely bestowed alms, hath a worth that a carnal man doth not see. Luther says, I had rather do the least truly good work, than obtain all the conquests of Cæsar and Alexander. If their good works shall be so rewarded, do you think a holy man can see them and not be taken with them? Many a wicked man when he hears a holy man make an excellent oration, wishes that he could do so too: it is not from the goodness he observes in it, or the principle from whence it comes, but from something of natural accomplishments that he is taken with it; so a godly man when he hears another pray excellently, and live holily, he wishes from his heart that he could do so too, his aim is to grow in holiness.

Fourthly, The present privileges of the people of God, not only what they shall have hereafter, but what they have here, they are freed from a world of evils that worldlings lie under. Whatever befals them turns to their benefit; they may be afflicted, but not hurt by affliction; the greatest hurt the world does to them, tends to their greatest good. Worldlings may take away their heads, they cannot their crowns. There is a real communication of a blessed interest in all that is good, for they have an interest in all that God hath, or is. The power of God is theirs to protect them, the love of God is set upon them, the righteousness of God imputed to them, so as to acquit them from sin; so that a child of God may not only appeal to the bowels of God's mercy, but to the bar of his justice, all the providences of God shall tend to their good. In Psal. xxv. 10. the Holy Ghost says, "All the ways of God are mercy and truth, to them that are in covenant with him:" they are mercy, because they are appointed to do them good; and truth, because they shall certainly do them good: Christ, and God, and all is laid out for the good of a godly man.

In this world they may go to God, and tell him wherein they are troubled, pained, or afflicted, and they are never more welcome than when they ask most from him. If thou ask great things from God, God is well taken with such requests; but if thou ask riches and honours, these are the low things of the foot-stool. God is exceedingly taken with thee when thou askest peace and pardon, peace of conscience, pardon of sin, strength against sin, power to overcome thy lusts, to withstand temptations. The people of God may have from God all that they want, and all that they can regularly wish.

Fifthly, These are such as have an incomparable dear and near relation to God; they are his delight, they are set apart by God as his own, his peculiar people. Though God have a propriety in all, yet he hath a peculiar propriety in, and a relation to these; therefore they are called his children, his house, his jewels, his garden. God's whole treasure and portion is his people; as God is his people's portion, so his people are his portion; they are those he hath been at a great deal of cost to purchase.

Sixthly, They are such as have the "image of God" imprinted upon them. Take notice of this word image, for the image of God appears in holiness. Now an image does not represent any thing of imperfection or deformity, but of excellency. If a man takes the picture of a man, he will not take it of his leg, or hand, or the like, but of his face, his beautifullest part is chiefly aimed at in the picture. Wicked men discover God's bounty in having wit and wealth; this is not the image of God; the image of God is that which is most excellent in a man, which is holiness: the power of God, is the hand of God; the wisdom of God, is the eye of God; the holiness of God, is the face, the beauty of God. The people of God resemble God in purity. "Be ye holy, as your heavenly Father is holy," there is the pattern, they have the divine nature: 2 Pet. i. 4. "Whereby are given unto us exceeding great and precious promises, that by these you might be partakers of the divine nature, having escaped the corruption that is in the world;" as it is in Ephes. iv. 18. "Having the understanding darkened, being alienated from the life of God, through the ignorance that is in them, because of the blindness of their heart." Rom. iii. 23. "For all have sinned, and come short of the glory of God." There is more of God in grace, than in all the works that ever God did in the world beside: there is much of God seen in making the Sun, Moon, and Stars: but in giving a man a new nature, a renewed understanding, in changing of a man from being a vessel of wrath and vessel of Satan, in making of him become a new man, a vessel of glory, God shews more of himself, than in making ten thousand worlds.

Use. Here I shall raise these following inferences. 1. If it be so, that there is such an excellency in the people of God here, then first, what excellency shall there be seen on the people of God in heaven? If they are so beautiful in their rags, what will they be when they appear in their robes? The glory of Christ shall be admired in them that believe. Oh what a head is he that hath such members? what a Lord is he that hath such attendance? The people of God are in a state of non-appearance now, hereafter it shall appear what they are; the very wicked themselves shall admire them.

2. *Inference.* What have we to think of those that have no regard either for religion, or for religious ones, any farther forth than it is decked and adorned with advantageous beauty, and outward glory? If religion be not looked upon with a favourable eye from authority, farewell religion, and religiousness. These love the child for the nurse's sake. What is the thing in fashion these are for; what authority commands, they will creep and cringe to; when the deer is shot, the herd flies from her; when religion is shot at, then farewell religion. What is this but to have the faith of God in respect of persons? If I love religion for the countenance of authority, then it is certain I love religion for the authorities sake: this is a sign thou shalt not have communion with those hereafter, that thou contemnest here. If the people of God are too bad for thee when they are in trouble and affliction, they will be too good for thee in glory.

3. *Inference.* Note here the excellency of holiness above worldly glory. Here a man is dignified by what is conferred upon him; when outward honour ceaseth, the man is contemned; but holiness it dignifies a man, and shall remain here and hereafter. Set a giant in a

valley, he is a giant still; a pearl is a pearl though on a dunghill; a holy man is a holy man, though never so much disgraced and contemned by men. John Baptist had a leathern girdle, and had locusts for his food, yet there was not a greater than John Baptist born of women. He was the fore-runner of Christ, the friend of the Bridegroom. On the other side, Herod, that was like the voice of God, and not of man, what was he in God's account? The angel smote him, and he became wormsmeat. There is a silent dignity in reproached piety, and a silent ignominy in advanced iniquity. As it was with Christ, so it is with the servants of Christ. When he was on earth, no man had more ignominy poured upon him; yet there was a secret glory attended him in all that befel him. Though born in a manger, yet worshipped there: sometimes he was driven to be hungry, the fish brought him money: sometimes a weary, at that very time converts a woman; sometimes laid hold on by his enemies, at that very time his enemies fell down before him. Look through the whole course of his life, there was a secret glory under all ignominy. Just thus it is with the servants of Christ, they are in trouble and disgrace, but there is a secret glory and dignity shines in them, the Spirit of God and of glory rests upon them: " If ye suffer for righteousness sake, blessed are ye." To be in high place, and yet to be a drunkard, a swearer, or profane, this spoils all thy glory, be thou never so high.

4. *Inference.* This is the way for a man to have a good name. Wouldst thou gain a good report living and dying? Take heed of sin, take heed of dishonouring God; then God will have thee in everlasting remembrance.

5. *Inference.* Note here the certain happiness of those beholders, that do see certain excellency in holiness, though disgraced and undervalued. If there be any thing in the world that is a sign of sincerity, it is this, to love holiness when disgraced, abused, and spit upon; to cross the stream, and thwart the multitude, is a sign of the truth of grace, and strength of grace: this is a sign of

true sight, and strong sight. To see beauty in a godly man in sufferings, the Lord will certainly have an eye upon thee in times of trouble. Here is comfort in thine infirmities. Dost thou love holiness when compassed about with sufferings and persecution? God will take notice of thy grace, though compassed about with abundance of infirmities; the Lord will take notice of a little of his, in a great deal of ours. Here is comfort in sufferings; if you regard his in their sufferings, the Lord will remember you in your sufferings; the Lord will remember what thou didst for such and such a servant of his own in trouble or distress. God doth not cast away any in their lowness, that have kept close to him in their highness; and this will be comfort in inward trouble, when thou canst find nothing from which to fetch comfort. And this will be comfort in the last day; though we can say nothing in that day, by way of merit, yet will it be comfort to be able sincerely to say that thou hast owned God and his people in the midst of sufferings. Do ye think that judge would not save that malefactor that had saved the life of his wife? If thou hast owned Christ when he was in his rags, do not fear but he will own thee when he comes in his robes.

6. *Inference, and last.* The people of God should learn not to be discouraged under any misery or affliction that can befal them in this world. At this very time God hath a high esteem of you; at this time you are his delight, his garden, his spouse. The saints of God are the wise men of the world, they have chosen that which cannot be taken from them. I profess, Sirs, the love of one saint makes amends for all the hatred you undergo for sinners. The very wicked themselves have a good opinion of you, when you do not basely comply: their consciences cannot but have an high esteem of you, when peradventure their tongues might speak against you. If all this will not do, remember, your own consciences are more than a thousand witnesses for you, will then comfort you. No man is a miserable man for any thing in the world that

is done to him, or said of him. No, it is a good conscience that will give the best acquittance. For thee to have the whole number of God's people to look upon thee as an unworthy wretch, and as a vile person, I look upon it as a greater ignominy and disgrace, than to have all the disgraces of wicked men cast upon thee. That man that hath a godly man to be afraid of him, had need to be very much afraid of himself. I shall conclude all with this one word, There is great reason to look narrowly to your hearts and ways, when they stand at a distance from you, and are afraid to come near you.

MR. JENKIN'S AFTERNOON SERMON.

Preached August 17, 1662.

EXOD. iii. 2, 3, 4, 5.

And the Angel of the Lord appeared unto him in a flame of fire out of the midst of a bush, and he looked, and behold, the bush burned with fire, and the bush was not consumed. And Moses said, I will now turn aside, and see this great sight, why the bush is not burnt. And when the Lord saw that he turned aside to see, God called unto him out of the midst of the bush, and said, Moses, Moses. And he said, Here am I. And he said, Draw not nigh hither: put off thy shoes from off thy feet, for the place whereon thou standest is holy ground.

LET us take a short view of the foregoing verses: and that this may be the more useful and profitable to us, we may take notice, that as in the former chapter there is described Moses' preservation to his future employment, so in this chapter there is described his preparation, and his fitting for that employment, *i. e.* by a vision, or rather a suitable apparition, in which God discovered unto Moses his care of his people, of whom Moses was to be a speedy deliverer. You have here in the words read unto you, the preparation afforded to Moses for the great work of being called to be Israel's deliverer; and in this preparation you may take notice of three principal parts.

I. An apparition that is here presented to the view of Moses, "a burning, though not a consumed bush."

II. Moses's care to observe it, "I will turn aside and see this great sight, why the bush is not burned." And then,

III. God's monitory precept, or admonition, which he afforded unto Moses, when he was drawing near to see this wonder, in which we have principally considered two parts.

1. This precept propounded. 1. Negatively, "That he should not draw near." 2. Affirmatively, "That he should put off his shoes from off his feet."

2. You have considerable, the reason or argument, whereby God doth back this precept or admonition, *i. e.* "because the place whereon he stood was holy ground." The time would fail me if I should go over all these parts, we shall only touch on the two former. The apparition which Moses saw, and Moses's desire to observe it: of the first I shall speak transitorily, and insist on the latter more fully, which I chiefly intend.

1. For the apparition, or emblematical discovery of the estate of the church in the burning, and yet unconsumed bush. And herein take notice of three things.

1. The lowness and weakness of the church, represented by a bush.

2. The cruelty of the church's enemies, signified and represented by fire.

3. The eminency of its preservation; though in the fire, yet unconsumed.

And in this only take notice, that the church is compared to a bush, for two reasons: 1. In regard of its deformity and blackness, and uncomeliness. 2. In regard of its weakness and brittleness. The church is uncomely in regard of sin, and weak in regard of suffering; and God sees it best that it should be thus with them to humble them, and to shew his goodness to accept them, and to love them, and make them long for their future beauty. And hereby God makes them more conformable to their head, hereby he makes them endeavour to look after inward beauty and glory. Hereby he puts them on a life of faith, and takes them off from living by sense, and creature-comforts, and from being intangled with creature-comforts. And hereby he shews how little he regards the beauty and glory of this life, which he denies to the best of his people. And hereby he shows, that there is a better state of appearance and glory approaching: and therefore the people of God are not to be censured under their blackness and deformity, either in regard of sin or suffering. Their happiness is not to be judged by its outward appearance: because this life is but the obscurity of the church: we see them like the tents of Kedar, but we do not see how like the curtains of Solomon they shall be. 2. The people of God should take heed of expecting that glory of this world, which is not promised to them, and to set their hearts on heaven. And you may see the reason why wicked men stumble so much at the outside of God's worship, because there is no outward bravery and beauty to allure them to the true worship.

2. The church is compared to a bush, in regard of its weakness and brittleness. Note, that it is not compared to a strong sturdy oak, but to a weak brittle bush. God loves to bring his church into a low estate and weak condition; as it is here compared to a bush, so other-where to a vine, a dove, a lamb, and a sheep, all weak creatures. Sometimes the church is said to be fatherless and destitute; as our Lord Jesus Christ, the head of the church, was said to be weak, a worm, and no man; and as the apostle said, "suffered through weakness." And this

makes them to trust in God, and puts them to rest on his strength. "When we are weak, then we are strong." Outward weakness will make us look the more to Christ for spiritual strength; the weakness of our state doth shew the spiritual strength God gives to his people for the upholding of them. And this weakness of his church doth exceedingly confound his enemies, when so weak a company shall be delivered, not only against, but by the strength of men: and hereby God doth gain to himself the greater glory in their deliverance, for remembering them in their weak estate. Hereby the people of God are made more thankful, both for their preservation in, and deliverance from their powerful adversaries. You see, here is a large field opened unto me, for the discoursing upon the church's weakness, which whether it be more suitable to the text, or to the times, I leave to you to judge.

2. Consider the cruelty of their opposition, that is set forth and represented by "the fire that burneth in the bush." Afflictions, and especially persecuting ones, are in the Scripture, frequently set out by fire, as "The fiery trial, the fire of afflictions." This doth not only discover the rage and cruelty of men, but also the benefit and utility that comes to the church by affliction; for the afflictions of the church are not as consuming, but trying fire. As the fire in the furnace is to gold, it only takes away the dross: not like the fire of hell, which hath heat without light; but the school of persecution hath light as well as heat: the school of affliction is the school of teaching. God teacheth his saints excellent lessons by the light of that fire. But I pass by, that I might now insist upon the third thing.

3. Consider the eminence of their preservation, "It was not consumed;" the church of God was hot, but not altogether and wholly consumed. Let the fire be never so hot and spreading, the church of God shall have a being. If the church be less in one place, it will be greater in another. What it loses in one place, it gets in another:

and God will have a name among his people on earth: A man may as well attempt to blow out the light of the sun with a pair of bellows, or batter it with snow-balls, as to root the church out of the world; for it is impossible to root Christ's church out of the world. And if you take notice of particular believers, " it is not consumed" in a way of hurting and destroying them. And consider, their graces are not consumed, their welfare is not destroyed: this fire cannot burn them up, though it burn upon them: but as he will mitigate and allay the fire, so as that it shall not decrease their strength, so he will cleanse his people by the fire, so as it shall burn up nothing but their dross, and what makes them offensive unto God, and what may make them hurtful to one another. But I pass by these things to the second general part, viz.

2. Moses's care to observe God's admonition, "That he would turn aside and see this great sight, why the bush was not burnt." Moses was an excellent naturalist, and yet here he was posed; he could see no reason in nature by all the learning of the Egyptians, how this thing should come to pass, that a flaming fire should be in a brittle bush, and yet the bush not consumed. And yet I do not conceive (as some jesuitical expositors upon the place do) that Moses did turn aside so much out of curiosity, as to understand what it was that God did intend by it, and would have to learn by it. And, doubtless, when God's works are great, our observations should not be small; when his providence is eminently lifted up, we should not be cast down; when the hand of God is upon us, we must not shut our eyes. I am very far from being a fanatic, and to give credit, or be led by unscriptural revelations: but yet, let me tell you, the times wherein we live are strange times, in regard of strange sights and apparitions, and I question if there have not been some as wonderful as this in our times; but I shall not now mention them; though it be a forfeiture of your modesty to give a reason for them, yet they do portend some

strange things. The hand of God is not to be neglected, though it cannot be perfectly conceived; and it is the nature of a wicked man to have " God's work far out of his sight." Be sure to lay them up in your hearts. And thus far you may take notice of them, to trust the God that hath all the elementary meteors in his power, and at his command; and this learn, to tremble and dread before that God that hath you in his power, and can do with you and all other things, as he pleases.

3. You have here considerable, the admonition of God, or the monitory precept God lays down to Moses, i. e. he forbids him to draw nigher, and then bids him to "pull off his shoes:" the reason of the former will be easily understood in the opening of the latter. I shall, therefore, in it, briefly take notice of two things.

1. An injunction, " put off thy shoes."
2. The argument whereby he doth back this, "Because the place whereon he stood was holy ground."

For the opening of the former, the injunction, " Put off thy shoes," I shall not give the divers glosses, and divers interpretations, which men, with more wit than weight, have endeavoured to make of this Scripture. The plain meaning is this, which is given us by Theodoret, " Put off thy shoes." God's scope, and drift, and intent hereby was, to require of Moses reverence, when he was to receive a message of very great concernment and importance about his church. The design of God was in this, to prepare him to obedience, therefore God required that of him then, which servants were wont to do when they came to their Lord and Master, to shew their reverence to them. Servants use to come bare-foot to their masters, to testify reverence to the commands of them on whom they waited: *Nudare pedes signum reverentiæ.* And the putting on the shoes is in Scripture, as well as among other writers, held a token of domination or masterly power. Hence some conceive, John spake of Christ, as one that had his shoes on; and of himself, as one that was unworthy to untie his shoes. And the prophet

Isaiah, by a sign of " putting off his shoes," is commanded by God to put off his shoes from off his feet, and to walk naked and bare-foot, and he did so, Isai. xx. 2, which denoteth the servility of the people, in token that God's people were to be in a low condition in captivity. So we read of mourners, in Ezek. xxiv. 17, " that were of a low spirit," they are said " to go without shoes," or " unshod." And my brethren, on the other side, when God would shew the freedom of his people, and their deliverance from servitude, he is said to " put shoes on their feet," Ezek. xvi. 10, and the reception of the prodigal into his father's house, and the freedom and privilege his father intended him, (according to some learned men, intended by that expression in Luke xv. 22.) is set forth by putting on shoes upon his feet. So that I take the meaning of this command to be so much: Shew by this thy reverence, thy humility, thy due submissiveness, thy subjection of spirit, together with thy servile readiness to do whatsoever I shall command thee. Calvin hath this note upon the text: "If so excellent a servant of God as Moses, had need to be quickened to reverence and obedience by such a ceremony, certainly we that are more backward to humility and obedience, should, by our reverent behaviour, when we come into the presence of God, signify both the reverence of our souls by our outward expression, and likewise quicken and fortify the inward graces of our souls, by the inward gestures of the body; especially in prayer, as kneeling, and lifting up the hands, uncovering of the head, and the like: for the presence of God is great, and it is the presence of the great God indeed." We that are not only by the law of creation, so infinitely below him, but also in regard of that illegal law of sin, so much against him, should testify our humility before him, and subjection to him, when he calls for it by our reverence.

2. The reason by which this is backed, " Because the place whereon Moses did stand, was holy ground." The meaning I take to be this, it is holy in regard of that visible

and miraculous token, symbol, and sign of his presence, that is here discovered in this place; not because the place was (as I do not understand how any place is) of its own nature holy, but God did testify, that the place being the place of his special presence, had thereby a holiness; there being now a sign given by God to Moses, that he was extraordinarily and miraculously there. And thus I have opened the second branch, whereon this injunction was backed, "This place was holy," so it was then. Now I do not understand how I can discourse of this so profitably unto you, concerning the holiness of places, unless we take notice of the holiness of places in the time of the gospel, and consider, whether, and how in these times, one place may be said to be holy, or holier than another. And truly I am not put on this employment willingly, nor the handling of this subject; and if it were not extorted from me by something, I do not say that I have seen, but that I have read, that was written by men, and those none of the meanest neither, the learnedest of the papists, I should not now have chosen to have entered upon this task, concerning the holiness of places; in opposition to whom, I have entered upon this discourse. I will give you expressions, which one of the devoutest, and the other of the learnedest of them hath; the learnedest of them, accounted so at least, (though blessed be God, his weapons have not been formidable to the church; is Bellarmine, his words are these, *Templum consecrandum merito venerabile et divina virtute præditum est:* The temple consecrated is deservedly holy, and venerable in worship, and endowed with divine virtue and efficacy; the temple ought to be looked upon as honourable and venerable. And for the other, Durandus he tells us, "So great is the religion and holiness of churches, that those things should be, and may be forbidden to be done in them," (he means perpetually, or else said nothing, for we grant as much) "which in other places may duly and lawfully be done."

In the handling of this question, "How are we to

judge and conceive of the holiness of places, in the time of the gospel? I shall endeavour, first, to explain it, and then faithfully and truly endeavour to resolve and determine the same.

First then, for explanation, I shall here endeavour to open these two things to you: first, what it is for a place to be holy, or wherein the nature of the holiness of the places consists; secondly, what that is, that is the foundation or cause of the holiness of places; and both these must in our discourse, and likewise apprehension, be accurately distinguished.

1. What it is for a place to be holy, this is two ways to be considered : 1. Generally; 2. More particularly.

1. More generally. The holiness of a place doth consist in the separation thereof, the setting it apart, the distinction and discrimination in the way of some excellent pre-eminence, or the exalting of it before and above all other places. Thus the notion of the holiness of places is taken in scripture, Exod. xxx. 31, 37, 38. you shall there read, that the Lord tells them in the 31st verse, concerning the ointment that he prescribed, and likewise the composition of it for his service, " This shall be an holy anointing oil unto me throughout your generations." Now see how God doth discover this to be holy, " On man's flesh it shall not be poured, neither shall you make any other like it, after the composition of it." Here was a discrimination, as well to the using of it, as to the making and composition of it. As none was to make such an ointment as this was, so none was to use it in their ordinary and common employment, so that now the holiness thereof did consist in the distinction and discrimination of it from other uses, and likewise from all other ointment. And this is further expressed concerning the holy perfumes, in the 37th and 38th verses, there was to be a difference betwixt this and other perfume; and this was the holiness thereof. And so you shall find it not only concerning holy things, but likewise concerning holy persons, Lev. xx. 24, 25. " I am the Lord your God,

which have separated you from other people; you shall therefore put a difference between clean beasts, and unclean." Mark ye, herein is the holiness of the people, that they were a differenced and several people. And hence it is you read in Deut. xxvi. 18, 19. that God is there said to "avouch his people," openly to discover himself, to assert it, "that they are his people;" their holiness was a discrimination, a separation from the rest of the people. And in Deut. vii. 6. and xiv. 2. you have there the very same things described and discovered unto you. And now for this, I shall desire you to take notice of comparing two places of scripture, which discovers the holiness of places; in Deut. xix. 2, 3. "Thou shalt separate three cities for thee in the midst of thy land, which the Lord thy God giveth thee to possess it." And at the seventh verse, " Wherefore I command thee, saying, Thou shalt separate three cities for thee." Now you shall have this again propounded to you in Josh. xx. 7. "And they sanctified Kadesh in Galilee in Napthali, and Sichem in mount Ephraim, and Kiriath-arba (which is Hebron) in the mountain of Judah." Mark, the scripture that was called separation in Deut. ix. 2, 7. is here called sanctification; therefore the word in the Hebrew is, "And you shall sanctify," or make holy these places; that is, holy by the separation of them unto that employment that I shall appoint. Hence a thing is said to be unholy in scripture, when it is common, is not separated and set apart to holy employments and services; and from every thing that is of a civil concernment. And hence you read in Acts x. 14. in the vision that Peter had, God bids "Peter, kill and eat." But Peter said, "Not so, Lord; for I have never eaten any thing that is common or unclean." That is, unclean and unholy, in a way of legal unholiness, is said to be common, not set apart, Heb. x. 29. you shall there read this notion clearly discovered to you in the New Testament: " Of how much sorer punishment, suppose ye, shall be thought worthy who hath trodden under foot the Son of God, and hath counted the blood of the covenant wherewith he was sanctified, an unholy thing?" An unholy thing is a common thing. So that now what is sanctification in the former part of the verse, is called commonness and uncleanness in the latter part. But not to give you any more instances of this nature, the general nature of holiness is discrimination or separation.

2. To answer it more particularly, this setting apart, or discrimination, or separation of places for holy uses, must have these two properties.

1. A place that is holy must have such a separation from other places, as that it must be alienated from all uses but holy uses, it must not at all be employed to civil uses; for the employing of it unto civil uses, must be looked upon as sinful and unlawful. Thus in the scripture, when times, things, persons, are reputed as holy, they are to be exempted from common employment: the sabbath-day, a holy day, " in it thou must not do any manner of work." The vessels and utensils of the temple were holy, and therefore were not to be used to ordinary uses; and this, as some do think, was the great sin of Belshazzar, that he would offer to drink in the vessels of the temple. And so the garments of the priests were holy, and not to be used by secular persons. And the tabernacle and the temple were holy, and not to be used in civil employment.

2. More particularly concerning this holiness, I desire to shew you what it is, by shewing you it must be such a holiness and separation as that the service done to God in those places must be accounted and looked upon as a better service, and more acceptable than if so be it had been elsewhere, more acceptable to God, and advantageous to ourselves. Now, as places are said to be holy in regard they are only to be for holy purposes, so

2. Holy, in regard that holy services are only to be done there, with acceptation or advantage, at least with so great acceptation. And therefore I desire you to take notice, that places in scripture are said to be holy,

which did sanctify the worship which was done in them, and sanctify the worshippers, and so the very places are part of worship; and so not only places in which God was worshipped, but by which God was worshipped. And thus the sabbath was sanctified, and so the performance of God's worship therein, made God's service more acceptable and sanctified. And so the altar, when it was holy, it made the gift the more holy and sanctified, and so the more acceptable, the altar sanctified the gift, Matt. xxiii. 18, 19. And so the incense was acceptable to God, as being put into such a censer: and so the service done to God in such garments was more acceptable, because done in them which God had instituted and appointed for Aaron and his sons to wear. And so I have opened the first thing in the explanation, and that is to shew you wherein holiness consists, and how it is that places or things may be said to be holy; and I think I have sufficiently cleared the notion to you.

2. To shew what the cause or the foundation of this holiness is; for this, my brethren, I shall desire you also to take notice of it more generally, and then more particularly.

1. More generally, that the cause and the foundation of a place, or any other thing's holiness is its belonging to God, God's peculiar relation to it, and propriety in it, declared as he shall please; and therefore to be holy, and to be God's, are the words of the like importance, or equivalence; its being God's, and his having a relation to it, is the foundation and cause of its holiness. And therefore if you look into Exod. xv. 2, you shall there find God commands that "they should sanctify to him all the first-born, it is mine." There now is that which is the cause, and reason, and ground of its being sanctified, or holy,—it is God himself; God hath a propriety in it. And therefore I desire you to look into Luke ii. 23; it will open this notion to you; there you shall see that this command is again repeated, but yet in other words. And therefore he saith, "As it is written in the law of the Lord, Every male that openeth the womb shall be called holy to the Lord." That which is

said in one place to be sanctified or separated, is here said to be holy, and therefore holy, because separated to God, Levit. xxvii. 30: "All the tithes of the land is the Lord's, it is holy unto the Lord;" it is holy, and therefore holy because it is the Lord's. So that here is the general answer. This is the foundation, ground, and cause of its holiness, God's peculiar propriety in it, it is the Lord's.

2. More particularly, that the declared propriety that God hath in any place, or his relation to a place, or its belonging unto God, that is the foundation of its holiness. This belonging unto God, or God's propriety in it, is declared two ways.

Its belonging unto God is declared,

1. From his presence.
2. From his precept.

1. By his presence. Now the presence of God, that was the foundation of the holiness of a place, was twofold.

1. Extraordinary.
2. Ordinary.

1. The extraordinary presence of God was by his miraculous apparitions, and discovering himself by some miraculous token, vision, sign, or manifestation of his presence, as now here in this "burning, and not consuming bush." Here was a miraculous token of God's presence. We shall find in the fifth of Joshua, and the last verse, God commands Joshua to put off his shoes: "Loose thy shoes from off thy feet, for the place whereon thou standest is holy ground. And Joshua did so."— And therefore, as I conceive, hence it is, the mountain in which Christ was transfigured is called "the holy mountain," 2 Pet. i. 18. "And this voice which came from heaven, we heard when we were with him in the holy mount." Why holy? Not as if it were holy at that time when the apostle writ that epistle, but it were manifest, there was an extraordinary manifestation and sign of God's presence, and so long as this extraordinary manifestation of God's presence continued, it was called holy. And this miraculous manifestation of the glorious-

ness of Christ's Godhead ceasing, the holiness of the place ceased also. And remember this place now, of God's extraordinary miraculous manifestation of himself in the bush, was holy for that time, and no longer, wherein he did manifest himself; for otherwise, in the time of the law, it were unholy to offer up sacrifice there.

2. As the presence of God was extraordinary, so it is ordinary, which is two-fold.

1. The presence of his standing residence in a place, by some visible or external symbol; or else,

2. The presence of God is a spiritual presence, in the religious services and performances of his people, in the place of their meetings and assemblies. Now concerning the first of these.

1. The presence of God by the more visible and lasting tokens of his presence, which was chiefly afforded in the time of the Levitical pedagogue; so the altar, temple, ark, and mercy-seat, were symbols of God's presence among that people. By them, God signified his presence, he recorded his name there by those visible tokens of his presence; and therefore the ark was said to be God's face. And when the ark was lifted up, it was said, " Let God arise, and let his enemies be scattered." Hence they so much rejoiced when the ark came into the city of David, because it was the sign of God's presence, and mourned when it was taken away captive. And God is said " to deliver his glory into captivity," that is, the token of his glorious presence; and as long as this continued, God was looked upon as there present, and thither the people went to pray, and offer sacrifice. And thus God more fixedly declared his durable relation to a place by these tokens, and while these continued in a place, he was looked upon to be there.

2. God's ordinary presence is considerable in the religious service of his people, and this I call the rather the more spiritual presence of God; that is, that presence of God in the ordinances, which we have, we hope this day, and which Christ did promise, Mat. xviii. 20 : " Where-

ever two or three are met together in my name, there am I present in the midst of them." Not in the midst of the place, but of them, when they do perform holy and instituted worship. This spiritual presence of God is that, that is afforded in the use of those ordinances of praying, hearing, and administration of sacraments; his presence is there to accept of these, and bless them, and make them operative, and to assist in these, and to enable both minister and people to go through their duty by his own power. Nor can God's presence be ordinarily expected, but in this his own way. Now then,

2. You must know, that as the presence of God is the foundation of a place's sanctity, and as it is several, so you must know, God's propriety in, and relation to a place, is declared by his precept; the precept of God is God's propriety in a place, as well as his presence; thus it belongs to him by command to make it holy, he may do what he will, and choose out what places he will to be holy. He to whom all things belong, surely may have some places and things more proper to himself and peculiar; so the Temple of old, and the Tabernacle, those places of Levitical and ceremonial worship were separated and set apart by God by divine institution. Hence we have many commands.

1. God commands that such a house, and such a tabernacle shall be built, and this had been unlawful to do had it not been commanded.

2. He directs the manner, and the mode, and that all things should exactly be done according to the pattern in the Mount. And,

3. God doth command it should be in such a place, in the threshing-floor of Araunah the Jebusite, and that place that himself had chosen.

4. He commands that he will be served in these places peculiarly, rather than in any other place, he would not have these places changed for others. Herein this place typified Christ, one that is only able to make our services acceptable. Hence it is said, Exod. xxiii. 17, " Three

times in the year all thy males shall appear before the Lord." And Acts xxvii. the eunuch there went unto that place that God had commanded.

5. He doth command, that he would have these places reverenced, and no civil employments used there when the holy service was doing; and that after the service was done, at that very time the place should be only for God.

6. And lastly, he annexed a promise unto that place, that he would accept of a duty done there rather than in any other place, even because it was done there; hence they prayed in the temple, rather than in their private houses, Luke ii. 27; and when they could not be present, by reason of God's providence, in the temple, if they do but look to the city and the temple, God accepted of their duty, 1 Kings viii. 48. So that God did promise that that place that he had instituted for his worship and service, that the service performed there should be more acceptable to him than elsewhere. This shews the reason and foundation of a place's holiness, the precept of God, and the promise and presence of God. And thus I have opened to you the second thing. Now having thus explained and opened the question to you:

2. I come to resolve the question, according to what I think in my conscience to be the truth of God; and this I shall do two ways.

1. By granting that which must not be denied.

2. By denying what must not be granted.

1. By granting what must not be denied: and here I grant willingly these four things.

1. That in the time of the gospel, it is not only lawful, but it is often very commendable and necessary, to design and dedicate places unto God. Now when I say, it is lawful to design them and to dedicate them, I pray you bear me witness, I do not say it is lawful to consecrate them, or to sanctify them; but I say it is lawful to design and dedicate them. Now for this take notice,

that between 1. The designing and appointing of a place; 2. The dedication of a place; and 3. The consecrating of a place, there are these differences.

1. Concerning the designation of a place, then is a place designed, when it is appointed to be made use of for the most convenience for such a service, as Tuesday and Wednesday may be appointed for lecture-days, not consecrated. Now you must know, that this designation of a day may be altered, and so may a place: if such a place be designed, it is in our power to make use of it, so as to leave off the use of it when we please.

2. As to dedication, I mean so lawfully to dedicate a place, which is of our own right to dispose of; so to dedicate it, as not again to be able to revoke it, or call it back from such a use and purpose. It is lawful and commendable for a rich man to dedicate so much ground, or money, for building a house for a free-school, or for the poor, and to give it away from ourselves, and from our own right and power: and if so be that a man hath power or propriety over a place or thing, it is lawful for a man to alienate such a thing. And yet this you must know by the way, that this dedication that now is in the time of the gospel, doth very much differ from that dedication of free-will-offering unto God in the time of the law; for they were dedicated to God in the time of the law immediately, that is, to his immediate worship; it was part of God's worship, it was a part of religion to do that thing; whereas it is not now dedicated to the immediate worship of God, but it is dedicated immediately to such a priest, or minister, or place, or company of people, that we have a good will to gratify ; and so it more remotely redounds to God's glory not immediately. For God hath not declared in his word the same acceptation in the gospel of things done in an immediate way, as he had in the time of the law, of which acceptation now we have no such promise. And therefore it is observable, as one speaks concerning that benefactor in the gospel to the Jews, " He hath loved our nation, and

builded us a synagogue;" it is not said, for God, but for us: this man out of love to us hath bestowed these things to God; which though a giving ourselves out of our own power, yet it doth differ from the free-will-offering in the time of the law. Aye, but now, Sirs, ye must know, that sanctification, or consecration, that is a great deal more; when we sanctify a thing, or consecrate a thing, this thing that is so consecrated, it is so holy, that there must nothing at all of unholiness, or of a civil or secular employment and concernment be done in it. Now we do not dedicate a thing, but there may be secular things in an ordinary and civil way done in them; and our services are not more acceptable for the place, nor the places less holy because of those civil employments. There is the first concession, that in the time of the gospel there may be a designment and dedication of places, and it is not only lawful but commendable.

2. I grant, that in times of the gospel some places are to have religious services performed in them, rather than in other places; I mean places of natural conveniency and fitness for the meeting of people together, whereby they may be free from disturbance, from the violence of enemies, and from tempestuous weather. As public meetings, whereby we have the society of God's people, their examples to stir us up to zeal, and their joint help in prayer and holy performances, to go along with us, that we may join our forces together, and with a great force wrestle with God, and overcome him which is invincible. And therefore, my brethren, I desire you to bear me witness this day, that I plead for public ordinances, and for the purity of God's ordinances to be administered in public places, rather than other places; so that I do here profess, that I do avowedly and openly declare my judgment to be for public meetings in public places, and the purity of God's ordinances, if they may be enjoyed without human mixture, which may hurt and pollute them.

3. I grant, that in the time of holy service, we are not then to use secular employments at that time in those

places, as eating, drinking, and talking, it being unsuitable to the work in hand: and howsoever they may be lawful at another time, yet unlawful then, because against the apostle's command, "Let all things be done in decency, and in order;" and that which is unsuitable to the commands of God, the taking his name in vain. My brethren, I will go further with you, we are to abstain from all other religious services, when not in season; and therefore when the minister is in preaching, we must not run into our places and kneel down, as some people do, and fall a praying. And I cannot but wonder, that they that do so much cry up uniformity and sanctity of places, that yet they should confute their judgment by their practice, that they should pray secretly, when the whole congregation is a praying vocally; and it may be the congregation is singing a psalm, or the minister preaching, and then they go to their prayers. I pray, where is the uniformity, decency, and order they so much stand for?

Lastly, I grant, that after the performances of holy duties, in places wherein we meet for the worship and service of God, it is our duty to abstain, not only from filthy and indecent actions of a natural or moral filthiness, unseemly, as looked upon by men against God's laws; but from all those civil, moral, lawful actions, at other times, they may reflect dishonour upon the work that hath been done, or upon the work that shall be done, or that may render the place meet for religious services afterwards. And this is that, that one calls a negative, or private reverence, a reverence or not doing something; not because the place is more holy, but for decency and order, considering the religious duties performed in that place. So that things subservient to religion call for a negative reverence, and are not so to be used, as that the religious services which are there performed and transacted, should be made disgraceful and dishonourable; as the bread of the sacrament, after the sacrament is done, is not lawful to be cast unto unreasonable creatures, because it reflects dishonour upon the religious service which we were before doing; so, dirty water is not to be put into the communion-cup; not that the cup is holy, but because it is a reflection of disgrace upon that holy service wherein that cup is made use of; and that cup is not to be made use of to drunkenness. But in all this bear me witness that I say, all this is but a civil reverence, and so due to any place where there is any honourable convention, as in the parliament-house, or presence-chamber, or the like.——Having yielded this,

2. I must come now to deny what must not be granted, and I likewise deny four things.

1. It is not now in the times of the gospel in any man's power to set apart a place for religious duties, so as that it should be unlawful upon a due occasion to use it for civil employments, or that it should be always unlawful to alienate to other uses, besides those uses that are divine. The bread and wine sanctified by God's own institution, by the minister, after the public use and administration of them in the ordinance, are not now holy, but they may be eaten in a civil use and way as our ordinary and common food. The synagogues among the Jews were as holy as our churches; they were for holy duties, as prayer, preaching, and the like, and dedicated to God's worship, and yet you must know there were civil employments used in those places after the religious worship was done; and therefore in Matt. xxiii. 34, saith our Saviour, " Some of them you shall scourge in your synagogues." Hence we used to keep courts and consistories in churches amongst us, and some of them none of the best; and we use here among us in this city constantly in our churches, (and I doubt not but it is lawful,) for an alderman in his ward to meet about secular business, as to choose common councilmen, or the like. But where there hath been a dedication of a place to God's worship, it is only God that can make it so holy, as that it should be sinful to employ it to other uses; and

if the governors of the church, upon due occasion and reason, shall substitute other places more fit than the former for divine worship, then the former places may return to their former proper uses; but it is not so in things consecrated by God. If the font, table, or pulpit wax old, they may be laid aside, and looked upon as common things, and may be used for other employments. And suppose the surplice be a lawful garment in God's worship, (which yet I am persuaded none of you believe,) doubtless it is not to be burned when it is old and past wearing, and the ashes put into a pot, or some such like thing, and be buried under the altar; but it may be used as other linen may. And so the common utensils, as the cup, and the like, when they are come to be old, they may be used for other employments, without fear of sin. And therefore it is an excellent speech of one. Saith he, So to consecrate moveable or immoveable goods, as that it should be a sin for the church to use them in any secular employments, it is an execrable and abominable superstition. God hath not consecrated any thing in the gospel so, as that it is a sin to use it otherwise. It was a sin in them to make use of the cups in the temple in any secular way, but it is not so for us. The reason is, because those things were set apart by God's own institution. But there can be nothing so consecrated by men, as that it may not be made use of in secular things without sin.

2. A second thing I deny is, that no place now in the time of the gospel hath such an holiness, either from institution or use, as to sanctify or make more acceptable or effectual the services therein performed. This is not in the time of the gospel. God is present at places of religious performances, not with respect unto the place, but the performance by him instituted and enjoined; and therefore he doth not say, " Where two or three are met together, I will be in the midst of that place," but " among them." God will be present in the place for the duty's sake, not among them for the place's

sake, but the duty's sake in the place, to bless the ordinance for his own institution sake. Prayers and other duties in the ceremonial law were regarded for the place's sake, but now we must abhor this piece of Judaism. For a man to set a place apart by consecration, that this place makes the duty any thing the more excellent, or acceptable to God, this is to make the traditions of men equal to the institution of God. The temple sanctified the duty, but not the synagogue; and the altar did sanctify the gift, and the person and service, because it was by God's institution, and so the temple and altar did add efficacy and worth to the work; but for men to consecrate the church, it is to make the appointment of men equal with the institution of God. Our churches and meeting-places are not holy, if they be holy at all, without relation to the duties performed; but our duties are holy, without relation to the church or the place. None but God can consecrate a place to be an effectual means of worship. The Jews worshipped God by the temple, but we worship God in the church, as the place doth afford a natural conveniency for our meeting together. The place, then, hath no influence at all upon our duties; and if any of you should think so, you do err exceedingly. It is but only a physical act of duty, or a natural adjunct of duty, which is but at the most helpful to the body's conveniency.

3. The third thing I deny is this, that there is no place so holy as to exclude another place from being as holy in a way of proper sanctity and holiness, which we have been now opening. God now makes not one place properly more holy than another. There is not now properly any religious difference of places. We have not now the precept of God to sanctify and separate one place from another,—to prefer one place before another. We have not now the miraculous presence of God, his appearing as at the bush. God hath not given us under the gospel those symbols of his standing presence and residency, as by the ark, and mercy-seat, and altar of

old, he gave unto his people. And as for his ordinances, if they make a place holy in regard of performance of duty to God there, and his spiritual presence in that place, then my parlour, chamber, or closet are holy where I use to pray, and where God doth afford his assisting blessing and comforting presence. So that if you make the spiritual presence of God to make a thing holy, in regard of God's spiritual presence going along with those services, then your houses are holy, and the field is holy where you walk when you meditate; and praying by the river side makes it holy. Human consecration makes no place truly holy. If the spiritual presence of Christ makes one place more holy than another, then the communion-table and font are more holy than any other place in the temple. And so, when God's presence hath been enjoyed at the font, that is more holy than the communion-table; and so, when the presence of God hath been enjoyed at the communion-table, that is more holy than the font, and so you must bring in Judaism. If the presence of God makes a thing holy, a new communiontable, upon which the sacraments was never administered, cannot be so holy as the old table. Nay, by this the mouths of the communicants are holy, having eaten the bread and drank the wine which was dedicated to an holy use, and so it will be sinful for you to eat any other food.—I conclude all with this, that the difference and holiness of religious places in the times of the gospel, is not given, but taken away by the gospel, 1 Tim. ii. 8: "I will therefore that men pray every where, lifting up holy hands, without wrath and doubting." You may pray, and that with as much acceptableness to God, in one place as in another. John iv. 21, Christ saith, "The time comes when you shall neither in this mountain, nor yet at Jerusalem, worship the Father." That is, God's worship and service shall not be confined and limited to those places, as if others were not as good and holy as they. 1 Cor. i. 2: "To them that are sanctified in Christ Jesus, called to be saints, with all that in every place call upon the name of Jesus Christ our Lord, both theirs and ours." One place for the calling upon Christ is as good as another; and therefore, " Where two or three are gathered together, I will be in the midst of them." And this is foretold in Zeph. ii. 11, and in Mal. i. 11. So that this is the sum of all : God's institution makes the Sabbath holy, and the bread and the wine set apart by God's own institution, after the duty, may be used in secular uses.

But fourthly and lastly, to name no more, no place is so sanctified by God, as that after the ceasing of that presence of God, any holiness should belong unto it, as now when the signs and tokens of God's presence ceased and was gone, the holiness of that place was gone, and then it was lawful for Moses to " put on his shoes."— And so when God's presence ceased in the ark, the altar, and mercy-seat, the places became no other than secular and civil. And now for us to go about (as the Papists do,) a pilgrimage to Jerusalem, as if that place had any more holiness than others, is a foolish and abominable thing. How many bloody battles have been fought, to the disgrace, as well as the loss, of Christianity, for the regaining of the Holy Land !

Nay, let me add, those places where the presence of God hath been formerly, when it hath taken away, and those places have been used to idolatry, they are the worse, and the more unholy; for this is turning the house of God into vanity.

The conclusion of all is this—whatever places are in holy duties, out of them they lose and leave all their holiness; and therefore I say it is boldness for us to go about to tie God's presence to a place where God hath never tied it. I cannot but wonder how it is possible for men of reason and learning to be so blind as to hold that the Lord's day (which was set apart by God for the sabbath, as you may see in the fourth commandment, and afterwards by Christ and his apostles, which doth amount to no less than an institution) is not holy after the service or sermon is ended, but then you may go play at football and cudgels, and drinking, and what not; and yet they should say that the place of performing religious duties in, is so holy after religious performances as that you cannot come into it without bowing the knee, and putting off the hat, and bowing to the altar and communion-table, and the like; this I cannot apprehend how it should be, and I wish any of you that are of this mind, would privately give me your reasons for it why it should be so.

Now having explained the point, and given you a resolution of the question, in these particulars, give me leave to wind up all with some uses.

First, We infer the great difference that is between sanctity of places under the Old Testament, and sanctity and holiness of places under the New Testament. They under the Old Testament had the immediate presence of God, the standing symbols, and visible signs of his presence, so long as these lasted: which was set apart by God's special commandment, and so they were holy, though they were not employed in a way of worship; but you cannot say so now, our places for performance of holy duties have no such holiness; places now differ from places then.

Secondly, By way of inference, I note the great goodness of God to give us such a sweet and gracious indulgent dispensation in the time of the gospel under the New Testament, as that he doth not tie us to ceremonies or places; he doth not bind us as he did the Jews to go three times in the year to the furthermost part of the nation to worship. No, my brethren, no land, no ground, is now unholy, as famous old Doctor Reynolds said, every place is now a Judea, no coast but is a Judea, every house is a Jerusalem, every congregation is now a Zion. See here the goodness of God in indulging us so far as to take any service done by us in a solemn and real manner, as if it had been done in those places which were formerly appointed for it to be done in.

Thirdly, I infer hence, there are several persons to be reproved.

1. We find hereby that all the holiness of relics of saints doth fall to the ground, and we see the folly of those that make pilgrimages unto saints and relics as the papists do. There was a time (say they) when such a saint's relics were laid up in such a place, and these are more holy than other places: so that this you see falls to the ground in itself. I might tell you concerning their lying about their relics, as one said, that there were as many relics as would fill an hundred carts: but supposing so, all that would not make that place the more holy.

2. Hence the superstition of those is to be reproved, which put holiness in place of burial, and make it more holy to be buried in one place than in another: it is more holy (say they) to be buried in the church than in the church-yard; and more holy under the communion-table than in any other part of the church.

3. This reproves them which cannot pray any where but in the temple, and they that use private prayers in churches. If you have houses and rooms at home, what is the reason that if Paul's or any other church stand open you must run in thither, and drop down behind a pillar to say your prayers.

4. This reproves them that have reverence towards any place more than another, as if they did deserve more holiness in one part than another, as bowing to the altar, or communion-table, or the like.

5. It reproves those that have reverence for situation of these places, they must stand east and west, and why not north and south? All these things fall off, like fig-leaves, if what I have said be true, that there is no holiness in places; and this I have made known to you not only as my judgment, but as my duty.

Now for exhortation, I shall desire you to take notice of four things, and I have done, and shall leave you to God, and commit you to the word of his grace. If this be so, that there is no holiness in places, then first of all, be the more encouraged to serve God in your families, in those places where God hath set you, where God is as well pleased with your service as in public places, serve God upon your knees with devotion, humility and reverence. And therefore, though I am against superstition, and popish practices, and those wicked cursed traps of innovations, that the men of the world have disturbed the church of God with; yet I am against putting on your hats in prayer; and sitting in prayer. Those that are for holiness of places, do not, with Abraham, in every place they come build God an altar. But let us in every closet and room build God an altar; let no morning nor evening go without a prayer in thy family, pray often, and pray continually, let your houses be as so many churches, as you read in Rom. xvi. 5. "Likewise greet the church that is in their house:" and in the second verse of Philemon's Epistle, "To the church that is in thy house." There the houses of the saints are called churches. This will bring a blessing upon your families. And if you be not willing to have that curse denounced against you, in Jer. x. 25. "Pour out thy fury upon the heathen that know thee not, and upon the families that call not upon thy name," then neglect not family-prayers, be much in prayer, and pray with frequency and encouragement, because God binds you to no place.

The second exhortation is this, labour to promote personal holiness, as well as family devotion. I am against local holiness: As one said, (that I heard once when I was a youth) happy are those garments that can carry away any of the dust of the temple; but they think not that any of their garments are unclean in wallowing in the mire of sin. But I say, do you labour to promote holiness in your lives, in your hearts and conversations. The Holy Ghost saith, "Unless you be pure in heart you shall not see God." And therefore put away sin, for if you regard iniquity, God will not hear your prayers: It is not your ducking, or bowing, or cringing never so much, or your going with your hat off through the church, that will make God hear your prayers, these will but dishonour you, because you live not accordingly.

3. Love the holiness of the living members, be not so much in love with the holiness of wood and timber, bricks and stones; but wheresoever you see the image of Christ, be in love with that soul. Wherever the presence of God shines, and wherever thou seest one that gives up himself to God in holy duties, do thou say, Oh! my soul, delight to come into the company of these men, "The righteous is more excellent than his neighbour." If there be a heaven upon earth, I tell you, it is in the company of godly men. I remember a famous man hath this expression, saith he, When I was in the company of the saints and people of God, I was as a living coal; but when I was separated from them, and was among the wicked swearers and drunkards, methought there was a spiritual coldness and frozenness went over my soul. Though the people of God are best company in Heaven, yet they are very good company here on earth. And Christians should stir up one another, and be provoking one another to love and good works; and wherever you have grace, be sure to impart it to others. Endeavour to love the holiness of saints, and be willing to impart your experiences to others, for this is your duty. Do not make a monopoly of holiness, but carry company with you to Heaven.

Lastly, to name no more, labour to preserve the holiness of God's true institutions, those things which are of divine consecration. What is human consecration, without divine institution? The sabbath day is of divine institution, labour to keep it holy; this is a holy day indeed, and this labour to keep your families from profaning of; but for other holy days, and holy things, they are much alike for holiness: the Lord's day is a holy day indeed, and for shame, do not let your children gad abroad on this day. Truly, I do verily believe, that though here be a great company of people in the congregation, yet they are but a handful in comparison of what are drinking in ale houses, and walking in the fields, that one can hardly get home to their house for the crowd of the people that are going thither. For shame let not this be told in Gath, nor published in Askelon. What! shall we stand up for the holiness of places, and yet oppose the holiness of the Lord's day, which God hath enjoined and instituted? Oh! that the magistrates of London—Oh! that England's king—Oh! that England's parliament would do something for the reformation of this, to oppose wickedness and profaneness, which will otherwise bring upon us the judgments of Sodom and Gomorrah, and make us guilty and worthy of a thousand punishments. And labour by prayer in your families to overcome that flood of profaneness, which you cannot by your strength prevent. And then for the sacraments of Christ, baptism, and the Lord's supper, these are ordinances of God's appointment, they are holy, and therefore should not be given to those that are unholy; and yet those who are so much for the holiness of places, do not care who come to the sacrament, if they have but a nose on their face, they shall come and partake of the ordinances, let them be what they will; this is to prefer man's institution before God's institution. And then for the Lord's message and word, that is a holy thing, and therefore love his messengers: the messengers of God delivering his message with fear and reverence, you are to hear them with the same fear, reverence, and resolution to be holy, as if Christ were present. And for the word of God, it is not enough for you to have a choice sentence written upon the walls of your churches, but let God's law be written in your hearts and consciences, and practised in your lives, that all the world may see you live as men dedicated to the true God, in all the duties of his ways and obedience. Many of these things might have been enlarged. What

I have given you with the right hand, I pray you christians, do not take with the left; for if you do, you will make yourselves guilty of a double sin.

First, because you do not obey the truth you hear.

And secondly, for putting a wrong construction upon it.

But I have better hopes of you, my beloved hearers, and hope that the Lord will be better unto your souls than his ministers, than his word, or any thing else can be. God bless you and his ordinances, and discover his mind and will at this time to you.

MR. BAXTER'S SERMON,

Preached August 17, 1662.

COLOSS. II. 6, 7.

As ye have therefore received Christ Jesus the Lord, so walk in him.

Rooted and built in him, and established in the faith, as ye have been taught, abounding therein with thanksgiving.

OMITTING the division, and in part the opening of the words, the observation is; "That those that have received Christ Jesus the Lord, must accordingly be rooted, built up in him, and established in the faith; and walk in him as they have been taught, and abound therein with thanksgiving."

This receiving of Christ signifies to believe in him. It is not only to receive his doctrine or benefits, but to receive his person, to receive him as related to us, for the uses and end for which he came into the world, and for which he offers himself to souls, by the preaching of the gospel. Sinners have lost and undone themselves; Christ comes to be the physician of souls. He will not save the unwilling, and despisers of his grace, while they continue in their unwillingness. He will save them by the way of covenant, while he consents and tenders them his grace, he will have them " consent to the terms of his covenant." The consent of the heart expressed by our covenanting with him, is this receiving of Jesus Christ. He is willing to be our physician, and when we take him to be so, we receive him. He is willing to save us from the guilt and power of sin, willing to be our Lord, head, intercessor with God, justifier, and all unto us; and if we consent to this, and take him as offered, this is receiving Christ; with whom his benefits are also received, the remission of sins, in-dwelling, renewing, comforting spirit, title to everlasting life, &c. In receiving Christ all this is received.

Receiving of Christ contains these two things, or these two things are essentially contained to make up the nature of saving faith, that is, to believe the doctrine of the gospel concerning Jesus Christ to be true, and to consent that the goodness that is therein revealed and proposed, shall be ours. To believe what Christ is, and what he hath done : so far to believe it, as here we are resolved to venture our souls, (though there may be some weakness through our faith's imperfection) and believing the gospel to be the certain word of God. Then next, to entertain the Christ that is offered in this gospel to be ours, with all the benefits that accompany, and to all the blessed ends to which he is revealed. Thus the water of life is freely rendered to all that are athirst, and there is no more required, but come and drink.

Then there are two things implied, that are the immediate products of saving faith, and inseparable from it, that is, trusting on him as the Redeemer, and obeying him as a Lord. To rest upon him as a Redeemer, Romans xv. 12. And here as far as the soul feels entertainment and encouragement by Christ, overcoming his doubts that Christ will reject him, &c. so far he hath quietness of soul in Christ, and will trust his soul upon

Christ. And then, the obeying of him in order to our full recovery, as a patient must obey his physician in using his remedies, and means he prescribes for killing our sins, restoring our souls to God's love, and being with him to eternity.

The nature of faith is to receive Christ; the sincerity of it lies in the suitableness of the act to the object; that we receive him as he is. Now, in Christ there is something essential to this act; that he be a Saviour, and our Saviour, &c. and there is something makes unto the well-being and fuller attaining of the end. The first are "the objects of faith itself," as it is of absolute necessity to salvation. The second sort are, "the objects of faith as it is strong," and makes to the well being of a christian. All that is essential to Christ as a Saviour, and Redeemer, is to be believed by him that will approve himself a true believer. And thus to receive Christ "as the eternal Son of God, made man, the Redeemer of the world," ruling us upon the right of redemption, justifying us before God, bringing us to God, and interceding for us. And thus Christ must be received according to his offices, and as those uses for which he is given to the soul do import and imply.

For the application of this point;—

First, Let us begin with those that our business at present doth not mainly lie on. Must men "walk in Christ as they have received him?" What shall we say to those that "have not, will not receive him?" stop us at the door, that we cannot bring in the doctrine of Christ, that "will not receive the principles of Christ?" How can we bring them, and build them up, that will not suffer the foundation to be laid, the seed to be received? Hast thou not received Christ? then thou hast refused Christ, been a despiser of the gospel of Christ, which will prove thy great condemnation. What is it for thee to hear the name, and not to have the spirit of Christ? Do not go upon conjectures; it is one thing to number thyself with those that are christians, as to outward appearance, and another thing to open thy heart, and deliver up thyself to Christ's government, and as a lost sinner, to receive him to those ends a Saviour must be received. And remember, this was no small work, God sending Christ into the world, no small thing to fetch thee from hell and Satan, to wash guilty souls from all their sins, and to bring them to everlasting glory. If these great things be rightly understood and believed by thee, if Christ be understood well as Christ, it must be done with a weakened, humbled, self-resigned heart, making the greatest matter in the world of these things. Hath thy soul been seriously taken up about thy own recovery? And hast thou received Christ as a man that was ready to be damned; as one that had a load on his soul heavier than all the mountains of the earth, to ease and deliver him? as one that was under the frowns of God in a state of enmity, receives reconciliation? Hast thou received Christ as if thou hadst received heaven in him? Believe it, these are great transactions, and will affect thy heart; and it is not a sleepy or jesting matter thus to receive Christ. Consider what it is to receive Christ.

1. If you have received Christ, you have received the great reconciler that binds up the broken-hearted, quiets those that tremble under the threatenings of God, for he should forsake and cast them off for ever.

2. If thou hast received Christ, thou hast received a perfect enmity to all sin, that will never let thee rest in sin, but be persuading thee from it, and conflicting in thee against sin in thy soul. If thou hast received Christ, thou hast not received a friend for sin, that will plead for, or give thee leave to commit sin; but one, that though he bear with thee in thy weakness, yet abominates thy sin. If thou hast received a Lord and master to rule, to be consented and subjected to him, and to be ruled by none but in subordination to him, who will break those in pieces that refuse his government, obedience and not verbal profession, is the thing he requires. Hast thou entertained Christ to be the master of thy

words, thoughts, and deeds, whose government thou livest under, more than under any in the world?

3. If you have received Christ, you have then received the beginning of felicity, and full contentment to your souls. Having found none in your sins, you have it discovered to you where it is: therefore with gladness go you on; and so far as you have hopes of attaining it, so far you have great contentment, &c.

4. In a word, if you have received Christ, you have fallen out with sin, subjected pleasures, profits, and honours to him; and you have received his Spirit, and this hath made you new, and maintains the way within you against the flesh, &c. If this be not thy case, Oh that thou knewest what a case thou art in! For then,

1. What the better art thou for all his blood shed as yet, if thou wert this day to die? What would Christ's blood do to the cleansing and saving of thy soul?

2. How canst thou look thy sins in the face, and think on what thou hast done, and art? How canst thou look inward into thy defiled heart, and not tremble, when thou hast no more shelter from the wrath of God?

3. How canst thou look God in the face, who is a hater of sin? How canst thou read his attributes, think on his threatenings?

4. How canst thou think to have any duty accepted, and prayer heard, or rewarded, &c.?

5. How canst thou think on the day of judgment, on the time when thou must receive thy final sentence, if thou hast not received Christ? Oh what a thing is a Christless heart!

Q. What shall I do that I may receive Christ?

A. 1. Till Christ be thine, and hath brought peace from heaven to thy soul, let no peace be there to keep him out. I do not say, overwhelm thyself with sorrow, but let sorrow dwell there, and let holy cares and solicitousness about thy spiritual state be there, till Christ come, and quiet, and reconcile thee to God.

2. Read and believe the gospel. See there what Christ

is, and thy necessity of him. Believing will open the door to entertain him; assent will procure thy consent.

3. Keep up no idol in thy heart against him. Turn out that that keeps out Christ, how dear soever it seems now, at last thou wilt see it more necessary to detest than keep it.

I come now to exhort all poor weak christians, that they would make after confirmation, and grow to a greater measure in grace, as they have received Christ. It is not enough to be conceited that you have been converted; and it will not be enough to the assurance of your conversation, or safety of your souls, that you think you are converted, and you sit down there. He that is content with the opinion he hath grace; therefore desires to have no more, because the promise of salvation is made to the truth of grace, it is a sign he never had grace. Strength in grace is your own felicity, it is part of your happiness. Your eternal happiness will partly consist in your personal perfection; and without personal perfection, all heavenly glory will not be a perfect felicity. If you have fixed your anchor in God's promises, this engages you to look up, make after, and proceed, &c.

Take these motives.

1. Consider, there is the same reason to move thee to grow, and proceed, as there was to move thee to thy first believing. Why do you become christians, but because of the necessity of the riches and excellencies of Christ, and that there were better things in Christ, than in the world? And are they not so still? Is the case changed? If christianity was reasonable then, it is reasonable now. If it was necessary to begin, it is necessary to hold on, and proceed in your race till you have obtained the crown.

2. Your receiving Christ essentially, contains in it an obligation to proceed and go farther; actually to trust and obey him, whom you have taken for your Lord and Saviour, from the very offices and relations of Christ received.

If I be a father, where is my fear? If I be a master, where is my honour? If I be a saviour, where is your confidence in me, submission to my saving work, obedience to my healing precepts? If I be your lord and master, why do you not learn of me your master, &c.?

Your first covenant engages you to proceed in fulfilling the things promised in your covenant, &c. Better not have promised to be his people, than to promise and break this promise. The very mercies also, you have received from him, pardoning your former sin, entertainment in his church, and all the blessings there found, are as so many obligations to proceed.

3. Ever since we came home to Christ, we have had an addition of reasons, besides the first reasons we had to believe. Every day brings in new, &c. Certainly if a little were desirable, more were more desirable. If the people that stood afar off, and never tried what Christ and grace is, were bid to come in, those that have tried and tasted are bound to proceed much more. You have the spirit of God, experiences of his love, tasted the bitterness of sin, have had some trial of the truth of such things of which we speak, when others have eyes and see not, &c. and will you turn back that have tasted, &c.?

4. Consider how much hath been lost upon many a soul for want of care to take rooting, and to proceed; how much labour of the ministry, mercies of God, pains and care of their own? I speak of those that have seemed sincere, not indeed so; that have many times comforted the hearts of their ministers and friends, and have had some kind of comfort to themselves in that taste they have had of the good word of God. How many times hath the preacher been gladded to see such a one come to him, seemingly with a broken heart, seeming to set themselves in the way of life! Yet the flesh prevailed for want of confirmation. How many years have some spent in duty, in hearing, prayer, gracious society, profession of religion! Yet afterwards the world hath drown-

ed all. What cause have you to see you lose not the thing you have wrought.

5. Consider how much of the works of your own salvation when you are converted, is yet undone. Though you are sure your conversion is true, how many temptations to resist, enemies to conquer, duties to perform, and heaven to be taken upon all those terms, as the tenor of your christianity! Therefore you had need to stand fast, and having done all, to stand, you have need not only to believe, but to wait and be patient in believing, and to proceed in the way you have chosen.

6. The want of strength and building up, makes the lives of many full of lamentable languishing weakness, scandals unto others, pain, calamity, and trouble to themselves. How long in healing? And how much smart and pain, while the fruit of their own folly is cured? How little, and how frequently do temptations prevail? And hence as in a wilderness, they are going one step forward, another backward; no evident keeping in God, and all through the fruit of their own languishing weakness. The fruits of the sins of professors have been such, that it should make you do all you can possible to escape the troubles at home, and reproaches abroad.

7. A life of spiritual weakness, is usually a burden unto him that hath it, it doth not only occasion his falling into sin, and so renews the wounds of this soul, but is a constant burden to him. Not that any measure of grace is troublesome, but that which consists with so great a measure of remaining corruption: this is the burden: sickness is burdensome, though there be life. Methinks you should not then be reconciled to your fears; you should, methinks, see so great difference between the sick and the well, that for your own peace sake, you should seek after confirmation. Every duty they do is their pain, which is another's pleasure, prayer, &c. their burden; sometimes tired, wearied, dull, &c. presently overwhelmed with temptation: every duty is a grievance

to them through the weakness of their grace and their corruption.

8. Christians that are weak and not confirmed, lose abundance of the fruit of God's ordinances that are improved by others. How many a truth that taste exceeding sweet to others, have no great relish to them, nor growth by it? A healthy man hath more relish in ordinary fare, than a sick person in varieties, the full stomach loaths the honey-comb.

9. The weak and unconfirmed christian is unprofitable comparatively unto others. Not that the church would wish the weakest member out, but comparatively unconfirmed christians are very unprofitable unto others; like little children in the family that must be looked to, make work for a great many more about them. What doth a sick person? but the work of others is to feed, support, and be a help to him. The church of God hath need of strong christians that can pray in faith fervently for others, and you scarcely pray for yourselves. Consider when the church needs a great deal of help, will you sit down with low attainments, and little things, when so many hundreds about you need so great assistance?

10. Weak persons are many times the troublers, and very dangers of the church. Many calamities have been occasioned by them. The sins of professors have occasioned the displeasure of God on the church: their errors hindered truth, and made divisions. When christians have not so much strength as to know truth from error, that hearken to every one that speaks with likeness, what have these christians done in the church? what mercies have been driven away, so far, that I think the church of God, from the apostles' days till now, have suffered more by the sins of professors, than the malice of their enemies! And how canst thou expect God will save thy soul, when thou hast set the church on fire, and been so great hindrance to others, that many should perish occasionally by thy example? &c. The greatest

sufferings of the church have come from the miscarriages of the church.

11. Such have been the great dishonours of Christ; but the graces of ancient Christians, the glory of their professions, their charity, self-denial, heavenly-mindedness, patience, &c. have preached the gospel to the world more effectually than ever their words could do. God expects your lives should be a considerable means for the conversion of wicked men. The same God that hath commanded ministers to teach others by their doctrine, hath commanded you should live for the conversion of the world; that your zeal, humility, patience, charity, self-denial, should win souls to God; and if it be a sin to give over preaching when we may, surely so to give over living, &c. If " wo unto me if I preach not the gospel," then wo unto you if you by your lives preach not the gospel. How many sinners have you about you? and how do you wrong and rob the ungodly of that ordinance God hath appointed for their conversion and salvation? You are the persons that take the bread out of their mouths, the means that should save them out of their hands, while you deny them one of the commanded means of salvation, that is, the eminent example of your lives. And if it be so great a sin to stop preachers' mouths, how great a sin to neglect this ordinance? Nay, are you not a dishonour and disgrace to the church? Is it not because of professors' ill lives, that the profane deride religion, while they see not the glory in it that should overpower an unbelieving and denying soul, and should indeed effectually manifest its excellency? Are these the professors, that are proud, stubborn, passionate, censorious, self-conceited, contemptuous, and envious as any others? I know the world is apt enough to slander, and the servants of God to bear a world of unjust reproaches, but oh! that there were not this occasion, &c.

12. Those that are not confirmed and established in grace, the devil, when he hath prevailed by a temptation

on themselves, can easily make them his instruments to draw and tempt others from their duty, to discourage them in their religion, and to do that mischief in the world he hath done by temptation of their own soul. It is ordinary for Satan to make use of lapsed, distempered Christians, to be the instruments of his temptations to those that are better, &c. An honest Christian will not so easily hearken to a drunkard, swearer, as to a professor he had good thoughts of, Gal. ii. 23.

13. For want of strength and establishment in grace, poor weak Christians are a very great encouragement to the carnal hopes of wicked men. I think scarce any thing in the world hinders our preaching more than this; when the wicked see those that make the greatest profession no better than themselves, and in some things worse, this hardens him against all the convictions that can be brought against him. Tell him he cannot be saved without conversion, he looks upon professors, sees them contentious, worldly, peevish, passionate, &c. sees some sin or other, this makes him think he is as well as they. Must there be so much ado to bring men to this state? Is this the difference, &c.

14. Methinks it should be some trouble to an honest heart, that yet we must be so like to the children of the wicked ones; and the weakest Christians are the likest to the wicked; I do not mean weakness in gifts or knowledge, &c. but a weakness in practical saving knowledge, love of God, self-denial, mortification, heavenly mindedness, &c. They that are in these in the weakest Christians, are the next and likest to the wicked : and doth not this grieve thee, that though thou art not a child of the devil, thou art so like one? We should not be conformed to the world, nor like to them in any thing, no not in outward vanities. But to imitate the fashion of the world, as to outward corruptions, to go in their garb, when a palpable vanity, to have so much of their pride, peevishness, malice, worldliness :—Oh look upon thy heart with humiliation.

15. Consider what a dangerous and lamentable standing those have that be not established, &c. You stand, but it is as unrooted plants or trees that stand shaking in the wind; beholders are always looking when they fall. You stand, but it is as a sick man, wavering, reeling, like Lot's wife, looking back, and always upon every occasion ready to repent. You have been believers; little things perplex and trouble you; little tribulations and afflictions discompose and disturb you, little temptations make you question the scripture, the providence of God, his love and care of his people, and the great foundations of religion. Foundation seems to shake, because you are shaking and tottering, &c. And what is like to become of such a soul? If thou standest shaking under small temptations for want of confirmation, what wilt thou do when a papist or quaker, &c. shall so speak concerning religion which thou art not able to answer? and so the surest foundation seems nothing when thou hast so weak hold. Our greatest afflictions next to the misery of the ungodly, is to think of our weak ones, what will become of them: and verily we do expect a considerable part of our congregation should be carried away, those that are "Christians, and know not why," yet have not humility enough to make use of others, and to keep close to those that should assist them. Remember when you see such times, when seducers are able to say the worst, shall make the strongest assaults on the weak ones, how many will be like to fall? Again, sickness, death, dying times will come, when you shall find a little grace will not easily do your work; and though you perish not, yet you may faint, and to your sorrow find the want of confirmation. You cannot but know how the strongest are put to it in trying hours, or at death. Will slack unsettled hopes of another life, such distempered hearts fight and encounter with such trials? Never think of dying comfortably, if you follow not after confirming grace.

16. It should humble you the more, that you have been so long, so many years in the school of Christ, and

love God, &c. no better. Should not you in this apprenticeship have learned better your religion, and been teachers of others, when perhaps, if in the principles you are assaulted, you will shew your weakness as soon as any? May not Christ say, "Have I been so long time with you," and yet have you "known, lived, &c." no better? reached no higher, attained no further? weaklings still? Nay consider in this time what advantage you have had for growth. A tree planted on a barren wilderness may not grow so much as in a fruitful place; but you have had the plenty and power of the ordinances of God, the choicest of the means and helps of salvation.

17. Consider, the nature of true grace tends to this; will you cross the nature of it? shall we be such weaklings in religion, which cross so the nature of grace? for grace the more it is exercised, the more it increases.

18. Heaven itself is perfection, and the work of a christian is to press towards heaven, and therefore it is to press towards perfection. You should make towards the end in a manner and way that is suitable to the end. Persons that enjoy so much already, and hope for so much greater, should not put off God with such little things.

19. Little grace shall have but little glory. You know not how great a difference there is between the least and highest in the kingdom of God. Nay, it is not only for a christian to desire to be glorified, but to enjoy the highest degree in glory: to serve God with the best, and improve his talent to the utmost, that his heavenly reward may be according. A christian should not slight it when it is tendered to him, and in his eye.

Q. But how shall I know I have attained this confirming grace?

A. These signs following, shew a christian confirmed and strong in grace, which I will name that you may know what to aim at, and what to desire. There is not so great a difference between a king and a beggar, between the greatest health and sickliest man, as between a strong useful christian, and a poor languishing soul, &c.

1. A confirmed christian is one, " that can resist many subtle and strong temptations," not only a single temptation, but when Satan assaults on every side, with errors on both extremes, with importunities of several parties, with temptations of prosperity offered, of adversity felt or feared; strong temptations that seem to lay a necessity of yielding on a weakling, that makes him say, I must do it to save my liberty, family, life, &c. A strong christian can say, there is no necessity; he can make light of those temptations that seem to be a necessity to other persons: he can confute a subtle sophister, and deal with a cunning adversary. Satan cannot so easily go beyond and outwit him.

2. He can do great, excellent, and useful work, is serviceable to God, if he have opportunity in business of greatest consequence. He doth not serve God only in some little and inconsiderable thing, but in his place sets himself to the work of God, doth the great work of his majesty faithfully. The service of God to him is more easy and delightful: as to go ten miles is more easy to the healthful, than one to a sickly person, he can go through God's service with pleasure, ease, and delight, without tiring, fainting, sitting down, or giving over.

3. He can digest the hard truths and providences of God, that are ready to puzzle, perplex and over-set the stomach of a weak christian. He hath laid his foundation, to which he reduces all things of difficulty, and by the help of those great truths he hath received, he can easily see through the difficulties that are yet before him. He can tell how to reconcile those things in scripture that seem contradictions. Where he meets with a difficulty, he can easily discern the cause is in himself, and that there is an undoubted way of reconciling them, though he hath not attained to it. He can easily quiet his soul under the most difficult providences, and interpret them so as is consistent with the truths of God, which must expound them. He reconciles providence with providence:

and providence with scripture, whereas a weak christian is ready to say, " A hard saying, who can bear this and that ?" And it is the difficulty of these kind of truths that makes so many turn their religion, because not able to digest the hardest truths of God. Cross providences make them question God's love, &c.

4. He is one that can exercise various graces without setting one against another, destroying or contradicting one another: he can do many works, believe many truths, perform many duties at once. He can rejoice and sorrow at once, and make his sorrow a help to his joy, and his joy a help to his sorrow, and so exercise both in that nature as will not directly hinder or weaken one another. He can tell how in such a time as we are in to rejoice, yet to be humble, to be cast down at God's feet, in the sense of the sins we have committed, and of God's displeasure, &c. yet to rejoice in the mercies we have and do expect to possess. He doth not look all upon sin, all upon affliction, or all upon mercy, but can eye every thing, and give every thing its part, can exercise graces methodically, give truths and providences their proper place in his meditations and affections. And this makes his life orderly, beautiful, regular, and useful; whereas a weak christian, let him set himself against one temptation, he is taken in another; if he humble himself in soul, he can do nothing but humble, weep, grieve, fear, and be ready to cast away all comfort, all sense of the love of God: if he set himself to the consideration of the grace of Christ, he is apt to forget humiliation, and to be puffed up with spiritual pride, &c. Thus he hath not skill, strength, and ability to carry on all the whole work of grace together.

5. A strong christian sinks not under those burthens that would press down and overwhelm a weak christian; he can bear heavy burthens, and more easily away with them, making it a recreation to bear some things that another would sink under, and cannot bear. It is thy weakness that makes thee make such a stir, when God

lays on thee personal, family, public afflictions, that make thee shrink under them. Strength of grace would enable thee to see God and glory in the midst of them, and to say " All shall work for my good:" it would enable thee to get advantage, and be bettered by them. Hadst thou strength enough to improve them, thou wouldst take comfort from them, and support thyself under them ; but when thou hadst not strength enough to understand God's meaning, to see the duty then called for, to improve all for God, to do that service to God thou shouldst do in such a condition: no wonder if thou have not grace to support and comfort thee in that condition. Whereas the confirmed christian by strong faith, love, and patience, can carry great burthens, &c.

6. Is helpful to many, and troublesome unto few. They are the useful persons in the family and place where they live. It is they can counsel others in their doubts, help them in their straits; that can bear up the weak when ready to sink; that can hold others by the arm when not able to go upright; that tend God's little ones : and if it were not for these what would God's little ones do? They are so furnished with patience, which God hath given them for the use of the weak ones in his family, and though they are troublesome, or do that which might be a disturbance to them, they will not thrust them out. It is they that comfort the feeble, support, provide for, strengthen and confirm the rest. And were it not for these, what backsliding hearts should we have? &c. And they are comparatively troublesome to few (though while corruption cleaves to them, they shall sometimes :) It is not they that are censuring their brethren, that are stirring up divisions, and make all that feud that is in the church. If they might be hearkened unto, and regarded, there would be quietness and composure, (for if ever there be peace, it will be by the strong ones :) but weak ones in grace are the burthens and troublers of the family. You may know they are the weak ones in God's house, in that they are those that are

always crying, complaining, making firework in the family, back-biting, censuring their brethren, quarrelling with one or other, &c. These peevish troublesome souls, are the weak ones, &c.

7. The strongest in grace are the best able to stand, work, and suffer alone. Though in duty they should not be alone when they can have society, and though the rest are most humble, therefore are sensible they have need of others, and will not throw away any of their helps; yet if all forsake them, they will stand to it still. They go not to heaven merely for company sake; they be not christians merely because such and such are christians; if all the world forsake Christ, they will stick to him, unless Christ leave them to their own weakness. But the weak christian hath a great deal more need of comfort and support, and lives a more dependent life: they cannot stand, work, suffer alone; if their minister fall, they fall: if their relations change, they change: if there be not somebody at hand to confute an adversary, they yield; if there be not somebody to keep life and warmth, they grow cold in every duty; in affliction they can step on no longer than led by the hand, &c. Have christians to support, and to quiet, and to moderate their passions, and to teach them the doctrine of patience: they can hold up no longer than they are refreshed with cordials. What would become of you, should God let you stand by yourselves, &c.?

8. The strong christian is one that can best live without creatures upon God alone (and a weak christian is one that hath most need of the creature, and can least live upon God alone) under the censures of the godly, frowns of the wicked, without riches, honours, pleasures, can have the quietness and contentment in God, whether he have anything or nothing wherever he is, &c. The more necessity thou art in of having something besides God for thy consolation, the more weak thou art, there must be supply: I know not how to be poor, disgraced, &c. This impatient soul is the feeble soul, impatience is nothing

but the fruit of weakness. The strong christian can live upon God alone : therefore if men make as if they were undone, if lost in their estates, it is a certain sign of a lamentable weakness of a sick soul.

9. That is the best and strongest christian, and most confirmed in grace, who is most employed and abides in the love of God, in love to God : that hath the fear of God, but goes beyond fear, and loves most, and abides most in the love of God : that makes it his great business to feed upon, and study the love of God to him, and to return love to him again. The more God's love is on thy heart, and the more thou lovest in the fruit of that love, the stronger christian. But he that lives most by a kind of constraining fear, though he may be sincere, he is but weak. Where there is nothing but fear and no love, there is no sincerity ; but where there is some little measure of love, fear is such a tyrant, that it will many times cloud it, so that almost all his life seems to be moved and managed by fear : and in this there is much loathness and unwillingness, and they had rather do otherwise than they do. According to the measure of love is the strength of grace.

10. He is the strongest christian that hath most pure and most universal love to others, that can love all men, even an enemy, with true unfeigned love, even with such love as belongs to a christian : that can love every christian, and not a party only, with the pure and fervent love which belongs to believers : that can love every child of God, and not those only that are of his opinion, or have done him good, but all, because they are children of God, with a sincere and special hearty love. That is the weak christian that picks and chuses, that is staggering when he comes to loving an enemy ; that takes in those that agree with him in judgment, and makes those almost only the object of his love ; that would confine his affections to some narrow society, some little sect, party, or parcel of believers, and cannot love christians as christians : and hence it is, division is the effect of enmity, or

of weakness in grace, for want of the universality of love. I would make no question to prognostic the healing of all divisions within this nation, could I but advance all that are concerned in it to the right temper of christian love. It is the weak children in Christ's family that fall out, when we have not enough love to reach to all, and to love a christian as a christian, &c.

Q. What must be done by those that are converted, to keep them where they are, to help them unto growth, to make them better, to further their confirmation, to secure their salvation, that they may after all attain the crown?

A. I shall leave with you twenty directions; and as many as there are, there are not more than you must practice: and take them as if they were the last directions I shall give you; and take them as practicals, not as notionals, that you must live upon as long as you live.

1. See that the foundation be surely laid in your head and heart, in matters of your religion. In your head, that is, that you well understand what religion is, what the christian religion is: what God is, what it is for God to be yours, in his attributes and relations unto you: what he is, and will be unto you: what you are, and must be unto him: what sin is, how odious, wherein its evil consists: what is sin, and what not: what sin hath done in the world, and what estate it hath brought transgressors into: what Christ is, what he hath done for man's recovery and redemption: what he hath wrought, gives and offers to the world: the end and design of God in the work of man's redemption: the tender of the gospel covenant of grace, freeness, largeness, and excellency of the grace of this covenant: the end of our religion, the everlasting glory that is revealed in the gospel, what it is, how sure, and how great. When you understand these things, get a sound and redicated belief concerning the truths of the holy scripture, revealing all these things: and think it not enough that the scripture is true, or that you are resolved so to believe, but get the best grounds for your belief:

be well established on those grounds: read the scripture much, till you are acquainted with, and relish the matter and language, and feel the power, and till all be delightful to your souls in reading, and be not ashamed to understand the fundamentals; look to your catechism: the fundamentals of religion you must understand and receive. And when you have got them into your head, be sure you get them into your heart, and never think any truth received as it ought, till it hath done some special work on your heart; till you believe that God is almighty, just, holy, &c. and all the attributes of God have made their holy impressions on your heart: that the sanctifying knowledge of God hath warmed your affections, captivated your souls, that God be enthroned in your hearts by the belief and knowledge of your minds: know yourselves so as to be humble: know Christ so as he may be sweet unto you, and exalted by you: set up Christ in your souls nearest to your hearts; know sin so as to hate it, &c. It is the entertainment of the good things of the gospel by the will, that is the principal part of your religion. It is a matter of lamentable consequence in all your lives, when there is not a sound work at the heart: how little life will there be from any truth in reading or hearing? The fundamentals of religion must be so received, as not only to have an old heart mended, but a new heart made. Thus understand, believe, and give up thy heart to that thou believest and understandest.

2. Know and remember the work of your salvation must be as long as your lives, and that you have never done, till you have done living. I give this direction, because I find something in christianity, the remains of carnality is apt to hinder, &c. And some professors, when converted, they are reconciled to God, and safe, &c. but there is a great deal to be done after, &c.

3. Understand well wherein it is your confirmation, stability, rootedness, and growth in religion, doth consist. The chief part of your growth in grace is not to know more things than you knew before; but to grow

in the knowledge, belief, entertainment, and improvement of the same truths, that at first you did receive; (not that you may not, or should not know more, for the clear knowledge of the fundamentals guide you unavoidably to the sight of many other truths, which a darker knowledge of those fundamentals will not discover to you.) It is not additional to your former knowledge, but the clearer known, sounder believing, heartier entertaining and improving of the truths you know at first; as the health of a man consists not in having every day variety of food, but in the parting and digesting of the same food, that is fittest for him. Get but a more perfect conviction, or concoction of what you knew before, and this is your growth. You may grow in the knowledge of God's attributes by knowing them more clearly, orderly, distinctly, satisfactorily, and believingly, than before. There is a world of difference in the manner of knowledge, between a dark and clear knowing things: grow in greater love to them, and greater skill in entertainment, improvement, and practice of them.

4. Grow downward in humility, and inward in the knowledge of yourselves; and above all, maintain a constant abhorrence and jealousy of the sin of pride; grow in humility, and fly from man; keep a constant apprehension of your unworthiness and weakness, of the odiousness and danger of sin, of spiritual pride (so called because exercised about spiritual things;) of being puffed up with pride of any thing in yourselves; of being too confident in yourselves; be low in your own, and expect not, nor desire other's good thoughts of you. Humility lies not in humility of opinion, of speech, garb, or carriage; but in opposition to high thoughts of our own parts—gifts, godliness, when we think of these above their worth. Still remember Psal. xxv. Prov. xxvi. 19. Isa. lvii. 15. John xx. 29. As ever you would grow in grace and be confirmed christians, keep a low esteem of yourselves, be mean in your own eyes, be content to be mean in others, and hearken

not to secret flatterers that would puff you up. Take heed of any thing that would puff you up, &c.

5. You must understand that you are disciples in Christ's school, where ministers are his teachers, and guides, the ordinances, his means for his people's good, and the scripture, the book you must learn; therefore keep in this order, keep under these guides, commit your souls to those that are faithful, and fit for souls to be entrusted with; and when you have done, with humble submissiveness to their teaching, keep in this school under those officers in their discipline, and dwell in the catholic church and communion of saints, and understand the duty of pastors and people, Heb. xiii. 17, 18. 1 Thes. v. 12. "Obey them that have the rule over you." If God had sent the poor Christians sufficient to support themselves, he would never have made it the duty of all to be marshalled and ranked in several schools, ranks, orders, and all to walk in this order to heaven. If you withdraw from under Christ's officers and ordinances, you are in danger of being snatched up as stragglers.

Q. What shall we do? Who shall we take for our guides, if God take them away? &c.

A. It is not the denial of public liberty that loses that relation between a pastor and his flock, nor any word from man should cause a poor soul to trust itself for guidance of salvation to one that is not able. A man's soul is not to be hazarded upon damnation by being deprived of the officers and ordinances of Christ, and cast upon the conduct of a blind guide merely for the pleasuring of a mere man.

6. Be sure you understand the nature of church-union, and necessity of maintaining it, and abhor all ways that are truly schismatical, that would rent and divide the church of Christ. As you must not, under pretence of avoiding schism, cast your soul upon apparent hazard of damnation, so you must maintain the necessity of church-union and communion. When Christ's members walk

in communion with Christ's members, supposing that which is singular to the generality of judicious men, take heed of any thing that would withdraw you from the communion of the generality of those that are found in the faith. Take heed of withdrawing from the main body of believers. Christ is the head of his church, he will never condemn his church. Walk in those substantials Christ's church hath walked in. Division among Christians is a sin God hath described as odious and tending to the ruin of Christians. Be very suspicious of any that would draw you from the main body of believers, and keep communion with the universal church of Christ, with the generality of the godly in love and affection, &c.

7. Be sure your own hearts and ways be the matter of your daily study; and when hypocrites have their work abroad, let yours be much at home; while they make it their business to censure this and that man, let the main of your business be in pressing the inward of your own hearts, in keeping all right between God and you. Observe your heart's inclinations. If any inordinate inclination after any thing, set a special guard; mark which way your thoughts go, that you may know your inclinations by your thoughts. In an especial manner preserve tenderness of conscience, fear of sin, lothfulness to displease God. Let truth have the mastery; maintain such a conscience that dares not sin to save your lives. Be sure you sin not wilfully. Obey the light.

8. Be sure to keep up continually a lively apprehension of the state and place of your everlasting happiness, to live by faith upon the unseen world. Know where your happiness lies, and what it is, that you grow not to carnal apprehensions of your happiness, live upon heaven, and let that be it that shall animate your faith to duty, and all that you may still be weary of vexation, and sensible of the vanities here below. Let your conversation be above. Be confirmed in your apprehensions of the certainty and excellency of eternal blessedness; grow

more in heavenly mindedness, and in satisfaction of soul, in the hopes you have of these things.

9. Understand the nature, method, and power of temptations, how to resist them, and live in watchfulness. Be not a stranger to Satan and his methods of tempting, what you have to watch against, and oppose, where you must be armed. Understand the nature of christian watchfulness; keep up a constant resolution and courage in resisting, especially the temptations you carry about with you, of your calling, constitution, company, and of the times. Set them down, remember them, keep a special observation of them all; and say, this and this it is I am in danger of; and it is my integrity and salvation that is in danger, and here place special guard, and make it your business to resist. The principal cause of christians' negligence in this, is the security of their consciences, and love of their sins; did you know your danger, you would better look after your safety, 2 Cor. ii. 11.

10. Especially understand how much the flesh and carnal self is an enemy to God and your souls, and how much you are engaged by the christian covenant to live in a warfare against yourselves, and against your flesh. You must not think the life of life-pleasing is consistent with religion. Understand how you are bound to take the flesh for your enemy, to watch against it, and to live in a continual combat with it, Col. iii. 5. The flesh is your chiefest enemy: the very senses themselves are all grown inordinate, and the work of faith is very much seen in its exercise this way. If you get an opinion, that you may eat, and drink, and cloath, &c. and do all things to gratify yourselves, &c. then no wonder if you find but little increase in spirituals, while you grow so carnal. Understand and practice the duty of self-denial, self is the very heart of sin; read it not under pretence of liberty in religion.

11. Give not way to a formal, heartless, seeming religiousness, customariness without the life: but keep

your souls in a continual seriousness and awakedness about God, immortality, and your great concernment. If duty be dead, take heed lest that incline you to a deadness in another, and so grow a customary deadness. Take heed of spiritual slothfulness, that makes you keep your hands in your bosom, when you should be doing for your soul; stir up to, and in duty, when you have but little time for life eternal: do not pray as if you prayed not, nor hear as though you heard not; but when upon duty, doing God's service, do it with all the seriousness and vigour you can. To grow lazy and negligent is the declining way: use such considerations as may stir you up, Rom. xii. 11. Tit. ii. 14.

12. Remember always the worth of time, and greatness of your work, and, therefore, so value time, as not negligently or slothfully to lose a moment; it will quickly be gone, and when you are at the last, you will better know its worth. Hearken to no temptation that will draw you to any trifling, abusing, wasting of your precious time. If thou hast no argument against thy sports, trifling pleasures, &c. but this, it loses my time, take it for a greater argument than if it lose thee thy money, friends, or any thing in the world, your youth, your morning hours, especially the Lord's day. Lose not any part of it, but improve it with yourselves and families; lose not a moment of the Lord's day, nor any of thy precious time thou canst spare and redeem. If thou hast lost any, be humbled for it, and be careful to redeem the rest: look back; do you approve of the time that is past? could you not have spent it better? remember what you have, let that quicken you; look before you, remember what is to be done, and do the first which must be done, and then leave trifles to that time you have to spare. It is ignorance and idleness, and not want of work, that makes any think they have time to spare, Eph. v. 16. Col. iv. 5.

13. Make a careful choice of your company. You cannot travel well to heaven alone, especially when you may have company, thrust not yourselves into every com-

pany, Eph. v. 7. Converse as much as you can with those that will help you, that are warm when you are cold, knowing when you are ignorant, believing when you are doubtful, &c. especially for your constant companions, live with those that will be a frequent help to you. Masters, choose the best servants, that fear God; servants choose to live with those that will help you in the fear of God; for husbands and wives make choice of those that will intend upon religion. Take heed of being unequally yoked, and of thinking to get well to heaven, while you presume to unite yourselves with those that with great advantage will hinder, not help, your salvation.

14. Keep a constant guard upon the tongue, especially take heed of those common sins that disgrace hath not driven out of the world, but have got some kind of credit amongst some professors; namely idle talk; that wastes precious time, makes us unfruitful to one another, backbiting especially, can they put but a religious pretence upon it, or if they back-bite those that differ in opinion. Remember that terrible passage, Prov. xviii. 28. James i. 26. Psal. xxxix. and xxxv. 28. Avoid idle talk, back-biting &c. watch over your tongues; and if they are by nature addicted to a laxity of tongue, and multitude of words, there lies a double obligation on you in point of danger and necessity above all others to keep a careful watch over your tongues. You should rather speak fewer words than others: and if you find yourselves inclined to speak against and behind his back, reprehend yourselves and avoid it.

15. Learn the holy skill of improving every condition that God shall cast you into; learn how to live to God in every condition. If you have skill and heart, there is advantage to be got by all. That prosperity may strengthen you in God, encourage you in his service, that adversity may wean you from the world, help you to repentance, raise you to God, and give you more than it took away, know the danger and duty of every condition, study them before they come upon you, that they do

not surprize you; learn to know what is the danger, duty, and particular temptation of every condition, and in that condition you are most likely to expect a fall into: prepare for affliction as the common lot of the saints, take it as no strange thing when it overtakes you; know how to abound and how to want. A great deal of a Christian's safety and comfort lies in this, to study the temptations and duty of every condition before it come, that so you may have your remedy at hand, and fall to your work, and commit yourselves to God.

16. Be as conscionable and strict in the duties of your relations, and dealings with men, proportionably as in the duties of holiness, more directly to be performed to God. Make as much conscience, care, study, diligence, about being just, that you wrong no man in buying or selling, as you do in duties of holiness, hearing, praying, receiving. In your trading make conscience of justice and faithfulness, as well as in the worship of God, and in your own personal behaviour; in your calling be diligent, not slothful in business, &c. And so in the duties of your relations. O that parents knew what a charge lies on them concerning the soul of their children, &c. So masters, look to your servants, and be as conscionable in doing your duty for their soul's good, and being faithful to them, and compassionate over them, as in your duty to God. Keep up family duties with life, seriousness, diligence, and vigour: the life of religion in the world must be kept up very much in families.

17. Make it your study and care to do all the good you can in the world. Let doing good be the principal part of your business. Think that the safest and happiest life in which you can do greatest good. Suffer not opportunities to slip out of your hands: take them where you have them, and seek where you may have them; look not only where you may get a good, but where you may have opportunity to do good to others. Every talent must be answered for, your knowledge, health, &c. use it as you will answer for it, and know, it is one of the greatest

mercies in the world, for God to give you hearts in doing good with that he hath given, Heb. xiii. 16. not for applause, but be good husbands for God, and consider which way you may attain your ends best, by what you give or do. Thus be rich in good works.

18. Live still as before the living God, approve your hearts to him, as knowing you stand or fall unto his judgment. Avoid carefully all offences unto men, for the Lord's sake, and their conscience sake, take heed of scandal, and receive all the good from others you can, but stick not too much on man's approbation : disregard not suspicions, or reproofs of godly men, but make not man's praise to be any part of your reward; it is a small thing for me to be judged of men. Be not much troubled at it if you cannot please all : the bawlings of the malicious should not disturb a soul that is quietly housed with God : that soul is not well stablished in faith, that can be so disturbed and distempered by the wrath or words of malicious men. Remember, God himself pleases not all : the most of the world are enemies to their Maker, upon the account of his holiness, justice, &c. and canst thou think to please all ? Withdraw from the world and yourselves unto God, for the consolation of his approbation, and for your felicity : this will save you from hypocrisy, and keep you from the temptations and vexations of the censorious world.

19. Be every day as serious in your preparations for death and judgment, as those that are always certain that it will come, and know not the moment when it will come, Mat. xxiv. 29. Use often to think seriously beforehand, what death is, what thoughts, what trials death will put a man upon : what temptations usually accompany our approaching death : what you shall most need at such a time as that : what thoughts are likeliest to possess you then : what you are likeliest to wish for when you must needs die, about spending your time, expending your estate, conversing with others, &c. Ask yourselves, What will I wish I had done, or been when

I come to die? Think what will be most dreadful to a dying man, for thus you have time to escape his judgment. Will it not be to think on a life lost in vanity, drenched in worldliness, unreconciled to God, or at least in utter uncertainty of his love? God hath not foreshewed what will be a dying man's terror to torment thee, but to get out of that terror; that which will be most terrible at death, conquer and destroy it presently. "They that were ready went in with the Bridegroom, and the door was shut," Mat. xxv. 10. Oh happy thou, if while the door is open, thou be found ready to go in; woe, if when the door be shut, thou hast thy preparation to make, thy graces to seek. Bethink what you will, either wish, or fear when you come to die, and when you will say, this should have been done, &c. let it be now done.

20. Rise speedily after every fall by sound repentance, and a fresh recourse to the blood of Christ, covenant of grace, and his intercession. Lie not secure in any sin, into which thou art lapsed; take heed of delaying and trifling, when thy particular repentance should be exercised. Renew thy covenant, and after thy rising deal faithfully with thyself and God; favour not thy sin, nor flesh; go to the quick, leave no corruption at the bottom. If called to make restitution, to shame thyself before men by confession, stick not at it. Take the plainest course, that is the way of God, and let not any thought of shame, dishonour, or loss hinder it; for the more it costs thee to rise from sin, the likelier it is thou art sound in thy conversion, and the more comfort thou wilt have; otherwise the fears and pains of thy disease will be upon thee, when the thorough cure would have prevented it. Quarrel not at any man's reproof, though they miscarry in it, have mentioned thy faults with passion, &c. Take that which is good, and be thankful. And after every fall sit not down in perpetual distress, but as Christ takes the honour of thy cure, take thou the comfort of thy cure when recovered. See thou art truly risen by repentance, and returned to him whom

thou hast dishonoured. Thy care must be to see thou be sincere in thy return, and then walk comfortably. See that Satan make not thee walk so as to rob thee of thy comfort, and God of his honour.

Thus having given you twenty directions, I shall reduce all to these eight particulars.

1. Do not think strength of grace will be got with ease: you must do that, that in other things is done for the attaining of strength, increase and confirmation. A man cannot attain knowledge in law, physic, or any art, without studying, diligence, unwearied labour, and patience, through that time that is necessary to attain it. Set yourselves to the reading of the scripture and other good books: study good truths. Think not to attain mastery in a day. And if ever such a conceit come in your minds that you are strong, confirmed Christians, do not easily entertain it; there must be time, industry, and diligence. Ordinarily suspect the conceit you may have of strength and confirmation; you must grow by degrees. God's method is to begin like a " grain of mustard-seed." We are not born men. Labour in the proper means with patience: infused gifts are given according to the manner of acquitting them. God gives as if our acquisition did attain it: never think of having this without patience, labour, and diligence.

2. Grow up in the church of God, and under his officers and ordinance, and among his people. Do not transplant yourselves from the garden and vineyard of the Lord, if you will thrive; no prospering in the commons where weeds will choke, &c. Keep within the church of God, in the communion of his people, among his servants, under the guidance of his ministers, for that is the duty of ministers,—to bring up, train up, and help the weak ones, till they grow to be strong. They are to be God's nurses, and helpers of the weak in the house of God. Do not think to prosper by breaking over the hedge, under pretence of any right of holiness whatsoever, following any party that would draw you to separation.

3. Make it, amongst others, the principal study of your lives to "study the love of God in the Redeemer," the nature of the new covenant, and the infinite goodness revealed in the face of a Mediator. How it was his design to attract the hearts of men to the love of God, by revealing his infinite love in the Redeemer, unto which end Christ came for, even to represent God's goodness in sinners' hearts, of their being reconciled to him, and ravishing them with his love. Study the glory and ravishing love of God, and unspeakable goodness in a Redeemer.

4. Live not by sense, or upon worldly hopes, nor in the exercise of it. See that you live a mortified life. Take heed of glutting yourselves with creatures, or letting your hearts out to any creature, or letting any creature be too dear to you. Live not too much on any sensible thing, or upon any worldly hopes or expectations. Shut your eyes to the world, let not your desires run out to the world, and live as much as you can upon the world to come.

5. Let holy self-suspicion always make you fearful of temptation, and keep you out of the Devil's way. Would you keep your standing? grow better and strong in grace. Let not the pride of your hearts, or confidence of your strength, make you meet among any unlawful communion, see any enticing spectacle, or thrust yourselves upon temptation. You are never safe if you thrust yourselves upon temptation. Think with yourself, my weakness is great, I must not gaze upon this enticing object, lest my heart take fire; I am not so strong as to be able to stand against such, &c.

6. When you cannot attain to that heat of internal affection you would, "be sure you walk uprightly with God." Sin not wilfully: keep your garments clean: set his law before your eyes. Sin not wilfully for a world: be but found in the way of duty, and God will bless you, and meet you in that way. Be as exact in obedience, as if you had that frame of soul you desire.

7. In a special manner keep all your bodily senses and

desires in subjection; mortify the flesh, keep under your carnal desires in due subjection to the spirit; let none of your senses take the reins out of your hands; keep a dominion over your senses.

Lastly, all your life long be longing to die. Let the work of your life be to learn to die. Consider what necessity to the safety and comfort of death, to consider frequently, " what assaults will be made upon dying men," that you may every day fortify against it; to consider what graces and duties will be most needful and useful then, that you may be most conversing with, and exercising those graces and duties. He that hath well learnt to die, is no weak christian. The strength of your grace lies in the exercise of these things; faithfully practice them, and you will stand when others fall, you will have comfort when others cast away their comfort, you will die in peace when others die in horror.

DR. JACOMB'S FORENOON SERMON.

Preached August 17, 1662.

JOHN viii. 29.

And he that sent me, is with me: the Father hath not left me alone: for I do always those things that please him.

THESE are the words of our blessed Lord and Saviour Jesus Christ, they are spoken by himself, and they are spoken of himself; though yet in a sober and modest sense they are applicable to all his members. That which Christ here affirms, is, that the presence of God was always with him, and this is first propounded, " He that sent me is with me," and then it is amplified, " and the Father hath not left me alone;" and then thirdly, the reason of this is annexed, "for I always do those things that please him."

I shall speak but very little of the words as they do refer to Christ: he tells us where his Father was with him, he did not leave him alone in all the troubles and difficulties that he met withal in the finishing the great work of man's redemption; still God was with him. It is true, there was a time when Christ was without the sensible manifestation of his Father's presence, when he cried out, "My God, my God, why hast thou forsaken me?" Why, but yet even then in truth and in reality his Father did not leave him; for though he had not the evidences of his Father's presence, yet he had the influences of his Father's presence. It would take up much time to shew you how in all particulars the Father was present with Christ. I will only speak this one word, and instance in this one thing, God's assisting presence was always with him, both in his active, and also in his passive obedience; and indeed he had that work to do, and those miseries to suffer, that if God had left him if he had not been mightily assisted by the divine nature, Christ as mere man, could neither have done, nor have suffered what he did; but the Father was with him, and to support him, Isa. xlii. 1. "Behold my servant whom I uphold." You shall find that Christ did act faith upon this, in Isa. l. 7. "The Lord God will help me, therefore shall I not be confounded," vers. 9. "The Lord will help me." So to the same effect is Psal. xvi. 9. And you shall find this made good to him in scripture, in his greatest necessities.

Take a double instance.

In the first place, after he had been engaged in the combat with Satan, you read in Mat. iv. the strongest combat or duel that ever was fought; wherein you have the Prince of Peace and the Prince of Darkness; the lion of the tribe of Judah, and the roaring lion that seeks how to devour; both of them putting forth their utmost strength, and endeavouring to overcome each other.

Now I say in this combat, the Father did not leave Christ, but he helps him; for he sends an angel to minister unto him, Mat. iv. 11.

So in Christ's bitter agony in the garden, just before his bitter passion and death upon the cross, the Father did not leave him alone, for he sent an angel unto him to strengthen him, Luke xxii. 43. and so in several other places, and in several other things I might instance; but I shall pass this by. Aye, but now why did the Father thus stand by Christ? He gives you the reason of it in the text, because he always did the things that pleased him. This I shall open in a double respect.

First, Christ's undertaking of the work of our redemption; it was very well pleasing unto his Father, that poor lost undone sinners should be brought back again unto God, and restored unto his love and favour: I say the Father was infinitely well pleased with Christ in this undertaking. Isa. xxxv. 10. The pleasure of the Lord shall prosper in his hand. The pleasure of the Lord, that is the work of our redemption; wherein God the Father took great pleasure or delight; therefore when Christ was publicly in the eye of the world to enter upon this great work, the Father sends him out with this witness, This is my beloved Son, in whom I am well pleased. He speaks not of this well-pleasing only to his person, but also of his well-pleasing as unto his undertaking.

Secondly, as the work itself was well pleasing unto God, so Christ managing of this work, was all along pleasing unto his Father; and that doth appear in this, that Christ in all things kept to his Father's commission, and to his Father's command. I say in all things he kept to his Father's commission. He did nothing here upon earth, but what was within the compass of his commission; for, saith he in the verse before the text, "I do nothing of myself, but as my Father bids me:" so also he acted in conformity to his Father's will; that was the rule and square by which Christ ordered all his actions; his eye was still upon his Father's will; whatever he willed him to do, that he did; whatever he willed him to suffer, that he suffered; and thus he always did the things that were pleasing to his Father. But I do not intend further upon the words in this reference; for my design is to bring down the words unto ourselves, to those that are the members of Christ; for there is the same disposition of heart in all believers to please God: in all things to please God. This was the frame and temper and carriage of Christ; so it is the frame and temper of every true believer: and this is a part of our likeness unto Christ; as you know there is a blessed resemblance and similitude between Christ and his members; they have the same spirit that Christ had, only in a different proportion; for he had it without measure: they have the same grace as Christ had for substance, though not for degree; "of his fulness we all have received grace for grace;" that is, as many interpret it, grace answerable unto grace. As the print in the wax answers to the print in the seal, and as face answers to face; so grace in believers answers unto that grace that was in Christ; they are to shew forth the virtues of Christ, 1 Pet. ii. 11. "Now this was the grace and virtue and holiness of Christ, that he always did the things that pleased his Father." Why this is in all believers, only with this difference; it was actual performance in the one, it is but endeavour in the other; it was perfect in the one, it is sincere, but imperfect in the other.

Christ always did things that pleased God, a believer endeavours always to do the things that please God, he doth not always do so; witness David in the case of his uncleanness, when he displeased the Lord, as it is in 2 Sam. xi.

The observation I intend to speak to, shall be this:

They that please God, and endeavour always to do the things that please God, such God will be with; such the Father will not leave alone; especially in times of suffering and trouble, for I will bring it to that case.

Indeed God will not leave such at any time; for

that promise is exceeding full, Heb. xiii. 5. "I will never leave thee, nor forsake thee." I do not know any one promise in all the Bible, that is expressed with such an emphasis as that promise is; such a multiplication of negatives in the original. But especially God will not leave such in an afflicted and suffering condition.

In the prosecution of this, I will speak to four things;

First, I will shew you when a man may be said to do the things that please God. 2. I will confirm the truth of the doctrine. 3. I will shew you in what respects God will be with them that desire to please him in a suffering condition. 4. I will give you the grounds and reasons of it; and then I shall come to an application.

For the first, we please God in what we do, when we act. 1. In a suitableness to God's nature. And 2. in subjection to God's law; for pleasing of God lies in these two things. As that pleases a man which is suitable to his disposition, and is correspondent with his command, we do the things that please God, when we do the things that God doth: and when we do that which God commands; when we hate sin, as God hates sin; when we are holy as God is holy. You shall find it in Col. i. 10. "That you may walk worthy of God, unto all well pleasing." Observe, this walking worthy of God, is walking suitably, or walking answerably to God, Mat. iii. 8, " Bring forth fruit worthy of repentance," or bring forth fruit answerable to repentance; so to walk worthy of God, is to walk suitable to God, to his nature: now then observe what follows, that you might walk worthy of God to all well-pleasing, then we please God when we walk suitably unto God: so also when we act in a blessed conformity to God, to his law; for nothing can please the good God, but what is good. Now the law being the measure, and standard of all goodness, nothing can be good, but what bears conformity to this law, which is the will of God. God is well pleased when his will is observed; as you know you that are masters, your servants please you when they do your will. That inference of the apostle for this is very apposite, Rom. viii. 8. "So then they that are in the flesh cannot please God." What is this same inference grounded upon, because the carnal mind is enmity against God: for it is not subject to the law of God, neither indeed can be: so that they that are in the flesh, cannot please God. Why? because there is that principle in them, as carries out a real enmity to the law and will of God; it is as if the apostle had said, they will not be subject to God's will, not obedient to God's command; there is a principle of enmity in them against these things, and so cannot please God. God is pleased when his will is fulfilled, and his commands observed; to please God, is in all things so to act, that whatever we do, we may express a likeness to God's nature, and a blessed subjection to God's revealed will, and this is the first thing.

A second thing is the proof of the doctrine; they that thus please God, he will be with them, he will not leave them alone, especially in an hour of trial. For, my brethren, assure yourselves of this, that which the Father did for Christ, he will do for all his members. It is true, Christ's sufferings being greater than ours possibly can be, and so his relation to God being higher than ours his; he a Son by eternal generation, we only by adoption: he had the presence of God in a more glorious manner than we can expect; but yet in our sphere according to the measure of our trials, and according to our capacity, we shall as really have the presence of God with us, as Christ had with him; that as we are partakers of Christ's sufferings, so we also shall be partakers of Christ's support. He that will be present with believers in heaven, as he is with Christ, he will be present with believers here on earth, as he is with Christ in all his sorrows and sufferings.

Now for the confirming of this comfortable truth, I need not speak much. Many promises you have in Scripture for it, and whatever God hath promised, he will certainly make good. Turn to that one promise instead of many, Isa. xliii. 2. " When thou passest through the waters, I will be with thee; through the rivers, they shall not overflow thee; when thou walkest through the fire, thou shalt not be burnt, neither shall the flame kindle upon thee." And you shall find too, that the saints have experienced it in all ages, God hath made it good.

Jacob was a man that met with many sharp trials. God exercised him with many troubles. You shall find that when he was going to Padan-aram, and was in a very afflicted condition, Gen. xxviii. 15, God comes to him, and saith, " Behold, I am with thee," Gen. xxxi. 5. His father frowned upon him, but the God of his father helped him, Joseph, Gen. xxii. 20. His master took him, put him into prison, a place where the king's prisoners were bound; he was in the prison, but the Lord was with Joseph. The prophet Jeremy was thrown into a dungeon, but the scripture saith, " God was with him." The three children were thrown into the furnace of fire, but there was a fourth with them, and that was the Son of God, Dan. iii. 25. Paul when he was brought to his trial, all men forsook him, but God stood by him, 2 Tim. iv. 16. So the Christians in all their sharp sufferings, 2 Cor. iv. 9. They were persecuted, but not forsaken; persecuted by men, but not forsaken by God. God hath abundantly made out this, and doth so still, that he will never leave those alone in a time of suffering, who desire unfeignedly in all things to please God.

Now the third thing is to shew you in what respect God is with such: why this presence of God is an active presence. God is not merely with his people, but he is with them in an active way: for this is a certain truth, God is working when the saints are suffering. I will open this in several particulars.

First, God is with such in his teaching presence. God's correction and God's instruction, they usually go together; and where there is the chastenings of God's hand, there is also the teaching of God's spirit. Psal. xc.

12. "Blessed is the man whom thou chastenest, and whom thou teachest." Christ, though he were a son, yet learned obedience by the things that he suffered. God teacheth his upright ones many lessons in a time of adversity, which they never learned in a time of prosperity. For we are like idle boys, or bad scholars that learn best when the rod is over us. In a prosperous condition God speaks to us, and we mind him not, Jer. xxii. 21. "I spoke to thee in thy prosperity, but thou wouldest not hear:" and this hath been thy manner from thy youth upwards. In prosperity God speaks once and twice, as Job speaks, but we will not hear; but in the time of adversity God opens the ears, Jud. viii. 16. As Gideon taught the men of Succoth with thorns and briers, so doth God teach his people by affliction; and oh the many blessed truths that they learn, when they are under the rod, when they want liberty! Oh what a mercy is it to have liberty then, when they have not ordinances as before! What a mercy is it to have ordinances then! Oh what an evil thing is it then for them, that they have departed from God! God teaches them these things then: sin is never so bitter, mercy is never so sweet, as in a time of suffering. Oh how vain and empty is the creature then! Oh how sweet is communion with God then! I say such things as these God teaches then.

Secondly, God is with such in his guiding presence, Psal. lxxiii. 24. "Thou wilt guide me with thy counsel, and afterwards receive me unto glory." When Israel was in the wilderness, then they had the cloud to guide them. It is a blessed thing to live under the conduct and direction of the wise God; we never have so much of this as in an hour of trial. Indeed the people of God never fly so much to God for direction, as at such a time: as Saul, when he was in distress then he calls for the ephod; and thus it is with us under affliction, then we look to God.

Thirdly, God is with them in his preserving and hiding presence. God is the saint's hiding place, their shield, their buckler, their rock, their defence; the scripture expressions are many to hold out God's protection as to his people. God hath a constant care over them to preserve them and save them; oh but especially in a time of trouble: as the mariner is never so careful of the ship, as under a storm; and God is never so careful of his church and people, as under affliction. Jeremy is in the dungeon, now God saves him. Daniel is in the den, now God saves him. The three children in the fire, now God saves them. Peter is in prison, now God saves him. The mother never tends the child so carefully as when the child is sick; and providence is never so tender to the people of God, as under a suffering condition.

Fourthly, God is with them in his comforting presence, 2 Cor. iv. 1. " Who comforteth us in all our tribulation," and usually we have most of consolation from God, when we have most of tribulation from without; as our sufferings do abound, so our consolations do abound much more. The child that is beaten when it is well, is cherished when it is ill. When persons are sick, then you give them cordials. God gives the best of comforts in the worst of times. When the burden is heavy upon the back, then the peace of conscience is great within. The worse it is without, the better it is within. When men discover most of anger, God discovers most of love.

Fifthly, God is with such in his strengthening presence to enable them and to support them to undergo whatever he is pleased to call them unto. This is the way of our good and gracious God. He always gives out strength, as he lays on affliction, he never leaves his children alone in this respect, he will be with them to support them. Though it may be not to deliver, yet he will certainly be with them to support: the rod and the staff they go together, Psal. xxiii. 4. the afflicting rod and the supporting staff: when one is upon the saint to afflict, then the other hand is underneath the saint to support: Isa. xli. 10. " I will uphold thee, I will strengthen thee, fear not, I will help thee: yea, I will uphold thee with the right hand of my righteousness. This David found, "I cried unto the Lord in my distress, he answered me, and strengthened me in my inward man," Psal. cxxxviii. 3. Oh! when men afflict, God supports: when men put the children of God into the deep waters, then God takes them by the chin, and holds them up, that they shall not sink and be drowned.

Sixthly, God is with them in his sympathizing presence, Oh he hath a tender sense of all the sorrows and calamities of his people! Oh it grieves him that they are grieved! They that touch Him touch the apple of his eye. In all their afflictions he is afflicted. "Saul, Saul, why persecutest thou me?" Every blow that is given to them, God bears a part of it himself. As they are sensible of God's dishonour, so God is sensible of their suffering. It pains him to the very heart to see his children wronged and abused by a malicious world.

Seventhly, He is with them by his sanctifying presence. All their troubles are to do them good, and to make them good: and therefore the furnace it is but to refine them from their dross: the pruning-hook of affliction it is but to cut off their luxuriant branches. God takes the sharp knife into his hand and lances them, but it is only to fetch out their corruption. By this shall the iniquity of Jacob be purged, and this is all the fruit, to take away his sin.

Eighthly, God is with them by his quickening presence, to make their prayers more fervent, to make their requests to the throne of grâce more importunate. The children of God cry most to him when they suffer most from men, and their prayers are best when their condition is worst. Prayer shortens affliction, and affliction heightens prayer. God is with them to hear their prayers. Oh the prayer of the afflicted that comes up to heaven! God hears the sighs and groans of his oppressed ones, their tears pierce the heavens, they call upon God in time of trouble, and pour out their sorrows before the Lord, and he doth hear them.

Ninthly, God is with them by his raising presence, to raise up their hearts higher, to elevate their souls, and bring them more near to himself. God's people when they meet with troubles in the world think nothing so sweet unto them as the enjoyment of God ; then no life so good unto them as the life of faith ; then they relish a sweetness in the promise : then every smile of God, oh how welcome is it ! Then all the affections of their souls center in God, and run to God : as in winter-time all the sap of the tree runs to the root : in summer time it spreads itself in the body, but in the winter goes to the root. When a man is sick, all the blood goes to the heart ; so in a suffering condition, all the affections of the soul go to God.

But now what are the reasons why God will not leave his people that thus desire to please him ?

Why, God loves them, therefore he will not leave them. Persons we love, we cannot leave, especially when they are in a distressed condition ; and as God hath set his love upon them, so they have set their love upon him. They love him, Psal. xci. 15. You have there an expression, " Because he hath set his love upon me, therefore I will deliver him : He shall call upon me, and I will answer him, I will be with him in trouble." God is a God of bowels, of great pity and compassion, and therefore he will not leave his people in a time of distress. You know bowels how they stand in you towards them that are in misery ; it goes to the heart of a merciful man to leave a person in misery. Oh how great are the bowels and compassions of God ! " Is Ephraim my son, is he a pleasant child ? Oh my bowels are turned within me, I will have mercy on him."

2. Such as please God, shall have his presence under sufferings, because now they need God most. If God will not leave his people as to temporal supplies, because they need such and such things : they need meat, and they need clothing : surely much more God will not

leave his children, as to spiritual supplies, under times of distress, because then they need God. Oh what can a believer do, or what can a believer suffer when God leaves him! His strength is in God; his support is in God; his comfort is in God, his all is in God: and therefore if God now leave him, what will become of him! He needs God at all times, but never so much as when his condition is dark and troubled. What was Samson, that man of so great strength, when his hair was gone? and what is a believer, when his God is gone?

3. God loves to see his people cheerful in a time of suffering, and therefore he is with them; he loves not that they should walk dejectedly. When God is present, Paul and Silas can sing in prison: the apostles can rejoice, that God honours them to be reproached for him. When God is present, the people of God are not only cheerful under tribulation, but can glory their cross is their crown; but if God be withdrawn, what can then be? drooping hearts and pensive sorrows.

4. God will not leave them, because they will not leave him; God will not leave them, because they suffer for his sake: were they not tender of God's glory, and careful to please him, they might be free from suffering as well as others; but it is for God's sake they suffer: "For thy sake we are killed like sheep, all the day long."

Lastly, It is thus, because God will make it appear to all the world, that he puts a difference between them that desire to please him, and other men. God hath a value for such. Do but see how Moses argues the case with God, Exod. xxxiii. 13. and so on, where he comes to God with a great request, that God will shew him his way, that he might know it; Why, saith God to him, " My presence shall go with thee." Moses said unto him, It is well thou art pleased to promise so great a mercy; " If thy presence go not with me, carry us not hence: for wherein shall it be known that I and thy people have found grace in thy sight. Is it not in this, that thou goest with us?" Observe, Moses pleads with God, how his fa vour, and love, and mercy should be with them, unless he were present with them! and so God walks with his people in trouble; for how should the world see God regarded them and did favour them, unless he manifested his presence unto them in a time of trouble and affliction!

DR. JACOMB'S AFTERNOON SERMON.

Preached August 17, 1662.

JOHN viii. 29.

And he that sent me is with me: the Father hath not left me alone: for I do always those things that please him.

I WAS upon these words in the morning. Having spoken something to them as they refer to Christ, who spake them here of himself; I then brought them down to his members, believers, and so propounded this observation from them—" That whoever they are that desire to please God and do the things that are pleasing to him, God will be with such, and the Father will not leave such alone, especially in a time of suffering and trouble." In the prosecuting of this point, I spake to four things, which I shall not now repeat, but come to the mark which I intend at present; and that is, to make some application. 1. Let me endeavour to prevail with every one of you, so to carry yourselves in your several places and capacities, that whatever you do, you may please God.

It was a blessed testimony that was given of Enoch, Heb. xi. 6. " Before his translation he had this testimony; that he pleased God." Oh! how happy will they be at the great day of judgment, which shall be singled out by Christ, before angels and men ; and Christ shall say of them, This was the man, or this was the woman that pleased God! There is a great deal of pleasing in the world, but there are but very few that make this their business, to please God; therefore I would have you shun that which is sinful, and press after that which is matter of duty.

1. There are some that mind nothing but to please themselves, to promote their own interest, to love their own ease, to indulge themselves in their own carnal delights, but they never mind the good of others, or the pleasing of God ; the apostle speaks of, and against these, Rom. xv. 1, 2, 3.

2. There are others that look no farther than the pleasing of men; if they can but keep fair with men, and shun the displeasure of men, that is all they aim at. But, my brethren, what a poor thing it is to have man to be your friend, and God to be your enemy ! to have the smiles of a poor dying perishing worm, and to lie under the frowns of the great God!

Indeed there is a good pleasing of men, to please them for their edification, as the apostle speaks, Rom. xv. 2. and so the apostle speaks of himself, 1 Cor. x. 32. " Even as I please all men in all things," that is, in all things that are of an indifferent nature, not simply evil, nor simply good, in all things.

This apostle was of a yielding and complying spirit, that he might thereby the better insinuate himself into the affections of men, and be more instrumental to the glory of God, in the work of the gospel, 1 Cor. ix. 22. " To the weak became I as weak, that I might gain the weak ; I am made all things to all men, that I might by all means save some ; and this I do for the gospel's sake."

But now in matter of duty, such things as are expressly determined by God, and so are either good or evil ; in these things the apostle would be no pleaser of men. " If I should please men, I should not be the servant of Christ." Gal. i. It is good to please others to their edification, but we must not please others to their own ruin and condemnation. It is good to please men when we can so do, and not grieve God. Instead of pleasing men, let it be your constant care and best endeavour in all things to please God. My brethren, this is a duty of so great importance, that was I now to take my leave of you, and should certainly know that I should never speak to you more, as we are come very near to it, for though I speak to you as a living man, yet I speak to you as a dying minister; this, I say, is a duty of that weight and importance, that I know not what to press upon you more material than this. Consult but two places of Scripture, Col. i. " For this cause we do not cease to pray for you." What was the thing the Apostle in this his constant prayers, did beg of God for them? It was this, that they might please God. And when he was taking his leave in the winding up of his epistle to the Hebrews, " Now the God of peace that brought again from the dead our Lord Jesus, the great Shepherd of the sheep, through the blood of the everlasting covenant, make you perfect in every good work to do his will, working in you that which is well-pleasing in his sight."

I need not go beyond the text for motives to stir you up to these endeavours: For,

Motive, 1. First consider what that God is, which I would have you endeavour to please. He is that God which made heaven and earth, that God before whom all the world is as nothing, but as a little dust in the balance, and as a drop of water to the bucket; that God whom angels adore and worship; that God who by a word from his mouth, is able to bring the whole universe into nothing. Will you not study to please this God? But further, consider what this God is to you. He is the fountain of your being, he is the God of all your mercies, he is your Creator and Sovereign, he is your Maker and Law-giver. It is he that by a smile can make you happy, and by a frown can make you miserable. It is he that hath heaven and hell at his disposal, " who openeth and none can shut, who shuts and none can open." He that must judge every one of you, either to eternal blessedness, or else to eternal torments; it is he in whose hands your breath, your life, your soul, your all is. Will you not endeavour to please this God? as the prophet argueth in point of fear, Isa. li. 12. "Who art thou, that art afraid of a man that shall die, or of the son of man that shall be made as grass, and forgettest the Lord thy Maker?" Oh poor creature! who art thou that goest about to please a mortal dying man, and dost not go about to please the great God, thy Creator and Sovereign!

2. Consider that relation wherein you profess yourselves to stand to God: he is your Master, you his servants; he is your Father, you his children; he is your Lord, you his subjects. You know all that are in close relations will study to please them that are above them; as the servant his master, the child his father, the subject his prince. All persons that are in a state of inferiority, will study to please their superiors, especially when they do depend upon them. Oh! how infinitely is God above those relations. Alas, there is but a very little distance betwixt you and your servants, and yet you expect they should please you, will you not, therefore, please God? especially considering your dependance upon him.

3. You shall not lose by pleasing God: that is enough to put us upon this. He that pleaseth God profiteth himself: in that very act wherein we please God, we profit ourselves. Men can do but little for us, yet for what they can do, we study to please them. Let me open this in a few particulars.

1. If you will sincerely endeavour in all things to please God, God will give you a gracious return to all your prayers. Oh what a mercy is this for a man to have his prayers answered by God! 1 John iii. 22. "Whatever we ask, we receive of him, because we keep his commandments, and do those things that are pleasing in his sight." Never expect that God should hear any prayers,

if we do not endeavour to do those things that please him.

2. Do you please God, then he will please you: mercy pleaseth us, and duty pleaseth God. Now when we please God in a way of duty, he will please us in a way of mercy. If we order our ways so as to please God, he will order his ways so as to please us.

3. Great is the benefit of pleasing God, even as to men: and this Solomon sets before you, Prov. xvi. 7, " When a man's ways please the Lord, he makes even his enemies to be at peace with him;" and he hath such another expression, Prov. xxii. 11. " He that loveth pureness of heart, the king shall be his friend:" the meaning of this scripture is this, when we keep close to God, and walk in compliance with his will, and make it our great design to please him, he will give us to find favour in the eyes of men. He that maketh God his friend, God will make that man's enemies to be his friends. Men are possibly full of anger, revenge, and exasperation; be it so. Do you desire to please God? God can turn their hearts towards you; God can sweeten them in their spirits, and take away that venom that is in them; so you know he did in the case of Esau to his brother Jacob.

4. This is the way to heaven and happiness. God will be pleased before the sinner shall be saved, Heb. xi. Enoch before his translation had this testimony, " That he pleased God." There is no way to heaven but this, the child pleases the father, and then the father gives him the inheritance. So it is here.

5. Let me return to the argument in the text; God will never leave them alone, that desire sincerely to please him. Methinks this should be a very prevailing motive to you, especially now; please God, and he will never leave you, no not in a time of distress and trouble. Here is the great difference betwixt a faithful God, and a false man.

In time of trouble and adversity men leave us and forsake us; in time of prosperity then they flatter us, and pretend a great deal of friendship and kindness: but as no man looks upon a dial when the sun is under a cloud; so these very men that pretend so much of kindness and friendship, if so be we do but come under a frown, or into trouble, then their friendship and kindness is at an end, as Paul said; no man stood by him when he came to be tried before Nero, all men forsook him, but God did not forsake him. The wise man hath an expression, Prov. xvii. 17. "A friend loves at all times, and a brother is born for adversity;" but where shall we find such a friend, or indeed such a brother? But now if you will please God, he will stand by you, when all men leave you, when you have the greatest need of God, he will then stand by you; if you be in a prison, he will be with you; if you be banished, he will be with you: if sin doth not part God and you, certainly no affliction shall part God and you.

Study to please God. Oh! is it not a sad thing for God to leave you! That is the saddest of all; when we lose God, then we lose all, Hos. ix. 12. "Woe unto them when I depart from them." What are all the mercies if God leave you? No more than if a man had a fair pleasant house, and should never see the sun more.

Oh do the things that always please the Lord, and he will never leave you. Under mercies, under afflictions he will be with you, and then your mercies shall be very sweet, and your afflictions shall not be very bitter. You know how earnest Moses was, Num. x. 13. with his father in law Hobab the Midianite; "Leave us not, I pray thee, forasmuch as thou knowest how we are to encamp in the wilderness, and thou mayest be to us as eyes." Oh keep God to you! especially when you are entering into the wilderness of trouble. God will be to you instead of eyes, he will be your counsellor, your comforter, your guide, your treasure, your portion, your all.

I might add one thing more in the last place,

Study to please God, because he is so easy to be pleased. This is a motive to us to endeavour to please those persons who are easy to be pleased. A child that hath a father that is easy to be pleased: a servant that hath a master that is easy to be pleased, will study to please them. Sincerity pleaseth God, though in the midst of much infirmity. He is so gracious and merciful, that whatsoever a poor sinner doth but desire to please God, he will accept of those desires. If we can but please God, it is no great matter whether we please men or not.

I shall conclude this branch with 1 Thes. iv. 1. "We beseech you, brethren, and exhort you in the Lord Jesus, that as you have received of us, how you ought to walk and please God, so you would abound more and more."

Use 2. By way of direction, I should here shew you how you are to please God. I told you in general in the morning, this pleasing of God lieth in two things,

1. In suitableness to his name. 2. In subjection to his law.

If you will please God in all your actions, look to this, that what you do may bear some resemblance to his nature, and hold forth obedience to his law.

Consult the will of God, and in all things act in conformity to that will. Do not allow yourselves in the commission of any known sin, for that will certainly displease God: as it was said of David when he took Bathsheba to wife: but saith the text, "the thing displeased the Lord." Do not baulk any known duty, for that will displease God.

In a word, be holy in all manner of conversation.

This being too general, I shall not insist upon it; only in a word more particularly.

Do those things now, make conscience of those duties which now lie upon you, in the doing of which you will certainly please God: and they are such as these.

Be stedfast in the ways of God, in the midst of a backsliding and apostatizing age, stand fast to the law of God, Phil. iv. 1. Contend for the faith which is delivered to the saints, ver. 3. of the epistle of Jude.

Be not ashamed to own Christ before all the world: if you be ashamed of him on earth, he will be ashamed of you in heaven; and woe be to that sinner whom Christ is ashamed to own.

Reckon reproaches for the name of Christ, better than the pleasure of sin that is but for a season.

When God calleth you to it, assert the purity and spirituality of gospel-worship. Do not place religion in a few shadows where the substance is neglected; but chiefly mind self-denial, mortification, crucifixion to the world, keeping up close communion with God, love the people of God whatever the world say or think of thee; for God is highly pleased when he seeth his children loved.

Keep up religion in your families, whatever scorn or contempt is cast upon you. Oh that you would labour to be of Abraham's spirit; "I know," saith God, "he will command his children and his household after him, and they shall keep the way of the Lord," Gen. xviii. 19.

I do not know any one better means for the keeping up religion in this nation, than for masters of families to be conscientious in the discharging of this duty.

Be good in bad times; be patterns of good works to those that shall behold you. Let no reproach or obloquy make you to abate your exact walking with God; whatever you meet withal in the ways of holiness and a strict life, say, if this be to be vile, I will be more vile. Make conscience of a strict observation of the Lord's day; take heed of that sacrilege of stealing away holy times; of prostituting that to common and evil uses, which is impropriated and dedicated to the service of God.

Pray for, and love all those that have been instrumental for your spiritual good in the work of the ministry, whatever dirt is now thrown in their faces, and though you never get more good by them.

Forget not to distribute to the necessities of God's people, that are many of them in a low condition; for this is a sacrifice of a sweet odour, and well-pleasing to him.

Carry yourselves with all patience and Christian meekness towards them that wrong you: pray for them that are your enemies, and when you are reviled, revile not again, but commit yourselves to that God who judgeth righteously.

Do your duty to your superiors, and to those that are in authority.

So carry yourselves that it may be with you as it was with Daniel; they had nothing against him, saving in the matter of his God.

Baulk not any duty for suffering; choose the greatest of suffering, before the least of sin.

In a word, so walk as it becometh the gospel. And finally I speak to you as the apostle spoke to them, Phil. ii. 16. " Hold forth the word of life, that I may rejoice in the day of Christ, that I have not run in vain, nor laboured in vain."

The *third use* is for comfort, to all those that do conscientiously endeavour in all things to please God: the comfort lies in this, you may suffer, but whenever you suffer, the Father will not leave you alone. Pleasing of God does not secure a man from suffering from men, sometimes it rather exposes a man to suffer from men: but now though it does not prevent suffering, yet it takes away the sting and venom of suffering; it makes it to be Samson's lion, when it was slain, he found nothing but honey in the belly of it. Oh! the presence of God in a time of affliction is exceeding precious, it turns gall into honey, thorns into roses. Be not troubled in your thoughts about what you may undergo: if God be with you, all will be well: if God comes when the cross cometh, the weight of it will not hurt you. What is a prison when God is there? My brethren, though estate leave you, relations leave you, all your comforts leave you, so long as God doth not leave you it will be well: therefore do not fear, be not dejected, or discouraged. Isa. xliii. 1, 2. " Fear not, O Jacob," why so? " When thou passest through the waters, I will be thee." We have more reason to be afraid of prosperity with God's absence, than of adversity with God's presence. A good God will make every condition to be good; it is not a prison but a palace where God is. They that do the things that please God, whatever condition they may be brought to, the Father will not leave them alone. Ministers may leave you, the means of grace and ordinance in a great measure may leave you, your creature-enjoyments and comforts may leave you; but here is a God that will never leave you: Oh! bless his holy name.

Fourthly, Is this pleasing of God, a duty of so great importance and benefit? then be tender and charitable in judging of those that do differ from you and others, upon this account because they dare not displease God. I may in this caution aim at myself and others of my brethren in the work of our ministry; but I am not here at present to take my last farewell. I hope I may have a little further opportunity of speaking to you: but if not, let me require this of you, to pass a charitable interpretation upon your laying down the exercise of our ministry. There is a greater Judge than you, must judge us all at the great day; and to this Judge we can appeal before angels and men, that it is not this thing, or that thing that puts us upon this dissent, but it is conscience toward God, and fear of offending him. I censure none that differ from me, as though they displease God: but yet, as to myself, though I do thus and thus, I should certainly violate the peace of my own conscience, and offend God, which I must not do, no, not to secure my ministry, though that either is, or ought to be, dearer to me than my very life: and how dear it is, God only knoweth. Do not add affliction to affliction, be not uncharitable in judging of us, as if through pride, faction, obstinacy, or devotedness to a party, or which is worse than all, in opposition to authority, we do dissent. The Judge of all hearts knows it is not so: but it is merely from those apprehensions which after prayer, and the use of all means do yet continue that doing thus and thus, we should displease God: therefore deal charitably with us, in this day of our affliction. If we be mistaken, I pray God to convince us: if others be mistaken, whether in a public or private capacity, I pray God in mercy convince them. But however things go, God will make good this truth to us; in this work he will not leave us, and our Father will not leave us alone; for it is the unfeigned desire of our soul in all things to please God.

DR. BATES'S FORENOON SERMON,

Preached August 17, 1662.

Heb. xii. 20, 21.

Now the God of peace that brought again from the dead our Lord Jesus, that great Shepherd of the sheep through the blood of the everlasting covenant, make you perfect in every good work to do his will, working in you that which is well pleasing in his sight, through Jesus Christ: to whom be glory for ever and ever.

IT would give light to these words, if you consider the scope and design of the apostle in this epistle to the Hebrews: the sum of which is, he writes to them that he might animate their spirits against "apostacy from the doctrine of the Gospel;" they were liable to this from you and others, upon this account, because they dare not displease God. I may in this caution aim at myself and other of my brethren, this upon a double account.

1. Partly in respect of those persecutions to which they were exposed: for the Jews were filled with a brutish zeal, for the ceremonies of the Levitical law, and ex-

pressed the greatest rancour against those who left Moses to follow Christ. This is the reason why the apostle lays down so many preservatives against their revolting from religion; and he spends one part of this epistle in a most passionate exhortation to perseverance, and doth in the tenth chapter insinuate himself into them: You have already tasted the first-fruits of affliction, ver. 3, 4. "You took joyfully the spoiling of your goods, knowing in yourselves, that you have in heaven a better and enduring substance." This is that temper that martyrs have expressed, who have not only parted with their goods, but with their lives for the gospel. When they came to the stake, they would not so much as shed a tear, to quench those flames wherein they should ascend to God, as in a fiery chariot. "You took joyfully the spoiling of your goods, knowing in yourselves, that you have a better and an enduring substance." Thus he insinuates himself, by representing what they had done, to encourage them to perseverance: and partly he fortifies them against backsliding, by those terrible judgments which he threatened against revolters, as you read chap. vi. 7.

2. As they were liable to this apostacy upon the account of persecution, so upon the account of the unsettledness and instability of their own spirits. There were several of those who had given up their names to Christ, who did compare the ceremonies of the law with the purity of the gospel. Now the apostle to secure them from this mixture, his great design is to represent the vanity and infectiveness of all the ceremonial law, and to express and prove the virtue and efficacy of the Lord Jesus his death, which was the substance of all the shadows. And this takes up one great part of his discourse with them.

Now in these two verses he sums up, by way of recapitulation, all that which he had discoursed of at large, and in them you may observe these two things.

1. A description of God, to whom he addresses this prayer.

2. The substance of the prayer itself.

The "description of God," that he amplifies by these two things: 1. From the attributes and qualities of God, (if I may so express it) "Now (saith he) the God of peace." 2. From the effects of his power and love; "That brought again from the dead our Lord Jesus, that great Shepherd of the sheep." And these titles, they are not here set down by the apostle to adorn his discourse merely as an ornament, but they have all a peculiar efficacy, as to the obtaining of the request which here he makes for them.

I shall begin with the first, the " description of God" from that attribute. " Now the God of Peace," the title that is used in the Old Testament frequently is this, "the Lord of Hosts," but in the New he is called " the God of Peace." There were darker representations of the mercy and love of God, the more full discoveries of his grace were reserved till the coming of Christ. Their discoveries under the Old Testament were but as the day-star, which ushered in the Sun of Righteousness. Now this title of the " God of Peace" imports two things—

1. That he is the author of peace, and works it.
2. That he loves and delights in peace.

First, that he is the author of it. And if you consider peace in all its notions and kinds, it is a fruit of God, and that which descends from him. 1. " Peace in nature" is the harmony that is between all the parts of the world, the union that is between the disagreeing elements that is from God; for without him the whole creation would presently disband, and return to its first chaos of confusion. 2. " Civil Peace," which is among the societies of men, that which is so amiable and lovely, and which needs no other foil to commend it, and set off its lustre than the miseries and cruelties of war—this peace comes from God likewise. Every rash hand is able to make a wound, or to cast a fire-brand, but it is only the God of Peace that is able to heal breaches, and to allay those storms that are in a nation. You know those showers, which render the earth fruitful, descend from heaven, from God; so all the counsels of peace descend from above. The fiery exhalations ascend from the earth, counsels of war and disturbance proceed from the devilish hearts of men. Or, 3. If you consider that "Rational Peace," which is in the spirits of men; that is, when the understanding exercises a coercion and restraint over our licentious appetites, when all our inferior faculties are under the empire and conduct of reason—this proceeds also from God. For since the fall, there is a great deal of tumult, many riots and disorders in the soul of a man. Reason hates a bad guide, and our appetites, those are evil instruments, and so many times hurry reason from its regular actings. But, 4. Much more if you consider " Spiritual Peace," that peace doth not only import an agreement of a man within himself, but the agreement of the soul with God. This is the fruit of the spirit, and it is only God that is able to convey this peace to us. And upon a particular account this title is given to him by way of eminency and property; as,

1. He is alone able to allow and dispense this peace unto us, for all our sins are injuries committed against him, against his crown and dignity; all the arrests of conscience are made in the name of God, and therefore it is only he that can speak peace. As in the civil state, it is an act of supremacy to give a pardon; only he that can condemn is able to speak pardon; so it is our God that is our judge. Provoked and incensed by us, he hath a judicial power to cast body and soul into hell-fire; is alone able to speak peace, and pass a pardon for us in the court of heaven; and this is experienced by a wounded spirit. It is just with such a person as with a malefactor, who stands condemned at the bar; he cannot receive encouragement from any of his spectators till the judge speak peace unto him. So if an angel from heaven should come and speak to a wounded spirit, it were impossible unless God did order, command, and dispense it, that the spirit should receive any peace, because our sins are immediately committed against him.

2. He is alone able to reveal and discover it. There is nothing harder in the world than to calm and quiet a disturbed conscience. It must be the same power that makes light to spring out of darkness that must cause a cheerful serenity in a dark and disconsolate soul. I know there is nothing more easy than that "false peace" which is so universal in the world; for the most among us cheat themselves with presumption, instead of peace with God, and security, instead of peace with conscience; but that peace, which is solid and true, can only be revealed by God himself. We have an instance of this in David, Psal. li. although Nathan had told him from God, "Thy sin is pardoned;" yet notwithstanding he saith, "Make me to hear joy and gladness, that the bones which thou hast broken may rejoice." He still addresses himself to God that he would cause him to hear the voice of pardon and reconciliation; for his soul could not be quiet by the voice of the prophet. There is so much infidelity in the soul of a man, that when he comes to take a view of his sins in all their bloody aggravations, only the spirit of God himself is able to allay the terrors of the conscience; and this he doth by an overpowering light, when he doth, in an imperative and commanding manner, silence all the doubts of the soul, and re-establish it in peace with God. Certainly, he that will but consider the terrors, the faintings, the paleness of a wounded conscience, when you shall see a person disrelish all the things of this world upon this account, "fearing lest God is his enemy," when all discourses that are addressed to him are ineffectual, and but like warm clothes to a dead carcase, cannot inspire any heat into him—this shews only God is able to reveal peace. So Job, " If he hide his face, who is able to be at peace?" There needs no other fury to complete the misery of a man than his own accusing conscience. Conscience is a verier devil than the devil himself, and able more to torment and lash the creature. Therefore, if that be once awakened, it is only God, to whose tribunal conscience is liable,

which is able to speak peace to the soul. Now you see in what respect this title, " the God of Peace," is attributed to him as he is the author and worker of it.

2. As he loves and delights in peace. This is that which is so pleasing to him, that he adopts those into the line of heaven, who are peacemakers, for they shall be called the children of God, Mat. v. 6. This characterizes persons to be his children, to be allied to him. God he only delights in the reflection of his own image; for those things that we admire in the world, and delight in, do not affect his heart. " He delights not in the strength of the horse, he takes no pleasure in the legs of a man: the Lord taketh pleasure in them that fear him, in those that hope in his mercy." Nothing attracts his eye and heart, but his own similitude and resemblance; and therefore where he sees peaceable dispositions, that is that which endears the soul to him, and makes it amiable in his eyes. You may judge of his delight in peace by this. It is that grace which in an especial manner prepares us for communion with him: for we can never really honour or enjoy him, unless we bring to him those dispositions which (if I may so speak) are in himself. And therefore it is no wonder that those have little peace of conscience, who make so little conscience of peace. You know when God appeared to Elijah, he did not appear in the storm, nor in the fire, but in the small still voice, and when Elisha was transported with anger, he was fain to allay that passion by music, that so he might be prepared for the holy motions of the spirit, he called for an instrument, and then the spirit moved in him. I bring it for this end, to shew, " how God delights in peace," and he will only maintain communion with those that are of calm and peaceable spirits. So much way as we give to anger, so much proportionably do we let in the devil, and cast out the God of peace.

Now, the reason why this title is given to God, is upon a double account partly with respect to the " blood of the everlasting covenant," which made peace between

God and us, partly with respect to the covenant itself, which is founded in that blood.

1. In respect of the " blood of the everlasting covenant." For it was the blood of Christ that hath sprinkled God's throne and made peace in heaven. You shall read therefore when Christ came into the world, it is said, (Luke ii. 14.) that the heavenly host appeared and sang, "Glory to God in the highest, and on earth peace," &c. Since the fall God and man are enemies, there is a reciprocal enmity between God and man: God hates the creature as it is unholy, and man hates God as he is just, the avenger of sin, the author of the law. Now Christ was the umpire that composed this difference, he was God and man in one person, and so being allied to both, he was a fit person to reconcile both. He was (as Job speaks) a day's-man between us. He hath paid every farthing that was due; for he did not compound with God, but paid the utmost that was due to him. He it is that hath reconciled us to God by the power of his spirit, in changing and renewing our natures, and creating in us those dispositions which are like to God; so that his blood is the foundation of this peace. And now, God appears to us not as a consuming fire, but as a refreshing light, full of calmness, serenity, and peace towards us. Christ hath brought more honour to God by his obedience, than we brought dishonour by our transgression; and therefore without any injury to God, he might be at peace with us. You know all our sins were but the acts of finite creatures, and only infinite in regard of the object against whom they were committed. But the blood of Christ was of infinite value in regard of the subject; for, he was God, and the enriching union of the Deity conveyed such worth and value to his blood, that he was able to appease God, and not only to free us from condemnation, but to make us the favorites of God. We are not only pardoned, but preferred upon the account of his blood.

2. He is the God of peace, as with respect to the blood

of Christ, which is the purchase of peace; so with respect to the covenant which is made between God and us, ["Through the blood of the everlasting covenant."] There are three sorts of covenants amongst men; some are covenants of friendship and amity, some are covenants of trade and commerce, and some are covenants of assistance and help. Now all these qualifications meet in this covenant which is made between God and believers: it is a covenant of peace and friendship, for now we stand upon terms of amity with God. Those who were strangers and enemies are now reconciled. And there is between God and us perfect peace; there is a league (as the scripture speaks) between God and the creature. It is the covenant of trade, there is now a way opened to heaven, we may now ascend to God in duties of holiness, and God descends to us by the excitations of his grace and influences of joy. And it is a covenant of assistance, for he promises not only to give us the reward of the covenant, but to secure unto us the condition, he promises to enable us to discharge the condition of faith and repentance. Now upon this account of that covenant which is founded in the blood of Christ, he is the God of peace to his people.

1st *Use*, is by way of conviction. This may discover us how distant their temper is from God, who are enemies to peace. We un-man ourselves. We unchristian ourselves so far as we are opposite to this blessed temper of peace. Certainly as disturbed water cannot make any reflection unto us of that face that looks into it; so when our spirits are disturbed by animosities, exasperations, heats and divisions, it is impossible for us to see the image of God, as he is the God of peace. And certainly there is no more doleful consideration in the world than this, That man whom God made so sociable a creature, who hath all the engagements and endearments laid upon him, which may cause him to live in peace and gentleness towards those who are of the same nature with him; yet that in the fierceness of our hearts, should exceed those of the most savage creatures. Man comes into the world naked, and altogether unarmed, as if he were designed for the picture of peace; but could you look into the hearts of men, you would find there such tumults, such divisions, such seeds of enmity against their fellow-creatures, that tigers and lions are calm and peaceable in comparison of them. Now how is this distant from the temper of the God of peace ? It is very strange to consider that when promises are made to bury all differences as rubbish under the foundation, that nevertheless the great work of many persons should be only to revive those former animosities, to make those exasperations fresh and keen upon their own spirits; but is this to imitate the God of peace ? These to promote divisions and disturbances amongst us, clothe their enemies with the livery of shame and reproach, that so they may be baited by their fury, that make it their design to represent that party which they think is dissonant from them, with the most odious appearances (you know this is the old art) and those showers of calumnies which are in the world, they usually precede the storm of persecution. The devil was first a lier, and then a murderer; and those who are of this seed, they follow his art. In the primitive times, all the persecutions of the heathens arose from the reproaches of Christians: so it is now. It is an easy thing to blast the name of those persons, who are designed for ruin. But if the contending parties would consider, (if I may call one party contending, which is only liable to penalties, and is resolved to bear them patiently) how unlike this is to that God of peace, methinks it should allay the rancour that is in men's spirits, and make an atonement between all the differences and divisions that is amongst them.

2. If only peace come from God, you may from hence take a trial of that peace that is within you, (for hitherto I have been only discoursing of civil peace) whether it be an effect of this God of peace. I know nothing more common in the world than presumption; there is a false

peace which doth not arise from the knowledge of a man's happiness, but from the ignorance of this misery. Peace, which is only like a torch to shine in the night, or like players that glitter only by torch-light: so is the false peace men cherish in their bosom, merely upon this account, because they do not bring their souls to the light of the word, they never had it from this God of peace, because,

1. God never speaks peace to a soul, but in the way of holiness and obedience. And therefore you shall find it is the counsel of the scripture, "Acquaint thyself with God, and be at peace."

Our peace is found in the way of duty; and there are none who are more blessed with the peace of conscience, than those who with the greatest fervour, frequency, and delight, maintain communion with God in holy duties. For, a friendship among men is cherished and preserved by visits and conversations, so our peace with God is preserved by those visits we make to heaven in our prayers.

2. That peace that comes from God, always causes in us a war with sin, for God's covenant with us is offensive and defensive, and therefore it is impossible any person should have true and solid peace, that waking tranquillity of soul, which is the reward of holiness and obedience, that entertains sin; for every sin thou dost wilfully commit, it is an act of hostility against God, it is that which makes him thine enemy, and makes thee an enemy to him. As Jehu said, "What peace, so long as the whoredom of thy mother Jezebel and her witchcrafts are so many?" So what peace can there be, so long as thou dost indulge thyself in sin, and make it thy business to gratify thy outward senses, though it be to the displeasure of God? It is the greatest mercy in the world to rob such persons of their peace, and to discover to them their danger; they are only capable of true peace, by the knowledge of that which is false. Therefore bring yourselves to this trial: whether or no doth that peace

which now you please yourselves in, cause in you an eternal hatred of sin? Doth it set you at a distance from your most beloved lusts; then it is that peace that springs from God. The greatest part of the world are in a state of war with God, though they do not feel the effects of that war. True indeed, God doth not always draw the sword, either of famine, pestilence, or war, against a nation, and yet they may be acting in a most hostile way against God: so for a person, God may not blast thy estate, or send diseases upon thy person, or raise a tumult in thy conscience, and make a conspiracy of thy thoughts and passions against thy peace. Thou mayest be quiet within, and yet have war with God; because, as in the world there may be a truce, when there is no peace, the war may still continue, though there is a truce between two princes: or rather, there is not a truce between God and the sinner, but as a town that is besieged for many days, may not feel the battery of their enemy, because he is undermining them to blow them up at once, so God doth not many times make his battery against sinners, but he is undermining them, and the fall at the last will be dreadful, if there be not a composition.

Use 2. By way of exhortation, let me press you all to follow peace, it is a duty which the gospel enjoins with the greatest force of words and expressions. The apostle when he is to seal up his affection to them, he doth it with that prayer, 2 Thess. iii. 16. " Now the God of peace himself give you peace always, by all means." What strange expressions! First, he gives you: hear the title of the God of peace, and then he saith (himself) " the God of peace himself." There is a great deal of force in that word. Peace is so excellent a blessing, and there is such an abhorrency in our corrupt nature to it, that it is only the Lord himself that is able to effect it. As if the apostle had said, the Lord must bow the heavens, he must come down himself to create peace among you; and to express the greater vehemency of his desire, he saith, give you peace always, by all means. So another Scripture, " pursue peace, follow peace with all men;" a word that imports our pursuit after it, though it runs from us. This is the strain and tenor of the gospel, and this becomes you as christians. When Christ came to purchase our peace, he came as a Lamb, an innocent and meek Creature: behold the Lamb of God. When the holy Spirit descended to seal the privilege of peace to us, he descended in the form of a dove; a guileless creature, in whom there is no rancor nor bitterness. What a strong engagement should this be upon all of us to pursue and promote peace? And for your encouragement consider,

1. That in the times of the gospel, all the promises do as it were empty themselves into this blessing, the blessing of peace. Thus Isa. xi. 6. you shall find there a gracious promise respecting the times of the gospel. " The wolf also shall dwell with the lamb, and the leopard shall lie down with the kid, and the calf, and the young lion, and the fatling together, and a little child shall lead them; and the cow and the bear shall feed, their young ones shall lie down together, and the lion shall eat straw like the ox." That which I observe from thence, is this, that God here promises to cause an universal peace and unity under the gospel, though it be as difficult as to persuade the most disagreeing natures to a peaceable cohabitation. For here the Scripture instances in those creatures between which there is the most natural, and, therefore, the most fierce animosities. The Lord will reconcile men, though their differences be never so great. What is too hard for the God of peace to effect? Is not God of infinite power, of infinite love? Then it should quicken us to pursue peace. 1. By prayer to him, because he is able to effect it; certainly that God that was able to bring order into the world, when it was a mere lump and mass of confusion, is able to bring peace, and to unite our spirits.

And it is observable, the greater our differences and divisions are, the more will the power of this God appear in reconciling them. It is said in the Psalms, that "God's throne is in darkness;" that is, his ways of providence are very difficult for us to trace and find out; and, therefore, when our divisions are at the highest, he is able by one word to allay the storm. This should encourage us in prayer. This is the course of God to glorify himself, by putting a stop to the greatest troubles when nearest to us, and to work out one contrary by another. To give you some instances, that so we may encourage our faith, and quicken our prayer to God for this blessing, consider how still God hath made "difficulties the way for enjoyment." For instance, the promise that Sarah should be the mother of a child; but he made way for that by her dead womb, for all that numerous progeny which like the stars of the sky descended from her. That he first maimed Jacob, and then gave him the blessing. He brought Joseph from the prison to a princely palace. First David was harassed with troubles, and then his head was decked with the imperial crown. So if you look into the kingdom of Christ, who would have thought that a few fishermen should have advanced the empire of Christ in the world? Had you lived to have seen those despicable beginnings, when a few unlearned men were the heralds and preachers of Christ, how would this have caused you to fail and sink in your spirits! And yet the gospel hath been preached in all parts of the world, and that by a few fishermen. The providences of God are like those plated pictures, if you look one way upon them, there is the appearance of a serpent; if you look on the other side, there is the appearance of an angel. So here, many times God is pleased to suffer exasperations to go very high, that so his power may appear more eminent in the composure of them. He it is that enables the faith of his people to draw water out of the rock, when the fountain is dry; that makes meat to come out of the eater (as in Samson's riddle) that is able to bring a peaceable harmony out of devouring differences, and therefore it should quicken our prayers to him.

2. To make us more serious in our endeavours after peace. Consider what a dishonour it is to the gospel, that those that profess themselves sons of the same God, members of the same Christ, temples of the same spirit, should be at deadly jars one with another. It is strange and unnatural that lilies should prove thorns to one another; that those who are saints in pretence, should be devils in practice to one another; that God's diamonds should cut one another; this is very strange; yet thus it is. But now especially it is most sad, when religion, which should restrain and bridle our passions, is made fuel and incentives of them: how far distant is it from the counsel of the apostle, Rom. xiv. 10. where he speaks concerning their lesser differences, " one values one day above another, another esteems every day alike?" What's his counsel? he speaks as a person that was filled with bowels and compassion. Oh, saith he, let not him that doth not esteem the day judge him that doth; " for we shall all stand before the judgment-seat of Christ." There we shall appear all upon a level, stand upon equal ground, and receive our final doom from him; this therefore should calm our spirit. Why may there not be some differences in judgment, without division in affection? For it is as impossible that all judgments should be of the same extent, as all our faces to be of the same colour and figure. Therefore consider what an injury it is to our profession, how doth it obscure the glory of God, and lustre of our religion?

3. Doth not the public enemy rejoice over us, I mean the papists? Do they not warm themselves at the sparks of our divisions? for you know the old maxim of divide and reign: therefore it should compose our spirits, and quicken us to labour after union. Unmortified lusts are thence, whence all wars and enmities spring in the world. The apostle Paul when he would compose their differences, he doth not lay down rules to decide their controversies, but to correct their secret passions, pride, self-seeking, revenge, &c. this being the seed of all dis-

turbances in the church. And although these lusts may not be conspicuous and visible to the eyes of men, yet they are certainly the fuel of our distempers.

The sum of all is this, those that have the spirit of God, they cannot but mourn and be sensible of these divisions. I know a great part among us are unconcerned. Some rejoice, those that are rather buried in the affairs of the world, and incumbered with much business, or those that are steeped in the pleasures of sense, are altogether unaffected with these things, stand as neuters, disregarding all events; but the saints of God cannot but mourn over them, when our divisions hinder the progress of the gospel, and are serviceable to nothing but the kingdom of darkness. Therefore I beseech you let what hath been spoken quicken you in your prayers to God, to pray for the peace of Jerusalem, (that is the least effect of our love and desires after peace) and by all endeavours to labour to bring back peace to us, that we may see that prophesy fulfilled in our time, that " the Lord should be one, and his name one amongst us."

DR. BATES'S AFTERNOON SERMON

Preached August 17, 1662.

Heb. xiii. 20, 21.

Now the God of peace that brought again from the dead our Lord Jesus, that great Shepherd of the sheep, through the blood of the everlasting covenant, make you perfect in every good work to do his will, working in you that which is well pleasing in his sight, through Jesus Christ: to whom be glory for ever and ever.

THE apostle describes God by the effects of his power and love, ("that brought again from the dead our Lord Jesus.)" The resurrection of Christ from the dead is one of the most transcendent testimonies of God's love and power towards us.

1. Of his love; because, as the anger of God was that which crucified our Saviour, so, on the contrary, it must be his love that should raise and restore him. Christ when he died, he looked upon God as a judge; and as those colours which we see conveyed to us, are answerable to the medium through which we see them; as, if we look through a coloured glass, we see the object of that colour: so the Lord Jesus, when he was upon the cross, looked upon God through the black cloud of our sins, and through the red cloud of his Father's wrath, and so died as a sacrifice to divine justice. But when he was raised from the grave, that was the testimony of God's love to him, and of his love to us, for he died as our surety, he was arrested for our debt, he was cast into the grave, as into a prison: but by his resurrection he was redeemed from prison and judgment. And therefore you shall find, when Christ was risen, he salutes his disciples with this, "peace be unto you," Luke xxiv. 31. There was the dawning of peace at the incarnation of Christ, for then the angels sung, peace upon earth; but the complete sunshine of peace was at his resurrection, when he had made full and complete satisfaction to God's justice: for this was a clearing of him before all the world, when God raised him from the grave. And in this respect it was very agreeable for the apostle to say, "The God of peace, that brought again from the dead our Lord Jesus."

2. It was the effect of infinite power. You know it is naturally impossible for a dead body to quicken himself, to revive; but for the Lord Jesus, who had the load of the sins of all the elect upon him, who was, as it were, secured in the grave by God's justice and power, for him to rise again, this must be an effect of infinite power in the great God. Thus raising of Christ, sometimes it is attributed to the Son, being God equal with the Father: but here it is attributed to God; and therefore when the

scripture would speak with the greatest magnificence of the power of God, it expresses it thus, "that power which raised Jesus Christ from the dead." When Christ wrought deliverance for the lost world, (all those who were committed to his charge,) this could be no less than the work of an infinite power. And upon this account also it is very proportionable to the design of the apostle, for that prayer he makes to God is for that which only can be accomplished by infinite love, and infinite power, i. e. to make the christian Hebrews perfect in every good work to do his will.

I come to a further description. He that brought again from the dead "our Lord Jesus," the title of the Lord Jesus was only given to our Saviour after his resurrection, he was called Lord before, and Jesus before: but these two titles were never united till after his resurrection. They came to see the place where the body of the Lord Jesus lay; the reason was this, because the resurrection of Christ was a solemn proclamation to the world, that Christ was the Son of God. It is true this title was given him immediately upon his conception, but it was never completely declared to the world, till after his resurrection; for before, Christ was a prince in disguise; the beams of the divinity were abated by the veil of his humanity; but then he was declared by power to be the Son of God.

It follows "that great Shepherd of the sheep." For the opening of this,

1. We will consider the title of Christ.
2. The person for whom this title relates.

First, this title " the great Shepherd." It is a wonderful condescension in Christ, that he will take upon him the title of a shepherd, that which rather expresses love and care, than power and dominion; yet he is pleased to assume this title to express his affection to us. For the opening of it, wherein he appears to be the great Shepherd, I shall lay down these particulars.

1. He is great in the dignity of his person; for, he

that is Lord of angels, is become the Shepherd of the sheep; and the humiliation of his person, in this respect, is the exaltation of his office. It is looked upon in the world as a mean and low employment, to have the care and inspection of a flock; but now herein appears the love of Christ, he was pleased to become our Shepherd, that so he might secure and bring us to the fold of heaven, and there make us to feed upon those pastures, and to drink of those rivers of pleasures which flow from the presence of God.

2. In the derivation of his authority: that authority which is communicated to him, whereby he is our Shepherd: and that is originally from God himself; it is not by any mediate deputation, but from God himself. He is our Shepherd, and hath a title to his flock upon a double account. 1. They are committed to him as his charge and custody, John vi. 37, &c. All the elect of the world were given by God the Father to Christ, not by way of alienation, but by way of opigneration, as so many pledges which he was to bring to grace and glory: and this charge he doth most fully execute, for there is none missing of those committed to him. 2. They are given to him by way of reward and recompence for all his blood and sufferings, Isa. liii. 10. The Lord put such a value on souls, that he purchased an interest in them by his own blood; and he thinks himself exceedingly recompensed for all his pains on the cross, agonies in the garden, temptations in the wilderness, &c. if souls will submit to his care. And here observe the course of heaven, God would endear souls to Christ upon all reasons, by virtue of his command, and that charge he gives to them, and by virtue of his own purchase.

3. If you consider, the extent of his care and affection, for all the saints of the world, those who are dispersed in all places, in all ages they are all his flock: and therefore it is the royalty of his administration, John x. 16. "there shall be one fold, and one shepherd." As Christ is the only Catholic king, so he is the only universal

Bishop; for all other shepherds have but particular portions of his flock committed to their charge, and they should be such portions as they have regard to, and are under their inspection, and at the last day, all his sheep shall congregate together, and stand at his right hand. All the saints of God that are now scattered, as so many stars in the firmament, shall be united in one constellation, when they shall appear in glory before him.

4. In respect of his endowments and qualifications, which fit him for the discharge of his office. And

1. Take notice of his affection and love to us, and that is the wonder of heaven and earth, "Christ laid down his life for his sheep." John x. 11. This is strange, that Christ should be " a sheep for the slaughter," that he might become our shepherd, that he should be a sacrifice before he could take his office upon him. Other sheep lay down their lives for the shepherd, but Christ laid down his life for the sheep. So great was his love that it brought him from heaven to "seek and find those that were lost." He left a palace to come to a wilderness; a throne of heaven to come to a fold here upon earth. We read of David that he exchanged a sheephook for a sceptre; but Christ quite contrary, he exchanged a sceptre for the rod and staff of a shepherd. It was said by one, There is nothing so conspicuous in Christ, as the prodigality of his love to us. Oh! do but consider how great love that was that should make him to die for us, that he might bring us home to his fold. We were all of us like erring sheep, who had strayed from him, and fell to the lord of the soil, as strange cattle; we were gotten into the possession of the god of this world. The Lord Christ would buy us off from thence. Though we forfeited our right in him, yet he would not lose his right in us, but he laid down his life that he might reduce us to his fold, that of wolves he might make us lambs, and fit us for the comforts of his presence.

2. In respect of his exact diligence and inspection over them. When but one sheep went astray from his folds,

we read, he left the ninety and nine, and went and sought for that one, Luke xv. where we have that parable, to express the diligence and watchfulness of Christ over his sheep. There is no person, be he never so mean, never so obscure, though lost in the number and account of the world, if he be one of Christ's sheep, he is always under his inspection and watchfulness. We read of the high-priest, that he carried the names of the tribes upon his breast-plate; the Lord Christ carries the names of all his sheep in his heart: therefore, Rev. xiii. speaking concerning the saints, all that dwell upon earth, "Whose names are written in the book of life." His diligence and care is so exact, that he hath all their names writ in his book. He that tells the stars, counts their hairs, and always exercises the most watchful providence over them for good. You know sheep are either liable to rage, or erring, and wandering. Christ's diligence is such that he protects them from the rage of Satan, reduces them from all their wanderings, and brings them home to himself.

3. In making proportional all their services and sufferings, to those degrees of strength which he gives to them, Isa. xl. 11. "He shall feed his flock like a shepherd, he shall gather the lambs with his arms, and carry them in his bosom, and shall gently lead those that are with young." Christ always makes a proportion between the services, sufferings, and strength he calls them to. He it is that with that tenderness speaks to Peter, " Peter, lovest thou me? feed my lambs." He hath provided for them the most ample, and most satisfying nourishment, the ordinances of the gospel, the word, the promises, which are the breast of consolation: these are all provided by him for his people. And in this respect he is the great shepherd, for he doth not only allow them means, but blesses the means to them. He is able to enlighten the dark mind. He can make pliable the stubborn will, and he can spiritualize the drowsy affection, which all other shepherds in the world are not able to effect.

4. He is the great Shepherd, if you consider his " power to preserve them from danger;" not only those dangers which respect Satan (for that fell under his care before) but those diseases to which they are liable, which threaten ruin. Other shepherds possibly may cure diseases, but not defend them from danger. Christ it is that " gives eternal life to his sheep;" he begins the "life of holiness," which though at present is but a spark in the sea, yet he keeps it alive till it shall break forth into a triumphant flame. That life that is encompassed with so many enemies, and liable to so many weaknesses, the Lord Jesus will " bring forth judgment to victory," and will make them to be powerful over spiritual and eternal enemies.

The sum is this. The Lord Christ is so perfect a shepherd, so compleat, as to all the qualifications of that office, that the prophet David breaks forth into exultation, Psal. xxiii. "The Lord is my shepherd," &c. and then afterwards expresses all those provisions which are made for him by God as a shepherd, " He makes me to lie down in green pastures, he leadeth me beside the still waters." So that you see Christ, whether for diligence, love, tenderness, for preserving us from danger, for securing us to life eternal, he only is the great Shepherd, he is the God of shepherds as well as the God of sheep, and all other shepherds are but inferior to him, and must be accountable to him for the souls of his sheep, which are more valuable than all the world.

It follows, " The great Shepherd of the sheep." I shall not spend any time in making any resemblance between the people of God and the sheep; Only,

1. They are sheep in respect of their innocency. You know, of all creatures the sheep are unarmed. Other creatures, either they are armed with strength, or skin, or swiftness to guard themselves, and offend others; but the sheep hath neither the strength of the lion, the craft of the fox, nor the swiftness of the deer; and of all creatures is most weak, inoffensive, and most liable to dangers and injuries. Of all persons, God's people are most

liable to danger, and when out of Christ's protection, the weakest persons in the world.

2. In respect of their meekness. A sheep is an emblem of meekness, that is their temper, and therein they imitate Christ, who hath propounded himself to be their pattern. " Learn of me, for I am meek and lowly." Both these qualities are expressed by the prophet, Isa. xi. where speaking concerning the times of the gospel, he saith, " The lamb shall lie down with the wolf." Now, where the prophet expresses their safety, there he expresses their innocency and meekness. This is the reason why the prophet saith, " For thy sake we are killed all the day long, we are counted as sheep for the slaughter;" because of all creatures most liable to injuries, that which doth least resent them. And wherever the grace of Christ comes, it sweetens the most cruel nature, and polishes the most rough disposition, and makes them to be like Christ, meek and lowly.

3. In regard of their profitableness; for of all creatures, they are most profitable, the food as to their flesh, the cloth as to their fleece. And the people of God, however they are exposed to the contempts and injuries of the world, they are the most profitable: for were it not for them, the whole frame of nature would fall into pieces, the stars would fall like leaves in autumn, and all the elements would fall into confusion. We see it by one Lot, who kept showers of fire and brimstone from falling on Sodom, till he was got out of it. And it is the people of God, for whom this frame of nature is continued, and when they are brought into the fold of Christ, the justice of God will have a solemn triumph over all the world.

4. As they are liable to wandering; sheep are wandering creatures, and when strayed, not able to reduce themselves. And in this respect the people of God are sheep, they have a thousand allurements to draw them from the ways of God; and if God should not guide them by his eye, it is impossible they should go in the way that

leads to heaven. Therefore David saith, "I have gone astray like a lost sheep, seek thy servant;" Psal. cxix. 176. This shall suffice to make the parallel and resemblance of the people of God to sheep.

The second argument is this, That he hath designed Christ to be the Shepherd of the church, "The great Shepherd of the sheep." This is another argument and evidence that he is reconciled to us, and that he is the "God of peace." For when God gave Christ to be our sacrifice, and raised him up to be our shepherd; these are the most clear testimonies of his love. For, although Christ now sits in Heaven, and "all the angels of God worship him," yet he doth not disdain to exercise the same care, and to express the same love to his people, that he did when he was upon the earth. All the offices of Christ express God's love to us, for he feeds us as a prophet, died for us as a priest, governs and defends us as he is a king; and all these meet together in this title, feeding of us, dying for us, defending of us; as he was God, he loved us; as he was man he died for us. This doth express the effects of his two natures in this title; and therefore an admirable evidence that God is at peace with us.

It follows, "Through the blood of the everlasting covenant." The blood of Christ is that which cements God and us together. For you must remember, our original peace with God was broken; that peace we have with him now, is called reconciliation; it is as a broken bone, which well set, is stronger than before, because nature conveys most liberal supplies to the weakest part: so now being reconciled to God, through the blood of his Son, we stand upon surer terms with him, than we did in innocency. The blood of Christ speaks better things for us than all our sins speak against us; it speaks peace to our souls, and that in heaven purchased by his death. Christ died as a testator, and bequeathed to the church a legacy of peace; he lives as the executor of that covenant, and now in heaven conveys to us that blessing of peace, which he bequeathed in his death. And as our peace was founded in his blood, so it is conserved by his intercession. He appears in the court of heaven as our embassador, to make up all those differences which fall out between God and us. For you know, amity and friendship is kept between foreign states, by their residents and agents, that are kept in their several courts; so we have an agent in the court of heaven, the Lord Jesus Christ, that was raised from the dead. And as a believer falls into sin, which is a breach of peace between God and us, so that peace is made up by the exercise of repentance on our part, and by sprinkling of Christ's blood upon us, on God's part. The renewed exercise of repentance, and application of Christ's blood, preserves that peace that is between God and believers. And (to sum up the force of the argument) when we had fallen from God, and it did not consist with the majesty of God to make peace with us, without satisfaction, then was he pleased to pay our ransom out of his own treasury, and redeem us by the blood of his Son. So that all his attributes might shine forth in their lustre, and glory in our salvation, and that upon sure terms we might be able to challenge an interest in his favour and love.

It follows, " through the blood of the everlasting covenant." It is called an everlasting covenant in two respects,

1. In opposition to the old covenant, which was made with Adam in innocency. But that covenant which secures to us the reward of that life eternal, did not secure to us the condition, that was perfect obedience; and in reference to this old covenant, sometimes the gospel is called a new covenant, sometimes a better covenant, because it supplies all weakness in the first covenant. Not as if the law of God was weak and faulty in respect of itself, for the law of God is just, and good, but weak in respect of us; for it is impossible that that covenant, by the breach of which sin and death, came in to us, should reconcile us to God, and appease his anger; and

therefore God contrived another covenant for us, a covenant in the gospel, that was made with us in Christ, and this is called an everlasting covenant, because it remains for ever, the tenor of it shall not be changed; for the first covenant is only abrogated and made null, while frustrated as to the intent it was first given.

2. It is called an everlasting covenant, as it brings to those that are parties in it an everlasting glory: so the Lord Jesus's blood is called an everlasting redemption, for it ransoms the souls of men from that eternal death to which they were liable, and gives them a title to everlasting life; for this covenant which now God hath made with us, it not only secures the reward, but the conditions to which the reward is made; for God saith, " I will plant my fear in your hearts, that you shall not depart from me."

I have now gone over the title, and that in order to the prayer which follows, " make you perfect to do his will, working in you that which is well-pleasing in his sight." The general sum of it is this: that God of peace who is reconciled to us in his Son, as he is the Father of mercies to us, so he is the fountain of holiness to us; and in this respect we can only expect from him the treasures of grace, as he is the God of peace; for God, as he is our judge, dispenses to sinners nothing but revenge; there is nothing to be expected but the curse of his law, the execution of that sentence of death from him. For, although the world despise holiness as a base and contemptible thing, they had rather be ungracious, than inglorious in the eyes of men, and upon this account they are afraid to be holy, lest they should be the public scorn and contempt of the place wherein they live: although holiness is of so low a price in the world, yet in heaven, next to God, Christ, and the spirit, holiness is the most rich jewel that God can bestow upon us; and therefore we must first look upon him as the God of peace, before we can beg any grace from him. And this is the reason why the apostle represents God by these titles, that he might encourage the Hebrews to believe God would grant his request. When Christ died for us, it was not his design only to quiet our conscience, but to quicken our souls, not only to free us from damnation, but from the domination of sin. And therefore you shall find these two are joined together, Tit. ii. 14. " Who gave himself for us that he might redeem us from all iniquity, and purify unto himself a peculiar people, zealous of good works." The death of Christ, as there was a value in it to purchase God's favour, so there was a virtue in it to restore to us God's image. And the account of his dying for us is it, that we must expect the least degree of grace and holiness from God. And this is the reason why the apostle prefaces this, " now the God of peace," &c.

I know you expect I should say something as to my non-conformity. I shall only say thus much, It is neither fancy, faction or humour that makes me not to comply, but merely for fear of offending God. And if after the best means used for my illumination; as prayer to God, discourse, study, I am not able to be satisfied concerning the lawfulness of what is required : if it be my unhappiness to be in error, surely men will have no reason to be angry with me in this world, and I hope God will pardon me in the next.

MR. WATSON'S FORENOON SERMON.

Preached August 17th, 1662.

JOHN xiii. 34.

A new commandment give I unto you, that ye love one another, as I have loved you.

WE are this day called to a love-feast; and nothing can be more suitable than to treat of christian love. Jesus Christ hath given us a great evidence of his love to us, he bled love at every vein; therefore we are to imitate him, and as becometh christians, to love one another. It is a general complaint, how true I know not, " That this is the great grace that is defective among christians." Although they pretend much love to Christ, yet they have little love one to another.

I have, in former sermons, discoursed concerning faith, how that by faith we must receive Christ in the sacrament; and now I shall speak something of love. Love is needful at a feast, it is requisite when we sit down at our own table. I remember it is said of Augustin, " He would not suffer any to feast at his table, that came in a spirit of rancor, and set down in passion." Sure I am, they are not fit to be guests at Christ's table, that come not in a spirit of meekness and love. It is true, we are to eat the passover with bitter herbs, but they must be the bitter herbs of repentance, not the bitter herbs of malice, wrath, and fury; we must come here with bitter tears, not with bitter hearts: hear what the text saith, " A new command I give unto you," &c.

Wherein, first, you have the command, " A new command I give unto you." It is not left to our discretion, but, we are bound to it by virtue of a command, " A new command I give unto you."

Secondly. This command is enforced by God's own example, " as I have loved you." It is called a new command, but love is an old command, this law is written in the nature of man. It is engraven in every man's heart by nature, and it is an old command, because found among God's ancient statutes, the ancient records of his law; aye, but it is a new command too, because pressed by a new example of Christ, " As I have loved you, so do ye love one another."

> *Doct.* Christians ought to make conscience of this duty of loving one another. Confident I am, we shall never see religion thrive in the world, until we see this grace of love flourish in the heart of christians.

For the illustration of this proposition, I shall do these two things. First, shew you the truth of this love: Secondly, the extent of this love.

First, Truth of this love. If you love one another, saith Christ, see you do it purely, not dissembling, but from the heart. 1 John iii. 18. " My little children, let us not love in word, neither in tongue, but in deed and in truth." Dissembling love is like painted fire that will never warm. We must not be like the bee, that hath honey in her mouth, but withal hath a sting in her tail. We must not pretend to love, to have honey in the mouth, but withal have the sting of malice in the heart: no, said the apostle, " Let us love in deed and in truth."

Secondly, Extent of our love. This fountain of love must run in three streams.

1. We must love all men, love their persons, although we must not love their sins. We have all the same make, the same lump and mould, and, therefore, must love. There is a natural love, that every creature bears to his own species and kind.

2. Our love must especially stream out to the saints of God, the household of faith. It is with our love, as it is with our fire. You keep fire all the day upon the hearth, but upon special occasions you draw it out larger, so our

love must always burn to all. Aye, but to the saints you must draw out the fire, enlarge your affections. We must love as God loves, he doth especially love the saints. Love every creature with a common love, but especially the new creature; and indeed there is that in every true saint, that may excite and allure our love. What are the graces of the spirit, but so many pearls to adorn the bride of Christ? What is holiness in the heart, but the embroidery and curious workmanship of the Holy Ghost? Here is enough to entice and draw out our love: and, beloved, if we love the saints for their graces, then we love all the saints.

And here I beseech you consider these six particulars.

First, We ought to love the saints in what condition soever they are, although they be poor in the world, low in their condition, for commonly so it is. They that have the lowest hearts, have the lowest condition too. I read of the king of the Moors, that he was offended at the christians because of their poverty; and truly when wicked men do fleece the saints, it is no wonder if they be poor. Methinks grace in a poor man, is like a pearl that lies in the dust, or like a cloth of gold that is hid under rags; you must love the gold, that is, the grace, notwithstanding the rags. The poorest saint alive hath the angel's riches; the poorest believer is a member of Christ, and shall we not love him? We love the picture of a friend, although it be hung in a mean frame; we must love a rich Christ in a poor man.

Secondly, We are to love the people of God although they have many weak infirmities. Shew me the man that is perfect, and let him throw the first stone, even the best. Saints like the stars they have their twinkling, they have their blemishes and their failings. In some there is too much pride, in others too much censoriousness, in others too much rash anger and passion, but we must love the grace that is in them, notwithstanding the infirmities that are in them. You love gold though in the ore, and mixed with much impurity. A saint on earth is like a diamond that hath its flaw, like to the rose that is sweet and perfumed, but yet hath its pricks. The best saints have some mixture and infirmity, and we must love them for the good that is in them. This is our great fault, we are apt to overlook all the good, and so take notice of the stain and blemishes in them; as those that see a little stain in a piece of scarlet, despise the cloth for the stain's sake; so do we. But God doth not do so by us; he is pleased to overlook many sad failings; he seeth the faith, and winks at the failings of his people. You that cannot love a brother because you see an imperfection in him, would you have God do so by you? Would you have him damn you for every blemish of sin?

Thirdly, We must love the children of God, though weak in parts. All are not born politicians; but though the saints of God have not always so good intellectuals as others, yet if they have good vitals, and the life of faith in them, love them for that grace; you do not despise your children because they are weak, but you love them because they are your children. Oh! do not despise a saint because he is of low parts, but love him as he is a child of your heavenly Father's.

Fourthly, We are to love the saints of God though in some lesser things they differ from us, if they keep the foundations of religion, and hold the head, Christ; yet we are to bear other things. One christian hath more light than another, and shall we unsaint all that cannot come up to our light? It is great wisdom to separate between the precious and the vile. O what a blessed place will heaven be, because there our light shall be clear, and our love shall be perfect. And that is the fourth.

Fifthly, Love the saints of God when reviled and persecuted. A bleeding saint should be the object of our love. Onesiphorus, saith Paul, was not ashamed of my chain: a sign he loved Christ's graces in Paul. Christ Jesus loveth no saints more than his persecuted saints. His martyrs have the highest thrones reserved in heaven for them.

We must love to see Christ's livery upon a man, though sprinkled with blood. He that is ashamed of a persecuted saint, will never suffer for a crucified Jesus.

Sixthly, We must love the saints of God, though their graces may eclipse and outshine our graces. Beloved, in the sweetest fruits worms are apt to breed, and in the best heart, the worm of pride is apt to be breeding. If God doth not keep us, we shall not only envy another's graces, if they outshine us, but their persons too. What though another's graces do outshine yours? yet love him, because the eminency of his graces bringeth much honour to the gospel of our Lord Jesus Christ.

And thus, my beloved, I have shewn you how you must love all the saints, 1 Pet. ii. 17. " Love the brotherhood, love the whole fraternity of believers." Oh! that this sweet spice of love might send forth its perfume among christians, that we could turn all our heart-burnings into heart-breakings, and quench the fire of divisions and contentions, and keep the fire of love burning upon the altar of our hearts. And, my beloved, as we must love all the saints, so we must shew this love by the fruit of it, for God doth not value that love that is invisible. The fruits of our love to the saints must be these four.

FOUR FRUITS OF LOVE TO THE SAINTS.

1. We must shew love to them by prizing their persons above others, Psal. xv. 4. spoken of a man that shall go to heaven, " in whose eyes a vile person is contemned, but he honoureth them that fear the Lord." The wicked are so much rubbish and lumber, but the saints are called the jewels, Mal. iii. 1. and we must prize these jewels above all the lumber in the world; as they said of King David, " thy life is worth ten thousand of ours." 2 Sam. xviii. 3. So is a godly man above a wicked man. God will give kingdoms to ransom his saints, Isa. xliii. 3. " I gave Egypt for thy ransom, Æthiopia and Sheba for thee;" and thus should we set the highest rate upon the saints of God, for that is to love them.

2. We must shew love to all the saints of God, by vindicating them, when they are traduced and slandered. It is a great sin to slander a christian, it is to go to pollute Christ's image, the throats of the wicked are open sepulchres, to bury the names of the righteous in. Now you that are christians must not be ready to receive a false and groundless report of a saint, but rather vindicate them, for that is to love them.

3. We shew our love to the saints by praying for them. You know not what good your prayers may do them. Ministers must pray for their people, and the people must pray for their ministers; for prayer commands God himself, Isa. xlv. 11. Prayer is the golden key that unlocks the heavenly treasure of God's bowels. "Oh pray one for another." We should not strive one with another, as is too frequent, but pray one for another.

4. Shew your love by being ready according to your abilities to relieve their wants; to love one another is to be a well-wisher to him, and to do all the friendly offices we can one for another. There are, my beloved, many of the dear servants of God in the ministry that have been already reduced to misery and want, and abundance more are like to be reduced to great necessities. Now I beseech you to shew your love to the household of faith, for that is a sign of your true love to God, and to the brotherhood, that when as myrrh drops freely from the tree, so works of mercy drop freely from the heart. If Jesus Christ should stand in the midst of the congregation, and say, "shew your love to me by your good works," I believe no heart here would be so hard as to deny Jesus Christ. Why, remember whatsoever you give ministers, and to his members, he takes it as given to himself.

That is the second, "Our love must extend to all saints."

3. Our love must reach to our enemies, we must love them that do not love us, Luke vi. 1. "Love your enemies, do good to them that hate you." I confess a mortal enemy I would be loth to make a bosom friend. But

though policy teach us not to trust our enemies, yet piety teacheth us to love them. Christ prayed for his enemies, and shed tears of compassion for them that afterwards shed his blood. So much for the doctrinal part. Now for a word of application, and I have done.

Uses.—And first, this may serve to reprove those who seem in other things to be excellent, and profess much love toward Christ and his gospel, but have no love to the saints of God. There are some that upon this very account have for these great many years absented themselves from the Lord's supper, because they pretend not to be in charity. This is a double-dyed sin, a sin with a witness; it is a sin not to come, and it is a sin not to be in charity. But let me say this to them, surely such kind of Christians are a shame to their profession. What, doth not the gospel teach you charity and love as well as faith? Surely that Christian hath no grace in his heart, that liveth out of charity with his brother; for as the philosopher saith, " All the virtues are linked together, and tied as with a string, and where there is one there is all: and where one is wanting, there is no virtue." So I say of the graces, they are linked together, and where there is one, there is all; and where one is wanting, there is none at all. Saith Augustine, " Thou braggest of thy faith in Christ, but shew me thy faith by thy love to Christ, for faith and love cannot be separated." For as in the sun, there is light and heat, and these cannot be separated one from the other, so faith and love is twisted together, and where there is one wanting, the other is wanting; as he that did so engrave his name on the buckler of Minerva, that whoever went about to take out his name, spoiled the buckler. So faith and love are so inseparable, that if you go to take away the one, you spoil the other. Oh! remember and mourn for it, thou that sayest thou art not in charity. It is a sad symptom thou art not in a state of grace, Titus iii. 5. " For we ourselves also were sometimes foolish, disobedient, deceived, serving divers lusts and pleasures, living in malice, envy, hateful, and hating one another;" that is, before conversion we were swelled with the poison of malice and wrath; but when once the grace of God came, then it was otherwise. That man that hath not love and charity in his heart, surely he hath nothing of God in him, for God is love; he knoweth nothing of the gospel savingly, for the gospel is a gospel of peace; he hath none of the wisdom which cometh from heaven, for that is meek and gentle, and easy to be entreated.

If there be any on the other side, that are not in charity, and yet will come to the Lord's table, remember this, you get no good by the ordinance, you do but defile the ordinance. The apostle calls it " the leaven of malice;" it doth sour all your holy duties, sermons, prayers, and sacraments; it is a little gall embitters a great deal of honey. So where there is a little of this gall of malice and hatred, it embittereth and spoileth all the honey of your graces and duties. The apostle bids us in prayer to lift up pure hands without wrath, 1 Tim. i. 2. " I will therefore that men pray every where, lifting up pure hands without wrath and doubting." What the apostle speaketh of the duty of prayer, I may say of the Lord's supper; when you come to see the body and blood of the Lord, lift up pure hands without malice, bitterness, and wrath. That is a sad speech of Augustine, " He that is full of rancour and malice, he is a man-slayer:" nay, the apostle saith it in the 1st epistle of John iii. 15. " whosoever hateth his brother is a murderer, and ye know no murderer hath eternal life abiding in him." Do not think this ordinance will profit you, if you do not come in love to the saints. Suppose a man drinketh down poison, and afterwards taketh down a cordial, surely this cordial will do him but little good; so thou that drinkest down the poison of wrath and malice into thy soul, and comest afterward to drink down the cordial of Christ's blood in the sacrament, why certainly this cordial will do thee but little good.

EXHORTATION.—Therefore, to conclude by way of exhortation. I beseech you in the Lord, that you would remember this text this day, when you come to the Lord's table, read over this lesson, "A new commandment I give unto you, that you love one another as I have loved you." Come to the sacrament in love to Jesus Christ, and in love one to another; be not full of bitterness, but full of bowels. The primitive saints were of one heart; you all expect, I know, one heaven, and will you not be of one heart? This I believe is a great reason, why the sacrament hath no more profited many receivers. You know if there be a stopping at the stomach, the meat taken in will never concoct and nourish. Why thou that hast wrath and anger, and malice at thy heart, there is an obstruction as it were at the stomach, and therefore it is that the bread of life doth not nourish thy soul. Why, Christians, are not we all soldiers in one regiment, under Jesus Christ, "the lion of the tribe of Judah," and the captain of our salvation? Are not we all branches of the same vine? and are we not all members of the same body? and shall there be a schism or rent in the body?

I shall only say this, we should do all as the serpent. Naturalists observe the serpent, that before he goes to drink at the waters, he casts up his poison; so before you come to the table of the Lord's supper, cast up your poison of bitterness, wrath, and malice, and then Christ's blood will be both a medicine to heal you, and a julep to refresh you.

MR. WATSON'S AFTERNOON SERMON,

Preached August 17, 1662.

2 Cor. vii. 1.

Having these promises, dearly beloved, let us cleanse ourselves.

IT is the title that I intend now, by the help of God, to insist upon, that sweet parenthesis in the text, "dearly beloved," wherein you have the apostle breathing forth his affections unto this people. He speaks now as a pastor, and he speaks to them as his spiritual children.

"Dearly beloved;" where you have,

First the title, "dearly beloved."

Secondly, the exhortation to holiness, "let us cleanse ourselves."

Thirdly, the means how we should be cleansed and sanctified, "having these promises."

It is the first of these that I intend, the title that the apostle gives to his children, "dearly beloved."

From hence observe this doctrine:

That the affections of a right gospel-minister towards his people, are very ardent.

"Dearly beloved,"—There are two things in every minister of Christ that are much exercised; his head, and his heart. His head with labour, and his heart with love; his head with labour in the work of the ministry. If done aright, it is a work fitter for angels than for men. It is our work to open the oracles of God, even those sacred profound things that the angels search into; and if God did not help us, we might soon sink under the weight of such a burden; and as a minister's head is exercised with labour, so his heart is exercised with love, and it is hard to say which of the two exceeds, his labour or his love. Thus is it here in the text, "my dearly beloved."

In these words we have St. Paul laying siege to these Corinthians, and labouring to make a happy victory, to conquer them with kindness, " dearly beloved." St. Paul's heart was the spring of love, his lips were the pipe, the Corinthians were the cistern into which this spring did run. This holy apostle was a mirror and a pattern of love towards the sinning Corinthians. Paul's tears did drop towards the praying Corinthians, his love did burn. Holy Paul was a seraphin, his heart did burn in a flame of affection to his people. How many passages do we find scattered in his epistles? He tells his people, which sometimes he did write to, and sometimes he preached to, he looked after their souls more than their silver, 2 Cor. xii. 14. " We seek not yours, but you:" as a tender nurse cherisheth the child with the breast, so St. Paul gave his people the breast milk of the world. In 1 Thes. ii. 7. this man of God did not only bestow a sermon upon his people, but was willing to impart his very soul to them if it might save theirs, 1 Thes. ii. 8. " We were willing to have imparted to you our own souls, because you are dear unto us." Such was St. Paul's affection to his people, that without a compliment he loved them more than his life. Phil. ii. 17. "And if I be offered upon the sacrifice and service of your faith, I rejoice with you all," that is as if he had said, if it be so, that my blood be poured forth as a sacrifice, if my death may be any way serviceable unto you, if it may help forward the strengthening and confirming of your faith, I am willing to die, I rejoice to do it: so full of affection was this apostle, that he could not choose but love his people, though the more he did love, the less he should be loved. In 2 Cor. xv. Oh! how did Paul sweeten all his sermons with love! 2 Cor. xii. If he reproved sin, yet he was angry in love, he dipped the pill in sugar, Gal. iv. 9, 10, 11, " How turn ye again to weak and beggarly elements? ye observe days, and months, and years. I am afraid of you lest I have bestowed on you labour in vain. Brethren, I beseech you, be as I am." See how St. Paul chides their sins, and yet at the same time courts their souls; no sooner did he launch the wound, but presently he poured in wine and oil into it. So did Paul love his people, that he would not justly give any offence to the weak believer, 1 Cor. viii. 13. "If meat make my brother to offend, I will never eat flesh more while the world standeth." Paul was like some tender mother, who forbears to eat those meats that she might, for fear of hurting the child that she gives suck to. Thus you see he was a spiritual father made up of love; and surely, my brethren, this affection in some degree, is in all the true ministers of Jesus Christ; they are full of sympathy and bowels unto those over whom the Holy Ghost hath made them overseers.

I shall only glance at the reason, why it will be thus, and why it should be thus, that such flaming affections there should be in all Christ's ministers to their people.

It will be thus, for these two reasons briefly.

First, From that principle within, that teacheth love. Grace doth not fire the heart with passion, but with compassion. Grace in the heart of a minister files off that ruggedness that is in his spirit; making him loving and courteous. Paul once breathed out persecution, but when grace came, this bramble was turned into a spiritual vine, twisting himself about the souls of his people with loving embraces.

Secondly, There will be this ardent love in a minister's heart, from the spiritual relation that is betwixt him and his people. He is a spiritual father, and shall we think him to be without bowels? 1 Cor. iv. 15. "Though you have ten thousand instructors, yet have ye not many fathers; for in Christ Jesus I have begotten you through the gospel." Some he begets unto Christ, others he builds up in Christ. Doth not a father provide cheerfully for his children? Can a father see bread taken from his child, and not have his heart affected with it? Is it not a grief to a parent to see his child put out to a dry nurse?

Thirdly, There should be this ardent love and affection in all God's ministers, for this reason, because this is the liveliest way to do most good. Knotty and stubborn hearts will soonest be wrought upon with kindness. The fire melteth the hardest metal; the fire of love, with God's blessing, will melt the most obdurate sinner. A Boanerges, a son of consolation, who comes in the spirit of love, is the fittest to do a piece of gospel-chirurgery, to restore and put such a one in joint again that is taken with a fault, Gal. vi. 1. "Restore such a one with the spirit of love and meekness." Thus much in short for the doctrinal part.

Give me leave now to make some application.

And first, here are several inferences that may be drawn from this: As

First, See here the right character of a gospel-minister. He is full of love, he exhorts, he comforts, he reproves, and all in love; he is never angry with his people, but because they will not be saved. How loth is a minister of Christ to see precious souls, like so many jewels, cast over-board into the dead sea of hell; a conscientious minister would count it an unhappy gain, to gain the world, and lose the souls of his people. He saith as the king of Sodom to Abraham, "Give me the persons, and take thee the goods," Gen. xiv. 21.

The second branch of information is this. Are true gospel-ministers so full of love? Then how sad is it to have such ministers put upon a people as have no love to souls? "The work of the ministry, it is a labour of love." Oh! how sad it is to have such in the ministry, that can neither labour nor love, that are such as are without bowels, that look more at tithes than at souls. It must needs be sad with a people in any part of the world, to have such ministers set over them, as either poison them with error, or do what in them lies to damn them by their wicked example. How can the devil reprove sin? How can the minister cry out in the pulpit against drunkenness, that will himself be drunk? Rom. ii. 22, "Thou that teachest a man should not steal, dost thou steal? Thou that sayest a man ought not to commit adultery, dost thou commit adultery?" We read that the snuffers of the tabernacle were to be made of pure gold, Exod. xxxvii. 23. Those who by their calling are to reprove and snuff off the sins of others, they should be pure gold, holy persons. In the law, God did appoint the lip of the leper should be covered. He ought to have his lip covered, he should not be permitted to speak the oracles of God, who though he be by office an angel, yet by life is a leper.

Thirdly, See from hence the happiness of a minister, who is placed among such a people as give him abundant cause of love. How happy is he that can say to his people from his heart, "Αγαπητι, my dearly beloved." And here let me speak by way of encouragement to you of this parish. I find St. Paul commending the good he saw in his people, 1 Thess. i. 3. "We are bound to thank God always for you, beloved, because your faith grows exceedingly." Here Paul is commending his people. In imitation of the apostle, let me at this time speak a commendatory word to you. I have exercised my ministry now among you for almost sixteen years, and I rejoice and bless God that I cannot say, the more I love you, the less I am loved. I have received many signal demonstrations of love from you, though other parishes have exceeded you in number of houses, yet I think not for strength of affection. I have with much comfort observed your reverent attentions to the word preached; you rejoiced in this light not for a season, but to this day. I have observed your zeal against error: and as much as could be expected in a critical time, your unity and amity. This is your honour; and if for the future there should be any interruption made in my ministry among you, though I should not be permitted to preach to you, yet shall I not cease to love you, and to pray for you; but why should there be any interruption made? Where is the crime? Some indeed say, that we are disloyal and seditious. Beloved, what my actions and sufferings for his majesty have been, is known not to a few of you: but, however, we must go to heaven through good report and through bad report, and it is well if we can get to glory, though we pass through the pikes. I shall endeavour that I may still approve the sincerity of my love to you. I will not promise that I shall still preach among you, nor will I say that I shall not; I desire to be guided by the silver thred of God's word and of God's providence. My heart is towards you. There is, you know, an expression in the late act, that we shall be now shortly, as if we were naturally dead; and if I must die, let me leave some legacy with you before I go from you. I cannot but give you some counsel and advice for your souls, and I hope there is no hurt in that. There are, my beloved, these twenty directions, that I desire you to take special notice of, which I would leave as advice and counsel with you about your souls.

First, I beseech you, keep your constant hours every day with God. The godly man is a man set apart, Ps. iii. not only because God hath set him apart by election, but because he hath set himself apart by devotion. Give God the *Auroræ filium.* Begin the day with God, visit God in the morning before you make any other visit; wind up your hearts towards heaven in the morning, and they will go the better all the day after! Oh turn your closets into temples; read the scriptures. The two Testaments are the two lips by which God speaks to us; these will make you wise unto salvation: the scripture is both a glass to shew you your spots, and a laver to wash them away; besiege heaven every day with your prayer, thus perfume your houses, and keep a constant intercourse with heaven.

Secondly, Get books into your houses, when you have not the spring near to you, then get water into your cisterns: so when you have not that wholesome preaching that you desire, good books are cisterns that hold the water of life in them to refresh you. When David's natural heat was taken away, they covered him with warm clothes, 1 Kings i. So when you find a chillness upon your souls, and that your former heat begins to abate, ply yourselves with warm clothes, get those good books that may acquaint you with such truths as may warm and affect your hearts.

Thirdly, Have a care of your company. Take heed of unnecessary familiarity with sinners. We cannot catch health from another, but we may soon catch a disease. The disease of sin is very catching. I would be as afraid of coming among the wicked, as among those that have the plague. Ps. cvi. 35. " They were mingled with the heathen, learned their works." If we cannot make others better, let us have a care that they make not us worse. Lot was a miracle, he kept fresh in Sodom's salt water. My beloved, take heed of the occasions of sin, evil company is an occasion of sin. The Nazarites in the old law, as they might drink no wine, so they were forbidden grapes, where the wine was made, as you read in Num vi. to teach us, that all occasions of sin must be avoided. Evil company is *belluo animatrum,* the devil's draw-net, by which he draws millions to hell. How many families, and how many souls have been ruined and undone in this city by evil company? Many there are that go from a play-house and from a tavern to Tyburn.

Fourthly, Have a care whom you hear. It is our saviour Christ's ounsel, Mat. vii. 15. "Beware of false prophets that come to you in sheep's clothing, but inwardly are ravening wolves." Let me tell you, the Devil hath his ministers as well as Christ, Rev. xii. 15. " The serpent cast out of his mouth water, as a flood over the woman;" that is, as the learned expounded it, Satan by his ministers and emissaries, cast out the flood of Arian doctrine to drown the church. There are some, who by the subtilty of their wit have learnt the art to mix error with truth, and to give poison in a golden cup. Take heed who you hear, and how you hear. Be like those noble Bereans, that searched the scriptures whether the things that they preached were so or not, Acts xvii. 11. Your ears must not be like spunges that suck in puddle-water as well as wine, but your ears must be like a fan, that fans out the chaff, but retains the pure wheat. You must be like those in the parable, Mat. xiii. 48. that gathered the good fish into vessels, but cast the bad away. The saints are called virgins for their wisdom: they will not let every one defile their souls with error, they have a judicious ear, and a critical palate, that can distinguish between truth and error, and put a difference betwixt meat of God's sending, and the devil's cooking.

Fifthly, Study sincerity, Isa. li. 6. "Behold, thou desirest truth in the inward part." Be what you seem to be, be not like rowers in a barge, that look one way and row another. Do not look heaven-ward by your profession, and row hell-ward by your conversation; do not pretend to love God, and yet love sin: *simulata sanctitus, duplicata iniquitas.* Counterfeit piety is double iniquity. Let your hearts be upright with God: the plainer the diamond is, the richer it is; and the more plain the heart is, the more doth God value his jewel. A little rusty gold is far better than a great deal of bright brass. A little true grace, though rusted over with many infirmities, is better than all the glistering shews of hypocrites. A sincere heart is God's current coin, and he will give it grains of allowance.

Sixthly, As you love your souls be not strangers to yourselves. Be much and often in the work of self-examination. Amongst all the books that you read, turn over the book of your own heart, look into the book of conscience, see what is written there, Psl. lxxvii. 6. "I commune with mine own heart." Set up a judgment-seat in your own souls; examine whether you have grace or not; prove whether you are in the faith; be as much afraid of a painted holiness, as you would be afraid of going to a painted heaven. Do not think yourselves good because others think so. Let the word be the touch-stone, by which you try your hearts: let the word be the looking-glass, by which you judge of the complexion of your soul. For want of this self-searching, many live known to others, and die unknown to themselves.

Seventhly, Keep your spiritual watch, Mat. xiii. 37.

What I say unto you, I say unto all, watch." If it were the last word I should speak, it would be this word *watch*. Oh! what need hath a Christian to be ever upon his watch! The heart is a subtle piece, and will be stealing out to vanity, and if we are not careful, it will decoy us into sin. We have a special eye upon such persons as we suspect; thy heart is a suspicious person. Oh! have an eye upon it, watch it continually: it is a bosom traitor; Job set a watch before his eyes, Job xxxi. 1. We must every day keep sentinel, sleep not upon your guard: our sleeping time is the devil's tempting time: let not your watch-candle go out.

Eighthly, You that are the people of God, do you often associate together, Mal. iii. 16. "They that feared the Lord, spake often one to another." Christ's doves shall flock together: one Christian will help to heat another; a single coal of juniper will soon die; but many coals put together will keep life in one another. Conference sometimes may do as much as preaching; one Christian by good discourse drops holy oil upon another, that makes the lamp of his grace to shine the brighter. It is great wisdom to keep up the trade in a corporation. Christians by meeting often together, setting good discourse on foot, keep up the trade of godliness, that else would decay and soon be lost. Is not the communion of saints an article in our creed? Do not then live so asunder, as if this article were blotted out. The naturalists observe there is a sympathy in plants; they say some plants bear better when they grow near other plants, as the vine and the elm; the olive and the myrtle thrive the best when they grow together: it is true in religion, the saints are trees of righteousness, that thrive best in godliness when they grow together.

Ninthly, Get your hearts screwed up above the world, "set your affections upon things above," Col. iii. 5. We may see the face of the moon in the water, but the moon is fixed above in the firmament: so though a Christian walk here below, yet his heart should be fixed above in heaven. There is our best kindred, our purest joy, our mansion-house. Oh! let our hearts be above, it is the best and the sweetest kind of life. The higher the bird flies, the sweeter it sings, and the higher the heart is raised above the world, the sweeter joy it hath. The eagle that flies in the air, is not stung by the serpent. Those whose hearts are elevated above the lower region of this world, are not stung with the vexations and disquietments that others are, but are full of joy and contentment.

Tenthly, Trade much in the promises. The promises are great supports to faith. Faith lives in a promise, as the fish lives in the water. The promises are both comforting and quickening, they are *mitralia Evangelii*, the very breast of the gospel; as the child by sucking the breasts gets strength, so faith by sucking the breast of a promise gets strength and revives. The promises of God are bladders to keep us from sinking when we come into the waters of affliction. The promises " are sweet clusters of grapes that grow upon Christ the true vine :" O! trade much in the promises, there is no condition that you can be in, but you have a promise. The promises are like manna, that suit themselves to every Christian's palate.

Eleventhly, To all you that hear me, live in a calling. Jerom gave his friend this advice, " To be ever well employed, that when the devil came to tempt him, he might find him working in his vineyard." Sure I am, the same God that saith, " Remember the sabbath day, to keep it holy," saith also, " Six days shalt thou labour." The great God never sealed any warrants to idleness; an idle professor is the shame of his profession: 2 Thess. iii. 11. " I hear there are some (says the apostle) that work not at all, but are busy-bodies, such we exhort, by our Lord Jesus Christ, that with quietness they work." Solon made laws to punish idleness; and Cicero saith of an idle man, *Spiritum trahit, non vivit.* He draws his breath, but doth not live, he is not useful; but a good Christian acts within the sphere of his own calling.

12. Let me intreat you to join the first and the second table together, 'piety to God, and equity to your neighbour. The apostle puts these two words together in one verse, δικαιως και ευσιβως, Tit. ii. 12. " That we should live righteously and godlily:" Righteously, that relates to morality; Godlily, that relates to piety and sanctity. Always remember this, every command hath the same divine stamp and authority as another command hath. I would try a moral man by the duties of the first table; and I would try a professor by the duties of the second table. Some pretend faith, but have no works; others have works but they have no faith: some pretend zeal for God, but are not just in their dealings; others are just in their dealings, but have not one spark of zeal for God. If you would go to heaven, you must run both sides of the table, the first and the second table, join piety and morality together. As we blame the papists for blotting out the second commandment, let not the papists blame us for leaving out the second table.

13. Join the serpent and the dove together, innocence and prudence, Mat. x. 16. " Be wise as serpents, and harmless as doves." We must have innocency with our wisdom, or else our wisdom is but craftiness, and we must have wisdom with our innocency, else our innocency is but weakness. We must have the harmlessness of the dove, that we may not wrong others, and we must have the prudence of the serpent, that others may not abuse and circumvent us. Not to wrong the truth by silence, here is the innocency of the dove: not to betray ourselves by rashness, here the wisdom of the serpent. How happy is it where these two are united, the dove and the serpent. The dove without the serpent is folly, and the serpent without the dove is impiety.

14. Be more afraid of sin than of suffering. A man may be afflicted, and yet have the love of God, but he cannot sin, but presently God is angry. Sin eclipses the light of God's countenance. In suffering, the conscience may be quiet. When the hail beats upon the tiles, there

may be music in the house; and when there is suffering in the body, there may be peace and music in the conscience; but when a man sins wilfully and presumptuously, he loseth all his peace. Spira abjured his faith, and he became a terror to himself, he could not endure himself, he professed he thought Cain and Judas in hell did not feel those terrors and horrors that he felt. He that will commit sin to prevent suffering, is like a man that lets his head be wounded to save his shield and helmet.

15. Take heed of idolatry. In 1 John v. 21. "Little children keep yourselves from idols." Idolatry is an image of jealousy to provoke God. It breaks the marriage-knot asunder, and makes the Lord disclaim his interest in a people. What kind of religion is popery? it is the mother of many monsters. What soul-damning doctrines doth it hold forth, as the meriting of salvation by good works, the giving of pardons, the worshipping of angels, popish indulgences, purgatory, and the like; it is a soul-damning religion, it is the breeder of ignorance, uncleanness and murder. The popish religion is not defended by strength of argument, but by force of arms; keep yourselves from idols, and take heed of superstition, that is the gentleman-usher to popery.

16. Think not the worse of godliness, because it is reproached and persecuted. Wicked men being stirred up by the devil, do maliciously reproach the ways of God. Such were Julian and Lucian. Though wicked men would be godly on their death-beds, yet in the time of their life they revile and hate godliness; but think not you the worse of religion, because it is reproached by the wicked. Suppose a virgin should be reproached for her chastity, yet chastity is never the worse: if a blind man jeer the sun, the sun is never the less bright. Holiness is a beautiful and glorious thing, it is the angel's glory; and shall we be ashamed of that which makes us like the angels? There is a time coming, when wicked men would be glad of some of that holiness that now they despise,

but they shall be as far then from obtaining it, as they are now from desiring it.

17. Think not the better of sin because it is in fashion. Think not the better of impiety and ungodliness, because most walk in those crooked ways. Multitude is a foolish argument. Multitude doth not argue the goodness of a thing. The devil's name is legion, that signifieth a multitude. Hell-road is this day full of travellers. Esteem not the better of sin, because most go this way. Do we think the better of the plague, because it is common? The plea of a multitude, will not hold at God's bar, when God shall ask, Why did you profane my sabbath? why were you drunk? why did you break your oath? To say then, Lord, because most men did so, will be a poor plea. God will say to you then, seeing you have sinned with the multitude, you shall now go to hell with the multitude. I beseech you, as you tender your souls, walk antipodes to the corruptions of the times. If you are living fish, swim against the stream, dead fish swim down the stream, Ephes. v. 11. "Have no fellowship with the unfruitful works of darkness, but rather reprove them."

18. In the business of religion, serve God with all your might, Eccles. ix. 10. "Whatsoever thy hand findeth to do, do it with thy might, for there is no device or work in the grave whither thou goest." This is an argument why we should do all we can for God, serve him with all our strength because the grave is very near, and there is no praying, no repenting, in the grave. Our time is but small, and therefore our zeal for God should be great. David danced with all his might before the ark, and so should we act vigorously for God in the sphere of obedience. Rom. xii. 12. "Fervent in spirit serving the Lord." Take heed of a dull lazy temper in God's service: you must not only say a prayer, or read a prayer, but you must pour out your souls in prayer; not only love God, but be sick of love to God. God in the old law would have the coals put to the incense, Levit. xvi. 13, and why so? to typify that the heart must be inflamed

in the worship of God; your prayers must go up with a flame of devotion. I confess hell will be taken without storm, you may jump into hell with ease, but it is all up hill to heaven, and therefore you must put forth all your might, Mat. xii. 11. "The violent take heaven by force." Heaven is not taken but by storm. Do you not see men zealous and very active for the devil, and for their lusts; and shall they take pains for hell, and will not you take pains for heaven?

19. Do all the good you can while you live to others. God hath made every creature useful for us, the sun hath not its light for itself, but for us. The fountains run freely, and so doth the myrrh drop from the tree. Every creature doth as it were deny itself for us: the beast gives us its labour, the bird gives us its music, and the silk-worm its silk. Now hath God made every thing useful for us, and shall not we be useful one for another? O labour to be helpful to the souls of others, and to supply the wants of others. Jesus Christ was a public blessing in the world, "he went about doing good." We are members of the body politic, nay, we are members of the body mystical, and shall not every member be helpful for the good of the body? That is a dead member that doth not communicate to the good of the body. O labour to be useful to others while you live, that so when you die, there may be a miss of you. Many live so unfruitfully, that truly their life is scarce worth a prayer, nor their death scarce worth a tear.

20. Every day spend some thoughts upon eternity. O eternity, eternity! All of us here are ere long, it may be some of us within a few days or hours, to launch forth into the ocean of eternity. Eternity, eternity is *status interminabilis*, says Boetius; no prospective-glass can see to the end of eternity. Eternity is a sum that can never be numbered, a line that can never be measured. Eternity is a condition of everlasting misery, or everlasting happiness. If you are godly, then shall you be for ever happy, you shall be always fanning yourselves in the light of

God's countenance. If you are wicked, you shall be always miserable, ever lying in the scalding furnace of the wrath of the Almighty. Eternity to the godly is a day that hath no sun-setting: eternity to the wicked is a night that hath no sun-rising. O I beseech you, my brethren, every day spend some time upon the thoughts of eternity. The serious thoughts of an eternal condition would be a great means to promote holiness.

The thoughts of eternity would make us very serious about our souls. O my soul, thou art very shortly to fly into eternity, a condition that can never be reversed or altered. How serious would this make us about our Heaven-born souls. Zeuxis being once asked why he was so long in drawing of a picture, answered, *Æternitate pigno*, I am now painting for eternity. Oh how frequently would that man pray that thinks he is praying for eternity! Oh how accurately and circumspectly would that man live, that thinks upon this moment hangs eternity!

The thoughts of eternity would make us slight and contemn all the things of this world. What is the world to him that hath eternity always in his eyes? Did we think seriously and solemnly of eternity, we should never over-value the comforts of the world, nor over-grieve the crosses of the world.

We should not over-value the comforts of the world. Worldly comforts are very sweet, but they are very swift, they are soon gone. The pleasures of the world are but for a season, just like Noah's dove, that brought an olive-branch in her mouth, but she had wings, and so did presently fly from the ark: so are all outward comforts; they bring an olive-branch, but they have wings too, with which they fly away.

The thoughts of eternity would make us not to over-grieve the crosses and sufferings of the world. What are these sufferings to eternity? Our sufferings, says the apostle, are but for a while, 1 Pet. v. 10. What are all the sufferings we can undergo in the world to eternity? Affliction may be lasting, but it is not everlasting. Our sufferings here are not worthy to be compared to an eternal weight of glory.

And thus, my beloved, I have given you these twenty directions for your precious souls. I beseech you treasure them up as so many jewels in the cabinet of your breast. Did you carry these directions about you, they would be a most excellent antidote to keep you from sin, and an excellent means to preserve the zeal of piety flaming upon the altar of your hearts.

I have many things yet to say to you, but I know not whether God will give me another opportunity. My strength is now almost gone. I beseech you, let these things which I have spoken, make deep impressions upon all your souls. Consider what hath been said, and the Lord give you understanding in all things.

MR. WATSON'S FAREWELL SERMON.

Preached August 19, 1662.

Isai. iii. 10, 11.

Say ye to the righteous, that it shall be well with him, for they shall eat the fruit of their doings.
Woe be to the wicked, it shall be evil with him: for the reward of his hands shall be with him.

THIS text is like Israel's pillar or cloud; it hath a light side, and a dark side: it hath a light side unto the godly, " Say unto the righteous, it shall be well with him;" and it hath a dark side unto the wicked, " Woe unto the wicked, it shall be ill with him." Both you see are rewarded, righteous and wicked; but here is a vast difference, the one hath a reward of mercy, the other a reward of justice.

I begin with the first of these, "Say unto the righteous, it shall be well with him."

This scripture was written in a very sad and calamitous time, as you may read in the beginning of the chapter. "The mighty man, and the man of war shall cease, the prudent and the ancient, both judge and the prophet shall be taken away." This was a very sad time with the church of God in Jerusalem. If the judge be taken away, where will be any equity? If the prophet be removed, where will be any priests? The whole body politic was running to ruin, and almost in the rubbish. Now in this sad juncture of time, God would have this text to be written: and it is like a rainbow in the clouds. God would have his people comforted in the midst of afflictions. "Say unto the righteous, it shall be well with them."

The great proposition that lies in the words, is this:

That howsoever things go in the world, it shall be well with the righteous man. This is an oracle from God's own mouth, and therefore we are not to dispute it, it is God's own oracle, "Say unto the righteous, it shall be well with him."

I might multiply scriptures, but I will give you one instance, in Eccles. viii. 12. "Surely I know it shall be well with them that fear God."

"I know it;" It is a golden maxim not to be disputed, "It shall be well with them that fear God."

For the illustration of this, consider two things.

1. What is meant by the righteous man.

2. Why, "howsoever things go, it shall be well with the righteous."

1. Who is meant here by the righteous man.

There is a threefold righteousness, a legal righteousness; and so Adam in this sense was said to be righteous, when he did wear the robe of innocency. Adam's heart did agree with the law of God exactly, as a well made dial goes with the sun; but this righteousness is forfeited and lost.

2. There is a moral righteousness, and thus he is said

to be righteous, who is adorned with the moral virtues, who is prudent, and just, and temperate, who is decked with the level of morality. But

3. There is an evangelical righteousness, and this is meant here. This evangelical righteousness is twofold.

1. There is a "righteousness of imputation," and that is when Christ's righteousness is made over to us: and, beloved, this righteousness is as truly ours to justify us, as it is Christ's to bestow upon us.

2. There is a righteousness of implantation, which is nothing else but the infusing of the seed and habit of grace into the heart: a planting of holiness in a man, and making him a partaker of the divine nature. This is to be righteous in the sight of God, a righteousness of imputation, and a righteousness of implantation.

The second thing is to shew you, why, "Howsoever things go in the world, yet it shall go well with this righteous man." It must be thus for two reasons.

1. Because he who is righteous hath his greatest evils removed, his sin pardoned, and then it must needs be well with him. Sin is the thorn in a man's conscience; now when the thorn is plucked out by forgiveness and remission, then it is well with that man.

Forgiveness in scripture is called a lifting off of sin, Job vii. "Lord, why dost thou not lift off my sin?" So the Hebrew word carries it; it is a metaphor taken from a weary man that goes under a burden, he is ready to sink under it, now another man comes and lifts off this burden; even so doth the great God, when the burden of sin is ready to sink the conscience. God lifts off the burden of sin from the conscience, and lays it on Christ's shoulder, and he carries it. Now he that hath his burden thus carried, it is well with him howsoever things go.

Forgiveness of sin and pardon, it is a crowning blessing, it is a jewel of a believer's crown. Pardon of sin is a multiplying mercy, it brings a great many mercies along with it. Whom God pardons, he adopts; whom God pardons, he invests with grace and glory.

So that this is a multiplying mercy; it is such a mercy that it is enough to make a sick man well, Isa. xxxiii. 24. " The inhabitants shall not say I am sick; the people shall be forgiven their iniquity." The sense of pardon takes away the sense of pain, and then it must needs be well with the righteous, for his greatest evil is removed.

2. However things go, it is well with the righteous, because that God is his portion, Psal. xvi. 5. " The Lord is the portion of my inheritance." The lines are fallen unto me in pleasant places. In God there are all good things to be found, and all that is in God is engaged for the good of the righteous ; his power is to help, and his wisdom is to teach, and his spirit is to sanctify, and his mercy to save. God is the righteous man's portion, and can God give a greater gift to us than himself? God is a rich portion, for he is the angel's riches. God is a safe and sure portion, for his name is a strong tower ; he is a portion that can never be spent, for he is infiniteness. He is a portion can never be lost, for he is eternity. " Thou art my portion for ever," Psal. lxxii. 26. and surely it is well with the righteous that hath God for his portion. Is it not well with that man that is happy? Why, if God be our portion we are happy, Psal. cxliv. 15. " Happy is the people whose God is the Lord."

Thus I have cleared up the doctrinal part. For the use to this,

Here is abundance of comfort for every godly man; for every person serving God in this congregation, God hath sent me this day with a commission to comfort you.

Oh! that I might drop in the oil of gladness into every broken heart, and rejoice every troubled spirit. Oh, here is good news from Heaven ! " Say unto the righteous it shall be well with him."

But here is a question must be answered. You will say to me, but how doth this appear, that it shall be well with the righteous? For we often see it is the worst with them in this world ; he is deprived of his comfort many times, he loses his very life in that quarrel, he is made the very reproach of the world oftentimes. How then is it well with the righteous?

To this I answer, yet still it is well with the righteous, though he meet with trouble in the world, and one follows on the neck of another, yet it is well with the righteous, as will appear in these three or four particulars.

1. The troubles that the righteous man meets with they turn to good, and so it is well with him. That is a most famous scripture in Jer. xxiv. 5. " Whom I have sent out of this place unto the land of the Chaldeans for their good." God's own Israel were transported into Babylon among their enemies; but it is for their good, saith the Lord. The troubles of the righteous are a means to purge out their sin. I have read a story of one who running at another with a sword to kill him, by accident his sword run into an imposthume, and broke the imposthume. Thus all the evils and troubles of the righteous serve but to cure them of the imposthume of pride, to make them more humble. When that the body of a saint is afflicted, his soul, that revives and flourishes in grace.

At Rome there were two laurel-trees, and when one withered the other did flourish; so when the body is afflicted, yet the soul, that laurel, doth revive and flourish.

God doth distil out of the bitterest drink his glory and our salvation: saith Jerome, that, that the world looks on as a punishment, God makes a medicine to heal the sore. Why then it shall be well with the righteous. The rod of God upon a saint is but only God's pencil, whereby he draweth his image more lively on the soul. God never strikes the strings of his viol but to make the music sweet. Then it is well with the righteous.

2. In the midst of all the trouble that doth befal the righteous, yet still it is well with them in regard of those inward heart-revivings that God doth give them.

We see a godly man's misery, but we do not see his comfort: we see his prison-gates, but we do not hear the music that is within his conscience. God doth sweeten to his people outward trouble with inward peace; it is the title that is given to God, 2 Cor. vii. 6. " God that comforteth them that are cast down." The bee can gather honey as well from the thistle and from the bitter herb, as from the sweet flower; the child of God can gather joy out of sorrow: out of the very carcass sometimes the Lord gives honey. When the body is in pain, the soul may be at ease, as when a man's head aches, yet his heart may be well; thus it is well with the righteous. God gives him that inward comfort that revives and sweetens his outward pain.

3. In the time of trouble and calamity, yet still it is well with the righteous: because God doth cover his people, in the time of trouble, he hides them in the storm. God hath a care to hide his jewels, and will not let them be carried away; and thus he makes good that scripture literally, Psal. xci. 4. " He shall cover them with his feathers, and under his wings shalt thou trust, no evil shall touch thee."

God oftentimes verifies this scripture literally. He makes his angels to be his people's life-guard, to hide them, and defend them. When a flood was coming upon the world, God provided an ark to hide Noah. When Israel is carried and transported into Babylon, God hid Jeremiah, and gave him his life for a prey, Jer. xxxix. 11. and in this sense the saints of God are called hidden ones, Psal. lxxxiii. 3. Why so? not only because they are hid in God's decree, and hid in Christ's wounds, but oftentimes God hides them in a time of danger and calamity: they are hidden ones. He reserved to himself seven thousand that had not bowed the knee to Baal. The prophet knew not where there was one, but God knew there were seven thousand. In this sense, it is well with the righteous in time of public misery.

Aye, but you will say, sometimes it fares yet worse than all this. Sometimes the righteous they die and perish, they are carried away in a tempest, why? yet still it is well with the righteous, and that in a two-fold sense.

1. Many times God doth take away the righteous by death, and that in great mercy: he takes them away, that they shall not see the misery that comes upon a nation. Virgil the heathen poet saith, "They are happy that die before their country." His meaning was, they die before they see the ruin of their country: and truly God many times takes away his people in mercy, that they may not see the ruin that is coming on a land. You have in scripture for this, 1 Kings xiv. 13. "He only of Jeroboam shall come to the grave in peace, because in him there is found some good thing towards the Lord God of Israel." God puts him in his grave betimes in mercy, because he should not see the evil coming upon the land: and there is a parallel to this, 2 Kings xii. last. It is spoken of Josiah, "I will gather thee unto thy Fathers, thou shalt be gathered unto thy grave in peace, and thine eyes shall not see the evil I will bring upon this place." Josiah died in battle: how then was it said he went to the grave in peace? We must understand the meaning of it is this; Josiah went to his grave in peace, because he was a holy man, and he had made his peace with God, and so he went to his grave in peace; and because he should not see the evil approaching, God gathered him to his grave in peace.

Jerom speaking of his friend Nepotian (you must observe Jerom lived to see some troubles before he died) saith he, Oh! how happy is my friend Nepotian, that sees not these troubles, but is got out of the storm, dies and is arrived safe in Heaven.

Luther died in mercy before the trouble in Germany broke forth: and thus you see the righteous though they die, yet it is well with them. God takes them away in mercy that they may not see approaching evils.

2. Though the righteous die, and are taken away, yet it is well with them, because death cannot hurt them:

death can neither hurt their body nor yet their souls, and then it is well with them.

1. Death cannot hurt their bodies, the body of a saint it doth not perish, though it die; the bodies of the saints are very precious dust in God's account: precious dust. The Lord locks up these jewels in the grave, as in a cabinet. The bodies of the saints lie mellowing and ripening in the grave till the blessed time of the resurrection. Oh! how precious is the dust of a believer; though the world mind it not, yet it is precious unto God. The husbandman he hath some corn in his barn, and he hath other corn in the ground. Why? the corn that is in the ground, is as precious to him as that is in the barn. The bodies of the saints in the grave, are God's corn in the ground, but the Lord makes very precious account of this corn. The bodies of the saints shall be more glorious and blessed than ever they were at the resurrection. Tertullian calls them angelical bodies, in regard of that beauty and lustre that shall be upon them. As it is with your silks, when they are dyed of a purple or scarlet colour, they are made more bright and illustrious than they were before; thus it is with the bodies of the saints, they shall be dyed of a better colour at the resurrection, they shall be made like a glorious body, Phil. iii. 20. Thus it shall be well with the righteous, their bodies shall not perish.

2. It will be well with the righteous at death, as to their souls too. Oh it will be a blessed time! Methinks it is with a saint at the time of death, just as it was with Saint Paul in his voyage to Rome. We read that the ship did break, but though there were so many broken pieces, yet he got safe to shore; so though the ship of the believer's body break by death, yet it is safe with the passenger, his soul that gets safe to the heavenly harbour. Let me tell you, the day of a believer's death, it is the birth-day of his blessedness, it is his ascension-day to Heaven: the day of his death, is his marriage-day with Jesus Christ. Faith doth but contract us here. In this

life is but the contract, but at death the nuptials shall be solemnized in glory, they shall see God face to face. It will be Heaven enough to have a sight of God, saith Austin, when the saints shall enter into joy; here joy enters into them, but then they shall enter into it. They shall drink of these pure rivers that run from the everlasting fountain.

And thus you see, it will be well with the righteous; however things go, though trouble come, though death come, yet it will go well with the righteous. And oh let those that are the people of God comfort themselves in these words! Oh what an encouragement is this to all you that hear me, to begin to be righteous! This text may tempt us all to be godly, Say unto the righteous, it shall be well with him; when things are never so ill with him, yet it is well with him.

We would be glad to have things go well with our relations, and in our estates. Why when the righteous things go well with us, thy person is sealed, thou art heir of all God's promises, thou art Christ's favorite, thou hast heaven in reversion, and is it not now well with thee? If you would have happiness, you must espouse holiness. Say unto the righteous, it shall be well with them: and thus much of the first proposition, the godly man's comfort in life, and death, it is well with him.

But now if all this will not prevail with you to make you leave your sins and become righteous, I must pass in a few words to the next branch of the text, to scare men out of their sins, to fright men out of their wickedness. "Wo unto the wicked, it shall be ill with him."

This, my beloved, is the dark side of the cloud.

It may cause in every wicked man that hears me, a trembling at the heart.

"Woe unto the wicked, it shall be ill with him."

The proposition that doth result out of these words, is this:

Doct. When things seem to be well with the wicked men, it shall be ill with them at last, though they have more than heart can wish, yet it shall be ill with them at last, Eccles. viii. 13. "It shall not be well with the wicked, nor shall he prolong his days, which are as a shadow." Because he fears not God, it shall not be well with the wicked, the God of truth hath pronounced this.

It is as true as God is true, " it shall not be well with the wicked."

Now that I may a little clear this to you, I shall demonstrate this to you in these four particulars.

1. It is ill with the wicked in this life.
2. It is ill with them at death.
3. It is ill with them at the day of judgment.
4. It is ill with them after judgment; it shall be ill with the wicked.

It is ill with the wicked in this life; a wicked man that hears me will hardly think so, when he hath the affluence and confluence of outward comforts. When he eats the fat, and drinks the sweet, he will hardly believe the minister that shall tell him, it shall be ill with him, but it is so.

For is it not ill with that man that hath a curse, yea, the curse of God entailed upon him? Can that man thrive that lives under the curse of God?

Floods of blood and wrath hang over the head of a wicked man; he is heir to all the plagues written in the book of God.

All God's curses are the sinner's portion, and if he die in his sin, he is sure to have his portion paid him.

Woe unto the wicked, every bit of bread he hath, he hath it with a curse, it is like poisoned bread given to a dog: every drop of wine he drinks, he swallows down a curse with it. Woe unto the wicked, there is a curse in his cup, and a curse upon his table. God saith woe unto him. We read of Belshazzar, Dan. v. 4, 5. that he did take the wine, and commanded to bring the gold and silver vessels out of the temple; and then they brought the golden vessels that were taken out of the temple, out of the house of God that was at Jerusalem, and the king and his princes, and his wives and concubines drank in them.

Belshazzar was very jovial; in the midst of his cups he was merry, but woe unto the wicked; for in the same hour came forth the finger of a man's hand, and reached over the candlestick, upon the plaister of the wall of the king's palace, and the king's countenance changed, and he was troubled. There was a hand and a woe written on the wall. Let a sinner live till he come to an hundred years of age, yet he is cursed, Isa. lxv. 20. " his grey hairs, they have a curse upon them."

2. It is ill with the wicked, not only in this life, but it is ill with him at his hour of death, and that in these two respects.

1. Death puts an end unto all his comforts.
2. Death is the beginning of all his miseries.

1. Death puts an end to all his comforts, no more indulging and pampering the flesh, then no more cups of wine, then no more music, Revel. xviii. 22. "The fruits thy soul lusteth after, are departed from thee." All things that are dainty and good, are departed from thee, the voice of the harper, musician, and trumpeter, shall be heard no more in thee.

As it is spoken of the destruction of Rome, so you may say of the wicked man, no more joy and gladness, no more mirth and music, all a sinner's sweet spices, his scarlet robes, his sparkling diamonds, they all at death depart from him.

2. As death puts an end to a sinner's mirth, so it lays a foundation for all his sorrows. Alas, before death begins to close a sinner's eyes, the eye of his conscience is first opened, every sin at the hour of death, stands with its drawn sword in its hand. Those sins that did in life delight him, now they affright and terrify him, all his joy and mirth turns into sadness. As sometimes you have seen sugar lying in a damp place, it doth dissolve and run to water: thus all the sugar-joys of a wicked man

at the hour of death turn into water, into the water of tears, into the water of sorrow.

3. It shall be ill with the wicked man at the day of judgment. When he is seated before God's tribunal, then he shall leave judging of others, and shall stand at God's bar, and be tried for his life.

I read concerning Felix, when he heard Paul speak of judgment, that Felix trembled. Josephus observes, that Felix was a wicked man, and she that lived with him, her name was Drusilla, whom he enticed from her husband, and lived in uncleanness with her. Now when Felix heard Paul preaching of judgment, he trembled. Now if he trembled to hear of judgment, what will he do when judgment comes? When all his secret sins shall be made manifest, all his midnight wickedness shall be written on his forehead, as with a point of a diamond? At the day of judgment shall be these two things.

First, There shall be a legal trial.

Secondly, The sentence.

First, A legal trial. God will call forth a sinner by name, and say, Stand forth, hear thy charge; see what thou canst answer to this charge!

What canst thou say for thy sabbath-breaking, for thy murders, and drunkenness, and perjury? for all thy revenge and malice? for all thy persecuting of my members? what dost thou say, guilty, or not guilty?

Thou wretch, thou darest not say thou art not guilty; for have not I been an eye-witness to all thy wickedness? do not the books agree, the book of thy conscience, and the book of my omniscience, and darest thou offer to plead not guilty? How will the sinner be amazed with horror, and run into desperation?

Secondly, after this legal process of trial, follows the sentence, go ye cursed into everlasting fire. What, to go from the presence of Christ, in whose presence is fulness of joy? to go from Christ with a curse. Why, saith Chrysostome, that very word depart, is worse than the torment itself. And remember this, you that go on in your sins, when once this sentence is past, it cannot be reversed; this is the most supreme court of judicature, from which is no appeal. Here on earth men remove their causes from one court to another, from the common law into the chancery. Oh! but at the last day of judgment, no appeals to remove the sentence, for this is the highest court.

4. It will be ill with the wicked that die in their sins after the day of judgment. Oh! then there is but one way, and they would be glad they might go that way; any way but to prison. Oh! but there is no way but to hell, Luke xvii. 23. " In hell he lifted up his eyes." Hell, is the very center of misery, it is the very spirits of torment distilled out. The scripture tells us, that in hell there are these three things ; there is darkness, there is fire, and there are chains.

1. Hell is called a place of darkness, Jude xiii. " To whom is reserved blackness of darkness." Darkness, you know, is the most uncomfortable thing in the world; a man that goes in the dark, he trembleth every step he goeth

Hell is a black region, nothing but blackness of darkness; and it must needs be a dark place where they shall be separated from the light of God's presence. Indeed Augustine thinks there shall be some little sulphurous light there: but suppose it be so that light shall serve only that the damned may see the tragedy of their own misery, and see themselves tormented.

2. In hell, as there is darkness, so there is fire ; it is called a burning lake, Rev. ii. 15. " Who was not found written in the book of life, was thrown into the lake of fire." You know that fire is the most torturing element, it makes the most dreadful impression on the flesh. Now hell is a place of fire.

It is disputed among the learned what kind of fire it is, and I wish we may never know what kind of fire it is. Augustine and others affirm that it is material fire, but far hotter than any fire upon your hearths, that is but painted fire compared with this. But I do rather think that the fire of the damned is partly material, and partly spiritual; and partly material to work on the body, and partly spiritual, which is the wrath of God to torment the soul: that is the lake, the burning fire. Oh! who knows the power of God's anger? Who can dwell with these burnings? It is intolerable to endure them, and impossible to escape them.

3. In hell there are chains, chains of darkness. Those sinners that would not be bound by any law of God, such shall have chains of darkness to bind them.

Quest. What should be the meaning of these phrases, chains of darkness?

Answ. I suppose it may be this, to intimate unto us, that the wicked in hell shall not have power to walk up and down, which perhaps might be a little ease, though very little; but they shall be chained down fast, not to stir, they shall be fastened to that stake with chains of darkness. Oh! this will be terrible indeed. Suppose a man should lie always on a down-bed, and might not stir out of the place, it would be very painful unto him. Oh; but to lie as the damned upon the wrack, always under the torturing scorchings of God's wrath, and to be tied, and not to move, how dreadful are the thoughts of this! And this is the condition of the wicked, they are under darkness, fire, and chains.

And to add unto the torments of hell, there are these two things more to shew you, " that it shall be ill with the wicked," let them die when they will.

The first is the worm. The second is the serpent.

First. There is the worm to torture the damned spirits, and this is no other than the worm conscience; the 9th of Mark, ver. 44, " where their worm never dieth." Oh! how dreadful will it be to have this worm?

Melancthon calls the tormenting conscience, a hellish fury. Conscience will be just as if a worm full of poison were feeding upon the heart of a man. Those sinners that would never hear the voice of conscience, they shall feel the worm of conscience. And then,

Secondly, as there is the worm to torment, so there is the serpent, that is the devil, who is called the old serpent, Rev. ix. As there is the biting of the worm, so there is the stinging of the old serpent.

First of all, the damned shall be forced to behold the devil. I remember what Anselm saith; saith he, "I had rather endure all the torments of this life, than see the devil with bodily eyes:" but now this sight the wicked shall see whether they will or no, and not only see but they shall feel the stinging of this old serpent the devil.

Satan is full of rage against mankind, and will shew no mercy: as he puts forth all his subtlety in tempting of man, so he puts out all his cruelty in tormenting of mankind. And this is not all.

"There are two things to set out the torments of hell."

First, these agonies, and hell convulsions, they shall be for ever: take that scripture for proof, Rev. xiv. 11. " and the smoke of their torments ascend for ever and ever, and they have no rest day nor night." Thus it is in hell, they would die, but they cannot; the wicked shall be always dying, but never dead: " the smoke of the furnace ascends for ever and ever." Oh! who can endure thus to be ever upon the wrack? This word " ever" breaks the heart. Wicked men now think the sabbaths long, when will the sabbath be over? They think a sermon long, and think a prayer long; but oh! how long will it be to lie in hell for ever and ever? After millions of years their torments are as far from ended, as at the first hour they began.

Secondly, which is another aggravation of hell torments, the damned in hell have none to pity them. It is some comfort, some ease to have our friends to pity us in our sickness and want: aye, but they have no friends. Mercy will not pity them, mercy is turned into fury. Christ will not pity them, he is no more an advocate for them. The angels will not pity them; but they rejoice when they see the vengeance; they insult and glory when they see the justice of God executed upon his enemies. Oh how sad is this! to lie down in the scalding furnace of God's wrath, and none to pity them! When they cry out, God will laugh at them. Oh! hear this all ye that go into sin, " it will be ill with the wicked ;" Oh! therefore turn from your sins, lest God tear you in pieces as a lion, and there be none to help you!

NOW FOR APPLICATION.

Oh! what an affrighting word is this to all wicked men, that go on desperately to sin, and add drunkenness to thirst! Never such an inundation of wickedness as now; men sin as if they would spite God, and dare him to punish them. Men sin so greedily as if they were afraid hell gates would be shut up ere they come thither. Oh! how manfully do many sin! They go to hell strongly in their wickedness! Oh! these are in a sad condition: is it not sad at the hour of death, and at the day of judgment, and after judgment with them? Wicked men live cursed and they die damned. Sinners are the very mark that God will shoot at, his standing mark, and he never misses this mark. You know what the scripture saith, " there shall be weeping, and there shall be gnashing of teeth ;" and saith Latimer, " that is sad fare, where weeping is the first course, and gnashing of teeth is the second course."

Quest. Whence is it that there is this gnashing of teeth?

Answ. First, it doth arise from the extremity of torment the wicked suffer: they are not able to bear it, and know not how to avoid it.

Secondly, the wicked gnash their teeth in hell at the godly to see them in heaven, them whom they persecuted and scoffed, and jeered, to see them in heaven, and themselves in hell, they are mad at it, Luke xiii. 18. " When they shall see Abraham, Isaac and Jacob, and all the prophets in the kingdom of God, and they themselves shut out;" they shall gnash their teeth at this. How may this amaze a wicked man? If all the curses in the Bible will make a man miserable, he shall be made so.

THE SECOND USE IS THIS.

Take heed that none of you here be found amongst the number of the wicked; take heed of being of this black regiment that wears the devil's colours, and fight under his banner. The sinner and the furnace shall never be parted. Oh! take heed of those sins, which will bring you to hell-fire!

There are (saith Bernard) fiery sins which bring men to hell-fire!

What are those fiery sins? Why, the fire of malice, the fire of passion, and the fire of lust and concupiscence, and the fire of revenge; these fiery sins bring men to fiery plagues, to hell-fire.

When you are tempted to any wickedness, think with yourselves, Oh! how can I bear the fierceness of God's wrath for ever? How can I lie in the wine-press of God's wrath for ever? Oh! take heed of those sins that will bring you into this place of torment.

I have read a story of a virgin, who being tempted by a young man to commit folly, saith she unto him, "grant me but one request, and I will do what thou desirest." "What is that?" saith he. "Do but hold your finger one hour in this burning candle." No, he would not do that. Saith she, "will not you for my sake hold your finger an hour in the candle, and will you have my soul lie burning in hell for ever?" Thus she rebuked the temptation.

Doth Satan tempt thee to wickedness, hold out this text as a shield to the devil to quench his fiery darts; say thus, "Oh, Satan! do I embrace thy temptations? I must be under thy tormenting to all eternity." Oh! therefore labour to be righteous, it shall be well with the righteous.

But take heed of sin, it shall be ill with the sinner.

I will conclude all with that saying of Austin—" When a man hath been virtuous, his labour is gone, but the pleasure remains; when a man hath been wicked, the pleasure is gone, but the sting remains."

MR. LYE'S FIRST SERMON.

Preached August 17, 1662.

PHIL. iv. 1.

Therefore, my brethren, dearly beloved, and longed for, my joy and crown, so stand fast in the Lord, my dearly beloved.

MY beloved, I do very well remember that upon the 24th of this instant month, in 1651, I was then under the sentence of banishment; and that very day did I preach my farewell sermon to my people from whom I was banished, because I would not swear against my king, having sworn to maintain his just power, and honour, and greatness. And now behold a second trial! Then I could not forswear myself, the God of heaven keep me that I never may! I am apt to think I could do any thing for this loving congregation, only I cannot sin. But since, beloved, there is a sentence gone out against us, that we that cannot subscribe must not subsist; this is the last day that is prefixed to us to preach. I shall now speak to you (God assisting me) if my passions will give me leave, just as if I would speak, if I were immediately to die; therefore hearken, "my brethren, dearly beloved, and longed for, my joy and crown, so stand fast in the Lord, my dearly beloved." Paul was now a prisoner at Rome, for the gospel of Christ; it was his second imprisonment, and he was not far from being offered up a sacrifice for the gospel he had preached. This gospel the Philippians had heard him preach, and the godly Philippians having heard of his imprisonment, they sent so far from Philippi to Rome to visit him, and to supply his wants. A gracious temper, which I hope the eternal

God hath given the saints in London, and for which, if for any thing, God hath a blessing in store for them. Paul is not so much concerned in his own bonds, as in the Philippians' estate. Epaphroditus tells him that there were heresies and false doctrines got in amongst them, but yet the Philippians stood fast: and herein Paul rejoices, writes this epistle, bids them go on, stand fast, keep their ground, and to be sure not to give an inch but to stand fast, knowing that at the long run, their labour shall not be in vain in the Lord.

I shall without any more ado enter upon the text; in which you have two things considerable.

A most melting compellation, and a most serious exhortation.

1. A melting compellation, "my brethren, dearly beloved," &c.

2. A serious exhortation; and in it first, the matter of the duty, stand, and stand it out, and stand fast. Secondly, the manner. First, so stand, so as you have stood, stand fast. Second, in the Lord; stand so, and stand in the Lord, in the Lord's strength, and in the Lord's cause. To stand in your own strength, would be the ready way to fall, and to stand in your own cause, for your own fancy, would be the ready way to expose yourselves to all manner of temptations: "therefore, my brethren, dearly beloved in the Lord, stand, and so stand fast in the Lord, my dearly beloved."

In the next place, by way of observation from the words; and if there be any wicked catchers here, let them know, that I shall speak no more than I shall draw from, and is the mind of my text; I would not give occasion to be a greater sufferer than I am like to be. But for the words.

First, For the melting compellation, " my brethren, my dearly beloved." Paul was an apostle, and a high officer in the church of God, and he wrote unto the Philippians, to all the Philippians, to the poorest of them; and see how he bespeaks himself to them, " my brethren." From hence take this observation, "that the highest officers in the church of Christ, though they are indeed by office rulers over them, yet by relation they are no more than brethren to the meanest saint." Here we have no such rabbies, to whom we must swear, because they say we must swear it. Paul calls them brethren, and so writes to them, Gal. i. 2. and James, a scriptural officer, one of the highest apostles Christ ever made, saith, "Hearken, my beloved brethren," Jam. ii. 5. So Peter, an apostle of Christ, "Wherefore the rather, brethren;" and John, the beloved disciple, "Brethren, I write no new commandment," &c. 1 John ii. 7. Well then,

1. If this be so, that the highest officers in the church, such as Christ approves of, are but brethren to the meanest saint, then certainly they are but brethren to their fellow officers. If no more relation to the toe in the body, then no more to the eyes. If there be any of a light spirit would bear rule, that love to have pre-eminence, I would desire them to read two scriptures, the first is, Luke xxii. 26. the second, Mat. xxvi. 27. Doth Christ say, whosoever will be chief among you, let him be one that will domineer over your estates, over your persons, over your consciences. Doth not Christ say so? No. But "Whosoever will be chief among you, let him be your minister—let him be your servant. Even as the Son of man came not to be ministered unto, but to minister, and to give his life a ransom for many." You have this also, Luke xxii. 25. "And he said unto them, the kings of the Gentiles exercise lordship over them, (i. e. over their slaves, over their vassals,) but ye shall not be so; but he that is greatest among you, let him be as the younger, and he that is chief as he that doth serve." Sure if Paul be but a brother to Philip then he is no more to Timothy.

2. If the highest officers in the church of Christ be but brethren to the meanest saint, then it is not for those brethren to lord it over their fellow brethren, lord it over God's heritage—remember, it is God's heritage. I hope,

your consciences will bear me witness, that I have laboured as much as in me lies, to be a helper of your joy, not to lord it over your faith," 2 Cor. i. 24. to press or cause you to believe this or that, because I believe it. If this may be allowed, then may I turn papist to-morrow. Saith Christ to him that would have had him speak to his brother, to divide the inheritance with him, " Man, who made me a judge over you?" Luke xii. 14. So say I, man, who made thee a tyrant, and lord over thy fellow brethren? 1 Pet. v. 3. " Neither as being lords over God's heritage," &c.

3. If the highest officers in the church of Christ be but brethren, and no more, then there shall be no discord between those brethren. Behold, how good and how pleasant it is for brethren to dwell together in unity: and truly I may comfortably speak that, and it is one of the greatest comforts I have in the world. I hope we have lived together in love, blessed be God. Let us not fall out, saith Abraham the elder, to Lot his younger cousin, for we are brethren. Beloved, the discords between pastor and people have made the best music in the ears of the Jesuits.

4. Are pastors, nay, the highest officers that Jesus Christ hath, and doth own in the church, but brethren? Oh! then let those brethren, if they will appear before the bar of their Father in heaven with comfort, take care of offending the souls of brethren; for at the hand of every brother, God will require the soul of his brother, Ezek. xxxiii. 6. " His blood will I require at the watchman's hand. We that are called by some the dogs of the flock, what shall we prove dumb dogs? what a comfort will it be to my dying brethren this day, if they can but say, Lord, we are clear from the blood of our brethren. The officers of Christ should never behave themselves so, that they should give their people occasion to say, we are brethren to dragons. But Jer. ix. 4. Take ye heed every one of his neighbour, &c. I would commend one scripture to all my brethren in the ministry, 1 Cor. viii.

13. A scripture that I would have writ in letters of gold on the lintel posts of all minister's doors. Wherefore if meat make my brother to offend, I will eat no flesh while the world stands, lest I make my brother to offend. Rather than to endanger my soul, I'll away with all these toys and gew-gaws.

2. From the terms of dearest affection, dearly beloved, longed for, &c. take this observation, that it becomes the highest ministers, much more the lowest, to bear a most tender, vehement, ardent, melting affection towards that flock or people that God hath committed to their charge. Thus Paul to the Philippians in the text: " my brethren, dearly beloved," &c. You shall find Paul in all his epistles, in a thawing frame to his people, melting in love unto them : the Corinthians were so in his heart, not only to live with them, but if God called him, to die for them ; so abundantly did he love them, 2 Cor. xii. 15. that he would very gladly spend, and be spent for them, carried them in his heart, and earnestly longed after them all. As for the Thessalonians, 1 Thes. ii. 8. he as a nurse, tendereth and nourishes them as children, and is so affectionately desirous of them, that he. is willing to impart to them not only the gospel, but his own soul, because they were dear to him. Then,

1. Is this so? ought the pastors so to love their people ? Give me leave to bespeak you in the words of Job, (in respect of those hundreds of ministers, that are to be plucked from their people : " Have pity upon me, have pity upon me, Oh ye my friends! for the hand of God hath touched me," Job xix. 21. What, will nothing serve but plucking out our very eyes ? our very heart (being so much the objects of the people's love ?) How sad is it for the father to be plucked from the child, the shepherd from the flock, the nurse from the child ? This is a lamentation, and ought to be for a lamentation, that there must be a parting between David and Jonathan, who loved one another as their own souls : this cuts them to their very heart, and this I may say, in respect to myself, I

bless God, I cannot say as she of her husband, "a bloody husband hast thou been unto me:" but a loving congregation have you been unto me. I know none of you have desired my destruction, nor to taint my name: never did I hear three in this congregation speak of pressing any thing against me, that was contrary to my conscience, nor can I say, that there are four in this parish that did ever deny to pay me my legal due, blessed be God for such a people. You have not encroached upon my conscience, as I hope I have not upon yours. Pastors must love their people; do not blame them if their hearts be almost broken, when they are to part with such a people.

2. Must the pastor love his people? then the people must love their pastor. It is true, it lies in the power of man to separate pastor and people, but not to separate their hearts. I hope there will never be a separation of love, but that will still continue; if we do not see one another, yet we may love one another, and pray for one another. I hope a husband doth not cease from loving his wife, because she is absent from him. But, oh! for my brethren, hundreds of them think that you are undone; but you are not undone, though you cannot see as far as other men, you may live in love and keep your conscience quiet.

3. Must pastors love their people? then you may see from hence what should be the grand object of the pastor's affection, i. e. the people, not what the people have. This is the great inquiry, What is the benefice worth? What is the preferment? Do they pay well, &c. Whereas we should not seek so much the fleece as the flock. We should not take oversight of a congregation for love of their pay, but of their souls: not, It is an excellent good living, as one said I have heard of, let me have their tythes, and let their souls go to the devil; but as the apostle, "I seek not yours, but you," 2 Cor. xii. 14. And I hope there may be many hundreds can say, it hath been the people's souls they have more loved and affected, than any thing that the people had.

4. Once more: we must love them, and love them tenderly; why and yet leave them? yes, my beloved, we are so to love our people, as to venture any thing for them, but our own damnation. I come not here to throw fire-brands; I bless God I have a most tender affection for all my brethren in the ministry; and though I am not satisfied myself, yet I condemn no man; I believe there be many of them do as conscientiously subscribe, as deny to subscribe. I protest in the fear of God, I cannot subscribe, perhaps it is because I have not that light as others have; for he that doubts, saith the apostle, is damned. My beloved, I hope you would not have us sin against God and our own consciences: it is not my living that I desire, but my office to serve my Lord and Master; but if we should, to keep communion with you, lose our communion with God, this is the ready way to have all our labour and pains lost; but as David said, (and oh that I could speak it with as good hopes as David!) " Zadok, carry back the ark of God. If I shall find favour in the eyes of the Lord, he will bring me again, and shew me both it and his habitation," &c. 2 Sam. xv. 25. Brethren, I could do very much for the love I bear to you, but I dare not sin. I know they will tell you, this is pride and peevishness in us, and are tender of our reputation, and we would fain all be bishops and forty things more; but the Lord be witness between them and us in this. Beloved, I prefer my wife and children before a blast of air of people's talk. I am very sensible what it is to be reduced to a morsel of bread. Let the God of heaven and earth do what he will with me, if I could have subscribed with a good conscience, I would; I would do any thing to keep myself in the work of God, but to sin against my God I dare not do it.

3. My joy and crown; therefore, " my dearly beloved and longed for, my joy and crown," my present joy and future crown; my joy which I value more than a crown, my principal joy. Hence observe this doctrine, that the fixed, standing, flourishing growth of saints in gospel

practice, and gospel obedience, is, or ought to be, matter of transcendent joy to their pastors. It was so to the apostle Paul. Paul heard how they stood, though there was a plague amongst them, yet they were not infected; and though he was in the gaol ready to be beheaded, yet this was his joy and crown that his people did stand; and I hope, my brethren, it will be our joy and crown to hear of your standing and growth in gospel-knowledge and profession; and,

1. If this be so, as John said, "I rejoice greatly, that I found of thy children walking in the truth." It should be the prayers and endeavours of all pastors, really to love the souls of their people, and to pray for them: that when they cannot look after the souls of their children, yet that good nurses may be looked out for them. What a joy was it that Moses's mother was made his nurse? and who can tell, it may be, though not out of any merit of ours, yet of their own clemency, our governors may give us to be nurses over our own children: but I cannot nurse my child myself, I will wish it well, and as good a nurse as I can: far be it that those that are to succeed, should not prosper. Lord, it shall be the prayers of thy servant, that those that are to succeed, may have a double and treble portion of thy spirit, that they may be both painful and faithful, &c.

2. If the people's growth in grace and knowledge, be matter of joy to a faithful pastor; then what do you think of those that hinder their thriving? I shall give you two scriptures, John xii. 19. "The Pharisees therefore said among themselves," (they durst not speak publicly; but who was it against? why, it was against Christ)" perceive ye how ye prevail nothing? Behold the world is gone after him." But we will order him for that, we will lessen his congregation; if we cannot do that, we will shut the doors against him; see Mat. xxiii. 13. "Woe unto you scribes and Pharisees, hypocrites for ye shut up the kingdom of heaven against men:" What! shut up the kingdom of heaven against men! What

the Pharisees, that pretended they had the keys of heaven, and to be the guides! Aye, that it is, because there is not room enough in heaven for us and them too? " No," saith Christ, " there is no such matter; for ye neither go in yourselves, neither suffer ye them that are entering to go in." I dare not tell you at this time, what it is to shut up the kingdom of heaven against men, you may better imagine it than I can speak it ; but thus did the Pharisees, " they would not go in themselves, nor suffer them that were entering to go in." I remember when I was a child, we had such a minister, that would one Lord's day preach up holiness, and the next Lord's day preach against the practice of holiness.

And now, my brethren, I come in the next place to speak to the last part, " stand fast :" and because I see a hurricane coming, keep your ground, stand fast, and live in the Lord here, that you may live with him hereafter.

MR. LYE'S SECOND SERMON.

Preached August 17, 1662.

Phil. iv. 1.

Therefore, my brethren, dearly beloved and longed for, my joy and crown, so stand fast in the Lord, my dearly beloved.

FROM this scripture you have these three doctrines.
1. That the highest officers of the church of Christ, though they are rulers of them, yet they are but brethren to the meanest saints. 2. That it becomes a true spiritual minister of Christ, to have a most vehement, ardent, strong, melting, tender affection, to that flock or people

which the providence of God hath committed to his charge. 3. That the fixed, standing, flourishing, and thriving of that flock in the profession and practice of gospel-knowledge and obedience, is matter of transcendent joy and triumph to such a godly pastor. The fourth, which is that I would now prosecute, is this, that it is the grand and indispensable duty of all sincere saints, in the most black and shaking seasons, to stand fast fixed and stedfast in the Lord."

This is a grand thing St. Paul had to say to the Philippians, when he was ready to have his head cut off; for so it was, he was beheaded for the testimony of Jesus: this is all he had to say, when in gaol, and in bonds, and that under heathen Romans; you are now my joy, you are now my crown. Oh! do but stand, and my joy, which is but two notes above gamut, will get to Ela. Oh! do but stand, and my crown is studded with diamonds. We live if you stand, though we die when you stand. It is the great and indispensable duty, &c. Whether these are black and shaking seasons, I have nothing to say, but I am wholly now upon your duty, beloved; and for God's sake let the words of a seemingly dying minister prevail with you. There is a kind of a maxim among some, that in case a person die seemingly and revive again, that the last words that were heard of that person, when in a rational temper, are the only things that that person will remember, when brought to life again. It is most probably, beloved, whatever others may think, but in my opinion (God may work wonders) neither you nor I shall ever see the faces of, or have a word to speak to one another till the day of judgment. Therefore I beseech you hear me as those that would, and may live with me to eternity: mark your duty, I have spoken something concerning the pastor's duty in the morning; now for the people's. It is the indispensable duty of all sincere saints to stand fast, &c. I confess, I have a love for the whole auditory. I have a mess for them, but my Benjamin's mess is for those I once called my own people:

you are my Benjamins, I wish I had a greater than a fifth for you. This proposition I shall first prove, and then secondly improve.

In the worst of times, in the most shaking seasons, and if I do not greatly mistake, there is an hour of temptation threatened by God, now beginning to be inflicted: if ever you would stand, stand now; and for your comfort let me but hint, that a Christian may stand comfortably, when he falls sadly, that is, he may stand by God, when he falls by man: I knew that a great many years ago.

First, then, *It is our duty to stand.* There be scriptures more than enough to prove this be your duty, Col. i. 12. "Stand perfect and complete in all the will of God." Phil. i. 27. "Only let your conversation be as becometh the gospel of Christ; that whether I come and see you," (alas, poor Paul! thou come and see them! thou wast beheaded before thou couldst come and see them! but) "or else be absent, I may hear of your affairs, that ye stand fast in one spirit, with one mind striving together" (not to pluck out one another's throats, no more of that: but striving together, not against one another, but) "for the faith of the gospel." So 1 Cor. xv. 58. "Therefore, my brethren, be stedfast, unmoveable, always abounding in the work of the Lord, forasmuch as you know that your labour is not in vain in the Lord." It is our duty to stand. But,

2. Wherein must we stand fast? I have no new doctrine to preach now. I shall but mind you of what I have formerly spoken, when you would not believe. I confess I do not begin to be of a new judgment now: and should I be continued in the ministry, (a mercy I can hardly hope for) I should be of the same judgment, and preach this doctrine, Stand fast.

God will certainly bring the people of God in England to his own terms, or else fare them well for ever. What is that we should be stedfast in? I would advise to a stedfastness, 1. Of judgment. 2. Of resolution. 3. Of faith. 4. Of conscience. So stand fast in the Lord in your judgment, in your resolution, in your faith, in your conscience.

1. I would advise you to a stedfastness of judgment. Strange doctrines are the greatest fetters that do assault a sound judgment; they are like waves, if they do not split they will shake the ship to purpose. Therefore your way is, to cast anchor well, to stand firm on the rock of truth, I had almost said all in a word protestant truth, though the market may rise somewhat high, yet stand firmly there. While strange doctrines like so many impetuous waves are beating upon you, break themselves in pieces they may, but if you stand, can never hurt you. I am not to begin to warn you against popery, not that I have the least reflection on any thing in the world, but on the scriptures. I am apt to think the wound of the beast must be healed; however, do not you spread a plaister for the beast, to heal his wound. Be no more children tossed to and fro, carried about with every wind of doctrine, with every wind of windy doctrine, by the slight of men, and cunning craftiness, that can cog the die; notable gamesters there are in the world, but you must stand steady in judgment, you must be firm to your principles. I would have you stars, not meteors; for meteors are carried about with every blast of wind. I hope better things of you. I shall pray God would make you stedfast in judgment. First, be sure to get good principles, and secondly, be sure to stand in those principles that you have got. And though I cannot say but some tares are sown among this parish, yet I bless the Lord for the generality; I hope I may say, I have an orthodox ministry.

2. It is not enough to stand in judgment, but we must be stedfast to our resolution, 1 Cor. xv. 58. "Be stedfast, unmoveable;" such as stand firm on some basis and foundation that doth not totter and stagger: if they find you staggering, to be sure the next moment they look upon you as falling. Be as they say of one or both of the poles

of the heavens, though all the world turns, the poles are immoveable. If I mistake not, you may see a great turn in the world, and behold, at this day the greatest turn that ever was in England; but yet you must not move, you must not stir, be true to your resolutions, but just to your first love; go on in the Lord's work, let nothing take you off. If I have preached any false doctrine among you, witness against me at the day of judgment; but if the things I have preached be true, stand to the truth; if you do not witness against my doctrine, (mine it is not) but rather witness for it; remember if you leave it, that very doctrine will witness against you at the day of judgment. Oh! the excellent heroine, queen Esther, thus and thus will I do, and if I perish, I perish. You cannot imagine against how many thousand temptations a stedfast resolution will guard you.

3. There is a stedfastness of faith too; when we so believe, as that we do not waver, or do not deviate. Will you give me leave to propose to you (my dear friends, though my congregation I cannot call you) that question which our Saviour did unto the Jews, (whom he hated, though I love you.) The baptism of John whence was it, from heaven, or of men? The doctrines you have heard, have they been from heaven, or from men? Answer me, if from men, abhor them. Man is a false creature, man would make merchandize of your faith and souls: but if from heaven, why then should you not believe them? I bless the Lord, my conscience bears me witness, I never did so far propose a doctrine to you, I would have you believe without scripture: if the doctrines have been from God, believe them. If not, abhor them, and any of those that shall dare to bring a doctrine, but dare not bring the authority of the scripture to warrant them. You may not be like those in Jam. i. 6. "That wavereth like a wave of the sea, driven with the wind, and tossed." The most godly man may stumble in his way (*i. e.*) tread away; but a wavering minded man is never settled concerning this way. Blessed be

God, I am not now (on this day, that looks as like my dying day, as can be in the world) to begin to fix upon a religion, fix upon my way; I know my way. If God will but keep my steps, and guide me in that way. If God be God (I appeal to your consciences) worship him. If Baal be God, worship him. Do not stand in disputing and doubting. Do not say, shall I? shall I? If the ways you have found be the ways of God, follow them; God hath but one way to heaven, there is but one truth. If Baal be God, follow Baal, do not stand wavering; do not consult with flesh and blood. It is an infinite mercy that God will give any of us to leave relation, estates, congregations, any thing for Christ. It is an infinite mercy we do not split upon a rock. Be sure to be either for God or Baal; a godly man many times halts in his way, but never halts between two opinions.

4. Stedfastness of conscience. Indeed the genius of my ministry hath lain this way, and here I could easily launch out, but I must be short. I would speak a word in season to those that are weak: it becomes you to be stedfast in conscience; then have a God-decreeing, a Christ-redeeming, a spirit-quickening, a gospel-promising, a heaven-prepared, a God infinitely more ready to save him, than he can possibly be desirous to be saved by him. Be stedfast in conscience against the guilt, the filth of sin, against the temptations of Satan, &c. Let us draw near with full assurance of faith; you can never believe God's love so much, as God's love doth engage you to believe, &c. I might add,

5. You must be stedfast in conversation. It is not the running well, but the running out. It is not the fighting, but the conquering that gives you title to the reward. For you to give a great deal of milk, and throw it down all at length with your foot, may argue you to have a good breast, but a bad foot. Never give those beasts of Babylon occasion to say, That a man may be a child of God in the morning, and a child of the devil at night; that we contradict that doctrine by our conversation, that we be stedfast.

But why must we be stedfast?

Alas, why? Would you have me marshal up all the reasons? Bid me count the stars, or number the sands on the sea-shore. There is not an attribute in God, not a precept, promise, or threatening in the word, not an ordinance, not a providence, there is nothing in God, or in the devil, or in sinners, or ourselves, but all would give a contribution of arguments to prove the saints should be stedfast. I must but hint at a few things. First, I would argue from Jesus Christ. Believers, you love Christ, and therefore you love the honour of Christ; now the honour of Christ is highly engaged in our stedfastness. We never cast a deeper blot on the honour of Christ, than when we grow unstedfast. I need not tell you so, the Jesuits, those meek Papists will tell you so, those that delight in nothing more than in milk of the Virgin Mary and in the blood of saints; they have enough if you be unsteady. 1. You dishonour Christ in his sufferings. Pray tell me, believer, why did Christ sweat blood? why did he die? why did he undergo what the wrath of devils could inflict, but for this end, to make you stand in conquest triumphing? Thus I remember as Joshua, Josh. xiii. " Come put your feet upon the neck of these kings, &c." So Christ hath died that you might live, that you might stand; and what dishonour to the Eternal Saviour of the world, to a dying Saviour, to see a flying christian. It was never heard of, that soldiers should fly before a conquered enemy, whose legs were cut off, whose arms were broken, whose swords were taken from them. 2. It is a dishonour to the spirit of Christ, the same spirit that was with Christ, in all his agonies, this very spirit he hath given to believers, that he might bring them through with some victory; therefore when we stand not, it is an high dishonour to Christ's spirit. 3. It is a dishonour to Christ's truth. Oh! let but a saint fall, and what dishonour doth it bring to the truth. I have but thought of some late experiments of poor ministers, that I have heard of, carried about in triumph, look here is the man, that hath done this, that, and the other thing; and now look here he is—I cannot excuse Noah for his drunkenness, yet methinks it is the part of a Cham to shew his father's nakedness. I remember that one hath told me (it is a great truth,) that religion never suffers greater wounds than by the hands of her professed friends. Oh! what advantage have the wicked Papists taken against us by the falls of English professors, both in principle and practice. 4. It is a very great dishonour to Christ's all-sufficiency. Tell me, man, is thy Christ able to protect thee against all evil? and is he able to supply thee with all good? or is he not? If he be not, then deny him, and whatsoever thou hast said concerning him; if he be, then stand close to him: in the mount he will be seen.

2. I would argue from saints; the infinite advantage, that at long run (I do not say presently) will redound to those that are steady in judgment, in resolution, in faith, in conscience, in practice, so far as all these are conformable to the word of God, and no further. The greatest advantage appears upon these four grounds,

1. Whatever you think, a steady condition is the safest condition.
2. The fullest condition.
3. The strongest condition.
4. The freest condition.

Oh! that I could beat this into my heart, as well as it is in my head. The safest condition in the midst of dangers; the fullest condition in the midst of wants; the strongest condition in the midst of assaults; the freest condition in the midst of straits. I profess in the presence of God, I have felt these things, and knew them to be truth many years ago.

1. It is the safest condition; never do the saints take hurt, but by declining, moving from their centre. While at their centre the devil cannot touch them; departing thence, is like the poor bird from her nest, every one hath a fling at them. Remember this, let but a man

once leave his scriptural station, and what temptation is he able to stand against? It is just like a man thrown down from the top of a house, no stopping till he come to the bottom, 1 John v. 18. "He that is begotten of God keepeth himself, and the wicked one toucheth him not."

2. It is the fullest condition. Oh, my brethren! saints living stedfastly on their foundation, are continually supplied by God, as the fountain doth continually issue out itself into the streams. I know it is best living upon a single God. How many thousands be there yet living in England, that can tell you, they never enjoyed more of God, than when they enjoyed least of the creature. Some have professed to me, their prison was to them as a palace, that were troubled more with these things, than ever you were, and the God of Heaven grant you never may.

3. It is the strongest condition. A man that stands stedfast, is like a man on a rock; the waters come, they may dash themselves in pieces, but never shall be able to dash him in pieces: he is fixed on a rock, and therefore stands. A man that stands steady to his scriptural principles, is like Samson with his locks about him: let all the Philistines come, what cares he? he is able to conquer them all.

4. It is the freest condition. A man that deserts his principles, is a slave to every condition, afraid of every humour, of every aspen leaf in the world, thinks all those are informers that converse with him, is afraid of some promoter or other; but he that stands fast, where the spirit of God is, there is liberty and freedom. Such a man in chains as Paul at Rome, is in a far freer condition than others, not in that restraint. Well then, it is rational that you stand; but it may be your lusts and interests can hardly swallow these things. If you stand you shall not fall; nay, if you do not stand, be sure you shall fall at last. The next thing I would do, is to apply this truth. Is it the most important duty of all sincere professors in the most shaking seasons, to stand stedfast in the Lord? Then

First, by way of lamentation.

1. Over our own souls. 2. Over hundreds of congregations.

Lord, we do say hundreds, nay thousands of congregations, that are this day, though they do not accompany us in person, yet mingling tears with us, and especially as I hear in the west of England.

1. Over our hearts. We must stand; that is our duty. Oh how should it cause us to lie low! by reason of the instability of our hearts, and their declining from the true foundation every day. Alas, beloved, this is that God complains of. They are a generation whose spirit is not stedfast with God; and therefore we have very much reason to complain of it. Oh what an unsettled people have we been! To-day we have been apt to cry Hosanna, Hosanna, to the Son of David; to-morrow our note is changed, Crucify him, crucify him, give us Barnabas. To-day the Lord is God, to-morrow Baal: any thing is God, provided we may keep our estates. Oh, Lord! what wilt thou do with such a people as this? Certainly it is a lamentation, and ought to be a lamentation. Believe it, beloved, I can now count seven years, if not something more, wherein I have most clearly expected the days I now see. No way but the severest ways to be taken with such a false people as we have been. Judge in your own thoughts, whether we have been true to God or man, to saints or sinners, to the church of God at home or abroad; whether or no this be not matter of lamentation?

2. With respect to our congregations. (It is not against the law yet to call them our congregations.) This I confess, I can rather weep than speak to. I cannot speak, my heart is too big for my head here. Lord, is it the duty of people, of saints to stand, to be stedfast? How then should we mourn over their poor souls, that because their pillars are taken away, must needs for ought we know fall, unless thou dost support them. What, Lord, dost thou complain of a flock of sheep that are scattered? There is no wonder in it, their Shepherd is gone. Do you

look on it as a strange thing, to see a poor ship tossed here and there in the sea, when her pilot is destroyed? Why, mothers, is it a strange thing for your children to fall, and knock their arms, legs, their brains out? why their mother is taken from them. Oh poor people! Good God, provide for this congregation! Aye, and for this city, that (let defacing, abominable wretches say what they will) is certainly one of the best cities God hath in the world; and therefore they hate it so desperately, because God loves it, and because they hate that God that loves it. I bless God, I can speak of my own people, they are not a mad pestiferous people for the most of them. How many thousand have their hearts at their mouths, now at this time before God in England? Alas, alas, that we should have our seers carried away from us; but what think you, when poor people shall be exposed to greater temptations, to an ulcer in the very kidneys, to a plague in the very heart or head; you now fear it, but when you feel it, what then?

2. By way of exhortation, beloved, I remember good Jacob, when he was come into Egypt, ready to die, calls his children together, and before he dies, blesseth his children. I cannot say you are my children, but I can say, in the strength of God, you are dearer to me than the children of my own bowels. I remember what poor Esau said, "hast thou but one blessing, my father? bless me, even me also, Oh my father!" Oh, beloved! I have a few blessings for you; and for God's sake, take them as if they dropped from my lips when dying; it is very probable we shall never meet more while the day of judgment; whatever others think, I am utterly against all irregular ways. I have (I bless the Lord) never had a hand in any change of government in all my life. I am for prayers, tears, quietness, submission, and meekness, and let God do his work, and that will be best done when he doth it. Therefore be exhorted to stand fast in the Lord. My own people hear me now: though you shall never hear me more, be exhorted to stand fast in the

Lord. You are not a schismatical, heretical people. I do not know the least person among you inclining to popery: therefore, be exhorted, as ye have been a people that have waited upon the ordinances of God, that have not persecuted your poor ministers, that have made it your design and business to live lovingly, quietly, and as it becomes Christians. I am confident a minister may live as comfortably among you as among any people in England. "So be ye stedfast, unmoveable, always abounding in the work of the Lord, forasmuch as you know that your labour shall not be in vain in the Lord." Here I had prepared, I confess, several arguments to have moved you to this stedfastness.

I could have told you, that withdrawing of any one of you back, you will meet with great temptations, which will very much unfit you for heaven. "If any man or woman draw back, my soul (saith God) shall have no pleasure in him." I could have urged you with examples from the heathens. Alexander, being in India, bid them tell him the greatest rarity in their country. "Sir, go tell them" (say they) "when you come to Greece, there are many here that cannot be forced by the prowess of Alexander to change their minds." I know there are some here, that cannot be easily persuaded to change their religion. Saith Lactantius, "Our very women torment their tormentors." I would never desire a more able disputant than a woman against a monk.

I could tell you of those enjoyments God hath put on you; our miseries have been great, but our mercies have been greater. I could tell you of six troubles and of seven; of six, wherein God hath stood by, and of seven wherein he hath not forsaken; and the truth is, he cannot forsake his people. He may forsake them as for comfort, he will never forsake them as for support. Let him lay on a burden, he will be sure to strengthen the back.

3. I hope, it is not dangerous if I tell you, you are engaged to God. There are vows upon you, baptismal

vows, to say no more; you have sworn to God, you have lifted up your hands; you are those that have undertaken that you would be true to God to your lives' end. If these vows have been any way strengthened, Oh, remember Zedekiah's case, Ezek.xvii. 18, 19. "Seeing he despised the oath by breaking the covenant (when lo he had given his hand) and hath done all these things, he shall not escape: therefore thus saith the Lord God, As I love, surely mine oath that he hath despised, and my covenant that he hath broken, even it will I recompsnse upon his own head." Remember it, you may play fast and loose with a man: you must not think ever to carry it away by playing fast and loose with God.

4. If you should not stand, you lose all you have wrought; all your prayers, tears, professions, practices, sufferings, all are gone if you give out at last, &c.

5. While you stand by God, God hath promised to stand by you; and the truth is, I have but one God, it is no great matter for all the tiles in Worms. There be a thousand devils, but all those devils are in one chain, and the end of that chain is the hand of one God. Oh! God will shew himself strong, 2 Cor. i. 6, 9. "For the eyes of the Lord run to and fro through the whole earth, to shew himself strong in the behalf of them, whose heart is perfect towards him."

Quest. But what shall I do to stand?

Answ. 1. If ever you would stand, if ever you would be firm standing Christians indeed, take heed you be not light and proud Christians. A feather will never stand against a whirlwind. Error and profaneness are most apt to breed in proud hearts. The proud and blasphemers are put together, 2 Tim. ii. 2. Be but humble Christians, that is the way to be standing ready Christians. If ever you would be steady in your stations, you must be low in your own eyes; do not you go and judge. And now, we shall have another kind of religion come up, as we have had it a great while, such a man cannot be an honest man.Alas, he is a Presbyterian, he is an Independent, he is an Anabaptist, &c. Now, all your great business will be, such a man cannot be a good, an honest man, for he doth not conform; on the other side, he cannot be an honest man for he doth conform. These are poor things. I bless God, I lay not the stress of my salvation upon these. It is true, I cannot in conscience conform, but I do not lay the stress of salvation on it, as I did not lay the stress of my salvation on being a Presbyterian. I confess I am so, and have been; it hath been my unhappiness to be always on the sinking side, yet I lay not the stress of my salvation upon it. It is my conscience, but it may be I have not so much light as another man; and I profess, in the presence of God, could I conform without sin to my own conscience, I would. If I should do any thing against my conscience, and all, and never see a good day. Do not then spend the strength of your zeal for your religion in censuring others. That man that is most busy in censuring others is always least employed in examining himself. Remember good John Bradford, he would not censure Bonner, nor Gardner; but, saith he, they called Joe Bradford, the hypocritical Joe Bradford, &c. Do not speak this as though I can or did in conscience approve of those things for which I must suffer, that I cannot approve of them, but take off people from those things that are so far from the foundation. "Look you but to the main things, look into your own hearts, examine them, and then you need not be much persuaded to look about to others."

2. You must take heed you be not loose christians. Will you remember one thing from me, (the God of heaven grant you never live to see it verified,) a loose protestant is one of the fittest persons in the world to make a strict papist. Tell me not of his protestantism, being a drunkard, it is because his king or country are protestants where they live. There is no religion in a loose liver; if ungodliness be in the heart, it is no difficult thing for error to get into the heart. A loose heart can best comply with loose principles: see, if they will

not be of any religion in the world that is uppermost. Let the Turk prevail, they would soon be of his religion.

3. Take heed of being a worldly christian. Oh! this is the David, that hath slain his ten thousands. A worldly heart will be bought and sold upon every turn to serve the devil's turn. Come to a worldly heart, and but promise him thirty pieces of silver, he will betray his Saviour. The temptations of the world are great upon us at this time: you that are husbands and parents know it; the world is a great temptation; but if we be overcome by the world, and the world not overcome by us, we shall never be able to overcome any one temptation that is offered to us. Therefore that is an admirable support, "in the world you shall have tribulation; but be of good cheer, I have overcome the world." I have overcome the world for you; and likewise I have overcome the world in you. Oh, Lord! if thou wilt but overcome the love and fear of the world; if thou wilt but arm us against the smiles of the world, then come what will, we shall stand steadfast.

4. Take heed you be not hypocritical christians; i.e. take heed you do not receive the truth, and only the truth, and not receive the truth in the love of that truth, 1 Thess. iii. 10. You have received the truth, but have you received the truth in the love of that truth which you received? Want of this, is that damnable occasion to popery; "and with all deceivableness of unrighteousness in them that perish, because they received not the love of the truth, that they might be saved," &c. It is just with God that they should fall into errors, whose hearts did never love real truths; better never received the truth, than to receive it, and not in the love of it.

5. Take heed of being venturous and God-tempting christians. What is that? When do I tempt God? I tempt God when I run into a pest-house and say God will preserve me from the plague. Take heed of running upon temptations to sin, whether it be in principles or in practice. I could tell you of two spiritual pest-houses in

England, if I had time; for principles one and for practice another. I do not say that I mean play-houses, on the one hand, or mass-houses on the other hand. Certainly, brethren, I read of Julian, that wicked bloodly apostate, that he sunk into that his apostacy first, by going to hear Libanius preach. Mistake me not, I am not against your going to hear the ministers of Christ; for a man may be a true minister, though he be a bad man; all the world can never answer the instance of Judas, who was a true minister, though a bad man. While I plead for the truth of his ministry, I do not spread a skirt over the wickedness of his life. The scribes and pharisees sit in Moses's chair; hear them.

But that which I mainly aim at is this, do not you go and run and venture yourself upon temptations. You have heard of a superstitious or idolatrous worship; you have a month's mind to see this; and what if so be when you are found in Satan's way, Satan should lay his paw on you, and claim to you, what do you there in Satan's ground? Would you be found, when you come to die, in a play-house? or in such a place where the true God is idolatrously worshipped? It is a great truth, if you would not be found in the devils' power, do not be found in the devil's pound. Brethren, we must know Satan is busy enough to tempt us, we need not go to tempt him. Eve lost all she had be hearing one sermon, but it was from the devil. Therefore, if you would not have your pockets picked, do not trade amongst cheaters, 2 Tim.vi. 3,5. "If any man teach otherwise, &c. (than that ye have received, and we preached) from such withdraw thyself," that is a good, honest, laudable separation; from such withdraw thyself.

6. Where God doth not find a mouth to speak, do not you find a ear to hear, nor a heart to believe. (Pray mind it, this I am sure is of concernment.) This is one of the grand points in my cards or compass, on which I hope I shall venture all. If any man come with a doctrine, not according to the word of God, let him carry it

whither he will. What have I to do with it? Either you come from God or no; if you do shew me his word and I will believe; if not, open your pack where you please, &c. Where God doth find a mouth to speak; where you have not a precept, promise, threatening, or example in the word of God, let them talk their hearts out, it is nothing to me, to my religion, to my salvation.

Object. But what ground have you for this?

Answer. Jesuit, I will tell you my ground: this is my great hold I have against popery. Could they convince me of this, that I must believe with an implicit faith, because they say it, I think it would not be long before I turned papist.

Question. But why must I not believe it with an implicit faith?

Answer. Look you into these three great scriptures, Mat. xv. 2. " Why do thy disciples transgress the traditions of the elders?" The Jews come and tell Christ, he was not a true son of the church of the Jews, he was disobedient to the church of the Jews: why? thou hast disciples that walk not as they ought. What do they do? They commit an unpardonable sin, they transgress the traditions of the elders, they break one of the greatest commandments. What is that tradition? They wash not their hands when they eat bread: this was the great sin, and they charge it on him, eat with unwashed hands. Why bring you in this tradition? What have you to say to it? What is that to the purpose? Prove, Jesus Christ, that there is any thing in the word of God that is against washing? But prove you out of the word of God, where they are bound to wash before they eat? If you will give out your imposition, make out your institution, and let me tell you, you talk of tradition, but first you set up an altar God never thought of; and secondly, you pull down God's altar. Why do you all transgress the commandments of God by your tradition? for God commanded, saying, Honour thy father and thy mother; and he that curseth father or mother let him die the death; but ye say, whosoever shall say to his father or mother, it is a gift, by whatsoever thou mightest be profited by me, and honor not your father or mother, he shall be free. Thus have ye made the commandment of God of none effect by your tradition. Ye hypocrites, you were told of it long ago. Well did Esaias prophesy of you, saying, This people draweth nigh unto me with their mouth, and honoureth me with their lips, but their heart is far from me, they draw near, wash their hands, wash their cups, and have filthy souls, they honor me with their lips, &c. But though their principle, their heart is bad, their worship is good, is it not so? No, in vain do they worship me, teaching for doctrines the commandments of men. So then, my brethren, remember, all those that teach for doctrines, the precepts of men, in vain do they worship God. Here is an innocent command, not against the word of God; but this command you must wash before you eat, if you do not wash, you do transgress the tradition of the elders. But let you starve father and mother, if you give but to the church, to a nunnery, friary, &c. it is all one. So that all those that will for doctrines teach the traditions of men, will render the commandments of God of none effect, in vain do they worship me. Look therefore wherever God doth not find a tongue to speak, do not you find an ear to hear, nor an heart to believe. Christians, if you expect Christ's benediction, always call aloud for Christ's institution. So Col. ii. 18, 19. one of the greatest steps you have against popery, " let no man beguile you of your reward in a voluntary humility, and worshipping of angels, intruding into those things which he hath not seen, vainly puffed up by his fleshly mind, &c." Deut. xii. 13. " What things soever I command you, observe to do it; thou shalt not add thereto, nor diminish from it." There are no wens in the body of God's precepts, therefore none of them to be cut off. You must not deal with God's ordinances, as that tyrant Procrustes did with men: if they were too long for his bed, he would cut them shorter; if too short, he would pull their limbs out of joint to make them longer. Never think yourselves in conscience bound to lend an ear to that which God doth not find a mouth to speak.

7. Would you stand fast? Beware of shaking doctrines. What are those? There are a great many of such doctrines, that are shaking. Give me leave to instance in three or four.

1. As you love your souls, beware of doctrines that tend to, and preach up licentiousness, looseness, and profaneness. Should any tell you, you may lawfully violate and profane the sabbath, do not believe it. The doctrine of the gospel, is a doctrine of godliness: it teacheth us to deny ungodly and worldly lusts, and to live soberly, righteously, and godlily in this present world. Therefore if you find any doctrine at any time, that should have the least tendency to encourage you in any sin, know it is a doctrine against the gospel.

2. Wherever you find any doctrine that shall tend to the lifting up of a man's free will, and debasing of God's free grace, know, it is a wicked doctrine, and against the genius of the gospel. Perhaps the papists will tell you, you are alive, Paul tells us we are dead. They say that we can do any thing; many things that we talk to the world, we cannot do. They say, that we can save ourselves and close with Christ if we will, whereas the apostle tells us, 1 Cor. i. 14. "The natural man receiveth not the things of the spirit of God, for they are foolishness unto him, neither can he know them, because they are spiritually discerned." It may, they will tell you, a natural man may love God with his heart really, as so, and savingly, whereas the apostle tells you, Rom. viii. 7. "The carnal mind is enmity against God, for it is not subject unto the law of God, neither indeed can be." Remember it in all those doctrines wherein we agree with those whom we call Pelagians, and Arminians, so far we agree with the Jesuits, and the worst of papists.

3. As you would avoid hell, avoid all those doctrines that would lift up self-righteousness, and debase the

righteousness of Christ. I fear I shall never be in that capacity that I would, to stand you instead in this particular. I confess I am against forty things in popery, but my soul is here engaged; if that doctrine be a truth, I never expect salvation by God. Either I must be saved by Christ alone, or else I must never be saved by Christ at all. Though Christ will never save me without sanctification, yet Christ never intended my sanctification should merit his salvation. Be as holy as you can, as if there were no gospel to save. Yet when you are as holy as you can, you must believe in Christ, as if there were no law at all to condemn you. Come and tell me of the merit of saints, &c. I will believe that truth, when I believe the whore of Babylon to be Christ's spouse, see Phil. iii. 9; 2 Cor. v. 21.

8. Why should you stand? you must be praying Christians. I confess when most of my strings are broken, there is yet one holds; there is a spirit of prayer (remember, Atheist) among the saints of God. I can pray yet: and I had rather stand against the canons of the wicked, than against the prayers of the righteous. Oh! pray that you enter not into temptation; or, if we enter into temptation, Lord, let not the temptation enter into us! Pray, if possible, let this cup pass from me, but if not, let it not poison me, but let me be bettered by it, and in due time deliver me from it. I believe, it would be a great temptation to you, if it should be said to you, you shall trade with no man any more, &c. You have enjoyed these and these comforts; bid them adieu for ever, you shall have no more to do with them; this would be a temptation. Temptations and trials are great, and certainly where they are so, prayer should be strong. There is no relief to be expected on earth: all our relief is to be expected from God, and that is to be obtained by prayer. Pray that God would be pleased above all things in the world to make you sincere. Would you be stedfast in your profession, you must be sincere in your practice. To him that hath shall be given, that

is a comfort; to him that hath but truth of grace, to him shall be given growth of grace. Would you be steady Christians, then make it your great work to attend the ordinances, that God hath prescribed to make you steady Christians. You were told of this many years ago, concerning attending the ordinances of God.

Quest. Pray what are those?

Answ. 1. There are secret ordinances: it may be thou canst not be so much in the pulpit as thou wouldst. Oh! be more in thy closet. It may be thou shalt not have so many opportunities to hear so many lectures: be more conscientious in thy meditations in secret. It may be thou shalt not have that freedom with God in public: be more earnest with God in private.

2. Mind your families more than ever. You have your children and servants call aloud upon you. How many grave faces do I see at this time, that can tell me, Sir, I remember some twenty or thirty years ago, you could not pass the streets, but here was one family repeating the word of God, another singing the praises of God, another praying to God, another conferring concerning the things of God. At that time we had not so much foolish absurd excursion into streets and fields as now. Oh! for the Lord's sake begin to take them up now. Let the Amorite, Perizzite, and Jebusite do what they will; but oh! for you and your children, and your servants, do you serve the Lord. Up again with those godly exercises. When we cannot hear a sermon, then read a sermon. If we cannot hear a sermon well preached, our godly parents would engage us to read a sermon well penned. If nothing new, let the word repeated and meditated call to mind what you have heard. Oh! reduce yourselves to your Christian frame. Let the debauched Atheists know, that they have something among you to be feared; that is your prayer. Let them know, that though you have not those opportunities you have had, yet you will improve those you have. And you, masters of this parish, for God's sake, keep in your servants on this day more than ever. You

are to be accountable for their souls; and they will give you a thousand thanks when they come to age, especially at the day of judgment. Oh! then blessed be God I had such a master. Blessed be God I had such a mistress. Blessed be God I had such parents!

Question. But then for public ordinances, what would you have us do?

Answer. 1. Wherever Christ doth find a tongue to speak, I am bound to find an ear to hear, and a heart to believe. I would not be mistaken. I bless the Lord I am not turned out of my ministry for being a schismatic; I know schism is a sin, nor know I any of my brethren that are so. Do not mistake us, therefore; do not go and tell the Jesuits we are schismatics, for we are none: but this I would advise, (I speak as though I were dying) do whatsoever lies in your power, to hear such whom you think to be godly. Beg of God, be earnest with him that he would give pastors after his own heart, and whom God hath sent: not such as may daub with untempered mortar, and not such as may prophecy lies in the name of the Lord; not such as may be clouds without water, but such as may be guides of the blind, burning and shining lights, faithful stewards. What shall you do? What did you twenty or thirty years ago? What did the good old Puritans do? They were not schismatics. But as much as lies in you possible, hear them whom in your conscience God doth hear. Oh! then expect the word of God should come to your hearts, when you have ground to believe it comes from your pastor's heart. I must confess, I intend to do the same, when put into the same condition with you. I acknowledge I am bound in conscience to hear the word of God, but I must take care whom I hear, hear those by whom God speaks. I hope God will grant several such.

Take but this advice more, and I have no more to say. Whatever abuse you find either in pastor, in people, or wherever you find it, do not go as your old use hath been, to rail, calumniate, backbite, and speak behind their backs. This is wicked and ungodly. But do every one according as God prescribes us that are members of any visible church. What is that? If I know any thing against my brother, do not go and make a sputter and a noise, and backbite; but take the rule of Christ: "If thy brother trespass against thee, go and tell him of his fault between him and thee alone. If he shall hear thee, thou hast gained thy brother; but if he will not hear thee, then take with thee one or two more; and if he neglect to hear them, tell it to the church;" and leave the blood at their door. Thou hast freed thine own soul. I hope by God's grace I shall do so. Thus I have now spoken something from this scripture. I cannot speak what I desire; for besides the exhausting of my spirits, there is something to be done after, viz. a funeral sermon. I shall say no more, but only this: the God of heaven be pleased to make you mind these plain things. I can truly say this, I have not spoken one word that I remember, which I would not have said to you if I had been a dying, and being to go to God as soon as gone out of the pulpit, and the God of peace be with you. Only mind that one thing, " when God doth not find a tongue to speak, do not you find an ear to hear, and a heart to believe."

MR. MEDE'S FAREWELL SERMON.

1 Cor. i. 3.

Grace be unto you, and peace from God the Father, and from our Lord Jesus Christ.

YOU will wonder, possibly, that I should pitch on the apostle's salutation for my valediction, and make that the conclusion of my preaching, which he made the beginning of his writing, and therefore I have made a double plea for it. I find that this was a form of blessing peculiar to this apostle, both in the beginning and end of this epistle; for as there is scarcely one epistle but begins with it, so many end with it likewise: as in Eph. vi. 24. " The grace of our Lord Jesus Christ be with your spirit." So in 2 Thes. iii. 18. " The grace of our Lord Jesus Christ be with you all." So that I find the apostle to use it frequently at the beginning and end of his writing. I thought as I made it the matter of my prayer for you in the beginning, so I might make it my farewell to you in the ending, and therefore " grace be unto you, and peace from God our Father, and from our Lord Jesus Christ."

Besides this, as Jacob said to his Benjamin concerning his venison, when his father asked him, how he found it so quickly? He answered, because the Lord thy God brought it to me: the same I may say of this scripture, for considering of what subject I should speak in my last labours here among you, the scripture came to my thoughts, and opening the book came immediately to my sight; and therefore I may say God brought it to me; which I no sooner looked upon, but methinks I saw the apostle on mount Gerizzim, and his mouth filled with blessings; for what greater blessings can a man wish, than that which comprehends all blessings, and that is grace and peace. Being therefore now to part, I thought to go to the top of the mount, and leave with you grace and peace from God our Father, and from our Lord Jesus Christ. In which words there are two generals.

1. A double blessing desired. 2. A double spring discovered.

1. A double blessing desired; and that is grace and peace. Grace is of all blessings the richest; peace is of all comforts the sweetest: both these the apostle begs for the Corinthians; and so do I for you. Beloved, " grace be unto you, and peace from God our Father, and from our Lord Jesus Christ."

2. Here is a double fountain discovered; and that is

the Father and the Son, God and Christ. The Father is called the God of Grace: the Son is called the Prince of Peace. Not that grace is from the Father without peace, nor peace from the Son without grace; but both grace and peace are from God the Father, through the Lord Jesus Christ.

The order of the words is worth nothing, "Grace be to you, and peace." First grace, then peace; for there can be no peace without grace, nor grace, but there will be peace. But there can be no true peace but from God; not from God, but as he is a Father; not from God as a Father, but as our Father; and he cannot be said to be our Father, but through our Lord Jesus Christ: and, therefore, he said, "Grace be unto you, and peace from God our Father, through our Lord Jesus Christ." Both are manifested as a golden chain linked together: not grace without peace, nor peace without grace; but both enjoined together, to fill the believers' souls with grace and peace. Now from the order of the words, we might raise several observations.

1. That peace is the fruit of grace.
2. That grace and peace are both from God.
3. That love which is the spring of grace and peace, is from God as a Father.
4. That we share not in his love, but only as he is our Father. All is from propriety. First, our Father, then grace and peace from God our Father.
5. That God is our Father only through Christ.

But before we draw any thing from the text by way of observation, we will speak to the terms by way of explication. "Grace be unto you." What is here meant by grace? This is a sweet word, it perfumes the breath, it cherishes the conscience, it warms the heart, it ravishes the soul. As the spouse was ravished with rays of Christ's glory, so Christ revives the soul with one of his gracious rays discovered to the heart. Grace is the life of the soul; thou art dead till grace quickens thee: thou art lost till grace find thee; undone till grace saves thee. Grace is the manna of angels, the spiritual bread which those that are wholly in being are nourished with, and subsist by. Angels live on grace, and stand by grace. Man that shares in the grace of God, is made fellow commoner with angels: eats angel's food, and shares in angel's blessings. Grace is the substance of the Scripture, the end of the law, the fulness of the gospel. Gregory calls it the heart and soul of God. I am sure grace is the heart and soul of the word: it is a little word, but it comprehends all good. Here is more than Homer's Iliad in a nut-shell; it is the epitome of all the good in heaven and earth. Name any word that signifies good in the soul here, or hereafter, but it is found in the index, in this little word grace. Grace comprehends God's love to us, and our love to God; and as God's love to us is the sum of all mercy, so our love to God is the sum of all duty. Grace is the new birth of the soul, whereby it takes up another nature, a new nature, a spiritual Godlike nature. As Christ was born, and thereby took on him the nature of man, and was made flesh, so man is born by grace, and thereby takes upon him the nature of God, and is made spirit: and here you have at once, the great mystery of grace in the lowest debasement of a Saviour, and the highest advancement of a sinner; for the Lord Christ could not be more debased, than to be born. It was nothing to so great an abasement for Christ to die, as for him to be born, for being once made man. It is no wonder for to die; but being the great God, it is a wonder that ever he should be made man. Lo, here is the debasement of Christ; yet if he had been born to a crown, to honour, it had been something, but he was born to shame, to sorrow, and death. But man by grace is born to a crown, to a kingdom; he hath a title to all the glory and blessedness of heaven, from the first moment of his new birth. So it is in the text, " Grace be unto you and peace."

Peace, in Scripture, is a very comprehensive term; it

carries in it, all happiness. It was the common greeting of the Jews, "Peace be unto you." Thus David by his proxy, salutes Nabal, "peace be to thee, and thy house." And the apostle here alludes to this form of salutation, that he might mix New Testament mercy, to Old Testament manners; he first styles grace, before peace, as Jacob did with his venison, he made it a savory meat, such as Isaac loved. Peace is the glory of heaven, in the bosom of God, and brought into the world in the arms of angels. The first peace you read of in the gospel, was peace by the administration of angels, Luke ii. 3, 4. "And suddenly there was with the angels a multitude of the heavenly host, praising God, and saying, glory to God in the highest, and on earth peace, good will towards men." And when our Lord Christ first sent out his disciples, this was the doctrine that he bid them preach, Mat. x. 12, 13. "When you come into a house, salute it, and if it be worthy, let grace and peace come upon it." Mark here by the way, our Lord Jesus Christ is no enemy to good manners, he would not have christians to be clowns, which is the use of some among us, who would have their religion quarrel with good manners; no, but "In whatsoever city or town you enter, salute it, and let grace, peace come upon it: that is, wish peace to them, saying, "the peace of God be upon this place, upon the head and hearts of all in it." So that peace is both a gospel-salutation when ministers and people meet, and it is a gospel-valediction, when the ministers and the people part. So did the apostle, and so do I now, grace be with you, and peace.

I observe in Mat. x. 13, 14. our Lord bids his disciples when they enter into a house, "If the house be worthy, to let their peace come upon it, but if they be not worthy, let grace, peace return unto you." Instead of leaving peace with them, to shake off the dust of their feet against them: that is, to show that God will shake them off as dust, and tread them under feet as fuel. My brethren, your diligent attendance on the word at this place hath comfortably prevented that part of my charge, to shake off the dust of my feet; for, how beautiful have the feet of a poor worm been unto you, being shod with the preparation of the gospel of Christ? And therefore seeing our Lord Jesus Christ said, If they be worthy of their peace, abide with them; on this account, I wish to you, grace and peace from God our Father, and from our Lord Jesus Christ. But what is that peace? It is the beauty of union, the harmony of the creation, the pleasure of life, the feast of a good conscience; it is that which makes life sweet, and death easy. Peace sweetens all our possessions, and all our afflictions. Without this the fulness of the world is a burden. With this, poverty and emptiness is a pleasant companion. Without this, our bread is gravelled with sourness, and our water mingled with bitterness. With this, green herbs become a feast, and our water is turned into wine. Peace is the most beautiful creature in the world, and therefore it is beloved of all, courted of all. Many seek her, but few there be that enjoy her; they do not go the right way to find her; for, "in the ways of righteousness is peace." Peace is the seminary of all blessings temporal, as grace is of all blessings spiritual. In grace you have implied all holiness, in peace all happiness; in grace all inward, in peace all outward blessings. Grace and peace are the Alpha and Omega of all blessings, as God is of all beings. No blessing comes before grace, and no blessing lasts longer. Then see in this phrase of speech, the apostle wishes upon them, as I do upon you all, the blessings both of time and eternity, and yet he wished not more to them, than God promised to give them, 1 Tim. iv. 8. "For godliness hath the promise of this life, and that which is to come; grace be unto you, and peace," &c. Not one without the other. Though a man may have peace without grace, as in a time of desertion or temptation; and a man may have peace without grace as in a secure and unregenerate condition. Grace without peace is often found in a troubled conscience, and peace without grace is often found in a seared conscience. As grace without peace is very uncomfortable, so peace without grace s very unprofitable; like Rachel, beautiful, but barren: therefore the apostle desires ye should have both grace and peace. We say the sun and salt are the most useful creatures in the world; the one for shining, the other for seasoning. (My brethren) grace and peace are the christian's sun and salt. Grace is the light of their souls, and peace is the savour of their comforts. Grace shines through all their faculties, and peace seasons all their mercies. The blessings of God are become as twins, as Christ said of the spouse, Cant. iv. 2. "She is like a flock of sheep that are even shorn, which come up from the washing, whereof every one bears twins, and none is barren among them." Grace and peace here are knit together by the spirit of God in a sacred knot not to be untied. As Castor and Pollux, when seen together, portend happiness to the mariner: so when grace and peace are found in a soul together, they portend the highest security and blessing to the believer. They are said in scripture to be bound together. Where God gives the one, he never denies the other. If he gives you the upper spring of grace, he will give you the nether spring of peace, for they go both together. If he gives you the dew of heaven, you need not question the fatness of the earth. If his right hand be full of mercy, his left hand shall not be empty. Therefore grace and peace be with you from God the Father, and from our Lord Jesus Christ.

Grace hath a double sense, either for the grace of God to us, that justifies us, or the grace of God in us that sanctifies us. Now there is a different flowing from each of these, but still it is grace and peace.

First, Justifying grace, hath a peace attending that. Rom. v. 1. "Being justified by faith, we have peace with God." So far as we have confidence in justifying grace, there remains no conscience of condemning sin. As there can be no bitterer war than between conscience and the ear, so there can be no sweeter peace, than when mercy and peace meet together, and when conscience and peace kiss each other. The former is the taste of heaven, the latter is the perambulation of heaven; both which the believer shares in upon his justification by faith. If Christ had peace, who was made our sin, needs must the believer have peace, who is made the righteousness of God in him.

Secondly, Sanctifying grace hath a peace attending it, and this peace differs from the former, as the root from the fruit. The peace of justification is a radical peace, the root of peace; but the peace of sanctification is the bud, the blossom of the tree: the former flows from the blood of Christ sprinkled on the conscience, the latter from the conformity that is between the word and the will, between the commands and the conscience. "As many as walk according to this rule, grace be unto them and peace," Gal. vi. 16. So that peace is the fruit of sanctifying grace. Now as the blood of the paschal-lamb, (which was a token of peace) was not to be struck on the posts of the Egyptians, but upon the posts of the Israelites; so neither is the blood of sprinkling, which brings perfect peace, to be struck on the posts of the carnal sinner, but on the posts of the true believer, an Israelite indeed, in whom there is no guile; no grace, no peace, that is God's law. How can a sinner have peace in a state of sin, when God and conscience, when word and conscience, when law and conscience, and all the attributes of God are against a sinner? No peace, saith my God to the wicked. Pray mark that chapter, it begins with the peace, and ends in no peace. In ver. 2. it is said, He shall enter into peace, that is, the righteous; in the last verse, There is no peace to the wicked. It is the state of grace that is the only state of peace. And thus I pass from the double grace desired, grace and peace; to the double fountain discovered, God our Father, and our Lord Jesus Christ.

But here is a question to be answered, if grace and peace be from God the Father, then how is it said to be from Christ? and if from Christ, how then from God the Father?

Answ. It is a known rule, that the transial external works of God are attributed to all the three persons in the Trinity; the same works that are attributed to the Father, are also attributed to the Son; and the same works are attributed to the Son, the same also to the Father: so grace and peace are here ascribed both to God the Father, and our Lord Jesus Christ; that is, they are both from mercy, and from merit. From mercy on God's part to us, from merit on Christ's part for us. They are from God the Father, because he wills them to us, from God the Son, because he works them in us. They are from God to Christ, from Christ to us. They are from God the Father originally, and from Christ derivatively, and to us actually. God the Father is the fountain of all grace and peace. Christ as mediator is the conduit of all grace and peace. Man in union to Christ is the cistern into which these streams of grace and peace run. God wills grace and peace to us, and Christ works them in us. God gives grace and peace to be applied to the creature, this is from the love of the Father, but the application of this peace to the soul, is from the merit of Christ the Redeemer. Thus you see there is a double spring of this double blessing. Time will not serve me further: the only observation, is,

That all the grace and peace which believers share in, is derived from God the Father through our Lord Jesus Christ. These three things opened will clear this; 1. That grace and peace are the believer's privilege. 2. That the fountain of this grace and peace is from God the Father. 3. That it is not given out from God the Father but through Christ.

First, That grace and peace are the saint's privilege: if grace is, then peace is. But grace is the privilege of every believer, and what whether you look upon it as taken from the love and favour of God to us; this is the believer's privilege. God can as well forget Christ at his right hand, as cease his love and favour to the soul of a believer. The believer's title to all their blessings arises out of his never failing love of God; or if you ask grace for the fruit of God's love to the soul, still it falls to the believer's privilege, vocation, justification, adoption, pardon of sin, purging from sin, strength against sin, holiness, faith, love, obedience, perseverance; all these are the privileges of every believer; nay, a man cannot be a believer without any one of them, they are as essential to the being of a christian as reason to the being of a man.

Secondly, As grace so peace is the believer's privilege. There is peace external, peace supernal, peace internal, and peace eternal. There is peace external, that is peace with men : there is peace supernal, that is peace with God : there is peace internal, that is peace with conscience : all these three are to be had here upon earth; and then there is peace eternal, and that is only to be had in heaven. The apostle here doth not exclude the former, but chiefly intends the latter. Peace with man is a good thing to be desired; but peace with God and conscience is much more to be desired. Peace with God is the spring of all things both within and without, both below and above, both in time and eternity : so saith Job, "If he gives peace, who then can make trouble?" Now this peace is the saints' privilege. It is a legacy left to every believer, by the last will and testament of a dying Redeemer. Will you see a copy of his will, then look in Job xiv. 27. " Peace I leave with you, my peace I give unto you, not as the world giveth, give I unto you." There is, it seems, a peace in the world's power to give, and there is a peace of Christ's bestowing. Now Christ would have us here not to mistake the world's peace for his, for the difference is very great; for, first, the world's peace is a false peace, it is counterfeit coin, it hath not the current stamp of heaven on it; but the peace that Christ gives to a believer, is true peace, and perfect peace : " Thou wilt keep him in perfect peace whose mind is stayed on thee."

Secondly, The world's peace is an outward peace, it is but skin deep, it wets the mouth, cannot wash the heart. Prov. xiv. 13. " In laughter the heart is sorrowful, and the end of that mirth is heaviness." The world's peace is but the shell of peace; their conscience lowers, when their countenance laughs: but the peace that Christ gives, is an inward and spiritual peace, Psal. iv. 7. "Thou hast put gladness in my heart, more than in the time that their corn and their wine increased. Thou hast put gladness in my heart." Peace is that gladness, or peace smooths the brow, but this fills the breast, as the sinner hath trouble within, in the midst of all his peace without. "In the world you shall have a trouble, but in me you shall have peace."

Thirdly, The world's peace has only a nearer spring arising out of the creature, out of worldly comforts; therefore it must needs be unclean; for an unclean fountain cannot bring forth clean water. But the peace of christians has an upper spring; it flows from the manifestation of the love of God in Christ : it is from the sprinkling of Christ's blood on the conscience, it flows upon the workings of Christ's spirit upon the soul, which is first a counsellor, then a comforter. Oh how pure must this peace be in a believer's soul, that flows from so pure a spring.

Fourthly, The world's peace is a peace given to sinners, it is a peace in sin, and it is a peace with sin, as the prophet Isaiah tells us, "It is a covenant with hell, and an agreement with death" (God delivers us from that peace.) Again, Christ's peace is given to none but believers; it is their privilege only, a stranger doth not intermeddle with his joy, Prov. xiv. 10. "The heart knoweth his own bitterness, but a stranger doth not intermeddle with his joy."

Fifthly, The world's peace is a fading, dying, transitory thing, it withers in the sand. "The triumphing of the wicked is short, and the joy of the hypocrite is but for a moment," Job xx. 5. Solomon doth elegantly liken it, to crackling of thorns under a pot, which is but a blaze and is gone, Eccl. vii. 6. so is the sinner's peace, it is for a spurt and is soon gone; but the peace that Christ gives to believers, is a durable and abiding peace.

Your joy no man shall take from you; it appears in life, in death, and after death. First it is our peace in life, grace brings forth present peace. It is said of the primitive Christians, "They walked in the fear of the Lord, and in the comforts of the Holy Ghost," Acts ix. 41. It is a remarkable expression, Psal. xix. 11. "In keeping thy commands there is great reward." He does not say for keeping them, which respects the end of the work, but in keeping them, which looks at the work itself. My brethren, every duty done in sincerity, reflects a peace in conscience, as every flower carries its own sweetness. It is possible, I grant, a believer may not always find and feel this peace; few do, some seldom find it, few find it always: the remains of corruption bringing forth to interrupt, or temptations to hinder, and God's desertion may darken and hide it, and a believer may seem to be totally lost. Yet in this condition, which is the worst a child of God can be in, he hath a double peace: first, a peace in the promises, in this very condition, and what you have in bonds and bills you account as good as money in your pockets; secondly, he hath it in the seed, "Light is sown for the righteous, and gladness for the upright in heart," Psal. xcvii. 11. Grace is the seed of peace, which Christ hath sown in the furrows of the soul, and therefore peace shall spring out of the furrows of the soul. Indeed this seed springs up sooner in some than in others, yet every saint shall have a reaping time sooner or later, Psal. cxxvi. 6. "He that goeth forth and weepeth, bearing precious seed, shall doubtless come again with rejoicing, bringing his sheaves with him. "If he stays long for the fruit, he shall have a greater crop at last; if he reaps not now, he shall be sure to reap hereafter," Psal. xxxvii. "Mark the perfect man, and behold the upright, for the end of that man is peace." Secondly, by this peace which is the peace of a child of God, it is a peace at death. Grace will minister to us then, and that ministration shall be peace. The sinner's peace leaves him when he comes to the grave: though in life it fills him, yet in death it leaves him. A believer hath a two-fold spring of peace, the first is from above him, the other from within him. That spring that runs with peace above him, is from the blood of Christ sprinkled on his conscience: the other that is from within him, is from the sincerity of his heart in the ways of obedience. My brethren, when we lie on our death-beds, and can reflect on our sincerity in all God's ways, this will be peace at last. So it was in Hezekiah, Isai. xxxviii. 3. "Remember now, O Lord, I beseech thee, how I have walked before thee in truth, and with a perfect heart, and have done that which was good in thy sight." There is nothing makes a death-bed so hard and so uneasy, as a life spent in the service of sin and lust; and nothing makes a death-bed so pleasant as a life spent in the service of Christ. Grace will bring forth peace, if not in this life: yet, thirdly, it will be sure after death. If time brings not this fruit to ripeness, yet eternity shall. Grace in time, will be glory in eternity. Holiness now will be happiness then. Whatever it is a man sows in this world, that he reaps in the next world. "Be not deceived, God is not mocked, for whatsoever a man soweth, that shall he also reap. He that soweth to the flesh shall of the flesh reap corruption; but he that soweth to the spirit, shall of the spirit reap life everlasting." Gal. vi. 7, 8. When sin shall end in sorrow and misery, grace shall end in peace, in joy, in glory. "Well done, thou good and faithful servant, enter into the joy of thy master." Mat. xxv. 21. Whoever shares in the grace of Christ in this world, shall be sure to share with the joy of Christ in the next world, and that joy is joy unspeakable, and full of glory. I will wind up all in a three-fold application, by way of exhortation, to three sorts of persons. 1. To such as have this grace and peace. 2. To such as have this grace and no peace. 3. To such as have neither grace nor peace.

First, To such as have both grace and peace. I will speak to them in two or three things. First, Admire thankfully the Father and the Son, the Father's grace, and the Son's love, for both had a hand in this; therefore bless both the Father for willing it to us, and the Son for working it in us. Grace and peace are the fruits of God's eternal election, for this blessing the Father gives, but the application of it to us is the fruits of Christ's redemption and intercession. How can you think of hell and damnation, and see yourself freed from it? And how can you think of the dreadful fury and vengeance of God, yourself not under it? How can you look on your state changed, your heart renewed, grace ratified and reconciled, and your conscience quieted? How can you think of these things, but must admire the love of the Father in giving this to you, and the love of the Son in purchasing this for you? All grace and mercy that is given to us, is by Christ purchased for us. Grace and peace are fruits of the redeeming blood of Christ purchased.

Secondly, Do not envy the conditions and possessions of the men of the world. They have riches and honours, profits and pleasures, but they neither have grace nor peace, therefore do not envy their happiness. There is a story of a Roman that was condemned by a court-martial to die for breaking his rank to steal a bunch of grapes; and as he was going to his execution, his fellow soldiers laughed at him, and others envied at him that he should have grapes and they none: "Now (saith he) do not envy me for my bunch of grapes, for you would be loth to have them at the rate I must pay for them." My brethren, you that are the children of grace and peace, do not envy at men of the world, at their riches and their comforts, their pleasures; for I am sure you would be loth to have them at the price they pay for them; for the end of these things is death.

Thirdly, Do not complain of the worst condition that the providence of God shall cast you into: in this it may be you shall suffer hard things; but remember, so long as thy soul is secure, never complain of hard things. My brethren, as God your Father brought you into a state of grace and peace, and thereby secured his love to your souls in Christ, can you complain of hard things? So let the joy of the Lord be your strength, "Rejoice in the Lord always, and again I say, rejoice," Phil. iv. 4.

The second use is, to such as have neither grace nor peace. May not I say, I speak to many such? I would I might not. Are there not many that are without grace, and therefore must needs be without peace? They may have the world's peace, but they have none of this peace. Let me beg of you to get out of this graceless state. Oh that you would believe the words of a dying man, for so I am to you, and such words use to be remembered. Oh remember this as a testimony I leave with you, that love of sin, and lack of grace, will ruin and destroy every soul at last. But you will say, how shall I get a share in this grace and peace?

I answer, first, break off all your false peace. We can never have true peace with God, when we content ourselves with false peace. You will never seek that peace which Christ hath purchased for you, while you content yourselves with that false peace which the old man hath wrought in you. Oh therefore break off all false peace, which is not the fruit of grace.

Secondly, Labour to see and be convinced of the miserable, and of the naked condition your souls be in, for want of the righteousness of Christ for a covering. Without this, soul, thou art miserable, wretched, poor and naked. Be convinced also what a miserable thing it is to have God our enemy. God is the sinner's enemy. "It is a fearful thing to fall into the hands of the living God." Oh be convinced of thy nakedness without Christ's righteousness, and thy emptiness without his fulness.

Thirdly, Labour to go out of yourselves to Christ for grace and peace. Surely in the Lord, shall one say, I have righteousness and strength; aye, there it is to be found. Labour for a thirsty frame of soul, for the promises run far to such, "That he will fill the hungry with good things." Go to Christ, soul, beg, pray, never leave God till he hath given thee an interest in Christ, "for none can come to me, except the Father draw him." There is no pardon for the least sin out of Christ, but there is pardon for the greatest sin in Christ. One sin can damn the soul out of Christ, but no sin can hurt the soul in Christ. Oh go to Christ, soul; never give rest to thy eyes, nor slumber to thy lids, till thou hast made peace with God in the blood of Christ. One sting of the fiery serpent was mortal, without looking upon the brazen serpent: so one sin will damn a soul out of Christ, but no sin can damn a soul in Christ.

Fourthly, To such as have grace, but no sense of peace, this is the counsel I would leave with all such. "Be much in the exercise of grace: frame much, believe much, use grace much, for the exercise and improving of grace will produce peace." There are ten duties which are to be the sphere of grace in activity, and in performing of them we shall have peace.

First, Make religion your business, the main design of your lives. Be Christians to purpose, be not only Christians by the by, but " let your conversation be as becometh the gospel of Christ," Phil. i. 27.

Secondly, Put forth renewed acts of faith on Christ every day, and remember it is as much your duty to believe in Christ to-day, as if you had never believed before. O live by faith every day, and this will bring peace to you.

Thirdly, Maintain a constant communion with God daily. This communion with God is man's chief good. The happiness of a child is in communion with his Father, and the happiness of a wife is in communion with her husband, and this is the happiness of a believer's soul, communion with God the Father, through Christ our head and husband. The seed of peace, it is true, is sown in the soul in union, but then it takes root downward, and brings forth fruit upward. Spiritual peace will never be obtained if communion with God be not maintained: that gives comfort in the midst of all sorrows, and satisfies all doubts, and recompences all wants. Lo, this is the fruit of communion with God.

Fourthly, Be good at all times, but of all best in bad times. Many Christians lose their peace by remitting of their grace, and let loose the reins of religion, to avoid the censures of a crooked generation. A Christian's zeal should be like winter fire, that burns the hottest when the air is coolest; or, like the lily, that looketh beautiful though among thorns; so should a child of God though among sinners.

Fifthly, "In all conditions choose suffering rather than sinning." If ever you would have peace, choose suffering rather than sinning. He that values peace with God, or peace with conscience, he must make this his choice. Daniel rather chose to be cast to lions than to lose the peace of his conscience. The three children chose rather to burn in the furnace than bow to the image. One said, "He would rather go to hell free from sin, than to live in heaven with guilt on his conscience." My brethren, let me a little enlarge, because sufferings may overtake us; for persecution is the genius of the gospel, therefore let me leave four short rules with you concerning sufferings.

See that your cause be good, your call be clear, your spirit meek, and your end right. Sufferings cannot bring our peace without either of them, but with them all our sufferings shall be peace.

First, Let your cause be good. It is not the blood, but the cause that makes a martyr. It is not for every cause a Christian should engage to suffer. Every cause will no more bear suffering than every little stream will bear a ship: nor will Christ let go sweetness to every suffering. 1 Pet. iv. 15. "Let none of you suffer as a murderer, or as a thief, or as an evil-doer, or as a busy-body in other men's matters." To suffer thus, is neither Christian-like nor comfortable. Some suffer rather as malefactors than as Christ's martyrs.

Secondly, Let your call be clear. It is not amiss to have a good cause without a call. Some may suffer for the cause of God, and yet sin in suffering for want of a call. Christ calls not all to suffer; to some it is given, to others it is not. If thy call be clear, thy peace will be sweet, though thy sufferings be never so great. But you will say, how shall I know when I am called to suffer?

Answ. 1. When truth suffers by our silence then are we called to suffer.

2. When our lives will be the denial of Christ, then are we called to deny our lives for Christ.

3. When sin and suffering surrounds us that we cannot get out, but we must either run through sin or suffering, then I may safely conclude, that Christ calleth me to suffer, and in this cause we may expect the peace and sweetness of his presence.

Thirdly, The third direction for suffering is this—our spirit must be meek: so was Christ, he went as a lamb to the slaughter.

It is possible a man may be right in his cause, and yet sinful in his carriage; and if so, no wonder if Christ be not sweet to us. To be fierce and raging, and reviling in suffering, it is not becoming humanity, and therefore much less like Christianity. A Christian should be like Christ, Acts v. 41. " And they departed from the presence of the council, rejoicing that they were counted worthy to suffer shame for his name." It becomes those that are found in the spirit, to give blessing for cursing. The more of Christ's spirit is in our sufferings, the more comfort and joy we shall receive from our sufferings.

Fourthly, See that your end in suffering be right. If it be self, or singularity, or schism, then Christ cannot be sweet to thee. Some have died that their ends may live. Socrates died in the defence of the truth, and to prove that there is but one God; but whether he died for honour, applause, or for God's sake, I think it is not hard to determine. But let thy cause be good, thy call clear, thy spirit meek, and thy end right, and then you shall have peace in all your sufferings: that is the fifth thing. Choose sufferings rather than sinning.

Sixthly, If you would have peace, be much in studying the scriptures. For as God is the God of Peace, and Christ the Prince of Peace, so the gospel is the gospel of peace, which God hath given to thee to lead thee in the ways of peace. " Great peace have they that love thy laws."

Seventhly, Take heed of apostacy, either in doctrine or principles. Though a believer is freed from apostacy in the state of grace, yet he is not freed from apostacy in the degrees of grace. He may fall sinfully, though he cannot fall finally. Demas fell by one, St. Peter by the other. Pray with David. Psal. xvii. 5. " Hold up my goings in thy paths, that," &c.

Eighthly, Make the word of God your rule in all things. Be sure you have a scripture warrant for all your practices; but especially keep close to scripture in matters of God's worship.

There are endless discourses about the mode of God's worship. I have no disputing time. It is good in difficult cases, always to take the surest side. For instance, if I follow the traditions of man for the worship of God, I may; but if I keep close to the directions of God in the scripture, I am sure I cannot sin; for this is the sure word of prophecy, to which you do well to take heed, therefore, in such a doubtful case, God's will is, that we take the surest side. Go to the law and to the testimony: labour to be fruitful and grounded Christians.

Ninthly, Keep up the power of godliness; do not let religion down into a lifeless formality. " The righteous shall flourish like a palm-tree: he shall grow like a cedar in Lebanon. Those that be planted in the house of the Lord, shall flourish in the courts of our God." Psal. xcii. 12, 13. My brethren, it is as much a duty in them that have grace, to improve it, as for them that have no grace to get it. If you sit under the daily means, the daily waterings of God, and do not grow, do you think this will be peace in the latter end ? Surely no, my brethren ; your fruitfulness under the gospel, is of very great concernment. It is unfruitfulness that makes God lay his vineyard waste. It is fruitfulness that procures the forwarding of your account in the day of grace.

Tenthly, Observe that excellent rule of the apostle, Phil. iv. 8. " Finally, brethren, whatsoever things are true, whatsoever things are honest, whatsoever things are just, whatsoever things are pure, whatsoever things are lovely, whatsoever things are of good report, if there be any virtue, and if there be any praise, think on these things." And now, my brethren, I commend you to God, and to the word of God, that is infinitely able to make you wise to salvation, with this benediction, which I shall make my valediction, " Grace be unto you, and peace from God our Father, and from our Lord Jesus Christ."

MR. NEWCOMEN'S FAREWELL SERMON.

Preached at Dedham in Essex, August 20, 1662.

REV. iii. 3.

Remember therefore how thou hast received and heard, and hold fast, and repent.

I BEGAN this scripture the last Lord's day in this congregation. I told you then, there were three doctrines obvious in the text ;—

Doctrine 1. That it is the duty of christians, to remember those truths that they have heard and received.

Doctrine 2. That it is the duty of christians to hold fast the truth that they have heard and received.

Doctrine 3. That continued repentance is the duty of christians, as well as initial repentance. Remember therefore how thou hast received, and heard, and hold fast and repent.

The first of these doctrines, I applied myself to, and applied to the people last Lord's day, and shall not now say any thing of it; but proceed to the next doctrine, that it is the duty of christians to hold fast the truths that they have heard and received. That which the apostle enjoins on Timothy, is, in proportion, the duty of all christians, 2 Tim. i. 13. "Hold fast the form of sound words, which thou hast heard of me in faith, and love, which is in Christ Jesus;" the whole entire body of divine truth. Hold it fast against all opposition whatsoever. Now if they that are themselves teachers of the truth to others, must hold fast the truth, according to the platform that hath been delivered to them; then much more is it the duty of private christians, who are supposed, not to have that latitude of parts and gifts that teachers have: and therefore you shall find, that Christ requires this not only of the pastors, but of the members of his church, Rev. ii. 24. speaking not only to the angels, but to the body of the church, " but to you, I say and to the rest in Thyatira, as many as have not this doctrine, and which have not known the depths of Satan as they speak, I will put upon you none other burden, but that which you have already; hold fast till I come. As if he should say, " this is all I require of you, my people: keep yourselves, and hold fast that which you have till I come." And so in Rev. iii. 11. "Behold, I come quickly; hold thou fast which thou hast, that no man take away thy crown." As if he should say, that divine truth, that thou hast heard and received, it is thy crown, thy excellency, therefore hold it fast. This duty of holding fast the truth, is urged in many other places of scripture, under other expressions; as that of continuing in the word of God. Christ says, if ye continue in my word, then are ye my disciples indeed. And continuing in the faith, Acts xiv. 22. Paul and Barnabas visiting the churches, exhorted them to continue in the faith. And so those terms of being rooted in the truth' of standing, of standing fast, and many others, they all enforce this duty. Now for the better handling of this point, I shall do these four things.

First, I will shew you, what christians are to hold fast.

Secondly, How they are to hold fast.

Thirdly, Why they are to hold fast what they heard and received.

Fourthly, I will apply it.

First, What christians are to hold fast. The doctrine says, " they are to hold fast the truths they have received." Now truths are of two sorts.

1. Some are natural and moral.

2. Some are supernatural and divine truths, called truths of God; because they come from God, and conform the mind and soul that receives them, to the image of God.

2. Now, though it is true, it is good for a man to be right in moral things, and to know, and cleave to that which is truth in morality; yet the truths that we are here called upon to hold fast, they are divine truths, supernatural truths, truths in religion, truths in the things of God.

Secondly, Again, religious and divine truths, truths of God: they are either such as are so in name, and in the estimation of some men, or else they are such truths as are truths of God, in the truth and reality of the thing. Now, when I say that christians are to hold fast the truths they have received, the meaning is not, that whatever any man, or company of men offer as truths, should be received, and held fast; for then we must hold fast many errors: but whatever men call truth, or offer as truth, we must examine it by the unerring rule of truth, that is, the word of God. In these things it is a clear canon which we have, 1 Thess. v. 21. " Prove all things, hold fast that which is good." Prove them, by the word of God, and if they hold truth by that then receive them, and hold them fast. Divine scripture-truths we are to hold fast.

Thirdly, Scripture-truths, truths that are grounded, and warranted in the word of God; they are either such as are immediately and expressly laid down in the scripture, or such as are mediately contained in scripture, and by deduction drawn hence. Now those truths are immediately and expressly laid down in scripture, we are without dispute to receive and hold : but those truths that are drawn thence, we may make use of our reason to examine them by the word ; and so far as we see them to be drawn from scripture, we are to receive them, and hold them fast,

Fourthly, divine truths from scripture are of two sorts: either the great and weighty things of the truth of God and of religion, which we call fundamental truths; or else they are those things that are of less weight than religion, and yet truths of God. Now we are not only to hold fast those truths of God, that are the fundamental truths ; as that there is a God, and but one God ; and that there is a Trinity of persons in unity of essence, Father, Son, and Holy-Ghost ; and that there is but one Mediator between God and man, the man Christ Jesus, and that he is both God and man in one person, and that he hath given full satisfaction to divine justice, for all that by faith close with him, and the like.

These are the great points in religion ; these we must be sure to hold fast. And not only these, but even the lesser ; those truths of religion that, comparatively, are far less than these, we must hold them fast. You know what our Saviour says of the commands : there are some that are the first and great commandments, and there are others that are the lesser : but, whosoever shall break one of the least of God's commandments, and shall teach men so, the same shall be least in the kingdom of God. So, whosoever shall renounce the least truth, God will be even with him for it. For those truths of God which are little and small comparatively, they may be of great weight and consequence in their sphere. Luther said, " let heaven run together as a scrowl rather than one filing of truth should be parted with." Surely those servants of God, the martyrs, were not so prodigal of their lives, but they knew what they did when they suffered for such truths, as men now call trifles, and not worth standing for ; the least truths of God must be held fast.

Thus you see what we must hold fast, divine truths, scripture truths, whether greater or lesser. We must hold fast what we have received. I should, but that I foresee the time will prevent me, answer an objection : is there nothing to hold fast but truth ? Doth not the apostle bid the Thessalonians, in the second of the Thessalonians, the second chapter, and the fifteenth verse, "hold the traditions which ye have been taught, whether by word or our epistle." The papists make much of this place for their unwritten traditions. In a word: know this, though there were some doctrines of faith, and matters of practice, which when Paul wrote this epistle, were not expressly to be found in writing, that had been preached by the Apostle ; yet this will not in the least infer, that now, when the canon of the scripture is completed, there should be such unwritten traditions, to which we are to give up our faith.

I go on to the second thing, and that is, to shew, how we must hold fast the truths of God, which we have heard and received.

First, in your judgments, being fully resolved and settled in your judgments concerning them, not wavering about them, nor suffering ourselves by any means and ways, to be removed from our stedfastness in them. Says the Apostle, 2 Pet. iii. 17. " Seeing you know these things, beware, lest you also, being led away with the error of the wicked, fall from your own stedfastness." Take heed you be not removed in your judgments ; hold fast what you have received, and suffer not every wind to blow you off from them.

Secondly, We must hold fast the truths we have heard and received in our wills and affections, in our love to the truth. We must receive the truth in the love of it, or else we should never keep the truth. Love is the strong holdfast in the word; no man will part with that which he loves. What makes the covetous man so unwilling to part with his money, but because he loves it? What makes the lustful sinner so unwilling to part with his lust, he will part with heaven, rather than his lust? Why, it is because he doth so love it. If men did love the truth, they would hold it fast.

Thirdly, You must hold the truth in the profession of it. Heb. x. 23. " Let us hold fast the profession of the truth or of the faith, without wavering." We must not only believe with the heart, but confess with the mouth, if we would be saved. When Peter denied his master with his mouth, and said, I know him not, I am persuaded, he denied him not in his heart. It is a dangerous thing in word, or outward profession, to renounce the truth or any part of it. " Hold fast the profession of the truth."

Fourthly, We must hold the truths of God fast in our life and conversation. This the apostle calls, " Walking in Christ;" and holding forth the word of life, in a blameless and harmless conversation, " We must hold fast the truths of God in our lives."

Fifthly, We must do all this constantly. Hold fast the truth in our judgment and affection, profession and conversation, constantly and at all times; as David, " I have inclined my heart to perform thy statutes always, even unto the end." We must not only in times of calmness and serenity, when we may have all the peace and applause of the world, hold fast the truth and profession of it; but in stormy times, when truth may burn a man's fingers if he hold it, yet even then we must hold it fast.

Sixthly, We must hold fast the truths we have received resolutely, against all oppositions whatsoever, whether of friends or foes. Paul would not bare an inch, no not to Peter his brother, his elder brother in Christ, and in the work of the gospel; he resisted him to the face, and gave no place to him, no, not for an hour.

Thus should we hold fast the truth that we have

heard and received in our judgment, in our wills and affections, in our profession, and in our lives and conversations, and thus hold them fast constantly, and resolutely against all opposition, on the right hand, and on the left, both of friends and foes; and that for these reasons, which is the first thing I have to do ; which is to shew you, why we should " hold fast the truth of God."

First, For the excellency of divine truth ; it is more precious than gold, better than rubies, and all that you can desire cannot be compared with truth. And it must needs be so, because it is the immediate issue of God himself, who is the fountain of truth, and the fountain of all perfection and glory. Natural men have said, truth is the daughter of time. Divines say, truth is the daughter of God. Divine truth is the child of God, the issue and birth of God. And whosoever therefore God hath pleased to deliver this truth unto, they must be tenderly careful that it be not deflowered and violated.

Secondly, It is our duty to hold fast the truth that we have received, because we have received it under the notion of those things that have a kind of constancy in them. I say, we have received the truth under the nature of those things that have a kind of constancy and perpetuity in them. The scripture speaks of the truths of God as an heritage, " thy testimonies have I spoken for mine heritage," saith David in the 119th Psalm. Though a man's personal estate may be alienated, yet that which is his heritage, this is unalienable in law; it is a wrong done to his posterity if he parts with that. Truth is the inheritance of the saints, therefore they are to hold it fast. Again, in scripture, the truth of God is called a thing committed to man's trust, 2 Tim. i. 14. " That good thing which was committed unto thee, keep by the Holy Ghost which dwelleth in us." That good thing! What was that! Why, the form of sound words, which in the verse before he had bidden him hold fast. This is but a reduplication of the same thing on him: the body of gospel-truths that was committed to thee, hold it fast; that good thing, a good thing: the author of it is good, and it makes us good; all that is contained in it is good matter, and it tends to a good end, the saving of our souls. This, saith he, hath been committed to thee, therefore keep it, that it may be re-delivered, and re-delivered entire and whole; and re-delivered to the same person that did commit it to us, else we cannot be faithful to our trust. The truth of God is committed to our trust; we must so keep it that we may re-deliver it, and re-deliver it entire and whole; and re-deliver it thus entire and whole to him that committed it to us, even to God. This is the duty of all christians thus to keep the word. There is a committing of the truth to all the church and saints of God; as Jude tells us in his epistle, verse the third, " That ye should contend earnestly for the faith, which was once delivered to the saints;" the faith, that is the doctrine of faith, the truth of the gospel, which was delivered to the saints. We have but one gospel, and it was delivered but once; God means no more to deliver his gospel, and the truth of it, therefore you had need strive hard to keep them, and hold them.

Thirdly, We should hold fast the truth that we have received; because, if we do not hold it fast, we do wrong God, and if we wrong ourselves, and we wrong the truth, and we wrong our posterity.

1. It is our duty, " To hold fast the truths we have received;" because, if we do not, we wrong God; for truths are more God's, than ours. They are ours as to the use of them; but they are his, as he is the original and author of them. Truths are God's jewels; there is never a truth of religion, but God owns it as his; and for us to barter away any of these truths of God, it is sacrilege, it is a robbing of God, it is a wrong to God. This is that God complains of, by the prophet, in the second of Jeremiah, the eleventh and twelfth verses. " Hath a nation changed their gods, which are yet no gods? but my people have changed their glory, for that which doth not profit. Be astonished, O ye heavens, at this, and be

horribly afraid, be ye very desolate, saith the Lord." The people, indeed, speak of a total forsaking of God, and all his truths; but there is, in the forsaking of every truth, a proportion of wrong to God.

2. It is a wrong done to the truths of God, when men having received the truth, and embracing it, hold it not fast, but cast it off, this is a wrong to the truths of God. We say, it is less reproach to a man when he comes to my house, to shut the door against him, and not receive him in at all, than when he hath been in a while with me, I turn him out: all the world now think I find cause to be weary of him. They who have shut their hearts against the truth, and never gave any entertainment to it, they are less injurious to it, than they that have received it, and professed it, and yet turn from it. These tell the world, that the truths of God are not so sweet, and worthy of their entertainment, as they supposed them to be.

3. This is an injury and wrong to ourselves; this is a wrong to our credit and reputation. Now, though we may not make credit our end in religion, yet we may make use of our credit or reproach, as an argument to hold fast the truth; John viii. 31. " Then Jesus said to those Jews which believed on him: If ye continue in my word, then are ye my disciples." Indeed, here Christ doth seem to distinguish his disciples; he hath some that are so in name, that are not so in deed, and he hath some that are so in deed and in truth; and of these he gives a character here, " If ye continue in my word." You now profess to believe my word; but if you hold fast, and continue in my word, then you are my disciples indeed. But if you continue not in my word, you have the name of disciples only, and that will not save you. You can never be saved, unless you be indeed the disciples of Christ; and you can never approve yourselves to be the disciples of Christ indeed, if ye continue not in the truth. 1 John ii. 24. " Let that therefore abide in you, which you have received and heard from the beginning." If that which ye have

heard from the beginning, shall remain in you, ye shall continue in the Son, and in the Father. Hold fast the truth of God which you have received, then shall you continue in the Son. If the truth of God, which you have received and believed, remain in you, and be held fast by you, ye shall continue in the love of the Father and Son, but not else. According to what he expresseth again, " Whosoever transgresseth, and abideth not in the doctrine of Christ, hath not God, therefore he cannot be saved. He that abideth in the doctrine, hath the Father and the Son." Therefore, as you would be saved, hold fast the truths you have received.

Now here (but I have not time to speak to it) is a case of conscience. Whether every error doth cut a man off from God? I answer, No, God forbid. But this we cannot speak to now.

Fourthly, They that hold not fast the truth of God, are injurious to their posterity. Our forefathers holding fast the truth of God in the day of their trial, and sealing it with their blood, was the means of transmitting the purity of the gospel to us their posterity; and if we, in our generation, hold not fast the truth of God, but carry it loose in our consciences and judgments, and we let it fall out of our hands and hearts, we forfeit the truths of God, not only from ourselves, but also from our posterity. Thus you see, we shall wrong the God of truth, and the truth of God; we shall wrong ourselves and our posterity, if we hold not fast the truth we have received. Thus we have the reasons of the doctrine.

APPLICATION.

For application: here first, I might bewail the general want of the care of the performance of this duty, which hath appeared many years in this land.

We have had little care of holding fast the truths we have received, for holding fast the truth of our judgment. How many are there, whose judgments have been perverted with many errors?

This is that which the apostle calls "a turning aside to another gospel," in the first of the Galatians, and the sixth verse. And so for holding fast the truth in the love of it, how many are there that have failed in that, which Christ calls, "the forsaking of the first love," Revelations the second, and the fourth verse!

And we should hold fast the truth in the profession of it; and how many are there that have failed in that! This the apostle calls in the tenth of the Hebrews, "a drawing back unto perdition."

And for holding fast the truth in the practice of it, how many have failed in that, that have been professors, and now are grown loose and debauched! This the apostle Peter calls, "a turning aside from the holy commandments." All these things call for our lamentation.

EXHORTATION.

But the whole work that I will apply myself to, is, to exhort every one of you, to the care of this duty, "to hold fast the truths that you have heard and received." Hold them fast in your judgment, hold them fast in your will and affections, hold them fast in your lives and conversations, hold the truths you have received constantly, and hold them against all opposition on the right hand, and on the left, from friends and foes.

To press this upon you, I think I shall need to use no other motive, than what I have laid down before you in the doctrinal part; only this one thing more, and that is, take notice how urgent the spirit of God is in pressing this in scripture.

Now, saith Mr. Hildersham, "if in those days when the apostles were yet living, who taught the people of God with more power and demonstration of the spirit, than any of us do, or can." Yes, if then they had need of such exhortation to continue in the doctrine, and to abide in it, to stand fast, and hold fast the word and truth of God; how much more needful are these exhortations in our days!

If any say, no, there is not more cause; for then the magistrate was a mortal enemy to the gospel, and the professors of it; but we are, (thanks be to God!) under a christian magistrate, who doth not oppose, but countenance the gospel, and the professors of it. If any makes this objection, I will give you Mr. Hildersham's answer to it, which I find in a sermon of his, printed in the year one thousand six hundred and thirty-one; which is now one and thirty years ago. Saith he, "though through the great mercy of God, we in this land enjoy the gospel in great peace, and have it countenanced by authority; and though through the religious disposition of the king, we may have great hopes of the continuance of the true religion, and seem to be freed from all fear of the altering of it; yet (says he) there is need of this exhortation in these days," and that for these reasons.

Reason 1. First, because of the great danger we are in of being over-run, or over-spread with popery, and the fiery trail before we are aware: for, says he, " the great increase of papists that we daily hear of, and the great declining of many, who are ready to receive an error that shall be offered to them: these things give us a just cause to fear the danger of popery over-spreading us."

And brethren, if it were so in his time, so many years ago, what is it now?

Reason 2. Secondly, says he, "if so be there were no danger of popery, yet says he, there are so many errors newly sprung up, that do shew how needful this exhortation is."

Reason 3. Thirdly, says he, " there is such a general decay of the love of religion in all places, and amongst all sorts of people, and so much irreligiousness every where, that it is the general disease of the nation."

Therefore he concludes, that in these times of ours, though religion hath the magistrate, to countenance it, yet there is as much need of pressing this exhortation, as ever there was; namely, " To hold fast the truths that we have heard and received."

Now, if you ask what you shall do, that you may be able to hold fast the truths that you have received? I will give you some directions.

1. If you would hold fast the truth that you have heard and received, get into Christ, be rooted and established in him. Brethren, it is not all the learning in the world, and abilities that a man can have, that will enable him to hold out, and hold fast the truths that he hath received, if a time of trial come, unless Christ be his bottom and foundation, unless Christ be his strength. If a man stands upon his own legs, his own parts and abilities, to argue and dispute, and repel objections; alas! these things will fail in a day of trial. Prison, death and a stake, are such arguments, brethren, that all the learning, and parts of the world cannot answer, but only Christ and his spirit, and grace in the heart. Therefore, if you would hold fast the truth which you have received and heard, and not be beaten off from them in the day of trial, get into Christ, be rooted and established in him, then shalt thou stand, not else.

2. If you would hold fast the truths that you have heard and received, then take nothing upon trust in matters of religion: whatever preachers you hear, or whatever books you read, take not things upon trust, but examine them, and prove them by the scriptures, and judge what foundation and warrant they have from the scripture, and accordingly receive them, or receive them not. It is observable in 1 Thes. v. When the apostle says, " despise not prophecyings," in the next word he says, " prove all things, and hold fast that which is good;" as if he should say, though I would not have you despise prophecying and preachers, yet I would not have you to take things upon trust, in matters of religion, " but prove all things, and hold fast that which is good."

3. If you would be able to hold fast the truths that you have heard and received, get a clear, distinct, and certain knowledge of what is truth; that which you

would hold fast, get a clear, assured knowledge that it is the truth of God, 2 Tim. iii. 14. " Continue thou in the things which thou hast learned, and hast been assured of." If a man would continue in the things that he hath learned, he must be assured of them, that they are the truths of God. But how shall a man be assured that such and such things are the truths of God. He may know this; first, by the consonancy of them to the word of God. Secondly, by the power of them on his heart, to convince, or humble, and quicken it.

4. If you would be enabled to hold fast the truths you have heard and received, then get a valuation and esteem of the truths of God. Such as David had, Psal. cxix. 72. " The law of thy mouth is better unto me than thousands of gold and silver." Better in itself. All the gold and silver in the world, all the riches in the world, will never do a man so much good as that; and better in my estimation. I value it more, I had rather part with all than with the word. A man that is of this mind, he will hold fast the truth. Oh! that there were such a heart in every one of you, as to say, " The words of God's mouth, they are better than estate, and better than liberty, and better than wife and children." If there were such a heart in us, this would enable us to hold fast the truth of God, and part with all rather than them.

5. If you would hold fast the truth that you have received and heard, then make conscience to practice according to what you know; make conscience to obey the truths of God. Obedience is the sinew of constancy. Christ saith, Luke vi. 48. " Whosoever hears these sayings of mine, and doth them, he is like a man which built his house, and digged deep, and laid the foundation upon a rock; and when the flood arose, and the streams beat vehemently upon that house, it could not shake it." Mark ye, it could not be shaken. The conscionable practical hearer, and receiver of the truth of God, he is the man that is like to hold out, and to hold fast the word; he that hath been a careless hearer, and never

made conscience to hear for obedience and practice, he is blown over presently. It is a sad passage I have met with in that reverend man, Mr. Hildersham, and to me it seems to have much weight in it; what hopes, says he, can we have of many of our hearers in England, who are willing to give the word a hearing, and outwardly profess it? but what hope can we have, but that if a time of trial come, they will turn papists, or profane, or any thing; for they never loved the word when they heard it; and they never obeyed the word, but lived in known sins; they take up a form of godliness, and hate the power of it; what hope, but that if a time of trial come, these will fall from the truth?

6. If you would be able to hold fast the truth that you have heard and received, then take heed of not receiving the least truth of God; take heed, I say, of knowing, and willingly forsaking the least truth; and knowing, and willingly giving way to the least error; as the committing of the least sin, may render a man abominable unto God, as you find in Levit. xi. 43. " You shall not make yourselves abominable with any creeping thing;" that is, with the eating any creeping thing. Now this was one of the least commandments that God gave out, for the not eating of such and such things: yet by transgressing this the people might make themselves abominable. The committing of the least sin may make a man abominable to God; so the embracing of the least error, and the forsaking of the least truth, may make a man abominable to God. The least truth forsaken knowingly, and the least error embraced knowingly, becomes a great sin; and a little error makes way for a greater. If once a man gives way to one error, a thousand will follow after. If we would hold fast the whole body of truth, we must take heed we forsake not the least truth. If we forsake God and his truths, whether in lesser matters or greater, and if we turn back again to Popery, and conform to the Papists in lesser matters (saith Mr. Hildersham) know, of a certainty, that Popery shall return again.

7. If you would hold fast the truths you have heard and received, then shun all such persons as would go about to draw you off from the truth of God. Shun all seducers, confer not with them; have nothing to do with them and their ways, Prov. xix. 27. " Cease, my son, to hear the instruction that causeth to err from the words of knowledge." Thou hast been instructed in the words of knowledge, and if any would instruct thee otherwise, and seek to draw thee off from the words of truth and knowledge, have nothing to do with them. " Cease, my son, to hear the instruction that causeth to err from the words of knowledge." Now, my brethren, this advice I judge to be more seasonable, because it is in my apprehension, that this present providence of God, in taking off at one stroke so many of his servants (that have endeavoured in uprightness of heart to instruct you, and the people of God) from this work, it is on my heart to think and fear, this will give a great advantage to seducers, to seek to corrupt you, and draw you off from the truth to their party. When the shepherds are smitten, there is a great opportunity given to the foxes and wolves to make a prey of the flock. When God makes it dark and night, then all the beasts of the forest creep out. As the Psalmist saith, Psal. civ. 20. When there is a night and cloud on the ordinances of God, then all the beasts of the forest will go forth; many will undertake to be your instructors, and say here is Christ, and there is Christ, but believe them not: remember the things you have heard and received, and hold them fast: cease from the instructions of those that would turn you aside.

8. And lastly, If you would be able to hold fast the truths of God, then commend yourselves and the truths you would hold, to God in prayer, and beg of God to hold you, that you may keep his truth: Put up those requests to God, that David doth, Psal. xv. " Hold up my goings in thy paths, that my footsteps slip not;" and in the 119th Psalm, " Be surety for thy servant for

good; hold thou me up, and I shall be safe, and I will have respect unto thy statutes continually." And thus, my brethren, I have done with this doctrine, and this sermon, and as far as I know, with my preaching in this place. The day is at hand, wherein I, and many others of my brethren shall be (though not naturally dead, yet) civilly dead, dead in law, dead as to the work of the ministry. And, as I told them of this particular congregation the last Lord's day, so I tell you; know what I would be willing to speak to you, if I lay on my death-bed, and had the exercise of reason and memory that I have now: look, I say, what I would say to you, if I now lay on my death-bed, the same I shall speak to you now, through God's assistance; and first, I would, and in some measure do give thanks to God, the God of the spirits of all flesh, that hath called me, a poor unworthy creature, not only to the knowledge, but to the preaching of the gospel of his Son Jesus Christ, and that in this place, and in this part of the land; and hath pleased in mercy to continue life and liberty to me in my work here, almost twenty-six years. Secondly, I would be, and I hope I am in some measure, thankful to God, and to his people, both of this town, and of the neighbourhood, for a great deal of love and respect, and encouragement, that they have given to my person and ministry here; and particularly I do acknowledge myself to be greatly obliged to my reverend brethren, the neighbour-ministers, for the much love I have received from them, their readiness to help me, in supplying my place in the time of my sickness or absence, and sweet society I have had with them. I believe you think it is no easy thing for me to speak, or think of parting with such an auditory and society, the like to which I never look to have on earth again. But seeing for my sins, and your sins, God will have it so, we must submit, and lie at his feet. That which he hath made crooked, who can make strait? But before we part, give me leave to speak a few words to you; something by way of request, and something by way of advice. By way of request, I would speak this.

First, That if any of you have found any benefit by my poor ministry, that if any of you have been enlightened, or awakened, or strengthened, and built up in the truth, and encouraged in the ways of holiness, by any thing that God hath put into my mouth to speak to you, let God have the praise, and let me have some room in your hearts, and prayers, however God shall deal with me.

My second request is, That wherein soever you have seen any failings in me, or any failings in my ministerial duty, that you would please to pass it by, and to help me in prayer to God, for the forgiveness of them. These are my requests of you, and that which I have to say to you, by way of advice is much the same, with what I said to this particular congregation the last Lord's-day. Take it in these particulars.

1. I would advise you and entreat you, that we may all of us lay to heart this present dispensation of God towards us, and the nation, in this respect, that we may be sensible of it. I remember, when I was young, and my famous predecessor, Mr. Rogers, was taken off from his ministry in this kind, though but for a few weeks, these parts were wonderfully sensible of that providence, and laid it to heart, and were much in humiliation and in prayer; and I think I may say, they received an answer again within some weeks. Now, brethren, though he was worth some hundreds of us; yet now it is not the laying by of one man, but of multitudes, fifty in one place, and threescore in another, and fourscore in another, and this not by a single bishop, but by an act of parliament, which makes the wound the wider, and the more incapable of cure; and shall not we be sensible of this? Shall so many precious vessels be laid by, as vessels of no pleasure, and none take it to heart? Shall so many burning lights be quenched together, so many wells

of the water of life be stopt up together, and this not be laid to heart? I beseech you consider and be sensible.

2. In the deepest and saddest sense you have of this providence of God, watch over your own spirits, that you lay the blame of it no where so much as upon yourselves. Some blame the times, and charge it on their iniquities; others are apt to blame us ministers, and charge it on our niceness and singularity. Might my advice take place with this people, I would desire, that every one of us might lay the blame no where so much, as on ourselves; for certainly, we have procured these things to ourselves. I find our predecessors the martyrs, when by a law religion was changed in the nation, and idolatry set up, they lay the blame not on the law-makers, but on themselves, and their own hearts. One of them saith, "all this is come upon us, because we did not love the gospel; we were gospellers in lip, but not in life." Much more doth it become us, whose sufferings are far less, to blame ourselves more than we blame any others.

3. My third advice is this, and I beseech you take it in love, for it is out of love that it is given you; if you should perceive at this time a difference in opinion and practice among us, that are the ministers of the gospel in this nation; standing, and sticking at things that others can digest, and do; and others doing things, that some of their brethren cannot come up unto: be not offended, thus it hath always been from the beginning; it is no new thing. Thus it was in King Edward's days. If there be any of God's servants that are learned and holy, and faithful, that do now for the enjoyment of their ministry, yield a conformity to all that is enjoined, I doubt not but many of them are grieved, that they cannot have the exercise of their ministry without this: and we who cannot come up to this, are grieved, that we cannot come up to it: the one, and the other have grief enough. Add not your censures to this grief, that is already upon them. It hath been all along a merciful providence of God,

that when some of his servants could not satisfy their consciences, and come up to the things that have been imposed upon them, without injuring their consciences; yet others have had a greater freedom given them, that they could yield; and if not so, what would have become of the people of God? therefore in those things, acknowledge there may be some providence of God, for good to you in it.

4. My fourth advice, I shall deliver to you wholly, in the words of that holy man and martyr of God, Mr. Bradford, in his letter to the city of London. Saith he," let us heartily bewail our sins and repent of our evils; let us amend the evil of our lives; let us every one be diligent in prayer, and attend with reverence on the reading, and hearing of God's holy word; let us reprove the works of darkness; let us fly from idolatry, and which is the particular I would indeed commend unto you, obey the magistrate, and them that are set over us in the Lord, in all things that are not against the word; and when they command any thing contrary to the word, let us answer, it is meet to obey God, rather than man. However (saith he) resist not the magistrate, nor seek to avenge yourselves, but commit your case to God; be patient, and submit to all that are in authority over you: but resist not, rise not against authority; but wait on God, till he pleaseth to cause the light to rise, and shine again upon you." This is my fourth advice.

5. Now it pleaseth God, that hearing opportunities, at least, some of them are taken from some of us, from many of us, for a time. My advice and counsel is, that the less now you hear, the more you will read; read the word of God much the more, and take all helps for the right understanding of what you read. The book of annotations is a great help to enlighten you to understand the scripture; and next to the reading of the scriptures, what spare hours you have, I would advise you to bestow your time in reading the Book of Martyrs; a book that hath formerly been more prized, than of late in Eng-

land. Especially, read that part of it which contains the history of Queen Mary's days; they will inform you of the great controversies that are between us and the papists; they will inform you what you shall answer. The reading how cheerfully they went to prison, and to the stake, will embolden you against the fears of sufferings, and death; and the reading of their letters, will be a great means to edify, and build you up. This reading of the scriptures, and other good books, is my fifth advice to you.

6. My sixth advice to you is, that seeing God hath taken away your week-day opportunities of hearing the word here, and in other places, you would be careful that the world may not devour God's portion; I mean that portion of time, which some of you have bestowed in hearing these lectures. It was a good speech of a gracious woman, now with God, when Mr. Rogers was silenced: " well," said she," by the grace of God, the world shall never have those hours that I was wont to spend in hearing heretofore." Her meaning was, she would spend them in her closet in holy duties. It was an excellent resolution, and worthy our imitation; and if I might after twenty-six years labour here in the ministry, now at my parting obtain thus much of you, that you having been pleased to be constant hearers here, would lay a law on yourselves, that so much time as you formerly spent in coming hither, sitting here, and returning home, that you will spend that time at home, either in praying, and reading, and meditating in your closets; or else in praying in, and with your families, and instructing of them: if I might but obtain this of you, at my parting, I shall believe that the devil and his kingdom would be losers by this our parting. If you would spend this time weekly in holy exercises, reading and praying for yourselves, and for the nation, and for your families, which you were wont to spend in coming to these lectures, and in attending here, and returning home; and that is my sixth advice to you, and therefore let me intreat this of you.

7. And my seventh advice and counsel is this, that seeing it pleaseth God to take away from you so many of your public instructors, that you would every one of you that are heads of families, be so much the more instructing and teaching your families: be so much the more in this, by how much the less is done in public. Read the word in your families, and catechise your families, and see that they may understand them. You have many helps for this, as Mr. Perkins, Mr. Ball, and the Assembly's Catechism.

8. And the last advice I have to give you, is this, that you would still continue your reverence of, and love to, and care for the observing of the Lord's holy sabbath. It is that, my brethren, wherein God hath been honoured in this town, and in these parts, I think as much as in most places in the world, and I pray do so still: and when you have not public ordinances, and public helps for the sanctifying of the Lord's day at home in your own congregation, if you have the word and ordinances in any comfortable manner abroad, travel for it, I say, travel for it; and when you have them not at home nor abroad, be so much the more earnest, and fervent, and abundant in your family and secret duties, in the sanctification of the Lord's day. I have some fears, lest if time should come to pass, that the magistrates should connive at the profaning of the Lord's day, giving way to sports and recreations on it, and preachers should cry down the strict observation of the Lord's day, and the like. I am afraid we have many youth, that in these parts, notwithstanding all the instructions that have been given them, would be ready to dance after these pipes, and run into the profaning of the Lord's day. Therefore you that are governors of families, remember the charge that God hath given you more expressly concerning this, than in any other thing that I know of: "thou, nor thy son, nor thy daughter, nor thy man-servant, nor thy maid-servant, nor thy cattle, nor thy stranger that is within thy gates, shalt thou suffer to violate the day of the Lord." Therefore, know

your authority, and do your duty ; and put on the holy resolution of Joshua, " Whatsoever others do, I and my house will serve the Lord." So say you, "Whatsoever others do, I and mine will sanctify the Lord's day, and keep it holy." So do, and the blessing of God shall be on you all the week long. And now, brethren, I commend you to God, and to the word of his grace, which is able to build you up, and to give you an inheritance among all them that are sanctified.

MR. BROOKS'S FAREWELL SERMON.

ALL that I shall do, shall be to answer two or three queries, and then I shall leave a few legacies with you, that may speak when I am not advantaged to speak to you.

The first query is this: What should be the reason that men make such opposition against the gospel, against the plain, powerful, conscientious preaching of it? This is not the principal thing that I intend, and therefore I shall only touch upon the reason of it.

1. Men's hatred and opposition ariseth against the gospel, because it doth discover their hidden works of darkness, Job iii. " They hate the light, lest their deeds should be removed." The gospel brings their deeds of darkness to light : and this stirs up a spirit of hatred and opposition against the gospel.

2d Ground is this; Because sinners under the gospel cannot sin at so cheap a rate, as otherwise they might do. The drunkard cannot be drunk at so cheap a rate; nor can the opposer and persecutor oppose and persecute at so cheap a rate as they might do, where the gospel doth not shine in power and glory.

3. Because the gospel puts persons upon very hard service, upon very difficult work; pulling out a right

eye, cutting off a right hand, offering up an Isaac, throwing overboard a Jonas, parting with bosom lusts, and darling sins. Herod heard John Baptist gladly, till he came to touch his Herodias, and then off goes his head. As they say, John vi. "This a hard saying, and who can abide it?" and from that time they walked no more with him. This is a hard gospel indeed, and at this their blood riseth.

4. Because of the differing and distinguishing work that the gospel makes among the sons of men, it softens one, and hardens another that sits next to him; enlightens one, and strikes the other blind; it wins on one, and enrageth another. The same sun hath different effects on the objects on which it shines. The gospel puts a difference between the precious and the vile, and this the vile cannot bear. It was never good days (say they) since such and such must be saints, and none else. We have as good hearts as any, and this enrageth them.

Lastly, It is from Satan. Satan knows that the very tendency of the gospel is, to shake his kingdom about his ears. Satan and Antichrist know that their kingdom must down by the power and light of the gospel; and therefore Satan and men of an antichristian spirit, do all they can to oppose, and shew their hatred against the everlasting gospel; and this makes them to be in such a rage against the gospel.

Quer. 2. When the gospel goes from a people, what goes? I shall give but a touch here.

1. When the gospel goes, peace, plenty, and trading goes. 2 Chron. xv. 3, 5, and 6. compared. "Now for a long season Israel had been without the true God, and without a teaching-priest." Why? They had priests, but they were Jeroboam's priests, as you may see, chap. xiii. verse 9. "Have you not cast out the priests of the Lord, the sons of Aaron, and the Levites, and have made you priests after the manner of the nations of other lands? so that whosoever comes to consecrate himself with a young bullock, and seven rams, the same may be

a priest of them that are no gods." A little business will buy a priesthood, and so they are said to be without the true God, without a teaching-priest, and without law. Mark what follows, " And in those times, there was no peace to him that went out, nor to him that came in, but great vexations were upon all the inhabitants of the country; and nation was destroyed of nation, and city of city, for God did vex them with all adversity."

3. Safety and security goes, when the gospel goes; so in the text just now cited. The ark was taken away, their strength and safety was gone. When the Jews rejected the gospel, the Romans came and took away both their place and nation, John xi. 48. " If we let him thus alone, the Romans will come, and take away both our place and nation." About forty years after, Titus and Vespasian took away their city; they cried, " If we let this man alone, the Romans will take away our nation;" and this was the ready way to bring the Romans upon them.

4. When the gospel goes, civil liberty goes. When the Jews slighted the gospel, and turned their backs upon it, they quickly became bond-slaves to the Romans.

5. When the gospel goes, the honour and glory, splendour and beauty of a nation goes. It is the gospel that is the honour and beauty of a nation; and when that goes, all the glory goes. As old Eli said, " When the ark was taken away, the glory was departed from Israel," 1 Sam. iv. 22. Jer. ii. 11, 12, 13. " Hath a nation changed their gods, which are yet no gods? but my people have changed their glory for that which doth not profit;" that is, the worship of God into the traditions of men. What is it that lifts up one nation above another but the gospel? Above all nations of the earth, England hath been lifted up to heaven.

6. When the gospel goes, all soul-happiness and blessedness goes. The gospel, you know, is the means appointed by God to bring souls to an acquaintance with Christ, to an acceptance of Christ, to an interest in

Christ, to an assurance that he is theirs, and they are his. Now when this goes all soul-happiness and blessedness goes.

7. When the gospel goes, the spiritual presence of God goes, for that still goes with the gospel. There is a general presence of God, as the Psalmist speaks, Psalm cxxxix. "Where shall I go from thy spirit? Whither shall I fly from thy presence?" This presence of God reacheth from heaven to hell; in that sense God is included in no place, nor excluded out of any place. But alas! What is this general presence? "When the gospel goes, the special presence of God goes." This leads me by the hand to the third query.

Query 3. And that is this; Whether God will remove the gospel from England, or no?

It is the fear of many, but I humbly suppose, no. Whatsoever darkness may be upon it, yet that God will not remove it. If you please, I will offer a few things that signify something as to my own satisfaction, and it may be so to you.

1. The rooting that it hath got in the hearts of sinners and saints, in the judgment, affections, and consciences both of sinners and saints. Certainly, it hath got so deep a root in the hearts of many thousands of saints and sinners, that it shall not be in the power of hell to raze it out.

2. The glorious anointings that are to be found upon many thousands of God's servants in this nation, to preach the everlasting gospel, and who would be glad to preach upon the hardest terms, keeping God and a good conscience, to preach it freely, as the apostles of old did. And certainly, God hath not laid in the treasure, that it should be turned into a heap of confusion, but that it should serve to the end for which he laid it in.

3. The ineffectualness of all former attempts and designs to destroy the gospel. You know what endeavours of old there hath been to darken this sun, to put out the

light of heaven, in the Marian days, and in other days since them; and yet it hath not been in prisons, racks, flames, pillories, nor any thing else to extinguish the glory of it. And then,

4. All designs and attempts to extinguish the everlasting gospel, have turned to the advancement, flourishing, and spreading of the gospel.

5. God never takes away the gospel from a people, till the body of that people have thrust the everlasting gospel from them. When, indeed, they have been so bold, as to thrust away the everlasting gospel, God hath been severe unto them. But till the body of a people have thrust away the everlasting gospel, God hath not taken it away from them, 2 Chronicles, the 36th chapter, from the 15th verse to the end, God sent his messengers early and late; they abused, slighted and scorned them, till there was no remedy. So in the 35th of Jeremiah, from the first to the twelfth; it is a famous text for this. So in the thirteenth chapter of the Acts, and the 45th, 46th, and 47th verses; " Because you have thought yourselves unworthy of salvation, lo, we turn to the Gentiles." Till the Jews came to thrust away the everlasting gospel, the Lord continued it to them.

6. The spreading of the everlasting gospel, is the special means appointed by God, for the destruction of Antichrist. First, he is to be consumed by the spirit of his mouth, then destroyed by the brightness of his coming; the spirit of faith and prayer in them that would be willing to lay down any thing rather than part with the gospel. God will not put his blessed church to the blush; he will not make them ashamed of their confidence.

7. Are there not multitudes of the children of believers that fall under many promises? And will not God make good his engagements to them? " I will circumcise your hearts, and the hearts of your seed; and the seed of the upright shall be blessed," &c.

8. The strange and wonderful affections and tender-

ness, that God hath wrought in his children to the gospel. What meltings and mournings, and what a spirit of prayer hath God put upon his people?

9. There are many young tender plants and buds of grace; such in whom the spirit of God hath stirred a hungering and thirsting, and longing after the great concernments of eternity. I would, upon these grounds, and others of the like import, hope and believe, that the Lord will not remove his everlasting gospel, however he may correct his people for their trifling with, and slighting the glorious gospel. I have several times thought, what a day of darkness was upon the world, in respect of sin and superstition. When Christ brought the everlasting gospel, what a day of darkness and superstition was on the whole earth! But you know what the apostle speaks, 1 Cor. i. 21. "For after that, in the wisdom of God, the world by wisdom knew not God; it pleased God, by the foolishness of preaching, to save them that believe."

When it is nearest day, then it is darkest. There may be an hour of darkness, that may be upon the gospel, as to its liberty, purity, and glory; and yet there may be a sun-shining day, ready to tread on the heels of it. And so much for the resolution of these queries.

I shall proceed, as I said, and leave some legacies with you; which may, by the finger of the spirit, be made advantageous to you, when we are not advantaged to speak unto you.

Leg. 1. The first legacy I would leave with you shall be this, Secure your interest in Christ. Make it your great business, your work, your heaven, to secure your interest in Christ. This is not an age, an hour, for a man to be between fears and hopes, between doubting and believing.

Take not up in a name to live, when you are dead God-ward, and Christ-ward. Take not up in an outward form, and outward privileges. They cried, "The temple of the Lord, the temple of the Lord," that had no interest in, or love, to the Lord of the temple. Follow God, leave no means unattempted, whereby your blessed interest may be cleared up.

Leg. 2. Make Christ and scripture the only foundation for your souls and faith to build on: as the apostle said, 1 Cor. iii. 11. "Other foundations can no man lay than that which is laid, even Jesus Christ." Isa. xxviii. 16. "Behold, I lay in Sion for a foundation, a stone, a tried-stone, a corner stone, a precious stone, a sure foundation," Eph. ii. 10. Since it is a very dangerous thing, as much as your soul and eternity is worth for you to build on this authority, and that; on this saying, and that; take heed.

Leg. 3. In all places and company, be sure to carry your soul preservatives with you. Go into no place nor company, except you carry your soul preservatives with you; that is, holy care and wisdom. You know in infectious times men will carry outward preservatives with them; you have need to carry your preservatives about you; else you would be in danger of being infected with the ill customs and vanities of the times wherein you live; and that is a third.

Leg. 4. I would leave with you, is this: Look that all within you rise higher and higher, by oppositions, threatenings, and sufferings; that is, that your faith, your love, your courage, your zeal, your resolutions, and magnanimity rise higher by opposition, and the spirit of prayer. Thus it did, Acts iv. 18, 19, 20; 21, 29, 30, and 31. compared. All their sufferings did but raise up a more noble spirit in them; they did but raise up their faith and courage. So Acts v. 40, 41, and 42. they looked on it as a grace, to be disgraced for Christ; and as an honour, to be dishonoured for him. They say, as David, "If this be to be vile, I will be more vile." If to be found in the way of my God, to act for my God be vile, I will be more vile.

Leg. 5. Take more pains, and make more conscience of keeping yourselves from sin than suffering; from the pollutions and defilements of the day, than from the sufferings of the day. This legacy I would beg that you would consider, take more pains, and make more conscience of keeping yourselves from the evil of sin, than the evil of punishment, from the pollutions and corruptions of the times, Acts ii. 40. "Save yourselves from this outward generation." Phil. ii. 15. "The children of God must be harmless, and blameless, without rebuke in the midst of a crooked and perverse generation." Heb. xi. speaks full to the point in hand. Rev. iii. 4. "Thou hast a few names even in Sardis, that have not defiled their garments, and they shall walk with me in white, for they are worthy." White was the habit of the nobles, which imports the honour that God will put on those that keep their garments pure in a defiling day, Rev. viii. 4. "And I heard another voice from Heaven, saying, Come out of her, my people, that ye be not partakers of her sins, and that ye receive not of her plagues." If you will be tasting and sipping at Babylon's cup, you must resolve to receive more or less of Babylon's plagues.

Leg. 6. I would leave with you, is this: "Be always doing, or receiving good." Our Lord and Master went up and down in this world doing good; he was still doing good to body and soul, he was acted by an untired power; he still doing or receiving good. This will make your lives comfortable, your deaths happy, and your account glorious in the great day of the Lord. Oh how useless are many men in their generation! Oh that our lips might be as so many honey-combs, that we might scatter knowledge!

Leg. 7. I would leave with you, is this: Set the highest examples and patterns before your face of grace and godliness for your imitation. In the business of faith, set an Abraham before your eyes: in the business of courage, set a Joshua: in the business of uprightness, set a Job: of meekness, a Moses, &c. &c. There is a disadvantage that redounds to christians, by looking more backwards than forwards. Men look on whom they excel, not on those they fall short of. Of all examples, set them before you that are most eminent for grace and holiness, for communion with God, and acting for God. Next to Christ, set the pattern of the choicest saints before you.

Leg. 8. "Hold fast your integrity, and rather let all go, than let that go." A man had better let liberty, estate, relations, and life go, than let his integrity go; yea, let all ordinances themselves go, when they cannot be held with the hand of integrity. Job xxvii. 5, 6, " God forbid that I should justify you till I die. I will not remove my integrity from me. My righteousness I will hold fast, and I will not let it go: my heart shall not reproach me so long as I live." Look as the drowning man holds fast that which is cast forth to save him. As the soldier holds fast his sword and buckler on which his life depends. So (saith Job) " I will hold fast my integrity; my heart shall not reproach me. I had rather all the world should reproach me, and my heart justify me, than that my heart should reproach me, and all the world justify me." That man will make but a sad exchange, that shall exchange his integrity for any worldly concernment. Integrity maintained in the soul, will be a feast of fat things in the worst of days; but let a man lose his integrity, and it is not in the power of all the world to make a feast of fat things in that soul.

Leg. 9. That I would leave with you, is this, let not a day pass over your head, without calling the whole man to an exact account. Well, where have you been acting to-day, hands? what have you done for God to-day, tongue? what have you spoke for God to-day? This will be an advantage many ways unto you; but I can only touch on these legacies.

Leg. 10. Labour mightily for a healing spirit. This legacy I would leave with you as matter of great concernment. Labour mightily for a healing spirit; away with all discriminating names whatever, that may hinder the applying of balm to heal our wounds. Labour for a healing spirit: discord and division become no christian. For wolves to worry the lambs, is no wonder; but for one lamb to worry another, this is unnatural and monstrous. God hath made his wrath to smoke against us, for the divisions and heart-burnings that have been amongst us. Labour for a oneness in love and affection with every one that is one with Christ, let their forms be what they will. That which wins most upon Christ's heart, should win most upon ours; and that is his own grace and holiness. The question should be, What of the Father? What of the Son? What of the spirit shines in this or that person? and, accordingly, let your love and your affection run out: this is the tenth legacy.

Leg. 11. " Be most in the spiritual exercises of religion." Improve this legacy; for much of the life, and comfort, joy, and peace of your souls is wrapped in it. I say, be most in the spiritual exercises of religion. There are external exercises, as hearing, preaching, praying, and conference; and there are the more spiritual exercises of religion, exercises of grace, meditation, self-judging, self-trial, and examination. Bodily exercise will profit nothing, if abstracted from those more spiritual. The glory that God hath, and the comfort and advantage that will redound to your souls, is mostly from the spiritual exercises of religion. How rare is it to find men in the work of meditation, of trial and examination, and bringing home of truths to their own soul.

Leg. 12. "Take no truths upon trust, but all upon trial," 1 Thes. v. 21. So 1 John iv. 1. Acts xvii. 11. It was the glory of that church, that they would not trust Paul himself. Paul that had the advantage above all for external qualifications; no not Paul himself. Take no truth upon trust, bring them to the balance of the sanctuary; if they will not hold water there, reject them.

Leg. 13. The lesser and fewer opportunities and advantages you have in public, to better and enrich your souls, the more abundantly address yourselves to God in private. Mal. iii. 16, 17. "Then they that feared the Lord, spoke often one to another," &c.

Leg. 14. Walk in those ways that are directly cross and contrary to the vain, sinful, and superstitious ways, that men of a formal, carnal, lukewarm spirit, walk in. This is the great concernment of christians. But more of that by and bye.

Leg. 15. "Look upon all the things of this world, as you will upon them when you come to die." At what a poor rate do men look on the things of this world when they come to die! What a low value do men set upon the pomp and glory of it! Men may now put a mark upon them, but then they will appear in their own colours. Men would not venture the loss of such great things for them, did they but look on them now, as they will do at the last day.

Leg. 16. "Never put off your consciences with any plea, or with any argument, that you dare not stand by in the great day of your account." It is dreadful to consider, how many in these days put off their conscience. We did this and that for our families, they would have else perished. I have complied thus, and wronged my conscience thus, for this and that concernment. Will a man stand by this argument, when he comes before Jesus Christ at the last day? Because of the souls of men, many plead this or that. Christ doth not stand in need of indirect ways to save souls, he hath ways enough to bring in souls to himself.

Leg. 17. "Eye more, mind more, and lay to heart more, the spiritual and internal workings of God in your souls, than the external providences of God in the world." Beloved, GOD looks that we should consider the operations of his hand; and the despising the works of his hands is so provoking to him, that he threatens them to lead them into captivity, for not considering of them. But above all, look to the work that God is carrying on in your souls: not a soul, but he is carrying on some work or other in it, either blinding or enlightening, bettering or worsting; and therefore look to what God is doing in thy soul. All the motions of God within you are steps to eternity, and every soul shall be blessed or cursed, saved or lost, to all eternity, not according to outward dispensation, but according to the inward operations of God in your souls. Observe, what humbling work, reforming work, sanctifying work, he is about in thy spirit, what he is doing in that little world within. If God should carry on never so glorious a work in the world, as a conquest of nations to Christ: what would it advantage thee, if sin, Satan, and the world should triumph in thy soul, and carry the day there?

Leg. 18. "Look as well on the bright side, as on the dark side of the cloud; on the bright side of Providence, as well as on the dark side of Providence." Beloved, there is a great weakness among christians, they do so pore on the black side of Providence, as that they have no heart to consider of the bright side. If you look on this black side of the providence of God to Joseph, how terrible and amazing was it! But if you look on the bright side, his fourscore years reign; how glorious was it! If you look on the dark side of the providence of God to David, in his first year's banishment, much will arise to startle you; but if you turn to the bright side, his forty years reign in glory, how amiable was it! Look on the dark side of the providence of God to Job; Oh how terrible was it, in the first of Job! But compare this with the last of Job, where you have the bright side of the cloud, and there God doubles all his mercies to him. Consider the patience of Job, and the end that the Lord made with him. Do not remember the beginning only, for that was the dark side: but turn to the end of him, and there was his bright side. Many sins, many temptations, and much affliction would be prevented by christians looking on the bright side of Providence, as well as on the dark.

Leg. 19. Keep up precious thoughts of God under the

sorest, sharpest, and severest dispensations of God to you, Psal. xxii. 1, 2, and 3. "My God, my God, Why hast thou forsaken me? Why art thou so far from helping me, and from the words of my roaring? O my God, I cry in the day time, but thou hearest not, and in the night season, and am not silent." There was the psalmist under smart dispensations: but what precious thoughts hath he of God under all? "But thou art holy, O thou that inhabitest the praise of Israel: though I am thus and thus afflicted, yet thou art holy." Psal. lxv. 5. "By terrible things in righteousness wilt thou answer us, O God of our salvation."

Leg. 20. "Hold on, and hold out in the ways of well-doing, in the want of all outward encouragements, and in the face of all outward discouragements." It is nothing to hold out, when we meet with nothing but encouragements; but to hold out in the face of all discouragements is a christian duty, Psal. xliv. "Though thou hast sore broken us in the place of dragons, and covered us with the shadow of death; yet have we not dealt falsely in thy covenant; our heart is not turned back, neither have we declined from thy ways." It is perseverance that crowns all. "Be thou faithful to the death, and I will give thee a crown of life." Rev. ii. 10. "And he that endureth to the end shall be saved," Mat. xxiv. It is perseverance in well-doing that crowns all our actions. If you have begun in the spirit, do not end in the flesh; do not go away from the captain of your salvation; follow the lamb, though others follow the beast and the false prophet.

Leg. 21. "In all your natural, civil, and religious actions, let divine glory still rest in your souls," Rom. vii. 8. 1 Cor. x. 11. In all your hearing, in all your prayings, let the glory of Christ carry it: in all your closet-duties, let the glory of Christ lie nearest your hearts.

Leg. 22. "Record all special favours, mercies, providences, and experiences." It is true, a man should do nothing else, should he record all the favours and experiences of God towards him; and therefore my legacy is, record all special favours, peculiar experiences. Little do you know the advantage that will redound to your souls upon this account, by recording all the experiences of the shinings of his face, of the leadings of his spirit. Many a christian loseth much by neglecting this duty.

Leg. 23. " Never enter upon the trial of your estate, but when your hearts are at the best, and in the fittest temper. It is a great desire of Satan, when the soul is deserted and strangely afflicted, to put the soul on trying work. Come, see what thou art worth for another world, what thou hast to shew for a better state, for an interest in Christ, a title for heaven. This is not a time to be about this work. Thy work is to get off from this temptation, and therefore to pray and believe, and wait upon God, and be found in all those ways whereby thou mayest get off the temptation.

Leg. 24. Always make the scripture, (and not yourselves, nor your carnal reason, nor your bare opinion) the judges of your spiritual state and condition. I cannot see my condition to be good. I cannot perceive it. What? Must your sense, and your carnal reason be the judge of your spiritual state? Isa. viii. 20. " To the law, and to the testimony if they speak not according to this rule, it is because there is no light, no morning in them." John xii. 24. " The word that I have spoken, the same shall judge you at the last day." The scripture is that which must determine the case in the great day ; whether you have grace or no, or whether it be true or no.

Leg. 25. Make much conscience of making good the terms on which you closed with Christ. You know the terms, how that you would deny yourselves, take up his cross, and follow the Lamb wheresoever he should go. Now you are put to take up the cross, to deny yourselves, to follow the Lamb over hedge and ditch, through thick and thin, do not turn your backs on Christ. The worst of Christ is better than the best of the world. Make conscience of making good your terms, to deny yourself, your natural-self, your sinful-self, your religious-self, and to follow him; and if you do so, Oh! what an honour will it be to Christ, and advantage to yourselves, and a joy to the upright!

Leg. 26. Walk by no rule but such as you dare die by, and stand by in the great day of Jesus Christ. You may have many ways prescribed to worship by, but walk by none but such as you dare die by, and stand by, before Christ Jesus. Walk not by a multitude, for who dare stand by that rule, when he comes to die?

Make not the example of great men a rule to go by: for who dare die by, and stand by this, in the great day of account? Do not make any authority, that stands in opposition to the authority of Christ, a rule to walk by: for who dare stand by this, before Jesus Christ? Ah! Sirs, walk by no rule, but what you dare die by, and stand by, at the great day.

Leg. 27. And lastly, sit down, and rejoice with fear, Psalm i. "Let the righteous rejoice, but let them rejoice with fear." Rejoice, that God hath done your souls good by the everlasting gospel: that he did not leave you till he brought you to an acceptance of, to a closing with, and a resignation of your souls to Christ, and the clearing up of your interest in him. Rejoice, that you have had the everlasting gospel in so much light, purity, power, and glory, as you have had for many years together. Rejoice in the riches of grace, that hath carried it in such a way towards you. And weep that you have provoked God to take away the gospel, that you have no more improved it, that you have so neglected the seasons and opportunities of enriching your souls. When you should have come to church-fellowship, any thing would turn you out of the way. Oh! sit down and tremble under your barrenness, under all your leanness: notwithstanding all the cost and charge that God hath been at, that you have grown no more into communion with God, and conformity to God, and into the lively hope of the everlasting fruition of God. Here are your legacies, and the Lord make them to work in your souls, and then they will be of singular use to you, to preserve you so, that you may give up your account before the great and glorious God with joy. Labour to make conscience of putting these legacies into practice, of sucking at these breasts, which will be of use to us till we shall be gathered up into the fruition of God, where we shall need no more ordinances, no more preaching, or praying.

MR. COLLINS'S FAREWELL SERMON.

Jude v. 3.

Contend earnestly for the faith, &c.

THESE words contain two parts.
   1. A duty exhorted to.
  2. The manner of the management of duty.

The duty exhorted to, is, to retain the faith delivered to the saints.

The manner of its management is, that we should earnestly contend to keep it.

I opened the terms, what is meant by faith.

It is not so much the grace of faith, but the doctrine of faith; not special faith, whereby we apprehend special mercy upon a promise made to the elect, but the *fides que creditur*, the whole substance of the doctrine of Christ, as to things that are to be believed, and duties that are to be practised.

But why is it said, the faith that was once delivered? (that is) invariably, irrevocably, once for all. "To the saints," respects the privilege the saints of God had in the faith that God had left. It is the faith of the gospel, committed as a treasure: and the church is called a candlestick, not only to hold out the light, but to hold the light: whence the church is called the pillar, or the ground of truth. Not that they are to make doctrines, but to hold forth the doctrines of Christ, even as tables and pillars, upon which proclamations are hung and held forth to be made public: so is the church of Christ, it is that in which the truths of the Lord Jesus are kept, and will be kept from one age to another.

But what is the import of the word "earnestly contend?" It is a word used only once in the New Testament in the composition. The word in the root is frequently used, and imports a struggling with might and main, as those that use to run at games. It is used for Jesus Christ in his sufferings, he was in an agony; the same word from whence this word is compounded. The apostle would imply such a contention, such a struggling to keep the faith of the gospel, as one word in the English is not able to express it, and interpreters very much differ, what is the import. The best do center in this, that we should contend for the faith, as men that would contend to keep their very lives.

The proposition is this, that it is the duty of the saints of God to maintain an earnest contention, to struggle for, and to keep the faith that was intrusted with them: wherein doth this contention consist?

1. It is not a carnal contention; the weapons of our warfare are not carnal, but spiritual, the saints are not called to contend for the faith with carnal weapons, with carnal power and force: (not by might and power, but by the spirit of God) force and power, and a fleshly arm, prison, pillars, and chains, and taking away of men's comforts and estates upon the account of the faith of the gospel, hath been the usual way of error's defending itself: prayers and tears are the church's weapons.

2. It is not a contention of uncharitableness. This allows no murdering, either of the bodies or souls of men. Christians are so to contend against error and sinful practices, as to love their persons, and pity those they con-

tend with. There are some opinions, that there is no way to shew a holy way of zeal against, nor to be able to destroy them, but by a holy separating from the persons. There were such to whom it was not lawful to say God speed, or receive them into their houses: but yet this in order to the saving their souls: saving some, plucking them as brands out of the fire.

But positively, this holy contention consists in these four things.

1. In managing the sword of the spirit, the word of God, against errors and sinful practices, to be able to confute them mightily, as Apollos did, out of the scriptures, shewing the Jews that Jesus is the Christ.

2. By prayer: for to pray down sinful opinions and practices. That we mean when we pray, thy kingdom come, that the gospel may run on and be glorified: that these nights of darkness may be dispelled, that truth may shine to the perfect day.

3. By holy practising against them: by holding forth the word of life in your conversations; by striving together by a mutual provocation for the faith of the gospel in respect of holy walking.

4. By being able to suffer for them.

The reasons of the point I gave you.

I shall now sum up all in a word of exhortation, to press every one that bears the name of a saint, to take up this exhortation of the apostle, "Earnestly to contend for the faith that was once delivered to the saints." The sum of all is, to beg that you would be valiant for the truth of Christ; that whatever hath been delivered to you consonant to the truth, agreeable to the faith delivered to us, that you would struggle might and main, by all Christian courage, by argument, practice, prayer, by suffering, rather than let go those truths that God hath taught you by his faithful ministers; that Christ hath been preached to you. Those scriptures you have in your hands; those doctrines you have learned by experience, by prayer, by searching the word. Those ways of worship God hath taught you; those patterns of his house, and outgoings and returnings there, that he hath taught you. Be exhorted to hold them fast, and not let them go. "Contend earnestly for the faith," &c.

It is to be lamented, that there is so sad a spirit of indifferency among Christians, as we find at this day. Many do so carry it, as if there were nothing in the gospel of Christ that were worthy the owning by practising, or worthy owning by suffering. This lukewarm, indifferent temper hath done the church of God a great deal of mischief formerly, and if admitted now, will do you as much mischief again. It hath been one of the sins which the Lord at this day is judging, and punishing his poor people for, that our zeal hath been so hot against one another for mere circumstances, and so cold when we are like to lose the substance; that our contentions rise so high in matters hardly of any moment, and our spirits work so low when they are to gain the great things for which Christ suffered, and which he delivered to us. It is my work, therefore, to beg you, that you would put on a holy resolution, that there may be no contention among us (for we are brethren) but only that contention, who may most retain, and evidently witness the faith that is delivered to us. It is the trust God hath committed, and he doth expect and look how we will manage it with courage and confidence, to keep the faith of the gospel. There are very great oppositions against you, and there ought to be great resolutions of christians to maintain themselves against such oppositions. It is a very sad thing that christians should see the faith and the way of the gospel of God, as it were taken from them at any time, and they have not one word to speak, nor any thing at all to venture in suffering for the ways and truths of Jesus Christ. Moses had such a holy zeal that when Aaron was an example to the people to lead them to idolatry, he contended with him earnestly to his face. The zeal of God's servants is so small now, that though Balaam be about the work, we have not a word to speak.

Though the small prophets of Antichrist be about the business, yet no Christian hath courage to speak. The holy apostle Paul, when Peter walked with an uneven foot, and began to Judaize, he tells us, he did resist him to his face. Shall Paul resist Simon Peter, and shall not the saints of God resist Simon Magus? Shall they resist Hymenæus and Philetus, and shall not we contend with Alexander the copper-smith? It is but suitable to what God expects, and the exhortation here given us, that we should maintain with might and main, as that which is our treasure, which we will not let go, the faith once delivered to the saints.

To put you upon this, I might encourage you with several things. All the reasons mentioned are as so many motives to this holy spiritual contention. Shall I tell you of three words further?

1. The mercy of God delivering the truth to you, should engage you to this holy contention. It is such a mercy as is a non-such mercy, Psal. cxlvii. the two last verses, " He hath given his judgments to Jacob, and his statutes to Israel. He hath not dealt so with any nation." How many of the greatest part of those that we call Christians in the world, are put, like Samson, to grind among the Philistines! Superstition, popery, idolatry, will-worship, such things as Jesus Christ never delivered to his saints, having both their eyes out, the scripture light that should have shewed them the truth, taken from them, and their consciences, that should teach them, carried in the pocket of some base priest, that dare not think any other than what he will tell them. How many are there, even of the very reformed of the world, who only get upon some broken plank of shipwrecked truth, whereby they swim to the Lord Jesus? But God does not deal thus with us. You have had the whole counsel of God revealed to you; a glorious light set up in the nation for a hundred years past, which hath been like the light of seven days. For these twenty years past the running to and fro of men hath increased know-

ledge. You have learned the truth from God's faithful ministers. You have received it with much affliction, with many temptations. It hath cost Jesus Christ dear to send it, it hath cost you dear to receive it, and will you let it go? Your sin above all others will be most provoking to the Lord Jesus.

2. I might tell you that it is a time, wherein many let go the faith, and methinks the Lord Jesus does by his poor and unworthy messenger speak to this great congregation, as sometimes he did to his apostles, will ye also go away? There are many that have been forward and eminent professors of the faith delivered to the saints, that have made shipwreck of faith and a good conscience; will you split upon the same rock? God hath kept the truth for you, and kept you in the truth hitherto, and is coming to see whether you will cleave to it, and keep it or no. We have been sucking at the breasts of the ordinances, and dandled upon the knees of providences, and gone on in a smooth way of profession; but what will you do now, when you must come possibly to suffer persecution for it? to keep the faith, you may lose your liberty, life, estate. And there is a great deal of hazard upon this account, because it hath pleased God so to dispose it, as that those that should be your guides into truth, the Lord is removing them into corners. Possibly while they have been with you, you have kept the faith: but what will you do when they are gone? While Moses was with the people they cleaved to the Lord; when once he was gone into the mount, they fell into their idolatry, and worshipped a calf. While Paul was at Ephesus the flock kept pure, but (saith he) "I know after my departure grievous wolves shall break in, not sparing the flock," &c. So while you have heard of God, who sends voices and warnings to scare away the wolves and foxes from you, possibly you may keep the faith; but what will you do when God removes them?

3. God hath ever had in all ages of his church, a word of his patience to be kept, to try his saints; and therefore

it does concern you to be valiant for the truth. In all the series of God's dispensations with his church, there hath been something or other of the faith of Christ, that hath cost them resisting to blood, to sacrifice their lives, to lay down all that they have for it by suffering. Now even as they, so we; if not in the same thing, yet in the same faith. We have still some word or other of God's patience to keep, therefore we need to have on the armour of light. You must wrestle with the fiery trial, for there is some jewel that Jesus Christ puts upon you to wear, that persecutors and persecutions, heresies and heretics will scratch at, which you must hold out with loss of life to keep; and this must be till the latter part of the rage and reign of Antichrist is out; and even as you keep that, so will God keep you, Rev. iii. 10. As you honour the word of God's patience, so God will honour you. As you are faithful to him, so will he give you the crown, and no otherwise. Hence therefore it concerns us all to be armed with a holy confidence and resolution, as to this spiritual warfare, in contending for the faith delivered to us.

But the great thing I shall speak to, is, wherein may Christians be helped in this holy struggling and contention?

I shall only mention five or six things, some to fit you for it, others to help you in the management of it. I shall name them mixtly, and not distinct.

First, Bring all doctrines that are offered you to believe, and all practices that are put upon you to practice, to the scriptures, the word of God; try them there, whether they be to be retained, or to be rejected. You will have this double advantage by it; 1. To discover what is right, and what is wrong. 2. To have on the best part of your armour, whereby to contend against it.

1. To discover what is right, and what is wrong; for the scripture alone is the touchstone of doctrines, and the trial of spirits. The scripture does discover itself, and doth discover all things that are contrary to it.

When you are bidden to try all things, it is not by practising all things, as some poor giddy-headed Christians of late days have done; who have made the practising every opinion, to be their trying of it, till they have run themselves into all opinions: but it is the scripture you are first to try, and then to practice; who are like the noble Bereans, that were more noble than those of Thessalonica, because they searched the scriptures. To bring the truths that have or shall be taught you, or the doctrines that shall be imposed upon you, to the word of God; to see whether they be according to the truth, or no: for false doctrines and false worship, of all things they hate the scripture most. They are alike false coin, or false jewels, which go best in the night. False coin will not endure the touch-stone, nor false jewels the day. No more will false doctrines the scripture, therefore it will be a great way to discover them.

2. It will be a great way to vanquish them, Eph. vi. "Above all, take the sword of the spirit?" The word of God is the sword of the spirit, by which we slay heretical doctrines; and by which we are to slay sinful practices. All those stones that the Davids of God have flung at the Goliahs of error, they have been taken out of the brook of the scriptures: therefore reduce all doctrines offered you to believe, all worships that are taught you to practise, to the word of God.

1. All doctrines that are taught you to believe, reduce them thither; there is no profession of faith to be built, but the stones must be fetched from that mountain. If you believe divine truths, but not because the scripture propounds them, your faith is but human. If you believe any thing the scripture doth not speak, your faith is diabolical. The word of God, and your faith, must run parallel. All that is written, you must believe, and you must believe nothing but what is written. This was the rule of the Old Testament, Isa. viii. 20. "To the law and to the testimony; to the law, that is, to Moses; and to the testimony, that is, to the prophets: if they

speak not according to these, there is no light in them. When any thing was offered to Christ by way of enquiry, his common answer was, "How readest thou?" Luke x. 26. "How is it written?" When the apostle Paul would redress the abuse of the Lord Supper, he does not carry the Corinthians to these and these fathers, to this and that use and custom, but brings that, How it was delivered from the Lord. He reduces them to the institution, "What I have received from the Lord, that I have delivered unto you." The word of God is perfect, in respect of doctrine, and in respect of worship. So that whatsoever is offered you to believe, you must try it by perfect rules; for it is given by divine inspiration, to make the man of God perfect and wise unto salvation. It is such a canon about doctrines to be received, as nothing must be added nor taken from it, Rev. xxii. Therefore it is called a Testament. Now no man dares add to another man's last will and testament. Who shall dare to add a faith to the faith of God's elect, to that which Christ hath delivered? I will give you this as a certain observation, that there never was any thing of false doctrine brought into the church, or any thing of false worship imposed upon the church, but either it was by neglecting the scripture, or by introducing something above the scripture.

2. Bring hither all practices of worship, as well as doctrine, to be believed. Try the ways and forms of Christ's house, by the word of Christ. He shews us the patterns thereof, the out-goings, and returnings thereof. He was faithful in all his house, even as Moses was, who did not leave a pin of the tabernacle, but did appoint it. There is nothing decent and comely in the church, which is so much pleaded for, but what comes in by Christ's institution. Whatever you worship without a warrant from the word of God, or by whatever means you worship without a warrant from the word of God, you worship you know not what, John iv. 20. It is will-worship; and by the same rule you receive one will-worship, you may receive twenty. It is vain worship; it will never reach the

end of your communion with God; (for he is a spirit, and seeks such worshippers;) it will never bring you to the enjoyment of God; therefore, in point of worship, bring it to the word of God. And as to faith and worship, say, hitherto, my faith and my worship, shalt thou go, and no further. This rule rightly improved, will dis-entangle you from the hooks, and take you off from the baits of those cunning fowlers (for to such the apostle doth compare them in the New Testament) who seek to betray souls from the simplicity of gospel-faith. Never any did invent false doctrine, but to put up them, they put down the Scripture, and they put out the eyes of christians to make them bend to it. Before they use other means to compel them, their great work is to darken the light, or the truth; and in the room of the Scripture to be your rule, they set up other rules, which, because there are three marvellously popular, I desire to mention them in opposition to this rule I have given you.

There is a three-fold rule men would set up to deceive poor souls. The name of the church; ancient customs; the generality of those where they live.

1. The specious name of a church, to make that a rule to doctrine and to worship. It was the plea of the Popish party in the Marian days. What! will you not believe the church? Hath not the church power to make institutions and canons about this, and that, and the other? Will you not believe the church? Will you go out from the true church? Thus do men that go about to deceive; nothing like it, as to the catching and deluding many poor souls, by making the church their rule. It was the way of the Popish party of old, and if Antichrist ever hath power again over the church of Christ, in that measure and degree it has had, you must expect it again; therefore, let me caution you against it. Can we enquire who this church was? It was only the decree of the proud church, Antichrist of old, and the Antichristian clergy, who (as you may read in their stories) would lord it over the faith of God's heritage. I must

tell you, the name, and custom, and way of the churches of Christ, is a reverend holy thing, even of that that is a true church. It is a weighty argument, when the apostle saith, "We have no such custom, nor the churches of Christ." And therefore I do fully close with him that said, No sober man will go against reason. No christian against the Scripture: and no peaceable-minded man against the church. But then the church must shine by a Scripture-light. If that be a rule, it must be ruled by the Scripture. The church's power is not authoritative, as to give laws against the laws of Christ; it is only ministerial. We do believe the Scripture for itself, and not because of the church; we receive the Scripture by the church. Hence, therefore, when we set up the name of a church, let us see whether that church walk in the way of Christ, whether she be his spouse or no, whether she doth act according to his institutions, whether they bring his light, yea or no; then submit. For it is not what a church practices, but what they are warranted to practice: not what they hold for a truth, but what they are warranted to hold as the word of truth. The word was written after the church; but as it is the word of God, it is before it. This, therefore, will break the snare. If you be set upon by the specious name of the church, look that the church hath warrant from Scripture-institution, and then submit to church-institution.

A second means I observe men would set up to betray poor souls from the faith once delivered to them, is ancient custom: (our fathers worshipped in this mountain.) When they would hold forth that which the scripture is short in, they will send us to such and such customs, of so many hundred years standing. It is to be bewailed that the date, the standing of false doctrines, and false worships, is so ancient; for though at first they were but innovations, yet to succeeding generations they become old: and it is a very great truth, that what is the most ancient, is the most true; and therefore there lies a great snare in this. Therefore when antiquity is pretended, if you find not their hoary heads in the way of righteousness, there is little reason for you to reverence them, or comply with them, no more than there was reason so suddenly to be taken with the Gibeonite's mouldy bread and clouted shoes. When matters of antiquity are pretended, say as Ignatius, *Jesus Christus est mea antiquitas*, Jesus Christ is my antiquity. So say, truth is my antiquity: for though an opinion hath been practiced a thousand years, yet men may have the word of truth in their hearts that is more ancient than all.

A third guide that men would set up, is, The general course of the world, or place, the generality of those where they live. This was that the popish party did often mention to the witnesses of Jesus Christ? What! will you be wiser than others? Cannot you do as others do? Must you be singular? And this is a taking rule for to make you conformable to those things possibly the word of God will not warrant, if you bring not this custom to the word of God. It is not what the most do, but what we may do. It is not what the practice of all in general is, but what ought to be the singular care, and strict holiness of christians in particular, that the word of God will allow. Christians are not to be conformable to the present world, Rom. xii. 1. The word will tell you, It is no more safe to follow a multitude to do evil, than it will be sweet to be in hell with a great company. The word will let you know, the secrets of the Lord are with a very few, and those, them that fear him. As for the whole world it lies in wickedness. The word will tell you, The ways of Jesus Christ, and the profession of Jesus Christ, is commonly called a sect; it is every where spoken against, and men hath it every where; therefore set up a rule in your hearts, in your houses, in your meditations, in your practice.

RULE 2.

Be very well rooted and established in the faith that hath been delivered to you. I observe one of the great reasons why christians so easily let go the profession they have made, is, because they were never well built upon it, nor established in it. There are many christians that, through their own itching ears, heaping up teachers to themselves, have never been rooted or established in the truth; the Lord pity them and keep them this day. Many christians that have attended to establishing means, yet never seriously considered nor laid things to their heart, but are like those the apostle speaks of, Heb. v. 12. that had need to learn the first oracles of God. How many among us profess with the highest, but have little ground for their faith! only (with the Jews) the traditions of the elders, the custom of the place, education, and because such a party of men say so, because nobody denies it, because ministers commonly preached it; but to have any solid and serious ground, they are yet to seek. It is not with the things of God, as with other arts, as logic, rhetoric, astronomy; in these arts the principle is presupposed to be proved; no man goes about to prove there is reason, that there is number, that there are heavenly bodies, because sense and experience shews it. But it is quite otherwise in the things of God: for you are not only to run away with the notion, that there is a God, that this God is one, and that these are his words and his works; but you are to know this by experience, because the knowledge of these things comes by infusion, by faith, by a belief that God is, " for by faith we believe the worlds were made by the word of God," Heb. xi. 3. It is that therefore I would press you to, that you would labour for an established spirit. Do not only hear the things of God, but see them; the first will but blind you, or at best leave you at great uncertainties; the last will settle you. What was the reason of the holy apostle's zeal, when they were under the greatest threatenings of the high priests, and were forbid to speak in the name of Christ, and to speak of justification by faith, and the resurrection of Christ from the dead, and forgiveness of sins by him, (things that are further remote from sense and reason?) The apostle will tell you, Acts iv. 20. "We cannot but speak the things we have seen and heard." Hence it is that poor silly women, that in respect of their imbecility and infirmity of sex, the terrors of the fire and faggot, might have been such to have brought them to apostacy, yet they confounded the great doctors and rabbis when they were brought before them. They were able to burn, though they could not dispute; they beheld things that were invisible. It is an excellent thing not to take up the word upon notion, upon opinion, but to have an established heart through grace. I shall direct you in two words.

1. Get the Lord by prayer to teach you every truth. What Jesus Christ teaches once, is everlastingly taught; no word is abiding, but what the Lord Jesus teaches himself. Look as it is with Satan, when he comes to seduce men from the truth, he will present such a fine notion without, and commonly he darts in some dazzling light within, so that you never knew a heretic take up a false opinion, but it was with a marvellous deal of sweetness and comfort. So when the Lord Christ teacheth by his spirit, he comes with that light, that sweetness, savour, and relish of truth, as will be impossible for you to let it go. Hence when Christ would confute the Pharisees, who had the witness of his Father in his work, he saith, Job v. 37. " Ye have neither heard his voice at any time, nor seen his shape." It is an excellent thing to see the shape, and hear the voice of God.

2. Be well rooted upon Christ, or else you will never be established in any truth of Christ. If you miss the Lord Jesus by the grace of faith, you will never hold fast the doctrine of faith; you are built upon the doctrine of the apostles, (not their persons) upon which the Lord Jesus is the corner-stone. He that does not know Jesus Christ himself, will certainly lose his faith. What is the reason the stony ground in time of persecution fell away? Why, they had not root, they were not planted upon the Lord Jesus.

Rule 3. Those truths that God hath taught you, and those ways of worship God hath committed to you, love them as your lives, love them above your lives; for no man will ever contend to hold them, if he do not love them. Things of low price and esteem, are presently let go. He that loves the word above his life, will let life go rather than the word. If you receive not the word out of love, every impostor and false prophet, every fear and terror of men will rob you of it. "Hide the word in thy heart (saith Solomon) love the truth dearly." It was a great speech of Calvin. Never did any one apostatize from the truth of Jesus Christ, but it was because he did not love the truth. And I add this, that never did any apostatize from the ways and truths of Jesus Christ, but it was because they did not receive them in love, or else they have lost their love; for there is a decay of affection, as well as having no affection. If you love them, what will you not suffer for them? (but more of that by and bye.)

Rule 4. Guard all the truths of God, and those ways of God that have been taught you; guard them strongly, especially truths that are most material and fundamental. For leading truths are like captains of armies, if they be routed, the whole rout follows them. There is great opposition that will be made against your faith. The whole power of darkness, of Antichrist, of his seducing spirits, likely and probably enough, will overspread the whole face of christianity once more. For she must sit as a lady, before she be desolate and forsaken for ever. The apostle bids you beware of dogs; beware of the concision; beware of evil workers; guard yourselves against them; guard the truths you have learned, by argument, by Scripture, by reason, that you may have wherewithal to confute them by the word of truth mightily, out of the scripture, as the apostle did.

Three things you are to guard against.

1. Your own deceitfulness; especially in a rash and sudden forsaking of those ways that have been taught,

and the profession you have taken up; for christians would never be so mad to apostatize, were they but seriously to deliberate, about the weight of them. Gal. iii. 1. " O foolish Galatians, who hath bewitched you, that you would not obey the truth ?" &c. and i. 6. " I marvelled what ailed you, that you soon turned away to another gospel." One would have thought they might have spoken with Paul first, and sent to him, and reasoned the case with him. There is a marvellous bewitching in false doctrines, to take men presently, who are not watchful over themselves. It is in disputations and practising truth, as it is in contentions. If you make a judgment before you hear both parties speak, you judge unrighteously. If you forsake the ways and truths of Jesus Christ, before you can hear what can be said for them, you do unrighteously.

2. Guard them against the lusts of your own hearts. The great work of a Christian, is contention; it is not so much against Antichrist, those that are without him, as that which is within him. If all heretical doctrines and ways were rooted out of the world, not only the being, but the memory, the heart is bad enough in one day to set them all on foot again; therefore guard the truth. Men of corrupt minds will presently grow reprobate, as to the faith, 1 Tim. iii. 6. Such doctrines and worships as shall suit with our lusts, as shall suit with exalting self, and laying Christ low, as shall suit with an easy way to heaven, when the scripture saith, Straight is the gate; as shall suit with self-preservation. So I might secure my estate, my liberty. I would suspect such doctrines as these, before I take them up for the ways of Christ.

Guard the truth against false teachers, such as shall come among you in sheep's cloathing, yet are wolves in heart; men that creep in at unawares among you, to subvert souls. I will not here describe them, you know them well enough by their fruits. Only this let me tell you in opposition to those; though you cannot come at the public ministry, or those God hath set over you, yet make conscience for to take fences, to take defences from them, as you may by their counsel, prayer, help, and assistance, for to guard you against false teachers. When the church of Christ is in the wilderness, you will find this is that the Holy Ghost advises them to, Cant. i. 8. You are to guard yourselves by communion one with another; as to go forth by the footsteps of the flock, so also you are to go and feed your kids by the shepherds' tents; for though it is not the work that God calls for, to pin your faith upon their sleeves, yet it is your duty to enquire of the Lord by them; for he is the messenger of the Lord to you.

Rule 5. Arm yourselves with resolutions to suffer for the faith of the gospel, and for the ways of Jesus Christ. As you should love the truth above your lives, so labour to be made willing to part with life, estate, liberty, any thing for to keep the ways of Jesus Christ. It is not the honour of the gospel of Christ to hear Christians to break out into murmurings, passions, discontents, contentions that are carnal and sinful. Your work is, humbly, meekly, and patiently to lie under the hand of God, and under the hand of man too; that becomes Christians. Suffering is that that will restore the glory of religion, that will keep the truth delivered to you, that will honour the cause of Christ best of all. Follow the example of blessed Paul. His expression is worthy of consideration, 2 Tim. ii. 9. he gives a charge of keeping and propagating one of the most glorious truths, (that Jesus Christ was risen from the dead) yet a thing that is farthest off from sense and reason, (wherein I suffer trouble,) Mark, Paul does not say, wherein I make trouble; no, but wherein I suffer trouble, as an evil doer, unto bonds, but the word of God is not bound. If this blessed and glorious apostle would have had the faith of God bound, and have contented himself with sinful silence, and not propagated the gospel, Paul might have been free; but Paul would not have the word of God bound, therefore Paul would suffer for it. Shall we go higher a great deal than this?

You have the glorious commendation of the Lord Jesus Christ upon this account, that he gave a free and full account of the doctrine of his Father, and of his glorious person, before Pontius Pilate, a bloody persecutor. It was not by saying to his disciples, fight; nor by saying, my kingdom is not of this world: but he gave a glorious confession before the face of Pilate, of the righteousness of his truth, doctrine, gospel, and of his person. Fear to ensnare the freedom of the truth, with your own liberty; do not ensnare it to your own lusts, nor to the will of any man. Oh! that we could study, and improve these scriptures more! it would make us fear God more, and man less. This is that that would make us to say, as holy David did, Psal. cxix. 161. "Princes have persecuted me without a cause, but my heart standeth in awe of thy word." For he that hath the most fear on you, and upon you, you will be more afraid to fall into his hands. It is a childish thing for a Christian to tread down the belief of any doctrine, or practise any worship for fear of man, who hath no more power to hurt us, than we give him ourselves by our fear; Fear not him that can kill the body, &c. It was the way of God's people formerly, that they came to divide between duty commanded by God, and commanded by man. You may read in all the days of Antichrist's persecution, from the beginning they came to divide in matter of obedience to God and his truth; and worship and obedience to man. Christians! nothing but a suffering spirit will help you to this, for there is no other way of obedience in this case to authority, but to suffer under it meekly, patiently, as lambs. This made the three children to divide between the command of the king, and the command of God. What says Nebuchadnezzar? "Every knee that bows not, shall be cast into the furnace." Very well. "As for that matter, (say they,) O king, we are not careful to answer thee; for we will not bow down," &c. What, will they not obey him? Yes, they will obey him; by suffering, as becomes Christians, and is the example of Christ: as if they should say, Truly we are terrified with the burning furnace, but we are terrified with hell too. We are terrified by the threats of the great king, but we are likewise terrified with the threats of the great God. He is able to deliver us out of your torments, you are not able to deliver us from his torments. So in the case of Daniel. Arm yourselves with this resolution of suffering, and lying down patiently and meekly under those things that you cannot do, so that God may be honoured by your holy resolution upon this account. For truly, you never do contend successfully for the faith of the gospel, till you contend by suffering; for it is said, They overcome by the blood of the Lamb. You never make religion your business, till the world see you can let such great things go, as life, estate, liberty, to keep it. Then wisdom is justified of her children. You never glorified the truths of God so much by practice, or writing, as by suffering for them. Those glorious truths against popish justification, mixing of works with faith, transubstantiation, purgatory, idol-worship, against all those things that were superadded contrary to God's institution, there is such a glory upon the truths, that is hard for the popish power ever to darken them again, because we see them written in the honourable and blessed scars of the witnesses, and burnings of those glorious martyrs. If you would take one another by the hand, when God takes away our faithful guides, and say, brethren, sisters, friends, come let us hold together. There is no way in the world to hold on together like suffering; for the gospel really would get more advantage by the holy, humble, sufferings of one gracious saint, merely for the word of righteousness, than by ten thousand arguments used against heretics, and false worship. Compare Phil. i. 12, 13, 14. with the 27, 28, and 29th verses. How are Paul's bonds a furtherance of the gospel? Paul no doubt was called an evil doer, that sowed heresy, and was hated every where. Saith he, "Many of the brethren of the Lord waxed confident by my bonds, and were much more bold to speak the word without fear."

Here is the great encouragement: and that is in the 27th verse, and he speaks it as one that was leaving of them, "Only let your conversation be as becometh the gospel of Christ, that you may stand fast in one spirit, with one mind, striving together for the faith of the gospel, and in nothing terrified by your adversaries, for unto you it is given, not only to believe, but also to suffer," &c. It is given to you as a duty, given to you as a privilege. O that you would confirm one another, and in slippery times hold up one another by the hand! Do it in going after God's call, and in this way, suffering for those truths you cannot otherwise hold and maintain.

Truly, Christians, you had need be armed with resolutions; for the world is always counting the things God's people have suffered, for very little, and they count it prudence not to meddle therein. Those men that have easy, soft terms to comply, that they have a latitude to do any thing, I believe some Christians are of that opinion, that they would even think the saints of God were ill-advised to venture their all upon those truths they see others died and suffered for.

It is a sad thing, many Christians study to draw out the lines of obedience as far as the honesty of the times will give them leave, but no farther: that they would go on with the Lord Jesus to the high priest's hall, and there deny him: or that would be willing to do any thing for Christ, but are willing to suffer nothing for Christ. You do very little honour Jesus Christ in this, and you will very little honour yourselves at the last. It is upon this account that Christians, if they see even against plain conviction of conscience, and the word, that there are super-instituted things broken in, as in conscience they cannot submit to, yet they cannot comply, why? they may be used lawfully, though not superstitiously. But saith the apostle Paul, "Do I yet strive to please men?" Gal. i. 10. "Am I then the servant of Christ?" You cannot be the servants of Christ, if you strive to please men. Woe be to you that please men, and displease

God. "He that would be my disciple, let him deny himself, and take up his cross," &c. What is that? Deny wife, children, relations, comforts, he must be willing to go out of all. Those duties the Lord Jesus Christ is most glorified in, they are either those our slothful hearts are most unwilling to do, or that our fearful hearts are most unwilling to suffer for. Therefore arm yourselves with resolutions to suffer.

I intended to have taken up four appearances and coverings that saints usually take up for to hide themselves, as under a covert, to beat down the gospel-warrants and commands, to suffer for the faith delivered.

1. The notion that a christian hath of indifference of things, that they are but toys and trifles, that they may be done, or not done. It is not my work to tell you what is indifferent, or name any thing in particular. As I remember in the book of martyrs, the usual argument was, why cannot you worship the idol? Why cannot you bow down as well as others? It is a small matter. Cannot you shew your outward reverence, and keep your heart to yourself? Indeed if there were any thing that is indifferent, a christian hath a marvellous latitude in point of doctrine, in point of worship. I would caution you therefore. The term of indifferent, I suppose it is devised as a pillar to rest the conscience on, which otherwise would startle, and look with a broad face upon them. Things that come under this notion, had need well to be weighed and considered. If they tell you plainly they came out of Rome, and had the plague of popery upon them. They came from hell, were hatched there, and the curse of God is upon them; nobody will entertain them. They must pretend they came from the church, from the apostles, descending from the scriptures; and hence they are entertained with the freedom and willingness, as that most christians take no notice, but fall down under them; and so the very power and life of religion and holy practice is eaten out. The devil hath three ways whereby he makes men seek after him. First, commonly he doth

cover holiness with other names. Secondly, he persuades that sins are but little. Thirdly, that they may repent hereafter. The first is suitable to my purpose, that virtue or grace is covered with other names: therefore if a man be holy, he is called precise; if zealous, he is said to be rash; and if it be really a sin, it shall come under the name of indifferency, a toy, a trifle, and things of that nature. Therefore you had need be cautious; for it is not so much what name the sin has, what title it goes under, as what it is really. As to things of doctrine and worship I know there is no medium; every man must give an account to the Lord what he does; therefore I do not tell you what is indifferent, and what not; but search the scripture, take heed what you receive for indifferent.

The second thing christians will say, is, I hope without danger I may comply with them, considering I bear them as my burthens. This is very like the young man in the gospel; he came to Christ and would have him come up to his terms; and when Christ told him, yet he lacked one thing, go sell all, &c. he went away sorrowful. So, many christians they would follow Christ, but they cannot, because there is not such security in it, but they will go away sorrowfully. Thou hypocrite! art thou willing to forsake all for Christ, yet canst not leave life, liberty, and some of these small things? Will you wound the name of Christ, and pretend to be sorrowful for it? I conclude, thy pretence shall not excuse thee; for so was Pilate loth to crucify Christ; and, as a means and expedient, he calls for water and washes his hands, saying, " I am innocent from the blood of this just man." But do you think God excused Pilate? No more will he you. Whatever is brought to you, is either forbidden or commanded by God. If forbidden by God, why do you meddle with it? If commanded of the Lord, why are you burdened with it? why do you it heartily? For the Lord loves one that is cheerful in his service. Neither man nor God is pleased with such.

A third thing, which satisfies many, is, That they may follow in some things the opinions of wise men, holy men,

and good men; that they may do as they do. I shall say
but these two words: first, many men are reputed good,
wise, and honest, that are not so. A man may be accounted
an honest man, that yet may be covetous: he may be accounted
a very good man, yet be really corrupt in heart,
and in his lusts; therefore it is good to try men. I dare
not trust mine own heart, (unless God gives strength, and
grace, and assistance every moment) lest I should betray
the truth of Christ upon some advantage. When the
devil would set abroach an evil opinion or practice, it is
his common way to turn it up in some clean vessel. Men
of civil honesty and goodness: you read the old prophet
drew the young one in, though expressly forbidden by God
himself. When you do not fear a young christian, it may
be the example of an old minister shall draw you: therefore
it is good to mind who you follow. Secondly, grant
they are all good and real, they are men fearing God, (as
there are some;) yet God will not let his people know all
his mind. There are some that would, but cannot know
all his mind and will; the Lord is free and voluntary, he
reveals things necessary to salvation; but for other things
he withholds. But what is your rule? Call no man master.
You are to follow no man further than he follows
Christ: and indeed for a man to follow the examples of
others, wherein they sin and do not know it, it is just
like the case of holy Noah, (who was a gracious man) and
knew not the strength of the grape, he was drunk with his
own vineyard: but what was the fruit of it? His son Cham
saw his nakedness, and discovered it. If good and holy
men taste of the intoxicated wine that is too strong for
them, and know it, will you sip after them? Unless you
will discover your nakedness, and proclaim it from generation
to generation, and make yourselves Chams, not sons
of the prophet: therefore I know not what warrant you
have to follow such examples.

The fourth thing is this; christians usually do no
good by standing out. Answ. Whether we get good,
or do good or no, we are to do our duty. The Lord will

honour you for suffering for the truth, 2 Thes. i. 2, 3, 4, 5. And by suffering you shall confirm the saints, and bear testimony; you shall witness against all false doctrines, and false worship, before the whole world. By your humility and patience, when you suffer not as evildoers, but as those that suffer for the word of righteousness, the word of truth, for holding fast the Lord Jesus and his faith, that is more precious than heaven and earth, than any created thing. This will make your name as a sweet savour to all generations; when those that apostatize, persecute, and oppose Jesus Christ, their memories shall be left as a curse to the people of God.

MR. CALAMY'S SERMON.

1 Sam. iv. 13.

And when he came, lo, Eli sate upon a seat by the way side, watching; for his heart trembled for the ark of God.

THAT you may the better understand these words, you must know, that whatsoever God threatened against old Eli, in the second and third chapters, because he did not restrain his wicked sons from their lewd courses, is here executed in this chapter: therefore we read there were four thousand Israelites slain by the Philistines. And the elders of Israel met together to consult how to repair this great loss; they confess it was the Lord that had smitten them. For, say they, "Wherefore hath the Lord smitten us to-day before the Philistines?" And they conclude, the way to repair this their loss, it was, to fetch the ark of the covenant of the Lord from Shiloh, and carry it into the battle; whereupon they appointed Hophni and Phinehas to fetch it, whereby they imagined that the presence of the ark would save them from ruin, but herein they were miserably mistaken. For this judgment befel not because the ark was not in the camp; but because their sin was in the camp. The ark of the covenant would not preserve those that had broken covenant with God. And therefore there was a great slaughter of the Israelites, and were slain thirty thousand men, and Hophni and Phinehas were slain, and the ark itself was taken prisoner. But what was old Eli doing? He was ninety and eight years old, and was not able to go to the battle, but sits upon a seat by the way side near the battle; and there he sits, thinking what shall become of the ark: "And lo, Eli sate upon a seat by the way side, watching; for his heart trembled for the ark of God," for fear lest the ark should be taken.—He was not troubled, what should become of his two sons, or what should become of the people of Israel, but what should become of the ark of God.

In the words are three parts.
1. Old Eli's solicitousness for the ark.
2. Old Eli's heart trembling for fear of the ark.
3. Old Eli's preferring the safety of the ark before the safety of his two sons, wife, and children.

"He sat upon a seat by the way side watching, for his heart trembled for the ark of God."

But what was the ark of God? Why should old Eli's heart tremble for fear of the ark?

I answer, this ark was the holiest of all the things of God; it was so holy that it made every place holy where it came, 2 Chr. viii. 11. "And Solomon brought up the daughter of Pharaoh, out of the city of David, into the house that he had built for her, for he said, my wife shall not dwell in the house of David king of Israel, because the places are holy whereunto the ark of the Lord hath come." This ark was the dwelling-place of God, it was the habitation of God, Psal. xcix. 1. "The Lord reigneth, he sitteth between the cherubims." Now these cherubims were placed over the ark; it was the speaking place of God, he met his people there, and there he gave an answer to them. Exod. xxv. 21, 22. "And thou shalt put the mercy-seat, above upon the ark, and in the ark thou shalt put the testimony that I shall give thee: and there will I meet with thee, and I will commune with thee from above the mercy-seat, from above the two cherubims, which are upon the ark of the testimony, of all things I shall give thee in commandment unto the children of Israel." This ark was God's foot-stool, and all the people of God worship him before the foot-stool of God. Psal. xcix. 5. " Exalt ye the Lord our God, and worship at his foot-stool, for he is holy." The ark, it was the glory and the strength of Israel, Psal. lxxviii. 61. " And he delivered his strength into captivity, and his glory into his enemies hands; and it was the terror of the enemies of God." And therefore when the ark came into the battle, the Philistines were afraid, and said, " woe unto us, for God is come down into the camp." And indeed this ark was called Jehovah, Num. x. 35. " And it came to pass, when the ark set forward, that Moses said, Rise up, Lord, and let thine enemies be scattered; and when it rested, he said, Return, O Lord, unto the many thousands of Israel." In a word, the ark was a pledge and a visible symptom of God's gracious presence with his people. As long as the ark was saved, they were saved; and when the ark was with them, then God's presence was with them; but when the ark was gone, God was gone, his comforting presence, his protecting presence, and his preserving presence. And therefore no wonder that this good old man sat watching here for fear of the ark. I call him good old man, many are of opinion that he was not good, because he suffered his sons to be wicked; and indeed his fault was great, but surely he was a good man, and I have two reasons to prove it. First, in that he took the punishment of his iniquity so patiently, " It is the Lord, let him do what seemeth him good." And secondly, he was a good man, as appears by the text, his solicitousness for the ark: "he sat trembling for fear of the ark."

Now this ark was a type of three things.

First, it was a type of Jesus Christ; for God spake from the ark; so God speaks to us by Christ.

Secondly, it was a type of the church of Christ; for as the ark was the preserver of the two tables of the law, so the church of Christ is the preservative of the scriptures.

Thirdly, the ark was a type of the ordinances of Christ; for as God did communicate himself by the ark, so God by his ordinances communicates his counsels, comforts, and grace unto his people. The ordinances of Christ they are the oraculum by which he conveys himself unto his people. Thus I have shewed you what the ark was.

I shall gather two observations from the words.

1. That when the ark of God is in danger of being lost, the people of God have thoughtful heads and trembling hearts.

2. That a true child of God is more troubled, and more solicitous what shall become of the ark, than what shall become of wife and children or estate.

I shall begin with the first doctrine.

That when the ark of God is in danger of being lost, the people of God have thoughtful heads and trembling hearts,

Or, if I may put this doctrine in a gospel dress, take it thus,

That when the gospel is in danger of losing, when gospel-ordinances are in danger of being lost, and gospel-ministers in danger of losing, that then the people of God have trembling heads, and careful and solicitous hearts about it.

Mark what I say. I say not when the ark is lost: for that was death to old Eli, that broke his neck, and it cost the life of Eli's daughter-in-law, when the ark of God was taken, she took no comfort in her child, though a man child ; she regarded it not. For the glory is departed from Israel, the ark of God is taken.

I say not when the ark of God is lost ; but I say when it is in danger of losing. When the gospel is in danger, the ministers of the gospel in danger, and the ordinances in danger to be lost, then the people of God have trembling hearts, and careful heads. When God threatened the Israelites, that he would not go with them, they were troubled for the loss of God's presence, and would not put on their ornaments, Exod. xxxiii. 3, 4. "I will not go up in the midst of thee, for thou art a stiff-necked people, lest I consume thee in the way. And when the people heard these evil tidings they mourned, and no man did put on his ornaments." 1 Sam. vii. 2. "And it came to pass while the ark abode in Kiriath-jearim, that the time was long, for it was twenty years, and all the house of Israel lamented after the Lord," that is after the presence of God, speaking from the ark, 2 Sam. xi. 10, 11. David would have had Uriah to have gone down to his house and made merry ; and Uriah said unto David, "the ark and Israel, and Judah abide in tents, and my lord Joab, and the servants of my Lord are encamped in open fields : shall I then go into mine house to eat and to drink, and to lie with my wife ? As thou livest, and as thy soul liveth, I will not do this thing," 1 King. xix. 10. and Elijah said, " I have been very jealous for the Lord of hosts : for the children of Israel have forsaken thy covenant, thrown down thy altars, and slain thy prophets with the sword, and I, even I only am left, and they seek my life to take it away." Thus you see when the ark is in danger, the people of God mourn and are sorrowful.

And there be four reasons, why the people of God are so much troubled when the ark of God is in danger.

Reason 1. Because of the great love they bear to the ark of God. " As God loveth the gates of Sion, more than all the dwellings of Jacob," Psal. lxxxvii. 2. so the people of God love the ordinances of God, and the faithful ministers of Christ, Psal. xxvi. 8. "Lord, I have loved the habitation of thy house, and the place where thine honour dwelleth," Psal. xxvii. 4. "One thing have I desired of the Lord, that will I seek after, that I may dwell in the house of the Lord all the days of my life, to behold the beauty of the Lord, and to enquire in his temple." Now love stirreth up the affections, as young Cresus, though he were dumb, yet seeing his father like to be killed, cried out, Do not kill my father. Such is the love of the saints of God to the ark, that they cannot be silent, they cannot but tremble when they see the ark in danger: and for Sion's sake, they cannot hold their peace: and they cannot be silent until the Lord make the righteousness thereof go out like brightness, and the salvation thereof as a lamp that burneth.

2. The people of God are troubled at this, because of the interest they have in the ark of God. Now interest stirreth up affection, as when another man's house is on fire; as you had a lamentable and sad providence this last week, and it is not to be forgotten, how suddenly in all our feastings, may God dash all our mirth. Now consider, how were they affected that had an interest in those that were burned: so the people of God have an interest in the ark. God is the haven of a child of God, the portion and inheritance of a child of God; and when God begins to forsake them, they cannot but be afflicted and troubled. The ordinances of God are the jewels of a christian, and the treasure of a christian; and the loss of them cannot but trouble them. And Jesus Christ is the joy of a christian, and therefore when Christ is departing, they cannot but be much afflicted at it.

3. The people of God are much troubled when the ark is in danger, because of the mischiefs that come upon a nation when the ark of God is lost. Woe be to that nation when the ark is gone. The heathens had the image of Apollo, and they conceived, that as long as that image was presented among them, they could never be worsted,

but be preserved; and the Romans had a buckler, upon which they had a tradition, that as long as that buckler was preserved, Rome could not be taken. Shall I give a hint, and set it out a little in five particulars.

1. "When the ark of God is taken, then the ways of Sion mourn, and none come to the solemn assemblies: it was the complaint of the church," Lam. i. 4. That is matter of sadness.

2. When the ark of God is taken, then the ministers of Christ are driven into corners. And this is matter of heart-trembling.

3. When the ark of God is taken, then the souls of many are in danger. When the gospel is gone, your souls are in hazard. There is cause of sadness.

4. "Then do the enemies of God blaspheme, and are ready to say, Where is your God? Then do the enemies of God triumph," Psal. xlii. 10. As with a sword in my bones mine enemies reproach me: while they say daily unto me, Where is thy God?

5. Then is Jesus Christ trampled under foot, and the ordinances of God defiled and trampled on; and then blasphemy and atheism come in like an armed man.

4. The people of God must needs tremble when the ark is in danger, because of their accessariness to the losing of the ark; and this was that which made old Eli so much troubled, because he knew it was for his sin that God suffered the ark to be taken. He knew that his not punishing his two sons, was one cause of that great slaughter the people of Israel met withal, and that made him tremble. There is no person here in this congregation, but his heart will tell him, he hath contributed something towards the loss of the ark. None of us so holy but our consciences must accuse us. We have done something that might cause God to take the ark from us. And therefore Mr. Bradford, that blessed martyr, said in his prayer, Lord, it was for my unthankfulness for the gospel, that brought in popery in Queen Mary's days: and my unfruitfulness under the gospel, that was the

cause of the untimely death of King Edward the sixth: and those that fled in Queen Mary's days, sadly complained that they were the cause of God's taking away the gospel from England. O beloved, it is for thy sin and my sin, that the ark of God is in danger; and therefore the Lord gave us trembling solicitous hearts, what shall become of the ark.

I come now to application.

Use 1. If this be the property of a true child of God, to be solicitous when the ark of God is in danger, and to have such a trembling heart for fear of the ark, then this is a certain sign there are but few that are the children of God in truth. O where is the man? And where is the woman that like old Eli sits watching and trembling for fear of the ark? And that will appear by these reasons.

First, In reference to the many sins in this nation; for let me tell you, there is not one sin for which God ever took away the ark from any people, but it is to be found in England. Did the church of Ephesus lose the candlestick, because they had lost their first love? And have not we lost our first love to the gospel, and to the ordinances? And did the church of Laodicea lose the candlestick, because of lukewarmness? And are not we lukewarm? Did the people of Israel, as here in the text, lose the ark, because they abhorred the offerings of God? and do not you do so? Are not the sins of Israel amongst us? the sins of Germany, and the sins of all other nations about us? And can any man here before God this day, in this congregation, that considers the great unthankfulness of this nation, and the great profaneness and wickedness of this nation, but they may conclude the ark is in danger, and God may justly take the ark from us?

I might tell you of the drunkenness, adultery, covetousness, injustice, and uncharitableness, &c. that doth abound among us; and I might tell you of sanctuary sins, profanation of sabbath and sacraments, our unthankfulness, and unfruitfulness, and unworthy walking under the gospel. And you of this place, God may very well take the ark even from you; and indeed it was the great interest I had in you, the which while I live I shall ever own; and that great affection and respect I had to you, that I would not send you home this day without a sermon, and let you go without a blessing. Now can any of you in this parish, and this congregation; can any of you say, God may not justly take the gospel from you?

Secondly, Shall I add, the discontents and divisions of a nation, as Christ saith, " A nation divided against itself cannot stand;" but I leave these things to your considerations. I believe there is none here but will confess the ark of God is in danger to be lost. But now where are our Elis to sit watching and trembling for fear of the ark? Where is Phinehas his wife, that would not be comforted, because the ark of God was taken? Where are our Moseses? our Elijahs, our Uriahs? Where are they that lay to heart the dangers of the ark? You complain of taxes, decay of trading, of this civil burden, and that civil burden; but where is the man or the woman that complains of this misery, the loss of the ark? Most of you are like Gallio, he cared not for these things; if it had been a civil matter, then he would have meddled with it; but for religion, he cared not for that. Every man is troubled about meum and tuum, about civil concernments; but who lays to heart, who regards what shall become of religion? There is a strange kind of indifferency and lukewarmness upon most people's spirits; so they have their trading go on, and their civil burdens removed, they care not what becomes of the ark.

There is a text of scripture, I shall not spend much time in opening it, but I would have you well consider it, Hos. vii. 9. "Strangers have devoured his strength, and he knoweth it not: yea grey hairs are here and there upon him, yet he knoweth not." Shall I say grey hairs are upon the gospel? I come not hither to prophecy, I say not, the gospel is dying, but I say it hath grey hairs: for you have had the gospel a hundred years and above, and therefore it is in its old age: and I dare challenge any scholar to shew me an example of any nation that hath enjoyed the gospel for a hundred years together. Now that grey hairs is to a hundred years, is no wonder. Well, grey hairs are here and there, and yet no man layeth it to heart.

Now shall I spend time to shew you what a great sin it is not to be affected with the danger that the ark of God is in. Consider but three particulars.

First, It is a sign you do not love the gospel. If you had any love to it, you would be troubled more for the danger of the ark, than for any outward danger whatsoever.

Secondly, It is a sign you have no interest in the gopel, for interest will stir up your affections. It is a sign you are not concerned in the gospel, for if you were concerned in it, you would be affected with it, as those that were interested in those persons that were in that lamentable fire the last week, it is impossible but they should be affected. And so it is a sign you have no interest in God and Christ, if your hearts do not tremble for fear of the loss of the ark.

But thirdly, There is a curse of God pronounced against all those that do not lay to heart the afflictions of Joseph, Amos vi. 1, 2, 3, 4, 5, 6. "Woe be to them that are at ease in Sion, and trust in the mountain of Samaria: ye that put far away the evil day: that lie upon beds of ivory, and stretch themselves upon their couches: that eat the lambs out of the flock, and the calves out of the midst of the stall: that chant to the sound of the viol, and invent to themselves instruments of music: that drink wine in bowls, and anoint themselves with the chief ointments: but they are not grieved for the afflictions of Joseph." Woe be to you that enjoy your fulness of outward things, and make merry therewith, and never consider the afflictions of God's people, and the danger of the ark.

Use 2. For exhortation, to beseech you all, that God by a providence hath so unexpectedly brought this day to hear me, and there may be a good providence in it; possibly I may do good herein. I say let me beseech you all to declare you are the people of God in deed and in truth, by following the example of old Eli, to be very solicitous of the ark of God, and let me exhort you to five particulars.

First, Let me persuade you to believe, that the gospel is not entailed upon England. England hath no letters patent of the gospel; the gospel is removeable. God took away the ark and forsook Shiloh, and he did not only take away the ark, but the temple also. He unchurched the Jews, he unchurched the seven churches of Asia, and we know not how soon he may unchurch us. I know no warrant we have to think that we shall have the gospel another hundred years. God knows how to remove his candlestick, but not to destroy it. God doth often remove the church, but doth not destroy it. God removed his church out of the east, as the Greek churches were famous churches, but God removed them, and now the Turk overspreads that country.

Secondly, I would persuade you that England's ark is in danger to be lost. Were it not only for the sins of England, those prodigious iniquities amongst us, and that strange unheard-of ingratitude that is in the land: but I will say no more of that, because I would speak nothing but what becomes a sober minister of the gospel.

Thirdly, I would persuade you, and O that I could raise you up to old Eli's practice: " He sat watching, for his heart trembled for fear of the ark:" he had a thoughtful head, and an aching heart, for the ark of God that was in great danger; and that I might move you to this, consider what a sad condition we are in, if the ark be taken. What will your estate do you good? or what will your concernments do you good if the gospel be gone? Wherein doth England exceed other places? There is more wealth in Turkey than in England, and the heathen nations have more of the glory of the world, than any christian king hath. What is the glory of England? What is the glory of christianity but the gospel? If the gospel be gone, our glory is gone. Pray remember Eli's daughter-in-law, the wife of Phinehas, she hearkened not, though a man child was born, and would receive no comfort, but called his name Ichabod: for the glory is departed from Israel, the ark of God is taken. O when the glory is gone, who would desire to live? I am loth to tell you the story of Chrysostom, he was but one man, yet when he was banished Constantinople, the people all petitioned for him, and said, "they could as well lose the sun out of the firmament, as lose Chrysostom from among them."

Fourthly, Let me persuade you not to mourn immoderately, neither be discouraged. I would willingly speak something to comfort you before I leave you. I know not by what strange providence I came here this day, and the Lord knows when I shall speak to you again: therefore I would not send you home comfortless. O therefore mourn not as without hope, for I have four arguments to persuade me, that the ark of God will not be lost, though it be in danger of losing.

First, Because God hath done great things already for this nation; and I argue like Manoah's wife, surely if God had intended to destroy us, he would not have done that he hath done for us. He that hath done so much for us, will not now forsake us. And therefore though our hearts tremble, yet let them not sink within us.

Secondly, I argue from the abundance of praying people that are in this nation, there are many that night and day pray unto God, that the ark may not be taken; and let me assure you, God will never forsake a praying and reforming people. When God intends to destroy a nation, and take away the ark, he takes away the spirit of prayer; but where God gives the spirit of prayer, there God will continue the ark. You all know, that if there had been but ten good men in those five cities, God would have spared them. We have many hundreds that fear God in this nation, that do not give God rest, but night and day pray unto God for this land. And who knows but for their sakes God will spare the ark?

Thirdly, Another ground of comfort is this, that God hath hitherto dealt with England, not by way of rule, but by way of prerogative. We have had unchurching sins all the reign of Queen Elizabeth, and of King James; and the godly ministers have been threatened ruin from year to year; but God hath hitherto saved England by way of prerogative. God hath spared us, because he will spare us. According to that text, "I will be gracious, to whom I will be gracious." God will not be tied to his own rule, and who knoweth but God will deliver us?

Fourthly, Another ground of comfort is, that God is now pouring out his phials upon Antichrist, and all this shall end in the ruin of Antichrist; God is pouring forth his phials upon the throne of the beast, and all these transactions shall end in the ruin of Antichrist; though some drops of these phials may light upon the reformed churches, and they may smart for a while, and God may severely punish them, yet it will be but for a little while but the phials shall be poured out upon Antichrist. God may scourge all the reformed churches before these phials be poured out, and persecution may go through them all; the which I call drops of these phials, but the phials are intended for Antichrist, and shall end in the time of Antichrist: and whatsoever becomes of us, yet our children, and our children's children, shall see the issue of the phials poured out upon the whore of Babylon. This I speak for your comfort.

Fifthly, I am to exhort you, that you would all of you contribute your utmost endeavour to keep the ark of God from being taken. And here I shall shew you,

1. What the magistrate should do.
2. What the minister should do.
3. What the people should do.

First, What the magistrates should do. I shall say but little of them, because I am not now to speak to them. They are to use their authority for the settling of the ark; for the ark of the covenant will be like the ark of Noah, always floating upon the waters, until the magistrates settle it. Thus David, 2 Sam. vi. 12. he gathered together all the chosen men of Israel, thirty thousand to fetch home the ark. So Solomon, he assembled the elders of Israel, and the heads of the tribes, the nobles, and the chief of the fathers of the children of Israel to Jerusalem, with a great deal of pomp, to bring up the ark of the covenant of the Lord into its place. O that God would encourage our nobles and magistrates that they might be solicitous to settle the ark. Magistrates must not be as the Philistine; they had the ark, but what did they with it? They set it up in the house of Dagon, but Dagon and the ark could never agree. Where false religion comes in at one door, the true religion goes out at the other. You must not put the ark and Dagon together.

Secondly, What must the ministers do to keep the ark from losing? They must endeavour after holiness. The ark will never stand steady, nor prosper upon the shoulders of Hophni and Phinehas. A wicked, profane, drunken ministry, will never settle the ark. It must be the sober, pious, godly ministers that must do it. How holy must they be that draw nigh to the God of holiness

Thirdly, What must the people of God do, that the ark may not be lost? There be five things I shall commend unto you, and then commend you to God.

1. You must not idolize the ark.
2. You must not undervalue the ark.
3. You must not pry into the ark.
4. You must not meddle with the ark without a lawful call.

5. You must keep the covenant of the ark.

First. You must not idolize the ark, that was the sin of the people in the text. They thought the very presence of the ark would excuse them, and keep them safe, and, therefore, they carried the ark into the camp. Though they reformed not, and repented not, yet they thought the ark would save them.

So many there be that think the ark will save them, though never so wicked. But nothing will secure a nation, but repentance and reformation.

Secondly, Do not undervalue the ark. This was Michal's sin, 2 Sam. vi. 14, 15, 16. "When David danced before the ark, and Michal mocked him, and despised him in her heart, (but, saith he) it was before the Lord, and if this be vile, I will be more vile." Some men begin to say, what need we any preaching, will not reading prayers serve? Others say, what need so much preaching, will not once a day serve? Now this is to undervalue the ark; therefore let us say as David, if to preach the word, if to fast and pray for the nation, " if this be vile, then I will be more vile."

Thirdly, We must not pry into the ark. This was the sin of the men of Bethshemesh. 1 Sam. vi. 19. " They loooked into the ark, and God smote them, and cut off fifty thousand and threescore men." Be not too curious in searching where God hath not discovered or revealed. For example, there be great thoughts of a heart, when God will deliver his people, and set his churches at liberty ; and many men talk much of the year 1666. That shall be the year wherein Antichrist shall be destroyed. And there are strange impressions upon the hearts of many learned men, as to this year. Some go to the year 1669, and others pitch upon other times. But, truly, if you will have my judgment, and I am glad of this opportunity to tell you, this is to pry too much into the ark. Remember the text, Acts i. 17. "It is not for you to know the times or the seasons which the Father hath put in his own power." And thus to conclude upon any particular time, if you find you are deceived, it is the way to make you atheists, and that afterwards you shall believe nothing. And those ministers do no service, or rather ill service to the church of God, that conclude of the times and seasons.

A Popish author saith, that in the year 1000, there was a general belief over the christian world, that the day of judgment should be that year; but when they saw it happened not, they fell to their old sinning again, and were worse than before, and believed nothing. Well God's time is the best, therefore let not us pry too much into the ark.

Fourthly, You must not meddle with the ark, unless you have a lawful call to meddle with it. This was the sin of Uzzi, 2 Sam. vi. 6, 7. the ark was in danger of falling, and he, good man, meaning no hurt, to keep up the ark, took hold of it; but, for so doing, he destroyed himself, and made a breach, and hindered the carrying home of the ark at that time.

We have had a great deal of disorder heretofore; and an abundance of well-minded people usurped upon the ministerial offices, they were afraid the ark was falling, and therefore they touched the ark, they laid hold on the ark; but their touching the ark hath undone the ark, and themselves too. O take heed of touching the ark.

Fifthly, If ever you would preserve the ark, then keep the covenant of the ark; keep the law which the ark preserves. The ark was a place wherein the law was kept, the two tables. Keep the law, and God will keep the ark; but if you break the law, you will forfeit the ark. The ark was called the ark of the covenant. Keep covenant with God, and God will preserve the ark; but if you break the covenant of the ark, the covenant made in baptism, and that covenant often renewed in the sacrament, if you break covenant, God will take away the ark.

JOHN GASPINE'S FAREWELL SERMON.

Preached at Ashpriors in the County of Somerset, the two last Lord's days before Bartholomew Day, 1662.

LUKE xii. 32.

Fear not, little flock, it is the Father's good pleasure to give you the kingdom.

IN this chapter we have the sum of a precious sermon which our Saviour makes to his disciples in the presence of the multitude. In which we have,

1. Several cautions in the first twenty verses of that chapter.
2. Some exhortations from thence to the end of it. The cautions are these.

First, To beware of hypocrisy, in the three first verses. Beware of the leaven of the Pharisees, which is hypocrisy; and the motive wherewith he backs this caution, is this, that all things should be opened and made known hereafter, how closely soever they may be carried, and how secretly soever their sins may be committed here. Men may think to varnish over the foulest of their actions by fair and plausible pretences, and so to hide their iniquities from the eyes of God and men; but they are much mistaken; for there is nothing " covered that shall not be revealed, nor hid, that shall not be known." ver. 2.

Secondly, He warns them to beware of timorousness and fearfulness in publishing his gospel, from the beginning of the 4th to the 12th verse, " I say unto you, my friends, be not afraid of them that kill the body, and after that, they have no more that they can do. But I will forewarn you whom you shall fear, fear him, who after he hath killed, hath power to cast into hell. I say unto you, fear him."

Thirdly, He cautions them to beware of covetousness, and this caution of his was occasioned by one that desired Christ to speak to his brother to divide the inheritance with them, verse 13. Upon this, Christ takes occasion to caution them against covetousness, verse 15. "And he said unto them, take heed and beware of covetousness." And that he might set out the folly of this sin of covetousness, he doth elegantly set it forth by a parable of a rich man, who was coveting after more and more of this world, and was casting, plodding, and contriving how to pull down his barns, and to build greater; and how to increase his estate in the world, when God said unto him, " Thou fool, this night shall thy soul be required of thee; and whose then will these things be which thou hast provided?" from ver. 15 to 20.

Having given them these cautions, he proceeds to give them several exhortations, as to seeking after the kingdom of God, to giving of alms, to watchfulness against the coming of Christ to judgment, and several other duties which I shall not now insist upon.

The text contains that exhortation of Christ, wherein he exhorts them to undauntedness and resolution in the ways of God. "Fear not, little flock, for it is your Father's good pleasure to give you the kingdom."

The words may be divided into these two parts.

First, Here is an exhortation.

Secondly, The reason of this exhortation.

First, An exhortation, "Fear not little flock." In the which here is,

1. A very loving compellation, in the words τὸ μικρὸν ποίμνιον, little flock.

2. The exhortation itself, μὴ φοβοῦ, fear not.

In the reason of the exhortation, viz. "For it is your Father's good pleasure to give you the kingdom." We have these things considerable.

First, Here is your Donor, your Father.

Secondly, Here is the donum or gift itself, which God will bestow upon his people, and that is the kingdom, by which is meant the kingdom of heaven.

Thirdly, The persons on whom God will bestow this kingdom, and that is you, you, my little flock.

Fourthly, The manner of God's bestowing the kingdom of heaven upon his little flock, and that is by gift, " It is your Father's good pleasure to give," &c.

Fifthly and lastly, The motive that prevails with God to give the kingdom of heaven to his people, and that is his own good pleasure, " It is your Father's good pleasure," &c.

So that you see every word hath its weight. Here is very much profitable matter contained in a few words; and many useful and profitable observations may be observed from it. As,

Doct. First, That Christ's flock is but a little flock, a very little flock. " Fear not, little flock."

Here be two diminutive words in original. First, μικρὸν, which signifies *little*; and then the word ποίμνιον, which also signifieth a *little flock*. Christ's flock is a little flock, very little in comparison to the rest of the world. The number of those that truly fear God, that are sincere christians, and that are by a true and lively faith really engrafted into Jesus Christ, is very small in comparison of the profane, the hypocrites, the unconverted and unsanctified, that are only christians by an external profession, that have only a form of godliness, but deny the power of it. " The way to heaven is narrow, and the gate strait, and there are but few that find it." Mat. vii. 13, 14. There may be many that make fair pretences to gion and holiness in a time of prosperity; but there are but few that will stick to Christ, and his holy ways, in discouraging times. There may be many that are rotten professors, but few that are sound in the faith.

Doct. 2. That God is a believer's Father; or that every sincere christian is a child of God, and hath God for his

Father. "It is (saith Christ to his disciples) your Father's good pleasure to give you the kingdom."

Doct. 3. That every true believer is interested in the kingdom of heaven. The great God will bestow the kingdom of heaven upon believers.

Doct. 4. That the kingdom of heaven is the free gift of God. "It is the Father's good pleasure to give you the kingdom." The kingdom of heaven comes not to a believer by his own merits, nor by his own deservings; but by God's free gift. The free grace of God is the great motive, it is God's good pleasure so to do. The saints cannot merit heaven by their holiest actions, though they walk never so closely with God. No, no, the kingdom of heaven is God's free gift unto believers.

Doct. 5. Lastly, That the consideration of a believer's interest in this kingdom of heaven, should make him cheerful and courageous in the practice of holiness, and keep him from being dismayed and discouraged at all the afflictions and tribulations that he meets withal in the world. This doctrine is gathered from the exhortation in the text, and the reason of it taken together. The exhortation, viz. "Fear not, little flock." The reason of the exhortation, viz. "For it is your Father's good pleasure to give you the kingdom." Intimating, that this one consideration that God will bestow the kingdom of glory upon his people hereafter, should make them with all willingness and cheerfulness to wade through all the calamities and incumbrances of this frail life. A believer's heavenly interest should make him rejoice in the midst of all his trials and tribulations that he meets with from the hands of men here on earth.

I shall choose out the second and last of these observations to go on upon, not having time and liberty to insist on them all. That observation then which I shall first of all insist upon, is this, viz.

Doct. That God is a believer's Father, or that every true and sincere christian hath God for his Father, and is a child of God. "It is your Father's good pleasure."

Before I come to the confirmation of this truth, I shall shew how many ways a people or person may have God to be their Father, and they may be his children.

First, A people or person may have God for their Father by creation. As God is the great Creator of the world, and they are his creatures, in this general sense God is a Father to all men and women in the world. To this refers that Scripture, Mal. iii. 10. Saith the prophet there, " Have we not all one Father? Hath not one God created us?" But it is a more peculiar sonship that belongs to believers; they have God for their Father in a more special and peculiar manner than this is.

Secondly, A people or person may be the children of God, and God may be their Father by profession. Thus God was a Father to the Jewish nation of old, because they among all the nations of the world did profess to own the Lord for their God, and to serve and worship him; and in this respect God doth profess himself to be a Father to Israel, Jer. iii. 9. " I am a Father to Israel, (saith God) Ephraim is my first-born." And thus God is a Father to all those that do profess his name. But if this be all the claim that we can lay to God as our Father, that he is so to us, and that we are his children only by an external profession, this will not entitle us to the kingdom, that eternal inheritance that God hath laid up in his people in the life to come; it is therefore yet in a more peculiar manner that believers have God for their Father.

Thirdly, A person may have God for his Father by adoption and regeneration; and thus true believers, and only such are the children of God, and God is their Father, 1 John xii. 13. " To as many as received him, to them gave he power to become the Sons of God, even to them that believe on his name, which were born not of blood nor of the will of the flesh, nor of the will of man, but of God." These are the sons of God, the strictest and most peculiar sons that shall be made partakers of all the privileges of the children of God, viz. Those that receive Christ into their hearts by faith, and such as are truly regenerate and born again. These are the true and genuine children of the Most High, the heirs of God, and co-heirs of Jesus Christ, as the expression is, Rom. viii. These are the children of God, of whom it was spoken, 2 Cor. vi. last, " I will be a father unto you, and you shall be my sons and daughters, saith the Lord Almighty." Having thus shewn unto you the several respects in which we may have God for our Father, I shall come to the confirmation of it, and shall prove that believers have God for their Father in this special and peculiar manner. There are abundance of scripture proofs for this, in which Jesus Christ speaking to his disciples, calleth God their Father, Mat. v. 16. " Let your light so shine before men, that they seeing your good works, may glorify your Father which is in heaven;" and ver. 48. " Be ye perfect as your Father which is in heaven is perfect," Mat. vi. 8. " Your Father knoweth what things you have need of, before you ask them," Mat. xviii. 14. " Even so it is not the will of your Father which is in heaven, those little ones should perish." John xx. 17. " Go, tell my brethren (saith Christ) that I ascend to my Father, and to your Father, to my God, and to your God." By these and other scriptures we may see that God is set forth to believers under the relation of a Father to them. And as God is called in scripture a believer's Father, so they are called sons, Gal. iv. 6. " Because ye are sons, God hath sent forth the spirit of his Son into your hearts, crying, Abba, Father, wherefore thou art no more a servant but a son; and if a son, then an heir of God through Christ." Again, 1 John iii. 2. " Now we are the sons of God, but it doth not yet appear what we shall be; when he shall appear, we shall be like him; for we shall see him as he is," Gal. iii. 16. The apostle speaking to the unbelieving Galatians, saith, " we are all the children of God by faith, which is in Christ Jesus." I shall no longer insist on the confirmation of this doctrine, but shall come to the application of it.

Use. Is it so, that all true believers are the children of God, and have God for their heavenly Father, then the first use may be of comfort and consolation to the godly, in that they are so nearly related to the great God; believers by virtue of their sonship, having God for their heavenly Father, have abundant ground of comfort and consolation upon these several accounts.

First, They are under his fatherly care and providence. Fathers take care for their children, to provide them things necessary, as meat, drink, and apparel; *ab iisdem alimur ex quibus generamur*, is a true maxim. We are nourished of those of whom we are begotten. Fathers when their children ask bread, will not give them stones; nor when they ask fish, will they give them scorpions, Mat. vii. 9. He that provides not these things for his children, is worse than an infidel, 1 Tim. iv. 8. And hath God commanded this from parents towards their children, and will not God much more provide for his children that are truly regenerate and born again, and that have his image by faith engraven on their souls? He would do it much more abundantly, Mat. vii. 11. "If ye being evil know how to give good gifts to your children, how much more shall your Father which is in heaven give good things to those that ask him?" This then is one great privilege that believers are made partakers of by virtue of this relation, having God for their heavenly Father. God will certainly provide good things for them, both for their being and well being here and hereafter; and they may come to God as a Father, with holy boldness of faith for all things that they shall stand in need of. God takes care for those that are strangers and enemies to him, and makes his rain to fall upon the unjust, as well as upon the just, Mat. v. 4, 5. "He giveth them rain from heaven, filling their hearts with food and gladness," Acts xiv. 7. "And will he not much rather feed his own children? he giveth food to all flesh," Psal. cxxxvi. 25. And will he not much rather take care for his own children that are engrafted into him by faith, that do love and serve him? If God's bounty be largely extended to those that are strangers and enemies to him, even to those that go on in sin and wickedness, as many times it is, then certainly he will kill the fatted calf for his own children, as the Father of the prodigal did for his returning son. Nay, in this the great God exceedeth earthly parents, as far as heaven is above the earth; for natural parents they give good things to their children when they ask them; but God the Father of spirits will do much more abundantly for his children, above what they are able to ask or think. The petitions of God's children may be large, their desires and thoughts larger than their petitions; for we are not always able to express outwardly what inwardly we desire; but God will do more abundantly for his people beyond all these. Let us look into the word of God, and we shall there see what noble provision he hath made for his people, what food, yea, angel's food he hath provided for them; what a feast of fat things (I mean of spiritual dainties and delicates) he hath dressed for them; "for their bread, they shall have the bread of life, he that eateth thereof, shall never hunger," John vi. 48. they shall have their fill of that hidden manna laid up in the sanctuary. We read of Benjamin's mess, Gen. iv. 3. last, that it was five times as much as any of his brethren; but the children of God, their food that they shall have from their heavenly Father, shall be a thousand times better, and more satisfactory than that which shall be given to the men of the world. They shall have their measures heaped up, pressed down, and running over, Psal. xxxiv. 10. "The young lions shall lack and suffer hunger, but the children of God, those that cry unto God their Father, shall want no good thing;" but especially spiritual good things, they shall be sure to have their fill of these, and shall be satisfied with them, even as with marrow and fatness; and for their drink, they shall have the heavenly nectar, the water of life, the blood of Jesus Christ, the which whosoever drinketh shall thirst no more, John iv. 14. They shall be abundantly satisfied with the fatness of his house, he will make them drink of the river of his pleasures; for with God is the fountain of life, in his light they shall see light, Ps. xxxviii. 8, 9. There is a river, the streams whereof shall make glad the city of God, Psal. xlvi. 4. and his children shall drink of this river of water of life, clear as crystal, proceeding out of the throne of God, and the Lamb, Rev. xxii. 1. It is for these especially that God hath provided the spiritual milk of the word, that they may grow thereby. They shall suck sweetness out of the promises, those rich breasts of consolation; and for their apparel, the children of God may say as the prophet, Isa. lxi. 10. "I will greatly rejoice in the Lord, my soul shall be joyful in my God; for he hath clothed me with the garments of salvation; he hath covered me with a robe of righteousness, as a bridegroom decketh himself with ornaments, and as a bride adorneth herself with jewels." What shall I say? They shall be clothed with the righteousness of Jesus Christ, a garment without spot or blemish, white as snow, even Solomon in all his glory was not arrayed like one of those.

Thus you have the first ground of consolation to believers, upon the account of having God for their Father, he will certainly provide for them those things that shall be necessary, both in this life, and in the life to come.

Secondly, Is God a Father to believers? Then another ground of consolation is this, that he will defend them from their enemies. How mightily doth it provoke natural parents to see their children abused? How quickly will their eye affect their heart, and stir them up to come in and rescue them? So will the Lord do for those that are his children by adoption and regeneration. He will defend them, he will be a wall of fire round about them, so that all their enemies, both spiritual and temporal, shall not be able to do them any real hurt. The devil, and all his wiles and temptations, the world and all its tempting allurements; yea, all the policy and malice of earth and hell, shall not be able to work their ruin. The Lord is on their side, and they have more for them, than they have against them. Upon this consideration it was that David tells us in his book of Psalms, "Though I walk (saith he) in the valley of the shadow of death, yet will I fear none ill ; for thou, O Lord, art my rock, and my fortress, and my salvation even for ever."

Would we not account him unworthy the name of a Father, that would suffer his children to be beaten and abused, and destroyed before his face, and not act in their defence ? And will God suffer his dear children so to be ? No certainly. " He that toucheth them, toucheth the apple of his eye," Zach. ii. 8, and God accounts what is done to them, as if it were done to himself in person ; "Inasmuch as ye did it unto those little ones, ye did it unto me!" Will Christ say one day as he tells us ? Matt. xxv. 40. and, " inasmuch as ye did it not unto the least of these, my brethren, ye did it not unto me," ver. 45. Beloved, there is a time coming, when the great God will reckon with ungodly men, for all the injuries and wrongs which they have done to his people, as if they were done to himself immediately.

Oh ! consider of this, you that are true believers ! Are you environed round with adversaries, either spiritual or temporal ? You have God for your defence, a God infinite in power, which is able to defend you from the hardest assaults of your most potent and politic enemies. His name is a strong tower, the righteous fly unto it, and are safe. Are you encountering with great temptations? The Lord being your Father he will protect you, and not suffer you to be tempted above what you are able to bear, but together with temptations, will make way for your escape, that you may be able to bear it, 1 Cor. x. 30. The Lord knoweth that his children are liable to many temptations from Satan, from the world, and from their own corruptions, and that they are subject to many afflictions and tribulations from the hands of men, and therefore he will be sure to be with them, and to be a very present help to them in the time of trouble.

Thirdly, Is God a believer's heavenly Father ? Then there is a comfort for them, that God will pity them and compassionate them in all their afflictions. A tender father pitieth his children when they are in any calamity. As for instance, in sickness, how will the groans of a child go near the heart of a loving parent? How do the agonies of pain in the child cause grief and sorrow in the parent's heart? What means would not a parent use to procure the health and ease of a child? "My life is bound up in the life of the lad," says Jacob concerning Benjamin. "O Absalom, my son, my son, would God I had died for thee!" says David concerning Absalom. What sympathizing and fellow-feeling will a dear and tender parent have of the miseries of his children? And as a father pitieth his children, so the Lord pitieth them that fear him, Psal. ciii. 13. The Lord is very pitiful, Jam. v. 11. The pity and compassion of the Lord towards his children, is excellently set forth in that scripture, Jer. xxxi. 20. Is Ephraim my dear son? Is he a pleasant child? For since I spake against him, I do earnestly remember him still; therefore my bowels are troubled for him: I will surely have mercy on him, saith the Lord." The bowels of the Lord do exceedingly yearn towards his people in all their afflictions and distresses, and he is full of pity and compassion towards them.

Fourthly, Is God a Father to all true believers? Then here is also for their comfort, that God doth and always will love them, and take delight in them. He loves them with an everlasting love; they are his chosen jewels, and he will certainly one day polish them, though he suffer them to be among the rubbish of the world for a while. They are his pleasant pictures, and he delights to be looking on them. The eyes of the Lord are upon them that fear him, and upon them that hope in his mercy, Psal. xxxiii. 18. God takes pleasure to be viewing the new creature which he hath framed by his own spirit in the hearts of his people, and his own image, which he stamped upon them; and herein the love that the Lord beareth his children, infinitely exceeds the love that earthly parents bear to theirs, in that he loveth them continually. Earthly parents, they love their children, but their love may be withdrawn from them again, and is oftentimes; but the love of God will never be withdrawn from his. Whom the Lord loveth, he loveth to the end; and although his loving countenance may be eclipsed for a time, and they may lose the sense of his love to them, by their failings and sinful infirmities, yet the Lord loves them still, there is nothing shall be able to separate believers from the love of God, Rom. viii. 25. and onward. The apostle Paul putteth the question there, (saith he) "Who shall separate us from the love of God? Shall tribulation, or distress, or persecution, or famine, or nakedness, or peril, or sword? As it is written, For thy sake are we killed all the day long, we are accounted as sheep for the slaughter: nay (saith he) in all these things we are more than conquerors through Him that loved us; for I am persuaded, that neither death, nor life, nor angels, nor principalities, nor powers, nor things present, nor things to come, nor height, nor depth, nor any other creature shall be able to separate us from the love of God, which is in Christ Jesus our Lord." It is not all the troubles of the world, nor tribulations, nor any thing that can render believers less lovely in the eyes of Christ. It is not all the devils in hell, that can withdraw God's love from his children, although they do endeavour it by enticing them to sin by their temptations, and then by accusing them to God for sin; yet all this will not rout them out of God's love. Though the Devil do labour to pick a quarrel between God and his people, yet it is not principalities nor powers, it is not all the power of hell, that shall be able to withdraw God's love from them.

Fifthly, Is God a Father to believers? Then they may take this for their comfort, that he will continually be mindful of them. Parents do remember their children, and are mindful of them; so the Lord, he remembereth his people, and will never forget them, Isa. xlix. 15. "Can a woman forget her sucking child, that she should not have compassion on the son of her womb; yea, they may, yet will I not forget thee." Earthly parents, though it be but rare, yet they may, and sometimes do forget their children; but God, he is more tender and mindful of his children, than earthly parents are of theirs—" yea, they may, yet will not I forget thee," &c. Though God's people do too often forget him, yet he doth never forget them, but remember them in all their conditions; even in their low estate, God is mindful of them, Psal. cxxxvi. 23. " Who remembered us in our low estate, for his mercy endureth for ever."

Lastly, Is God a Father of believers? Then they may take this for their comfort, that God will provide an inheritance for them hereafter. Fathers provide portions and inheritances for their children for hereafter; so doth God, Rom. viii. "Now" saith the apostle, " we are the sons of God; and if sons, then heirs, heirs of God, and co-heirs with Jesus Christ. How often is the kingdom of heaven called an inheritance, the inheritance of the saints, or them that are sanctified, Acts xx. 32. and xxvi. 8. There is an eternal inheritance laid up for the children of God for hereafter; yea, the kingdom of heaven is their inheritance, and it is now preparing for them, John xiv. 2. and they shall have assuredly one day an abundant entrance into their Father's kingdom. The children of God, while they are in the world, they are as heirs in their minority; they have not yet the possession of their inheritances, but it is theirs, and they shall have it in reversion; but hereafter, when they shall leave this earthly tabernacle, then they shall have the possession of it. Every true and sincere believer, he is heir to a crown, even a crown of glory that fadeth not away. " Their lines are fallen to them in a pleasant place, they have a goodly heritage; the Lord is the portion of their inheritance," Psal. xvi. 5, 6. It is the hope of this inheritance of theirs, that carrieth on the souls of the saints in the whole course of their lives; and maketh them joyfully and willingly to wade through all their troubles and difficulties that they meet with in their way to heaven. It is the consideration of this their portion and inheritance which they are entailed to by having God for their Father, that makes them forget the things that are behind, and press forward towards the mark for the prize of the high calling which is in Jesus Christ. It is their acting faith upon this, and having an eye to the recompence of reward, that makes them run with patience the race that is set before them; as knowing, that when they have finished their course, they shall receive a crown of life, which the Lord, the righteous judge, shall give them at that day.

Here the godly have the earnest of their inheritance, which is the spirit of God, Eph. i. 14. "After that ye believed, ye were sealed with the holy spirit of promise, which is the earnest of our inheritance, until the redemption of the purchased possession, unto the praise of his glory." Here believers have the promise of their inheritance. The word of God is a believer's patent for his inheritance, in which God doth as it were by promise make over heaven, and happiness, and glory to true believers, to be enjoyed by them for ever in the life to come; but hereafter, then they shall have the fruition and possession of it.

Would you know what a glorious inheritance this is, that the children of God by believing are entitled to? 1 Pet. i. 4. "It is an inheritance uncorruptible, undefiled, which fadeth not away." They are heirs to a crown of glory, they are heirs of God, and co-heirs with Jesus Christ, which is the heir of all things. Believe it, friends, it is such a glorious inheritance that the children of God are entitled unto, that all the inheritances and possessions in the world are but a trifle in comparison of it. To set out the beauty and excellency of the saints' inheritance, is a task fitter for some angel, than for a mortal creature; "for eye hath not seen, neither hath ear heard, neither hath entered into the heart of man to conceive what the Lord hath laid up for them that fear him," Isa. lxiv. 4.

Thus you see what abundant cause of comfort believers have upon this consideration, that God is their father, and that they are his children in every condition of their lives, in every trouble either outward or inward. Howsoever it be with a regenerate christian, one that is a true child of God, he hath cause to take comfort in this.

First, Is a believer in want here in the world? Is he in distress, and driven to straits, not knowing what course to take for the supplying of his natural wants, (as God's people are driven to such conditions sometimes) he can go to God as unto a Father, and make his wants and necessities known to him; he both can and will find out some way or other for a supply for you. He that hath promised so large a portion hereafter in heaven, will not deny so much of this world as is necessary for you in your way to heaven; "Your Father knows what good things you have need of," Mat. vi. 8. God which is the believer's Father, knows what things they need, and he is ready to hear them, and knoweth how to help them.

Secondly, Is a believer in danger? Is he environed about with his enemies on every side, and compassed about with those that seek his hurt? Oh! what comfort is this that he can go to God as unto a Father for help, even to him that is almighty, and able in a moment to defend them from their most powerful and politic adversaries? Is a godly man in danger, and hath he enemies that do wrongfully seek his life, as David had? Psal. xxxi. 13. yet he may have the same confidence that David had in that condition, and say, as he said in the following verse: "Yet I trust in thee, Oh Lord. I said, thou art my God, my times are in thy hand, deliver me from the hand of mine enemies, and from them that persecute me."

Thirdly, Doth a believer find his corruption within, to rebel against the regenerate part? Doth he find the law in his members which is warring against the law of his mind, to lead him into captivity to the law of sin and death? Doth he find his sins to be very strong within him, and that they begin to draw him away from God? Oh! what comfort is this to a child of God in this condition, that he can go and complain then to his heavenly Father, and be confident that this Father will hear him and help him, and make him more than a conqueror over all the enemies of his soul.

Fourthly, Art thou that art a believer, in doubt, and knowest not what course to take? Go to thy heavenly Father for direction; he is the infinitely wise God, and he will be sure to direct thee for the best.

Fifthly, Art thou slandered, reviled, and reproached in the world, and made the common scorn and derision of the ungodly? Go to thy Father, thy heavenly Father, and complain to him. He will certainly clear up thine innocency, as the light at noon-day, and wipe off all the reproaches that are wrongfully cast upon thee.

Sixthly, Art thou that art a believer, wronged by men, and knowest not how to right thyself? Go to thy heavenly Father, he will certainly set all things right one day. Neither is it all the power and policy of thine adversaries, nor their riches, nor any thing that shall be able to pervert him, and hinder him from redressing thy wrongs, and from doing thee right.

Seventhly, and lastly, Dost thou find thyself to be in a state of languishing, thou that art a believer? For to such I am speaking all this while. Dost thou find thy natural strength to decay, and thy sickness to increase, and thy pains to grow upon thee, putting thee in mind that thy body must be shortly laid in the grave, telling thee that thou mayest expect within a few days or hours to lay down thy earthly tabernacle, and to encounter with the pangs of death? Oh happy soul then, that canst make thy approaches to God, as unto a Father, and breathe out thy soul into the bosom of thy heavenly Father, and say as Christ did when he was on the cross, "Father, into thy hand I commend my spirit!" Believe it, Christian, thou that art truly such, it will afford thee more comfort that God is thy heavenly Father, and thou his child by adoption and regeneration, than if thou wert related to the greatest prince, and the most puissant monarch in all the world.

Thus I have done with the first use, which is a use of consolation to the godly, upon this consideration, that they are the children of God, and that he is their heavenly Father.

SECOND USE FOR CAUTION.

Secondly, If it be so, that all true believers are the children of God, and that he is their Father, then this should caution wicked men to beware how they meddle with God's children. Oh! have a care of afflicting, wronging, persecuting, hurting of the people of Gods, lest you be found fighters against God, have a care of annoying, and troubling those that are so near and dear to God, that are so tender to him as the apple of his eye; beware of vexing and molesting those that are so nearly related to the great King of kings, and Lord of lords. You may think it may be that you may do what you will to the godly, because they are low and mean in the world, as many of them are; but I must tell you, as mean and as low as they are in your esteem, they are near and dear to God. Carnal men may think they may oppress, and wrong, and do what they please to the people of God, because they are weak, and not able to help themselves; but little do they think how nearly the great God doth account himself concerned in their affairs. Little do the great ones of the world consider, what heavy reckoning will be laid to their charge one day for injuring, wronging, and molesting the poor servants of God. If they did, surely we should not have them so busily employed therein as they are. Thus for the second use.

THIRD USE FOR EXAMINATION.

Thirdly, Is it so, that believers have God for their heavenly Father, then here is matter of trial. How shall we know, whether God be our Father or no? and whether we be his children in this peculiar manner, by adoption and regeneration? It is true, God is a Father to us by creation, and we are his children by profession; but if this be all the relation that we bear to God, this will not entitle us to holiness and salvation, without we are regenerate and born again, and are become his children by regeneration, and God be our Father by virtue of the new covenant. "We are all by nature the children of wrath," Ephes. ii. 3. How shall we know then, whether we are gotten into the state of sonship, by adoption and regeneration, and whether God be our heavenly Father? There are many that pretend that they have God for their Father, when as yet they are under the dominion of their lusts, and are strangers to a work of true conversion and regeneration, and enemies to a life of holiness; and a groundless presumption, that men are the children of God, when there is no such matter, hath proved the bane of many thousand souls. I shall therefore give you these characters, whereby we may know, whether we are the children of God in this peculiar manner or no.

First, Whose image do you bear, do you bear the image of God? or else do you bear the image of Satan? Those that are the children of God by adoption and regeneration, they are such as bear their Father's image. The image of God which is created in righteousness and in true holiness, is engraven upon their souls. They are such as do bear the image of the heavenly Adam, 1 Cor. xv. 49. "And they have put on the new man which is created in knowledge, after the image of him that created him," Col. iii. 10. And is it so with thee, dost thou bear the image of God? Hast thou a new and holy nature put into thee, inclining thee to all holy duties, and to avoid all sin? Art thou renewed in holiness, then thou art a child of God, and God is thy heavenly Father? But if it be not thus with thee, if thou hast not this new and holy nature wrought in thee, but thy old corrupt nature is predominant, inclining thee to sin; whatsoever groundless presumption thou mayest have, yet thou art no true child of God by regeneration and adoption.

Secondly, Wouldest thou know whether thou art the true child of God or no, by whose spirit art thou led? By the spirit of God, or by the spirit of Satan? They that have God for their Father, are led by the spirit of God, Rom. viii. 14. " As many as are led by the spirit of God, they are the sons of God." Try thyself then by this, art thou led by the spirit of God? Dost thou live after the flesh, and not after the spirit? Dost thou mind the things of the spirit, and not the things of the flesh? If so, then thou mayest comfortably conclude that thou art the child of God, and that he is thy heavenly Father. We may know our sonship by our spirit; if we are the Sons of God by adoption and regeneration, then we are led by the spirit of God, which is a spirit of prayer, Rom. viii. 15. A spirit of liberty, making us free from the dominion of our lusts, and from the slavery of sin and Satan, 2 Cor. iii. 17. John viii. 32. A spirit of love to God, and to the people of God, 1 John v. 2.

Thirdly, We may know whether God be our heavenly father or no by this, do we labour to set forth the honour of God? Children, they are very tender of the honour of their parents. This is a great duty to honour earthly parents, Exod. xx. 11. much more should we honour God, which is the Father of spirits; "If I am your father where is mine honour?" (saith Christ.) If God be our father, where is that honour that we should yield to him? If we are the children of God by regeneration and sanctification, then we are tender of the honour of Christ. It will make our hearts rise to hear his name blasphemed, or taken in vain; his sabbaths profaned, his worship corrupted by human mixtures; his creatures abused into excess; his commandments broken. These things will grieve and trouble us more than any thing, if we are God's children in truth. But if we can see God dishonoured by the unholy lives of carnal men, his commands trampled under foot, and yet not be grieved at this; but can close in with those that make it their business to dishonour God, then thou art no child of God in this particular sense. The great dishonour that is brought to God in the world, is a sad sign that there is but few, very few, that are in truth the children of God: and the abounding and increasing of all sorts of sin, whereby God is exceedingly dishonoured. Drunkenness, swearing, sabbath-breaking, uncleanness, lying, extortion, oppression, scorning and deriding at holiness, contempt of God's ordinances, persecution of his faithful laborious ministers, and people. I say the abounding of these and such like abominations is a very sad evidence, that there are very few that have God for their heavenly Father, in this special and peculiar manner, and that are his children by adoption and regeneration.

Lastly, Wouldest thou know whether God be thy Father, and thou his child inquire whether thou art courageous in the ways of God, and in the practice of godliness? They that have God for their heavenly Father, they have a noble and heroic spirit. They are such as will not be ashamed, nor afraid to lead a holy life, notwithstanding all the mocks, and taunts, and threats of the world. They that are of a base timorous spirit, that are afraid of owning the ways of holiness, for fear of being reproached, reviled, or opposed, by the profane world, they that are afraid to cleave to the ways and people of God in discouraging times, they are not of the right strain. Say not then that thou art born of God, nnless thou canst prove thy noble extraction, by thy noble and heroic courage and resolution, notwithstanding all the trouble, calamity, and persecution, thou mayest meet with in the world. Thus much for examination.

FOURTH USE FOR EXHORTATION.

Fourthly, Is it so, &c. Then here is a word of exhortation.

First, Unto those that are unregenerate, that have not God for their Father in this peculiar manner; and that is that they would never be in rest, till they come to be united unto Jesus Christ, and to have him to be their Father by regeneration. It is a sad thing to be void of this, when we cannot go to God as to a Father, and cannot expect any thing from him, as from a father. Oh! how little do thousands think of this, whether they are the children of God, and have God for their Father, or no. They care not for it, they make not out after it, or take it for granted, when they have no true and real ground so to do. Oh! then labour to get into this state of sonship! Close with Jesus Christ by a lively, operative, heart-purifying faith, that thou mayest thereby be invested into God's family, and become his child. Consider, that before thou art thus by faith engrafted into Christ, thou hast woeful parents, thou art a child of disobedience, Eph. ii. 2. " A child of wrath," verse 3. " a child of Satan," John viii. 44.

Secondly, Here is a word of counsel and exhortation to the godly, that are the children of God by adoption and regeneration.

First, To those my first counsel is, that you would make it your greatest care and diligence to please your heavenly Father, and have a care of sinning against him. Consider, that the sins of God's children, are very grievous to him, αι σὺ τοκνον, said Cæsar to his son Brutus, when he saw him among his betrayers, What, and thou my son? So will God say to his children, when they grieve him by sin : What, and thou, my son, my child, one whom I have adopted my heir; what, will you sin against me? I thought you had more love. Have I loved you so much, and do you love me so little? Hath my spirit comforted you, and will you grieve it? Have my bowels yearned towards you, and will you kick against them? Have I been crucified for you, and will you crucify me again afresh by your sins? The nearer the relation is that the soul beareth to God, the greater is the aggravation of the sin against God.

Secondly, Labour to shew forth your noble extraction,

by your noble and raised affections. It is beneath the son of a prince to be taken up with trifles; it is beneath one that is heir to a kingdom, to set his affections upon low and base things, things of nought. So it is beneath the children of the great King of kings, the Lord of lords, to let their affections run out inordinately after the world, and the enjoyments thereof. They are born from above, and therefore should set their affections upon things above, and not on things on earth, Colos. iii. 2. What an unsuitable thing is it for a christian, to be taken up with the inordinate love of the world? It is a degradation to the heirs of heaven to have their minds taken up only or mostly with earth, and earthly vanities; they are *ad majora nati*, born to greater things. It is unbecoming such to soil their affections with earth, which are born to an inheritance incorruptible, which fadeth not away. Oh, that the children of God, and such as do profess themselves so to be, would manifest their holy and heavenly extraction, by their holy and heavenly affections; and that such as are the sons and daughters of God by adoption and sanctification, would not walk so far beneath that relation.

Thirdly, Labour to imitate your heavenly Father: " Be you followers of God as dear children," Ephes. v. 1." Be ye merciful as your heavenly Father is merciful; be ye holy as he is holy; be ye compassionate as he is in all things." Labour to imitate your heavenly Father! it is a christian's honour to be like God, and imitate him.

Fourthly, Labour more and more to obey your heavenly Father. Our natural parents may require obedience of us, and it is our duty to give it them; much more may him that is the Father of spirits require it of us, and it is much more our duty to give it him: " Walk as obedient children," 1 Pet. i. 14. Yea, you must obey him cheerfully too. The obedience of children is herein differenced from the obedience of slaves, in that slaves are drawn to their duty out of a slavish fear, but children come to it willingly, out of a filial affection. Oh therefore let your obedience to God be cheerful and voluntary. Take delight to do the will of your heavenly Father.

Lastly, Submit to your heavenly Father's chastisements. This is the exhortation of the apostle to the Hebrews, Heb. xii. 5, 6, 7. " My son, despise not thou the chastening of the Lord, nor faint when thou art rebuked of him. For whom the Lord loveth, he chasteneth, and scourgeth every son he receiveth." If ye endure chastening, God dealeth with you as with sons; for what son is he whom the Father chasteneth not? But if ye are without chastisement, whereof all are partakers, then are ye bastards and not sons. Let us not then murmur and faint under our afflictions and chastisements, but let us submit to them, and labour to grow the better for them. Thus much for the first observation, That God is a believer's heavenly Father. The other observation that I proposed to insist upon from this text, was the last of the five mentioned in the beginning, and it contains the chief sum and scope of the whole verse, and is most suitable to our times, and to this occasion, you may remember was this.

Doct. That the consideration of a believer's interest in the kingdom of heaven, should make him cheerful and courageous in the practice of holiness, and keep him from being dismayed at all the trouble and calamities that he meeteth withal in the world : " fear not (saith Christ) little flock, for it is your Father's good pleasure to give you the kingdom." In this observation, there are two things supposed.

First, It is supposed in this doctrine, that believers have an interest in the kingdom of heaven. This I need not now stand to prove, having spoken to it already in the handling of the former observations. God being their Father, he hath provided an eternal inheritance of glory for them, in his eternal kingdom.

Secondly, It is supposed in the doctrine, that believers are like to meet with opposition from the world; they are diligent in the practice of godliness, are driving a trade for heaven. They shall be sure to meet with abundance of trouble and hindrance from the world, and the prince of the world. This is a truth exceeding manifest, both from scripture and experience. "We shall be hated of all men for his name sake," Mat. x. 22. And because Christ hath chosen his people out of the world, "therefore the world hated him." John xv. 19. And experience makes this evidence in all ages of the world; those that are godly and walk with God, they have been sure to have their portion of afflictions and tribulations, from the hands and tongues of the malicious and ungodly world ; and my design is to shew what little cause the servants of God that have an interest in the kingdom of heaven, to be afraid or dismayed at any of these hindrances and oppositions, that they meet withal in their way to heaven. For the handling of this doctrine, and the fitting of it for our improvement by application, I shall speak to these three things.

First, I shall shew you by some instances from the word of God, how the saints that have had an interest in the kingdom of heaven, have been encouraged in the ways of God, and have had their spirits borne up in their lowest condition, and in their greatest trials and troubles here below.

Secondly, I shall shew you that believers are dehorted from despondency ; and being dismayed under their sufferings upon the consideration of their heavenly interest.

Thirdly, I shall give you some reasons, why believers, that have a title to the heavenly glory, should be courageous and undaunted, and not dismayed at all their eternal trials and tribulations that they meet withal from the world: and so shall come to the application.

First, For the first of these, I might give you many instances from the word of God, of the courage and magnanimity of the heirs of heaven in their trials; as David, how courageous was he in the Lord, even in his lowest condition, Psal. xlvi. 1, 2, 3, 4. "God is our refuge and our strength, a very present help in trouble; therefore (saith he) will we not fear, though the earth be removed, though the mountains be cast into the midst of the sea, though the waters thereof roar and be troubled, though the mountains shake with the swelling thereof Selah." Psalm cxviii. 6. "The Lord is on my side, I will not fear what man can do unto me." David had put confidence in God, and therefore was not afraid of man. Where the fear of God is, and where the hope of glory is, there the slavish fear of man will quickly vanish away. This no doubt was that which made the three children not to be afraid of the fiery furnace, nor Daniel of the den of lions, Dan. iii. 16. and 6. We have a notable example to this purpose, Hab. iii. 17, 18. "Although the fig-tree should not blossom, nor fruit be in the vine; though the labour of the olive should fail, and the fields should yield no meat; though the flocks should be cut off from the fold, and there should be no herd in the stall: yet will I rejoice in the Lord, I will joy in the God of my salvation." The consideration of his heavenly interest, and that God was the God of his salvation, was that which not only kept the prophet from being dismayed, but also made him to rejoice in the absence of all creature joys and comforts; the want of these worldly things, were not able to abate his heavenly joy, which he had in the God of his salvation. The consideration of their heavenly interest, and their title to the everlasting glory, was that which made the apostles of Christ so courageous and comfortable under all their sufferings that they underwent for Christ. This was that which made the martyr Stephen so fearless and undaunted, when he was on the brink of death, and when the stones flew about his ears, when he could look up into heaven, the place of his inheritance, where he was going, and take a view of that heavenly glory, Acts vii. 55. A believer that can look up by an eye of faith upon Christ and heaven, and take a view of the unseen world, the place of his eternal rest and felicity, will be able in some measure to undergo with comfort, the sharpest and bitterest persecutions that the malice of men or devils can expose him to. This was that which made Paul and Silas sing praises at midnight, when they were shut up in prison, and their feet in the stocks, Acts xvi. 25. This was that which caused the believing Hebrews to take joyfully the spoiling of their goods; even the consideration of their interest in the kingdom of heaven, Heb. x. 34. "For ye had compassion of me in my bonds, and took joyfully the spoiling of your goods, knowing that in heaven, you have a better and a more enduring substance." Their knowledge of this their interest in the heavenly riches, made them willingly to part with the earthly riches for the sake of Christ.

Secondly, The next thing to be spoken unto, is this. To shew that the people of God, upon this consideration of their interest in the kingdom of glory, have been dehorted from fear and despondence, and exhorted to courage and magnanimity in the ways of God. Upon this consideration it is, that Christ exhorts his little flock in the text, not to fear, because that God would give them the kingdom of heaven. How often are the servants of God in scripture, dehorted from fear, Isa. xli. 10. "Fear not, I am with thee; be not dismayed, I am thy God." Ver. 14. "Fear not, thou worm Jacob, and ye men of Israel. I will help thee, saith the Lord thy Redeemer." Isa. l. 7, 8. "Fear ye not the reproach of men, be not dismayed at their revilings, for the moth shall eat them up like a garment, and the worm shall eat them like wool, but my righteousness shall be for ever, and my salvation from generation to generation." And again, ver. 12. "Who art thou that shouldest be afraid of a man that shall die, and of the son of man that shall be made as grass, and forgetteth the Lord thy maker, that stretched out the heavens, and laid the foundation of the earth?" And our Saviour in the New Testament, to the supporting of believers under their afflictions and tribulations, tells them, that it is a blessed thing, thus to be dealt withal by the world, Mat. v, 10, 11, 12. "Blessed are they that are persecuted for righteousness sake, for theirs is the kingdom of heaven. Blessed are ye when men shall revile you and persecute you, and speak all manner of evil against you falsely for my sake: rejoice and be exceeding glad, for great is your reward in heaven." And Luke vi. 22. "Blessed are ye when men shall hate you, and when they shall separate from you their company, and shall reproach you, and cast out your name as evil for the Son of man's sake, rejoice in that day, and leap for joy, for behold your reward is great in heaven." The consideration of our interest in the kingdom of heaven, should keep us from being dismayed, though we are hated, persecuted, reproached by the profane world, but should make us rejoice rather, and leap for joy. Thus much for the second thing, which is, That the people of God are dehorted from fear and despondency, and exhorted to courage and magnanimity in the ways of God, from the very consideration of their interest in the kingdom of heaven.

Thirdly, I shall give you the reasons why believers, those that have an interest in the kingdom of heaven, should not fear nor be dismayed at any outward trouble, opposition, or tribulation that they meet with in the world.

First, It is very unsuitable for one that hath secured the heavenly interest, and his title to eternal glory, to be dismayed at a thing of nought. How unsuitable is it for one that is an heir of heaven, to be excessively grieved and disconsolate, because he meeteth with some rubs in his way thither? Oh how unseemly is it for a child of delight to walk in darkness and heaviness, because somewhat of the world falls a cross to his expectation or desire: for one that is to enjoy eternal happiness in the life to come, to be dismayed and perplexed at every petty cross that he meeteth here below? How unseemly is it for a child of God, and heir of heaven, for one that shall sit down with Abraham, and Isaac, and Jacob in the heavenly glory, to go up and down drooping at inconsiderable crosses and light afflictions, which are but for a moment.

For a worldling that hath all his good things here, and hath no other portion but in this life, to be grieved and perplexed at his external losses and troubles. This is not so much for such a one to be grieved when he is thwarted in his designs, and when the world falls a cross to him, this is but suitable and agreeable to such a one, because he hath placed his hope, his contentment, his joy and delight in these things, and therefore being deprived of them, he is deprived of his best things, his portion, his all.

But for a child of God, one that hath an interest in eternal life and glory, to be cast down and dismayed at such small things, as the affliction, trials and tribulations of the world. Oh what an unseemly thing is this, as if their heavenly interest did not give them greater cause of joy and rejoicing, than those external worldly afflictions, do give them cause of sadness and disconsolation.

The frantic mirth of the profane world, that are in the high way to damnation, and the groundless perplexities of the regenerate children of God, are both alike unsuitable and unseemly, although not both alike dangerous.

To see a worldling, that hath nothing else to comfort and support him, but the fading enjoyments of this present life, to be merry and jovial, as if all were well; and on the other hand, to see a believer, that is an heir of heaven, to live in a drooping and disconsolate state, because of these outward troubles, is cause of pity and lamentation.

Secondly, As it is unsuitable for a child of God that hath secured his eternal state, and made sure of his heavenly interest, to be dismayed at the afflictions of the world, so it is very unwarrantable. Believers are commanded to be much in holy rejoicing; " Rejoice (saith Christ to his disciples) because your names are written in heaven," Luke x. 20. " Be glad in the Lord, oh ye righteous, and shout for joy, all ye upright in heart," Psal. xxxii. 11. " Rejoice in the Lord, oh ye righteous, for praise is comely for the upright," Psal. xxxiii. 1. " Rejoice evermore," 1 Thes. v. 16. Oh how exceeding unwarrantable is it then for those that have an interest in the heavenly glory, to be discouraged at their outward afflictions, by which they do disparage religion, and frighten away others from the doors of grace.

Thirdly, It is irrational for one that hath secured his interest in the heavenly kingdom, to be afraid of his worldly afflictions and tribulations, seeing all the losses and crosses in the world, are as nothing comparatively to such an one. Let a child of God but weigh and ponder such things aright, and compare the cause of joy that he hath, by virtue of his heavenly interest on the one hand, with the cause of sorrow that he hath, by reason of the crosses of the world on the other, and he will see, that he hath a thousand times more cause of joy, than of sorrow; and therefore the thoughts of his heavenly interest, should swallow up those of his worldly troubles and disappointments. " I reckon (saith the apostle Paul) that the sufferings of this present time are not worthy to be compared with the glory that shall be revealed in us," Rom. i. 18. And the same apostle tells us elsewhere, " Our light afflictions which are but for a moment, work for us a far more exceeding and eternal weight of glory," 2 Cor. iv. 17. Now, is it not unreasonable for a believer to be grieved and disquieted with those light afflictions which shall be recompenced with an eternal weight of glory? What can a child of God lose, as long as his God, his portion, his interest in heaven is safe and secured to him? What are all the losses that he can sustain in the world, as long as he is interested in the eternal kingdom of glory?

I must tell you, believers, ye that walk holily and closely with God, and have a title to the kingdom of heaven, for you to be grieved and discontented because all things do not concur according to your desires in the world, is unreasonable and absurd; as if a rich man that hath a great estate, and fair houses and orchards, should be disquieted because the wind bloweth away a few leaves from his trees.

Is not the kingdom of heaven that thou art entitled to, enough to make thee amends for all thy troubles and calamities in the end? Art thou troubled by the profane world, and vexed up and down by thy enemies, and not suffered to rest in quiet? And is it not enough for thee that the kingdom of heaven is the place of thine eternal rest and happiness, where thou shalt be for ever advanced above their reach? Art thou exposed to the loss of thy place and estate in the world, and will not an incorrupted crown of glory, and an eternal inheritance among them that are sanctified, make thee amends for those petty losses that thou sustainest here? Art thou the off-scouring of the world here? And is it not enough that thou shalt be glorified in the presence of saints and angels hereafter? Art thou slandered and reproached by the world? And is not this enough to support thee that thou shalt be acquitted at the bar of Christ? Dost thou suffer the loss of liberty? And art thou under restraint and imprisonment, and is not this enough to comfort thee, that thou art free from the captivity and dominion of sin, and art rid of those chains and fetters by which so many thousands in the world are led captive by Satan at his pleasure, and that thou art free from the prison of hell? Put the case (which is the greatest trouble that a godly man can undergo in the world) thou art to lose thy life for the sake of Christ, and of a good conscience, however a believer's interest in the kingdom of heaven should keep him from being dismayed at that loss; an eternal life of happiness and glory will be enough to recompence thee a thousand fold for loss of this frail life. Thus you have the third reason, it is irrational for a believer that hath an interest in the kingdom of heaven, to be dismayed at those outward crosses and losses that he sustains in the world, because they are very little and inconsiderable while their God, their portion, their heavenly interests are safe and secure to them.

Lastly, one that is an heir of heaven, and hath a title to the heavenly kingdom, should be courageous in the ways of God, and not be daunted at his outward troubles, because of the short continuance of them, as the joys and pleasures of the world are but for a little moment of time, so the sorrows and tribulations of the world are but for a small moment of time; neither the troubles of the godly, though they may be sharp, yet they are but short, death will quickly put a period to them all; all the trials and tribulations of the saints will be at an end when they come to enter into their everlasting rest. The saints in heaven are perfectly freed as from the evil of sin, so from the evil of suffering; they will be out of the reach of their most powerful and malicious adversaries. Now what little reason hath a believer that hath an interest in the kingdom of glory, to be dismayed at his worldly troubles, which shall so soon be done away, when he hath a title to everlasting happiness to support him? Who is there that would be dismayed at the sufferings of a few years or weeks, if he were assured of an eternal weight of glory to make him amends for it? Thus much for the doctrinal part.

Use I.

Is it so, that a believer's interest in the kingdom of heaven should make him cheerful and courageous in the ways of God, and keep him from being dismayed at the sufferings and afflictions that he meeteth withal in the world?

Is it so, that one that hath a title to heaven, hath cause of joy in the midst of his greatest sorrows and troubles? Then

First of all, here is matter of trial and examination for us to try ourselves whether we have a title to heaven or no. We would all rejoice to have somewhat which might effectually support us, and bear us up under troubles and afflictions in the world, and it is sad when we are in trouble, if we have nothing to support us; but if we have secured our heavenly interest, and have cleared our title to the kingdom of glory, we have then the greatest ground of comfort and joy in the world, and we may upon right grounds rejoice under the sharpest tribulations that we meet with from the hands of men. I shall therefore give you some marks and characters how we may know, whether we have an interest in the kingdom of heaven, or no. And here I might refer you back to those characters propounded in the application of the former doctrine. If we can truly say that God is our Father by adoption and regeneration, and that we are his children, then we may safely conclude, that we are some of those that have an interest in the kingdom of heaven. If we are the children of God, then we are coheirs of God, Rom. viii. are entitled to heaven. Try then whether you can conclude that you are the children of God. But because I know not whether ever I shall have liberty to speak to you again from this place, I shall propose some other characters also to help us to pass a right judgment upon ourselves in a matter of so great concernment.

First, then, whosoever thou art that wouldest try thy title to the heavenly glory, thou mayest try it by this: If the design of thy life be to glorify God, and to promote their heavenly interest, then thou art one of those that are entitled to the heavenly inheritance; if thou drivest a trade for heaven, and if that the obtaining of heaven be the principal part of thy care and business, and the great design that thou drivest at in all thy actions, then by this thou mayest try thy title to heaven. Apply now this home to thy soul, what trade and design art thou now driving in the world? Is it thy main business here to promote thy temporal or thine eternal state? Art thou striving more after earth or heaven? If thy design here be after riches, honour, or greatness in the world; and makest all thy actions subservient to thy design, then thou art none of those that have a title to heaven. But if it be the business of thy life, and the trade that thou drivest in the world to advance God's glory, and thine eternal salvation, and dost care for no more of this world, than may tend to promote God's glory, and thine eternal happiness; then thou mayest safely conclude that thy name is written in heaven, and that thou hast an interest in that kingdom. It is the grand mistake of thousands of souls every where, that they pretend to seek after the kingdom of heaven, but they seek it only by the by, and their main design in the world is somewhat else, as to grow rich, or great, or honourable here. They do not make it their principal business, and their great design to secure their title to heaven; but they look upon heaven only as a reserve for them, when they can enjoy the world no longer. And therefore they will have some glances, and some faint endeavours that way; but if ever we will enter into heaven, we must first of all seek God's kingdom and his righteousness, Mat. vi. 33. Luke xii. 31.

Secondly, Wouldest thou know whether thou hast a title to the heavenly glory, or no. Thou mayest know it by thy heavenly mindedness. They that have an interest in the heavenly kingdom, they have heavenly hearts; if their treasure be in heaven, their hearts will be there also, Mat. vi. 20, 21. "Lay up for yourselves treasures in heaven, where neither moth nor rust can corrupt, and thieves break through and steal; for where your treasure is, there will your hearts be also." And is it so with us? Are our hearts taken up with the heavenly glory? Are our meditations and contemplations much on heavenly objects? Or else, are they taken up only or mostly with earthly vanities? Are our hearts on our riches, pleasures, &c.? Or else are they placed upon heaven, and heavenly things? If we have a title to the kingdom of heaven, our hearts, minds, and affections, will be heavenly, and taken up with heavenly objects, Col. iii. 1, 2. "If ye then be risen with Christ, seek those things which are above, where Christ sitteth at the right hand of God. Set your affections on things above, and not on things on the earth."

Thirdly, Wouldest thou know whether thou hast an interest in the kingdom of heaven, or no? How dost thou like the employment of heaven? If thou likest the employment of heaven, then thou mayest comfortably conclude, that thou hast an interest in the kingdom of heaven.

Canst thou say thou delightest to be employed in serving, and in glorifying God, and in worshipping of him in spirit and truth, according to his word? Canst thou say in truth, that thou delightest to do the will of God here on earth, as it is done by the angels in heaven, and the spirits of just men made perfect there? Dost thou take delight to be employed in that employment that the saints of heaven are, and shall be for ever employed in? Dost thou take pleasure to adore, and praise, and magnify the ever blessed God? Dost thou take pleasure in the duties of religion, and rejoice to be conversing with God in prayer, and in other holy exercises, and to be enjoying communion with him? If it be thus with thee as I have now described; this, this will evidently make out thy title for heaven. Many thousands pretend that their designs are to go to heaven, and they presumptuously conclude that they have an interest in that kingdom, when as they like not the heavenly employment in themselves or others, and they care not to get acquaintance with God here on earth, and are strangers to the duties of religion, and to a life of holiness, and perhaps spend an hour in a week, or it may be in a month in secret prayer, or in other holy exercises; and it may be neglect the worship of God in their families too; but if we are unacquainted with the employment of heaven, which is to praise and magnify, worship and adore God.

If thou delightest not so to do, thou canst not conclude that thou hast a title to heaven: but if thou hast an interest in the kingdom of heaven, then thou dost most of all delight in that employment which hath most of heaven in it.

Fourthly, If thou hast an interest in the kingdom of heaven, thou hast a special love to the heirs of heaven; and thou hast a near and dear affection to the people of God though they be despised, rejected, scorned, and persecuted by the profane world; and thou dost delight in the company of those on earth, which are like to be thy companions in heaven; and thou hadst rather have the society of those, howsoever mean and low in the world, that have the truth of grace in them, than of all the stately and glittering gallants of the world, that are strangers to a life of holiness; and the more holy and heavenly they are in their hearts and lives, the more amiable will their company be to thee, 1 Job iii. 14. Psal. xv. 4. Put thyself to the question whether it be thus with thee, or no, and thou shalt find out thy title to heaven thereby.

Lastly, If thou hast a title to heaven, then thou art so far at a point with all the riches, and pleasures, and enjoyments of the world, as that thou wilt rather forego them all, than forsake Christ; and rather part with them all, than that they shall hinder thee in thy way towards heaven; and if thou art brought so far at a pinch, as that thou must either forsake thy interest in Christ and heaven; or to forego thy worldly accommodations. Thou art very willing to forego them all that thou mayest stick close to Christ, and go forward in thy way to thy heavenly inheritance. Thus it was with the apostle Paul, Phil. iii. 7, 8. But what things (saith he) were gain to me, those I accounted loss for Christ; "Yea, doubtless I account all things but loss for the excellency of the knowledge of Christ Jesus my Lord, for whom I have suffered the loss of all things, and do account them but dung that I may win Christ." And is it so with us then, when riches, honour, and pleasure do stand in competition with Christ, and hinder us in our progress in grace and holiness. Are we willing and ready to cast them away, as we would cast away dung. If it be thus with us in reality, then we may conclude we have a title to heaven, and an interest in the eternal glory. By these things, beloved, you may try whether you have an interest in heaven or no. Having finished the use of examination, I shall come to the next use, which is the last that I shall speak unto, which is an use of exhortation.

Is it so, that the consideration of a believer's interest in the heavenly glory is enough to bear up his spirit under all the trials and tribulations of this life? Then oh that you which cannot upon trial find, that you have a title to heaven, that you would labour after an interest in the heavenly glory. If thou hast no interest there, what good will all the enjoyments of the world do thee? How quickly will all thy comforts and pleasures leave thee? And what little cause hast thou to rejoice in the abundance of outward things; if thou hast no title to the durable riches? If thou art void of the riches of grace here, and hast no title to the riches of glory hereafter; what wilt thou do in a day of trial, and in an hour of trouble and calamity? What wilt thou do when losses, crosses, troubles, and vexations shall compass thee about, if thou hast not an heavenly interest to support thee under them? What wilt thou do, when pains and anguish, when diseases, sickness, and death, shall seize upon thee, if thou hast not a title to thy heavenly inheritance? These things will certainly and speedily come upon us, how far off soever we may put them in our thoughts. The proud looks of the lofty will quickly be turned into an earthly paleness; though they look as big, and carry themselves as high, as if they had a protection from hell and the grave; and those bodies which we now take so much care to please and pamper, will shortly become a feast for worms. Though they may be adorned with all the ornaments that the pride of man can invent, and friends, and riches, and will but accompany us to the grave, and there leave us. And oh what will then become of us, if we have no interest in Christ and heaven, and cannot lay claim to the everlasting glory?

If you ask me, how we shall do to secure our interest in the kingdom of heaven? I answer, it must be by a thorough closure with Christ by faith, and chusing of him for our Lord and Saviour. God hath ordained that those that are united to Christ by faith here on earth, that they shall be with Christ and live with Christ in heaven. Heaven and glory is the dowry that God giveth with his Son Jesus Christ; and they that will marry the heir shall have the inheritance; and if we are Christ, then all will be ours, 1 Cor. iii. 22, 23. " Whether of Paul, or Apollos, or Cephas, or things present, or things to come, all is yours, and ye are Christ's." They that have an interest in Christ, have a title to all. Let us therefore contract ourselves to Christ, resolving to be no longer our own but his; and to live no longer to ourselves, but to him. Let us chuse him to be our Lord and Saviour, and take him upon his own terms as he is offered to us in the gospel, to be our king, priest, and prophet; and when we are once thus united to Christ by faith, we shall be coheirs with him of the heavenly inheritance. All this will be ours when we are Christ's by a self-resignation, and submission, and when Christ is ours by a believing choice and election; when we have thus made choice of Christ upon his own terms to be our Lord and Saviour, our portion and our all: and have given up ourselves to him to be wholly his, and at his disposal. This will undoubtedly give us a firm and an unquestionable title to heaven.

Secondly, The next address that I have to make is to those that are the heirs of his kingdom, and have a title to this heavenly inheritance. Is it so that a believer's interest in the kingdom of heaven is enough to bear up his spirit under all his troubles and afflictions, and to keep him from being dismayed under his sorest trials and tribulations that he meeteth withal from the world; then the exhortation that I shall give to you, is the same that our Saviour giveth in the text: " Fear not, little flock, for it is your Father's good pleasure to give you the kingdom." You that have an interest in the heavenly glory, oh, be not dismayed, nor affrighted at those outward afflictions and tribulations that you meet with here below. It is true, God doth often exercise his dear children with trials, afflictions, and tribulations. This is the way by which God doth discipline his children, while they are in their minority here. This believers must count upon beforehand; but there is not any of those things that should make a believing christian dismayed, seeing his eternal concernments are so safe, and his heavenly interest is secure.

And there is no trouble nor cross that the saints can meet withal, but that we are somewhere or other in the word of God exhorted not to be afraid of it. Do we meet with reproach from men? Is that the cross we undergo? This indeed is heavy, insomuch that the Psalmist complains, that his heart was broken by it, Psal. lxix. 20. Yet the servants of God, the heirs of heaven, are cautioned not to fear that, Isa. li. 10. " Fear not the reproach of men, nor be afraid of their revilings." Or is the affliction that thou meetest withal, imprisonment for the sake of Christ and of a good conscience, this is likewise grievous and heavy to be born; yet the heirs of heaven are exhorted not to fear that neither, Rev. ii. 10. It is Christ's advice to the church of Smyrna, " Fear none of those things which thou shalt suffer; behold the devil shall cast some of you into prison, that ye may be tried, and you shall have tribulation ten days; be thou faithful unto the death, and I will give thee a crown of life;" those that have an interest in the crown of life; imprisonment for the sake of Christ, if God should call them thereunto. Nay, put the case thou were to suffer death itself for the sake of Christ, this is the greatest and sorest of all sufferings. Yet the servants of God are cautioned not to fear that neither, for it can be but a bodily death, and it will make way for a better and happier life, Mat. x. 28. "Fear not them that can kill the body, but are not able to kill the soul. Whatsoever thy sufferings be, thou that art a believer, and hast an interest in the kingdom of heaven, thou art exhorted not to be afraid of it.

Oh, christians! I beseech you act faith upon your heavenly interest. I might tell you it can never be more seasonable so to do than now. The more you act faith hereupon, the more you will be enabled to live above the frowns of a troublesome and vexatious world. Oh, look up by an eye of faith upon the recompence of rewards, and you will be able to prefer the afflictions of the saints, before the vain and transitory pleasures of unregenerate sinners, which endure but for a moment, and to chuse the greatest affliction before the least sin, as Moses did, Heb. xi. 25, 26.

And let the joy that is set before you make you to endure the crosses of this world, and to despise the shame, as the Captain of your salvation hath done before you; and let the hope of the glory of God make you rejoice, notwithstanding all the scorn and contempt that you meet with from the world.

But because of our frailty and aptness to be afraid and dismayed at afflictions and tribulations, I shall set before you some considerations, which, if well weighed, might, by the blessing of God, do much to the curing and removing of those fears and discontents that are apt to seize upon us when we are exposed to trials and losses in the world.

First, Consider, christians, you that have secured your heavenly interest. Are you in sore troubles, and do you meet with hard dealings from men? It may be you may bring more glory to God by your afflictions, losses, and crosses in the world, than if you should always be in a quiet, prosperous, and serene condition. It may be God may have a greater revenue of glory by thy troubles and trials, than by thy prosperity in the world: and shall we not be willing to be in such a condition, howsoever unpleasant to our corrupt flesh, in which we may be most serviceable for God, and bring most honour and glory to him. It is a sign that we have little love to God, or indeed to our own souls, if we do not prefer the glory of God before our own ease and carnal contentment. What, do we but mock with God in our prayers, when we pray that his name may be glorified, if we are dismayed and discontented when God is glorified by us in our sufferings, because they are tedious and irksome to our flesh. If we are unwilling that God should be glorified by our sufferings; if we are unwilling to honour him in an afflicted state, why do we then in our prayers pretend to beg that God may be glorified? Oh, how much is God glorified many times by the sufferings of his people, when as he is dishonoured by the secure and sensual lives of many thousands that are in prosperous, calm, and quiet condition in the world! I might give you many instances from the scripture, to such that the sufferings of God's people have tended very much, to the setting forth of the high praises of the Lord. Oh, how much have the sufferings of the Israelites been all along! of Job, of David, of Hezekiah, of the three children, of Daniel: and so under the New Testament; how have the sufferings of Stephen, Paul, Silas, and the rest of the apostles and martyrs, resounded to the honor and glory of God, for whom they suffered!

Indeed, God's people do more honour and glorify God by their sufferings, than by their doings for him. Let us not then be dismayed, though we may be in a troublesome and suffering condition; seeing this is a condition, in the which we are most capable of doing service for God, and of bringing most honor and glory to him.

Secondly, Thou that hast an interest in the kingdom of heaven, art thou in an afflicted suffering condition in the world? To bear up thy fainting spirits, consider, that affliction and tribulation, is that, by which God is pleased to cleanse and purge his people from sin. Afflictions are like black soap, which doth seem to soil the cloth, and make it more filthy, yet it purgeth and cleanseth it, and maketh it more white at length. It is as the fire, into which the gold may be thrown, yet it is not consumed, but refined and purified, thereby it loseth only its dross; so the saints are not quite consumed by their afflictions, but sanctified, and they lose only that filth, dross, and rust, that doth mix itself with grace in their hearts. By this shall the iniquity of Jacob be purged, saith God speaking of afflictions: and this is all the fruit to take away his sin, and shall we be unwilling to have our sins purged?

It is true, as for those that are reprobates, God usually lets them alone to go on and die, and perish for ever. When as yet, God is leased to correct his people, and to cast them into the furnace of affliction, because he intends mercy to them; and surely it will be known one day, that there can be no greater judgment befal poor creatures than to be let alone without chastisements, to take their own swing in sin: and oh how many thousands are now in torment, for that they were let alone in their sins, and never chastised by afflictions in their life-time! When as God's people are chastened of the Lord, that they might not be condemned with the world, 1 Cor. xi. 32. And which is easier to be born, external tribulations in this life, or eternal torments in the life to come? One of these two will certainly befal every man and woman of us: either we shall be chastened here, or condemned hereafter. The wicked are oftentimes let alone here, they are not in trouble as other men, Psal. cxxiii. but they are condemned with the world. The godly, they are often chastised of the Lord here, but it is in mercy to them, that they may be purged from sin, and not condemned with the world. And David tells us, that by his afflictions he was reduced from going astray, and brought back again into the fold of God, Psal. cxix. 67. " Before I was afflicted, I went astray, but now have I kept thy precepts." And shall we be dismayed at the means whereby we are kept close to God, and are kept from falling away from God? A man is willing to take a bitter medicine to purge away that disease which would otherwise kill him. Nor is he troubled at the working of his physic, though he have many painful gripes, so long as it tends to the removing of those obnoxious humours and diseases which would otherwise bring him to his grave: and shall christians be afraid of the bitter cup of afflictions, which by God's blessing purge away their sins, which are the diseases of their souls, and so preserve them from eternal death? Thy trials here are to purge thee and cleanse thee, that thou mayest not lie in eternal torments in the world to come. And shall christians be dismayed at that which tends to their eternal health and salvation, and to the keeping of their souls from hell? We should rather rejoice to be in that condition whatsoever it be, by which we may be most purged and preserved from sin. Standing pools do usually contract filth and mud. So those christians that are settled upon the lees in a prosperous state and condition, they do very frequently get filth and corruption. The people of God are never made the freer from sin by their freedom from outward afflictions. This then is the second consideration to keep the saints from being dismayed at their afflictions in the world, because thereby they are purged from sin which would otherwise prove the bane of their souls.

Thirdly. You that are the heirs of heaven, and have an interest in the eternal glory, you are in affliction and tribulation in the world, be not dismayed; for consider these things do tend to the exercising and increase of our graces, and to the making of you eminent in grace and holiness. And will you be daunted at that which tends to the making of you more holy? will you be grieved at that which tends to the increasing of your faith, patience, humility, heavenly mindedness, and to the making of you more eminent for holiness and godliness? Believers are usually greater gainers by their afflictions in the world than by their external prosperity; yea, many times they are losers by their prosperity, when as they have been great gainers by their troubles and adversity. Oh how many have gained in grace and holiness by their losses in the world! The servants of God were never more eminent in grace, than when they were least and lowest in their outward estate. True graces are the diamonds that shine brightest in the darkest night, and these shine clearest in the obscurest night of adversity.

The saints in scripture were then most eminent for holiness, and godliness, and all other graces, when they lay under greatest troubles and tribulations from the world; and how exemplary in holiness, and how eminent in faith and heavenly-mindedness were the martyrs, when they were afflicted, tormented, imprisoned, burned and persecuted with the most grievous persecutions from the hands of wicked men; when as the prosperity and pleasures of the wicked did tend to the hardening of them in their sins.

Did we seriously consider how great hinderers, riches and pleasures, and worldly prosperity are to grace and holiness, we should not be so discontented at our mean and afflicted condition in the world, nor so over-desirous of those accommodations which have proved the bane of so many and the hinderers of their salvation. Peace and plenty, honour and prosperity, doth very often increase pride and covetousness, security, and earthly mindedness; whereas affliction, tribulation, want, reproach, being sanctified by God, doth tend to the exercising and increasing of patience, humility, and a heavenly conversation. And upon this consideration the apostle Paul "gloried in tribulations, because it wrought in him the grace of patience," Rom. v. 3. And not only so, saith he, "but we glory in tribulation also, knowing that tribulation worketh patience," &c. There are many souls now in torments for that pride, security, worldly mindedness, and other sins, which were nourished and fostered up in their prosperity in the world; and many souls now in heaven which were helped forward in their way thither by the exercise of those graces which were nourished and increased by their adversity, crosses, and calamities here below. Be not therefore dismayed and discontented, christian, with that condition, though it be grievous to thy frail flesh, which doth tend to the increasing of grace and holiness.

Lastly, Thou art a believer, and heir of heaven; art thou in affliction? Be not dismayed, because these things being sanctified by God will tend to the fitting of thy soul for, and to the bringing of thee nearer to heaven. Afflictions and tribulations do tend to the uniting of souls closer to Christ, and to the fitting and preparing them more and more for eternal glory; and hence it is that God hath ordained that through many tribulations we must enter into glory. Acts xiv. 22. God doth discipline his dear children by sorrows and troubles here, and so fit them for to reign with him hereafter; and shall we be dismayed at such a condition that doth tend to the fitting of us for our heavenly inheritance, and to the bringing of us nearer to Christ and salvation? Oh let not afflictions nor tribulations dismay you that have an interest in the kingdom of heaven to support you, but let the consideration of your heavenly interest keep you from fainting at all your afflictions and tribulations that you meet with in your way to heaven.

And now, beloved hearers, give me leave to trespass a little more upon your patience, seeing this is like to be the last opportunity that I shall have to speak to you from this place, being prohibited to preach unless upon such terms as I confess my conscience dares not submit unto. Being therefore enforced to lay down my ministry, I thought good to let you know that it is neither out of singularity nor stubbornness in opinion, which many it may be may conjecture, but because the things required are such as my conscience cannot close withal. Could I see a sufficient warrant from the word of God for those ceremonies and other things that are enjoined, I should readily submit unto them; for I can take the great God to witness with my conscience that nothing in the world grieveth me a hundred part so much as to be hindered from the work of the ministry, and to be disabled from serving my great master Christ in that employment. But seeing I cannot find my warrant thence, I dare not go against my conscience, and so do evil that good may come thereby. Those strict prohibitions recorded, Deut. xlii. and xii. 32. Prov. xxx. 6. And in other scriptures, wherein we are prohibited to make any addition to God's own institutions in his worship, and the terrible threatenings pronounced against those that shall transgress in this particular, hath such impression upon my heart, that I dare not give my assent nor consent to any thing in God's worship which is not warranted from his word; but I think it the lesser evil of the two to expose myself to sufferings in the world, rather than to undergo the checks and reproaches of a wounded and grieved conscience.

Dearly beloved, while I had liberty to speak unto you, I may say with the apostle Paul, Acts xx. 27. I have not shunned to declare unto you the whole counsel of God; but according to that strength and ability that God hath given me, have laboured to instruct you, and to press home upon you those great and saving truths which are of necessity to be known and practised, in order to salvation. And as the apostle Paul wrote to the Philippians, Phil. i. 8. so may I say to you, that God is my record, how greatly I have longed after you all in the bowels of Jesus Christ; your conversation unto God and eternal salvation, is that which I have had in my eye: for this I have prayed, for this I have preached, for this I have studied. Neither is there any thing more joyous to me, than to hear of any of my hearers that are walking in the truth, and that have set their faces towards heaven.

But seeing God is pleased (for ends best known to himself) to suffer my mouth, together with the mouths of many others, my dear and reverend brethren in the ministry, to be stopped, I desire to leave a word or two with each of you, which I would have you to look upon as the words of a dying minister, or of a dead minister, in a civil sense; and therefore suffer them to take the deeper impression upon your hearts. I shall therefore direct a word or two to three sorts of persons.

First, To those that do much rejoice at this time, and that have earnestly looked and longed for it: to such who hug themselves, and make merry because the troublers of Israel (as wicked men account the ministers of Christ to be) which have told them of their sins, and reproved them of their carnal, sensual, unholy lives, are not suffered to preach, nor to trouble them with the unpleasing doctrines of repentance, conversion, mortification of sin, and other truths which they dislike: to those who look upon the faithful, laborious, convincing preachers of the word of God to be their enemies, because they have told them the truth, and could not sooth them up in their sins, and rejoice as the inhabitants of the earth did rejoice over the witnesses, and make merry, Rev. xi. 10.

To you I say, whosoever you are, that none have more need of our labours, and of our preaching than you; and if you were but acquainted truly with your own state in which you are (which is a state of death and wrath, without you repent, and turn, and become new creatures) you would be of other minds than now you are, and turn your mirth and jollity into mourning. Consider, that it is never the better with any city when the watchmen are removed, nor for a traveller when the light is gone which should direct him in his way; and it cannot be but sad when so many thousands of godly ministers, which by their doctrine and lives have been as lights in the world, shall be extinguished and silenced. Believe it, Sirs, there is no good groping out our way to heaven in the dark, when as we know not whether our next step will be heaven, or hell; in eternal joy, or misery. A sick man is never the nearer health, because his physician is not suffered to speak to him of the danger of his disease; and carnal and ungodly men are never the nearer their salvation, because their faithful ministers are not suffered to preach to them of the evil and danger of their sins, which are the hinderers of it. I shall commend to your consideration that one scripture, which I would have you be often reading, and thinking on, as it is recorded, 1 Pet. iv. 17, 18. The time is come that judgment must begin at the house of God ; and if it begin at us, what shall the end be of them that obey not the gospel of Christ? and if the righteous scarcely be saved, where shall the ungodly, and the sinner appear ? If God begin with his faithful ministers to chastise and afflict them ; Oh what will then become of the wicked and ungodly world? If the godly drink first of this cup, it is because the wicked shall drink the dregs of it.

A second sort of persons which I shall speak to, are such who are halting between two ; that are like Agrippa, almost persuaded to be christians ; that have some convictions upon their consciences, of the excellency of the ways of God, but yet their interest leads them another way. They are unwilling to expose themselves to any troubles or tribulations, by going against the stream of the world; they are afraid that if they should be diligent in the duties of religion, and should walk holily and closely with God, that then they should be reproached and scorned, or persecuted by the world, and therefore they will go on a little way but no farther, than that they may retreat back again with ease and safety as to their carnal and worldly interest. To such, whosoever you are, I must tell you, first, that you must go beyond the common sort of the world; unless you will intend to come short of heaven, you must not take the example of the multitude to be a sufficient warrant for you to walk by; the broad way, though it be to your corrupt natures the most pleasant way, yet it is not the safest, but the most dangerous way : and the narrow way of holiness and godliness will be found at last to be " the way leading to life, though there be but few that find it," Mat. vii. 13, 15. They that are afraid of making too much ado for heaven, they are like to have nothing at all to do with heaven. It is a christian's duty, and should be his care, not to be " conformed to the world, but to be transformed by the renewing of their minds, that they may prove what is that good, and acceptable and perfect will of God." Rom. xii. 2.

Secondly, You must not stick at afflictions and crosses in the world if you intend to go to heaven. Christ's cross is the first that must be learnt by Christ's disciples, Luke xiv. 27. You must account upon it beforehand, that if you will live godly in Christ Jesus, you must suffer persecution, 1 Tim. iii. 5. You must not be afraid of the reproaches of the ungodly, nor flinch at oppositions and tribulations, if you intend to be everlastingly happy. The fearful are in the fore-front of them that march to hell, Rev. xxi. 8. " but the fearful and unbelieving and abominable, &c. shall have their part in the lake which burneth with fire and brimstone, which is the second death." The fearful you set down in the front in that black list there mentioned. "But the kingdom of heaven suffers violence, and the violent take it by force."

Thirdly, The end will pay for all; the kingdom of heaven will make you amends for all the tribulations that you meet with in your way to heaven.

Lastly, I shall speak a word to those that fear the Lord, and are diligent in the practice of godliness, that are very much grieved that their faithful teachers would be removed into corners. My advice that I have to give you, besides what I have spoken before, is the same with Paul's to the Philippians, Chap. iv. 1. " My brethren, dearly beloved and longed for, my joy and crown, so stand fast in the Lord, my dearly beloved." Consider your heavenly interest, and let that bear you up under all your worldly troubles and persecutions. Let not the terrors nor threats of men nor devils make you stir apart from the doctrine which is according to godliness. Though you may be scorned and afflicted by men, yet the day will come when you will be publicly owned and honoured by the Lord of glory, and when Christ which is your life shall appear, then shall you appear with him in glory? Be not affrighted at the sufferings of your ministers, though they should be far greater than now they are ; nor discouraged at the backsliding of hypocritical professors, who having formerly made fair pretences to religion and reformation, yet are turned with the dog to their old vomit again, and by their so doing do declare that it is their carnal interests only that they look unto, and therefore they will be for religion and reformation, so long as that may be promoted thereby, and no longer. But labour to imitate the heroic courage of Joshua, who resolved that he and his house would serve the Lord, though all Israel should forsake him and backslide from him. Stand fast, I beseech you, in the faith, quit yourselves like men, be strong in the Lord, and in the power of his might, put on the whole armour of God, that you may be able to stand in the evil day, and having done all to stand. Let not the enmity nor opposition of the ungodly make you to forsake the duties of religion, and the ways of holiness. Think not the better of that way, or of those persons merely because they prosper in the world, nor the worse of those merely because they are persecuted and afflicted. What were those that were tortured not accepting deliverance, that had trial of cruel mockings and scourgings, yea moreover of bonds and imprisonment, that were stoned, that were sawn asunder, that were tempted, that were slain by the sword ; they that wandered about in sheep-skins, and goat-skins ; being destitute, afflicted, tormented ? Heb. xxii. 35, 36, 37. "They were such of whom the world was not worthy," verse 38. True holiness and the fear of God are never the less lovely in God's account, because it is rejected, scorned, and condemned by the wicked world ; and sin and profaneness is never a whit the more pleasing unto Christ because it is in fashion and practised by the greatest or most of men. Finally, my brethren, commit yourselves and your way unto the Lord, and wait patiently for him, he will command deliverance for you in his own time. Snatch not after deliverance by any preposterous and unlawful courses, before God holdeth it out to you, lest you provoke him to detain it the longer from you.

To conclude all, I shall take leave of you in the words of the Holy Ghost, recorded Acts xxv. 32. Heb. xiii. 20, 21. And now, brethren, I shall commend you to God, and to the word of his grace, which is able to build you up and to give you an inheritance among men that are sanctified. And the God of peace which brought again from the dead our Lord Jesus Christ the great Shepherd of the sheep, through the blood of the everlasting covenant, make you perfect in every good work to do his will; working in you that which is well pleasing in his sight, through Jesus Christ, to whom be glory for ever and ever.

DR. SEAMAN'S FAREWELL SERMON.

Heb. xiii. 20, 21.

Now the God of peace, that brought again from the dead our Lord Jesus, that great Shepherd of the sheep, through the blood of the everlasting covenant, make you perfect in every good work, to do his will, working in you that which is well pleasing in his sight, through Jesus Christ; to whom be glory for ever and ever, Amen.

THE apostle, being now upon the conclusion of this epistle, after a very large discovery of Jesus Christ, in all those things that belong to his person, concerning his nature, as God, as man, and concerning his offices, especially concerning his priestly, and concerning the blessings and benefits, especially in matters of sacrifice, doth in this last chapter insist on matters hortatory; and in the words, draws near to a conclusion which contains a prayer, wish, or desire, which he puts up unto God, in the behalf of them, in order to their good and benefit. Now the God of peace, &c.

In which words, there are two two things considerable.

1. The matter of the apostle's prayer.
2. The grounds, which he doth insinuate for audience.

In the things he desires, the matter of the prayer is laid down in verse 21. and is summarily and generally propounded in several expressions; yet nevertheless, so as they have their specialties belonging to them. In the beginning he shows what he aims at, make you perfect, &c. In general it refers to their sanctification, and that they be thoroughly sanctified, as to their inward man, and outward conversation, as to those things that belong to them, in the habits of their minds, and eternal carriage.

The grounds which the apostle uses, by way of insinuation for audience, are contained in the words of the 20th verse, wherein we have a very large description of the person prayed unto; " the God of peace, that brought again from the dead our Lord Jesus, &c." He describes him under such notes and mark, as serve much for enlargement and enforcement, in the matter of prayer.

But here a question may arise ; seeing grace is the thing the apostle principally desires, and it is usual with holy men, both under the Old and New Testament, to chuse out such attributes as suit most with their particular occasions, and are most agreeable to those requests they have, why he doth not apply himself to God, as the God of all grace, but rather, the God of peace?

Therein first the apostle seems to make use of that same liberty which belongs to holy men. As there is in the general, a liberty left to God's people from God himself, Paul in this place makes use of that liberty he had, as to the manner of prayer, using such a description of

God, as seemed good to him at present. But secondly, if he be the God of peace, it follows, he is the God of grace. If God hath glorified himself so far among the Hebrews, as to reconcile them to himself, by the blood of Christ, then there is no question, God will proceed further; and having provided for those things which appertain to their justification, no question but he will for those things that are necessary to their sanctification. Therefore the apostle argues plainly from justification to sanctification. He that justifies his people through the blood of Christ, sanctify you by the spirit of Christ, make you perfect to do his will, working in you that which is well pleasing in his sight, &c. so desires we should be sanctified, on the consideration of our justification. Having provided for justification, by the blood of Christ, follows sanctification by the spirit of Christ, 1 Thes. 23. " And the very God of peace sanctify you wholly," &c. That God who is allied to you, the God of peace, and hath provided for you peace, I desire he would further provide sanctification; for sanctification is nothing else, but the effect of that grace, which is procured for believers through the blood of Christ. There is no access to God, for sanctification of our natures, until we prevail with him for the justification of our persons, and he first shews himself to be a God of peace, by way of justification, before a God of grace and sanctification. But to proceed.

First, for the description of the person; wherein take notice of him:

1. By one of his attributes. 2. By one of his special works, whereby he hath manifested that attribute.

1. The attribute of God, is implied, under those words, that he is called the God of peace. The gracious God that provides for reconciliation between himself and sinners, that finds out ways and means to win those who are by nature children of wrath, to be the children of God. There is no peace, but God is author of, whether natural peace, or civil peace, or political peace, he is pleased to provide for them; but there

is a transcendent kind of peace, which doth with a peculiarity belong to God's people, i. e. Spiritual peace between God and sinners, and that inward peace that we enjoy, if our conscience hath been troubled with terror of sin, wrath, &c. Peace belongs so to God as none of the creatures can have any glory of it, Psal. iv. 7. The peace, is God's peace: none can effect it, or devise it but God; and with respect to this, he is more especially called the God of peace, because he hath found out a way to make reconciliation between God and his sinful perishing creatures, 2 Cor. iii. 19. Ephes. ii. 14. &c. Col. i. 13.

2. There is a special work of God attributed to him, that the apostle takes into consideration, i. e. That he "brought again from the dead our Lord Jesus, that great Shepherd of the sheep, through the blood of the everlasting covenant;" wherein we have many words, and every word its weight, and we shall scarce be able to weigh every one so as to take the full sense and emphasis of them. In the words there is,

1. Something implied. 2. Something expressed.

1. Something implied; namely, that the Lord Jesus Christ was sometimes in a state of death; and that being in a state of death, it was not any ordinary power, way, or means, could ransom him. He was in the state and condition of the dead. He was for a while, under the power and dominion of death. His body for the space of three days lay in the grave, and in that sense, he was under the dominion of death, as all dead men are. The great Shepherd of the sheep could not have his own life, in some sense. No interest he had in God, by virtue of sonship or any of his offices, could save him from death, though the Son of God, and Head of the church; and Christ looked upon it so far from being below him, that he thought it necessary for him, and it was his glory, John x. 11, 12. "I am the good Shepherd; the good Shepherd giveth his life for his sheep: but he that is an hireling, and not the shepherd, whose own the sheep are not, seeth the wolf coming, and leaveth the sheep and fleeth, &c.

Hirelings have no spirit or principle in them, that they should lay down their lives for the sheep; but he so much respected his Father's glory, and good of his flock, finding there was no way to bring them to salvation, as he denied himself in all other respects, for their good: so in this respect lays down his life for them. And herein the church of God seems to have a deadly kind of wound, to be at a deadly loss, Zach. xiii. 7. " I will smite the shepherd, and the sheep shall be scattered." But herein lies the wonderful goodness and wisdom of God, he is pleased to improve, as the life so the death of Christ, for the good of his church, Luke xxiv. 16. " Ought not Christ to have suffered these things?" It was very expedient that seeing the sheep could not otherwise be saved but by the shepherd's dying, that the shepherd should lay down his life for the sheep; and seeing no other way to make reconciliation to God, it was very expedient Christ should die. Therefore it is to be taken notice of, that it doth not mis-become the head, therefore not the members of the body. They must be content to lay down their lives for the flock, for so did the great Shepherd.

2. *Something expressed*: Where take notice, First, of the person spoken of: Secondly, of that which is given us to be taken notice of in particular.

1. The person to be taken notice of, is, our Lord Jesus Christ. That which we have considerable, is,

First, The title that belongs to him in his church; in this regard, called the great Shepherd of his sheep. The Shepherd of the sheep, yea, the great Shepherd of the sheep. Whatsoever glory was to be communicated to any member of the church, it was first put into the head, before they were to be made partakers of it. Some were to be made inferior ranks, Eph. iv. 11. but it was not fit any should have such glory, to be called shepherds, before he had that honour of him. Therefore it is the great Shepherd, he that is shepherd not of a particular congregation, but of the whole church of God, he is the Saviour of all his body, he hath the full number of all the elect, both among the Jews and Gentiles, committed to his charge to save.

2. What betides this great Shepherd, through God's grace towards him, that is, that he is brought again from the dead, i. e. that he doth attain to a state of resurrection; and here take notice of this by the way, for consolation. The great Shepherd of the sheep doth die, but the great Shepherd of the sheep rises again. Herein argues God's love, that though he would suffer him to die, yet not to see corruption, Psal. xvi. 10. Because he is the great Shepherd, therefore he must die; but because he is the great Shepherd, therefore he cannot continue in the state of the dead. Death must not triumph over the great Shepherd of the sheep, no, not by any means. As it was necessary that he should die, much more that he should rise again. We read Rev. xi. concerning two prophets. When they had finished their course they die, and their dead bodies are cast into the streets, &c. But we read also of their resurrection. There is a twofold state incident to those persons, one state of dying, another state of rising; and so it is not peculiar to Christ only, but to others with him. The great Shepherd of the sheep dies; no wonder if the little shepherds die too. But the great Shepherd is raised, so shall the little ones in their order, and in their time, 1 Pet. v. 6. "When the chief Shepherd shall appear, ye shall receive a crown of glory that fadeth not away." Resurrection is that which Christ exemplifies first in his own person, in order to assure all his members, they shall attain to the same state with him; and God is as easily able to provide, when he sees expedient to raise them from the dead, as to suffer them to die. Christ he brought again by a high hand, and in a triumphant manner; he did not with so much sorrow and trouble to himself, and his disciples, go to, but as triumphantly come from the grave. So can God, with a word, in a moment, bring them to life again.

2. By what means the great Shepherd comes to have this honor conferred upon him, that he should be raised

from the dead. There was worth enough in his person, but it is not altogether ascribed to this; but through the blood of the everlasting covenant, i. e. by, and in, the virtue and efficacy of it. He had died as a priest, and his blood was a blood of sacrifice, and it was shed for the remission of sins, and salvation of souls; because Christ did die for so noble an end as this, and in such a manner as that his death became a sacrifice, and did seal the everlasting covenant wherefore Christ is the mediator: therefore with consideration of this blood of Christ, and of the ends, uses, and benefits of it. Hereupon it is that Christ is raised from the dead. In Zac. ix. the resurrection of Christ was prophesied of, but by virtue of his blood shed, so that Christ was more fit to be raised, who died for such noble and honourable ends, as the glory of God, and salvation of his people, in the virtue of that covenant God hath made, and in the virtue of the blood of Christ, shed for the sealing of that covenant.

Now, what this covenant is, is worthy to be considered, because of its epithets, called here everlasting covenant. There was a temporal covenant God made with the people of Israel, and that was sealed and confirmed by the blood of bullocks, &c. Christ took not on him this covenant, he did not bind men to stand by those terms contained in the covenant; for indeed, Christ came to make it void. There is an eternal covenant, and that is nothing else but those terms of grace and favour, which are proposed to us in the doctrine of the gospel, which amounts to this, whoever repents shall be saved. He that repents and forsakes his sin shall find mercy; and that he will be merciful to all on these conditions in all parts of the world; for these terms God will not repent of. If men repent they shall have the benefit of it, and whoever believes shall be saved. It is called everasting, because God will abide by it, both here and hereafter. The states of all shall be determined according to the terms of this covenant. Now Christ shed his blood to procure those terms contained in that covenant. For the case of poor sinners was so miserable, that they could never come to have all their sins pardoned, and their souls certainly saved, unless Christ had died and shed his blood, and so to satisfy God's justice, that it might be free for him to be merciful where he would be merciful. The covenant is founded in the blood of Jesus Christ, that blood being the blood of the everlasting covenant; therefore the apostle so magnifies it, of all the great and gospel-blessings that belong to the New Testament, to the condition of a child of God, there is not any like unto this, the blood of the everlasting covenant. They that come to this, and have the benefit of this, they shall be surely justified, and eternally saved in the virtue of this blood. In the business of being saved by faith, it contributes nothing more, but as it is an instrument to bring us to be made partakers of the benefit of this blood. We are saved not by virtue of our believing, but by the virtue of his blood; so that, it is not so much the act, as the object of faith that saves. Christ rose in the virtue of his blood; and all our comforts and hopes are found in his blood. The blood of Christ was of so much value with God, as that he will raise him from the dead, and it is of so much virtue to us, that through it we shall have justification, and sanctification, and salvation, God being so good and gracious a God to Jesus Christ and his church. Hereupon the apostle emboldens himself to desire his further manifestation of his love, that where he hath so bountifully provided for the justification of sinners through the blood of Christ, that he would provide for their sanctifying by his spirit. Hence observe,

1. God is with some singularity, the God of peace.

2. To the end that God might show himself to be the God of peace, he hath provided an all-sufficient Saviour for his people, here called the great Shepherd of the flock; and God being of a gracious disposition towards them, provides to that end Christ shall take care of them, and to all those things that pertain to their eternal welfare.

3. It was expedient this Person should die, though the great Shepherd. Nay it was necessary, that it might

be so much more verified and manifested that he was the great Shepherd of the sheep, that he should lay down his life for his flock.

4. It was as necessary that Christ should be raised from the dead, as that he should die. Therefore his continuance was but a temporary, nay a momentary time to him. Now Christ is risen, yea all power in heaven and earth is committed to him; and if he was able to do any thing for his people before, much more now.

5. The resurrection of Christ doth arise partly from the tenor of the covenant God made with man, and partly from the virtue and benefit that was in the blood of Christ. God put himself into a covenant, Christ was mediator of it, and in virtue of that covenant sinners must be saved; but the Saviour must first save himself, raise himself from the dead, and then hath all power committed to his hand; &c. There are two things that I would have you further observe and carry away:

1. That Christ is indeed the only great Shepherd of the sheep. Whatsoever others there are, they make to his own interest. Whosoever there be that may possibly entitle themselves under the name and notion, yet this is undeniable, that Christ is the only great Shepherd of the sheep. Therefore in the concernments of the church, there is none christians should honour as Christ, and whose voice they ought to hear before his, or by whom they should be ruled and governed, but by him. If Christ be the great Shepherd, then the church must hear his voice, "for my sheep hear my voice," &c. And if he be the great Shepherd, then the church must be ruled by him, for the shepherd must have the ordering of the flock, and the flock must be at the disposal of the shepherd. And then, thirdly, The flock of Christ must be careful to please him, for fear he set his dog upon him, that we provoke him not to exercise his correcting power. He hath his correcting power. He hath his rod of discipline, as well as his staff and crook, which is to perform by others as seems good to him, for he hath many ways to let loose

the devil on his own children. Satan had a desire to afflict Job, and God gave way to it, &c. The church of God is God's spouse, and there is a great deal of love between the husband and the wife, between Christ and the church: yet Psal. iv. 5. This she is solemnly charged withal. God hath made Christ a head to his church, therefore his church must be ruled by Christ; and it is not for the church to say, the inferior shepherds would order me thus and thus, we must in the meanwhile say, but what doth Christ say in such cases? It is not for the church to go aside by the flocks of his companions, Cant. i. 7. The companions of Christ pretended to be shepherds of the sheep as well as he, but have not that power Christ had. They have their societies, and would have the ordering of them; but the church desires to know where she may hold communion with Christ, that she may not turn aside by the flocks of her companions. There are many disputations among inferior shepherds; but this is out of all dispute, that Christ is the great shepherd of the sheep. That great man at Rome never pretended higher, than to be the vicar of Christ, and successor of Peter. Now we know that the principal is more to be regarded than the vicar; therefore if Christ be the great Shepherd, surely the sheep of Christ must hear his voice before all other shepherds, especially since Christ hath spoken so signally in the case, "My sheep hear my voice, and they follow me: a stranger will they not follow, for they know not the voice of strangers." And God having so solemnly commanded, Mat. xvii. 5. "This is my beloved Son, in whom I am well pleased, hear ye him." The great Shepherd must be heard before all little shepherds. The little shepherds have their divisions, Acts xx. 29. "After my departure shall grievous wolves enter in among you, not sparing the flock, also of your ownselves shall men arise, speaking perverse things, to draw away disciples after them." True shepherds are always careful to make disciples for Christ, and to bring all disciples to Christ. All John's work was to make disciples, to put them over to

Christ, not to make disciples to him, but to make over all his disciples unto Christ. If any man will gather, he must gather for Christ, not himself. Others would draw men to any matter or manner of doctrine, government, &c. But our eye must be upon Christ, and our ear open to his voice, and our hearts awed with his will and mind in scripture, made known to his church; and they love not Christ as they ought, that desire not to hear his voice before any others in the world, for he is the great Shepherd of the sheep.

2. Though he be the great Shepherd of the sheep, yet he died; and though he die, yet because he is the great Shepherd of the sheep, he is raised again. The great Shepherd dies, the little shepherds must not think much of it, if they be called to die. We must be contented, if it be exemplified in us, if occasion serve; for if God spared not the great Shepherd, what have the little shepherds to plead for themselves that they should be spared? If the case fall out, while I labour to serve the church as I can, I come to suffer for the church in the end, I do rejoice, and I will rejoice. And truly we had need to pray for such a spirit as this; for if this was the great Shepherd of the sheep, it will very well become the little shepherds. But against the fear of death here is the comfort. The great Shepherd of the sheep dies, yet is raised from the dead; so shall the little ones; not one member of the flock, death can always triumph over. In this respect Christ will have all his members to be raised, in that he got the victory over death; for Christ arose as the first fruits, and ascended into heaven as a fore-runner. Though we may have denial as to the advancing of Christ's service, &c. yet the resurrection of the dead is that we must take into our thoughts, and it is our solid comfort, God will one day bring all the sheep together into one fold, and David shall be their king, and have the ruling and ordering of them to all eternity. There is a resurrection to little shepherds, when we come to lay down our

natural lives, we can look for no other recompence for it but our resurrection, and the thoughts of it must be our comfort. And oh! how doth this encourage us to come unto God, though sin be heavy upon us? Remember, there is a God of peace, that takes to himself this name, for this very end, that sinners may know for their encouragement, that reconciliation is wrought out between God and them, through Jesus Christ; and if they will but come and take hold of the blood of the everlasting covenant, Christ hath said, they shall have all the blessings and benefits promised in the covenant of grace, and that the blood of Christ can procure for them; they shall have forgiveness of sins, and salvation of soul. Therefore, when we consider Christ hath died to have a flock, and for saving of the flock, and to make himself the God of peace through his blood, this should comfort us.

It remains, we come to consider of the matter of the prayer. This is very full, " make you perfect in every good work to do his will, working in you that which is well-pleasing in his sight," &c. Here we are to observe two things; first, the matter of the apostle's desire: Secondly, the measure of it. The matter of his desire, is, that the Hebrews may be made perfect in every good work to do the will of God, i. e. that they may be fully and thoroughly regenerate, sanctified throughout, both in soul and body, and that they may be furnished with all graces, and enabled for every duty. Take notice of every one of the expressions. First, make you perfect. It is the duty of christians to perfect every good work, to cleanse themselves from all the impurity of flesh and spirit, and to perfect holiness in the fear of the Lord, 2 Cor. vii. 1. Secondly, in every good work, in matters of piety, righteousness, charity, sobriety ; for within these heads, most of these things may be comprehended that belong to christians, they will go a very great way to make a perfect christian, but that christian cannot be perfect, that is not sanctified in every one of these. Thirdly, to do his will; that you may be ready, cheerfully willing to do his will on all occasions.

But how is it possible flesh and blood should attain to this, that they should be perfect in every good work? Why, saith the apostle, working in you that which is well pleasing in his sight, through Jesus Christ, working in you. You see thereby all our works depend on God, and it is in vain for us to build on any foundation but this; for it is God that worketh in you, both to will and to do of his good pleasure, &c. Col. ii. 12 Through the faith of the operation of God; working in you, or doing in you, or causing in you, or making in you, that which is well pleasing in his sight. Our work is to depend on God's work; our outward working depends on God's inward working.

Again, that which is acceptable in God's sight, but it is only through Jesus Christ. Good works themselves, though never so good, agreeable to the law and gospel, yet if God look not on our persons and works through Christ, they will not serve the turn, ye cannot be accepted; "working in you that which is well pleasing in his sight, through Jesus Christ." Will God be pleased with nothing, but only for Christ Jesus's sake? And if it do not please Christ, it will not please God. It is truly, plainly, verily so. That which God cannot accept of though Christ, he doth not accept at all: but now things are so ordered, that God hath put all things into Christ's hands. Christ Jesus hath the ordering of the worship and government of the church, he hath the making of all the articles of the christian's creed. A christian is bound to believe nothing, but what Christ teaches, as necessary to salvation; so that in Christ we are complete, if we believe as he teaches us to believe; and if we worship God as he teaches us to worship God, and have such order and government concerning his house, and walk so as we desire in all things to please our Lord and master, and have him before our eyes, then are we returned unto

Christ, the shepherd and bishop of our souls. But if we present God with any kind of creed, model of worship, or government, that hath not Christ's image and stamp upon it, God will say, as Christ concerning the money, whose image or superscription doth it bear? If we can say Christ's, the way of worship we have learned from Christ, that order and government in the church we have learned from Christ, then the Father and Son will own it. If it have man's superscription upon it, not God's or Christ's, I cannot tell how we should presume it can be acceptable to God, through Christ; for God hath so confined himself, he will not be pleased, but through Christ; and that all matters of religion in the New Testament should be ordered according to Christ's mind, as the old according to Moses. It is necessary we enquire after Christ's mind in what we do. If we can do any thing, and in doing it, are sure it will be acceptable to God through Christ, well and good; otherwise not. This is the apostle's prayer, " that God would make them perfect in every good work to do his will, working in them that which is well pleasing in his sight, through Jesus Christ."

The doxology. Whether we refer it to God or Christ, it is all one; we have nobody to honour and glorify in the church, but God through Christ. We cannot tell how to divide those that are so nearly united. Therefore when we glorify God, we glorify Christ. And this we must observe. God hath ordered all men's concernments so, that we have nothing to plead for our soul's salvation, but God's grace. The rule in his word, is his gospel that he hath made known to us; and therefore let the word of God dwell in you richly, in all wisdom. There is a great deal of do in God's church, about this and that. He that must determine the business is Christ; and there are but two ways—the determining things for the present, and for the time to come; hereafter by questioning the matter of fact; for the present, by making of our rule. When the question comes concerning the matter of fact, there he receives our rule. What hath Christ said? How hath Christ provided in things of this nature? It is plainly so and so: but in dubious matter and customs, and the like, I know not how to answer them, when we shall come to answer Christ, when he shall put the question, Did you not know whom you was bound to fear? Did I speak nothing at all in the case, neither generally nor particularly? Could you not by any means come to understand my mind? I doubt we shall not be able to answer this. But we must say we found a certain state in the word; but having laws and customs among ourselves, therein were at a stand. Why (saith Christ) were your laws and customs above or below my word? Must your law be ruled by my word, or my word by your doctrine? Did not all christians hold out this, that the word of Christ was above all authority, in the matters of Christ? Shall the members of the body become greater than the head? Therefore you could not be ignorant in this case. Your own professing me to be so great, in all my natures and offices; but when you come to practice, then you will deny me. Shall we be able to answer this? We must consider of this, that if we would please God, it must be through Christ; and then we must carry ourselves, as directed by Christ Jesus in his word; and nothing can take us off that principle, no pretence whatsoever; for the christian religion is such a thing in the nature and substance of it, as Jesus Christ is the author of. Therefore if Christ be the author, all that belongs to the christian religion, as to its substance, we should account nothing of moment in religion, but only that which we can ascribe to Christ, as the author of it. The care of the church is in the hand of Christ, whatsoever providences are let in on the church, to exercise or try the church, all must be borne patiently: but every member must worship him. God hath made Jesus Christ a shepherd, &c. In what he finds fault, we must not justify; what he commands, we must approve; what he calls to be done, we must practice; what is not his, we must not own as his. Much may be drawn from this, both for instruction and consolation, that Christ is the great Shepherd; though he die in his members, he shall rise in his members. I may say, though he die in his ministers, he shall rise in his ministers, Isa. lix. 21. "As for me, this is my covenant with them, saith the Lord, my spirit that is upon thee, and my words which I have put into thy mouth, shall not depart out of thy mouth, nor out of the mouth of thy seed, nor out of the mouth of thy seed's seed, saith the Lord, from henceforth and for ever." This is a part of the covenant, that the word and spirit of Christ shall be continued among the members throughout all ages. God will provide. His children shall not live without a spirit, neither without his word. God hath engaged himself for both, for the one as well as the other, that there shall be a super-addition, and perpetuating of them; and herein we must depend upon the faithfulness of the great Shepherd of the sheep.

A FAREWELL SERMON, PREACHED AT GREAT AYTON IN THE COUNTY OF YORK, BY GEORGE EVANKE, CHAPLAIN TO SIR GEORGE NORWOOD, BART. AT CLEAVELAND, IN YORKSHIRE.

MATTH. xxvi. 39.

Nevertheless not as I will, but as thou wilt.

THE subject of this chapter is a sad story, and tragical relation of a dying Jesus. In the beginning of this gospel, you may see him coming into the world in a shower, Matth. ii. 13. And now in the end of it, you find him going out in a storm, Mat. xxvii. 22.

MR. EVANKE'S SERMON. 413

Alas! that so good a guest should find so bad a welcome, and that the Lord of life should so soon be put to death! When the angels, those heavenly choristers, first sang that Christmas carol, of a Saviour that was born into the world, Luke ii. 10, 11, 12, 13, 14. one would have thought the world should have fallen a dancing after such evangelical music, and that all hearts should have like the babe in Elizabeth's womb leapt for joy, at the news of a new born prince. But it was quite contrary; for instead of joining in that heavenly choir in gratulating the happy arrival of this young king into their country, they take the alarum of his birth as if an enemy had landed in their coasts. And hereupon Herod presently heads an army, goes out against him, and makes the poor prince to fly the country, Mat. ii. 13, 14.

But though the meanness of his birth, extraction, and descent may give them distaste at first, yet when he begins to display his divinity among them, by working such amazing miracles, as none could work, and preaching such moving sermons as none could ever preach. Oh, then they will recant their error, and own their Saviour, "and the joyful shout of a king will be heard amongst them:" as it is expressed in Numb. xxiii. 21.

Truly one would think that it would have been thus; but Oh no! the rocky hearts of these marble wretches would not yield, nor melt, nor thaw, nor take impression, but still they continue in their unbelief and hardness of heart, disowning the Lord that bought them, and consulting his death, who was contriving to bring them to life.

All the displeasure he would have done them, was to take their sins from them, Mat. xi. 28. And all the pleasure they meant to shew him was to take his life from him, Mat. xxvi. 59.

All the hurt that ever Christ did them, was to pray for them, " Father, forgive them, forgive them." And all the good they ever did him, was to cry, " crucify him, crucify him." And crucify him they did before they could sit down.

Whose death and crucifixion is described and represented to your view,
1. By the antecedent, or things before.
2. By the consequents, or things following after.

The antecedents were,
1. The several preparatories to it.
2. The judicial progress about it.

The prerogatives were,
1. The Jews conspiring, ver. 3, 4, 5.
2. Judas's covenanting to affect it, ver. 14, 15, 16.
3. Christ's own preparing and fitting himself for it, that he might without reluctance submit to it, and without the least symptom of desponding, encounter and go through with it. And this is the argument of the latter part of this chapter at large, and of my text in short.

Father, if it be possible, let this cup pass from me, yet not my will, but thy will be done.

Which words I may call, The pious soul's sequestring itself for dying: or, Our Saviour's preparatory to his passion. Wherein you have two observables:
1. Here is an humble petition presented: Let this cup pass.
2. Here is an hearty resignation promised: Not as I will, but as thou wilt.

First, An humble petition; Let this cup pass from me. Our Saviour was at this time very apprehensive of death. "The sorrows of the grave had compassed him about, and the pains of hell had taken hold upon him."

And now in this dark condition and spiritual damp that his soul lay under, he gets himself out into the garden alone, and there he sits weeping, as Elijah under the juniper-tree; and like dying Hezekiah, he lays his case open, and spreads his condition before the Lord, imploring him, Samaritan-like, to shew him some pity in this his extremity: Father, saith, he, Let this cup pass from me.

Now in that Christ betakes himself to God for help in this hour of heaviness, you may learn hence "It is better to intrust and interest God, for our help and comfort than man." For man, yea, the best of men, are but men, and when they have done the best for us, it may be they can do no good to us.

When the man, in the Kings, had made his misery known to his neighbours, and cried to them, Help, help, you know what an answer he got, How can we help, except the Lord help?

When Job had told over the sad story of his great losses to his three friends, expecting some redress to so unparalleled grievances, you know how long they sat by him, without giving him one word of counsel, or administering the least word of comfort, which forced him into that passionate resolve, Miserable comforters are ye all.

When Judas lay under the convulsions and corrodings of a grumbling conscience, and ran to the priests for absolution, a "look thee to that," was all the comfort he could get from them. Ah! that man's condition is most to be pitied, who runs to none but man for pity. When all is done, God is our surest stay. He is usually the last, but always the best refuge: Therefore, when we have read over the sad lecture of our losses, and poured out our wants and wrongs into the bosom of our safest and firmest friends, then is this apostrophe, this turn, the sweetest turn the soul can take, when it can turn to God (as you see Christ doth here) and say, "Father, if it be possible, let this cup, this cross, pass from me."

II. Secondly, Here is an hearty resignation in these words, "Nevertheless not my will, but thine be done." And if he had said, it is true, it is ease which this nature, this human nature of mine would have, but if thou, Lord, art otherwise resolved to continue me in pain, I have no more to say but only this, Thy will be done.

It was the saying of a good woman in her sickness, when asked whether she was willing to live or die, she answered, I am willing to do whether God pleaseth. But said one, if God should refer it to you, which would you chuse? Truly, said she, if God should refer it to me, I should even refer it to him again. Here is the picture of Christ's patience (drawn here in this text) where as you see, he refers to his Father's pleasure, "Not my will, but thine be done." Paraphrastically thus—if thou wilt have me suffer a while, lay load on me, and spare not—if I must be spit on thus shamefully, and buffeted thus basely, and that by my own creatures, whom I could send to hell with a word speaking; if I must climb to the ladder, and be hung up in gibbets as a spectacle of sadness to my friends, and object of laughter to my enemies; if it be so that my honor must lie in the dust, and my blood lie in the dust, and my sacred body go to bed with worms; if it must be thus, let it be thus, and no otherwise than just thus. In a word, if he that never stole any thing, unless it were men's sins from them, must now be numbered with transgressors, and hanged with thieves? If the redemption of the world be so costly, that I cannot hug a poor soul to heaven with me at a cheaper rate, I am content to come up to God's terms, and to buy the life of the nation though it be with my own death. Thus much is meant in this expression: "Thy will be done," or "as thou wilt."

From which branch, we may shake this fruit into your lap.

Doct. A gracious soul will endeavour the crossing his own will, when he sees that it crosses God's.

Or, thus, A true Christian dare not, at least ought not, to gratify his own humour when it stands in opposition, or cometh in competition with God's honour.

In the improvement of which, I shall

1. Premise some precedents of it.
2. Annex some reasons to it.
3. Infer some use from it.

The first precedent I shall pitch upon is Abraham, Gen. xxii. 2. Here God calls Abraham out to very hot service, even to lay the sacrificing knife to the throat of his dear child. Come, saith God, " Take thy son, thy only son Isaac, whom thou lovest, and offer him up for a burnt-offering." Alas! how many considerations might have stept into Abraham's head, at this time, to have made him refuse obedience to a command so grievous and ungrateful to flesh and blood. " Alas! Lord, Isaac is my son, the only staff of my old age. And if my son die, it will be enough to bring my grey hairs with sorrow to the grave. Nay more, Isaac is my only son, I have none else to keep up my family, and to preserve my name in everlasting remembrance; and if he die, all the hopes I have of a flourishing posterity die with him. Nay more, Isaac is the son of promise. In his seed all nations are to be blessed; Christ, the Messiah, is to come, of his line; Sion's deliverer is to spring out of his race; and if he die, the world, for ought I know, must want a Saviour, and Israel his Redeemer. Besides, if Isaac must be sacrificed, is there none to lay bloody hands upon him but myself? Must an indulgent father be his own child's executioner? Must I that gave him life, be the cruel instrument of taking it away?" Thus Abraham might have expostulated the case with God. But no, no, instead of replying, he falls to obeying, Gen. xxii. 3. without either disputing the justice of God's precept, or distrusting the truth of his promise, for he considered " That God was able to raise him up again from the dead." Heb. xi. 19.

See here an eminent piece of self-denial; his sin must go, his son must go, any thing, yea, every thing must go when God calls for it.

It was Abraham's will, and wish too, that Isaac should live; but Abraham would not own his will, when he saw it did not own God's; and what lost he by it?

Take this, Christian, as an axiom, and put it as an article into thy creed, That there is never any loss in obeying God, let the command be ever so dangerous costly, or difficult. The way to keep Isaac, is to give up

Isaac; and the way to enjoy thy will, is to deny thy will. The promise is clear, Matt. xix. 29.

A second precedent you have in David, 2 Sam. xv. 26. who in that great cross, his chasing from the crown, thus expressed himself; " Behold, here I am, let the Lord do with me as seemeth good in his sight." As if he had said, If the Lord please to change the nature of my unnatural son Absalom, who seeks to usurp the crown, and ravish the kingdom from me, and to settle and re-establish me on the throne again, if God please thus to honour me, it shall content me; but if he use his negative vote, and deny me that mercy, saying, I have no pleasure in thee, I will be content still; Let him do (saith David) what seemeth good in his sight. Not what seems good in my sight, but in his. His will shall be my will, and his pleasure my delight. See what another self-denying saint here is, that God and he, should have but one will betwixt them both. If God would favour him, he would be for it; and if God would afflict him, he would not be against it. Which disposition mindeth me of that passage which I have read of Socrates, when a tyrant threatened him with death, I am willing to die, said Socrates. Nay then, replied the tyrant, you shall live against your will. No, said Socrates, whatever you do with me, it shall not be against, but with my will.

O friends, I question whether some of you, who pretend to grace, may not go to school to this heathen, who had no other pilot but nature, to steer him. Could not the tyrant, by altering the man's condition, make him to alter his countenance? And is your condition up and down, as your comforts or discomforts ebb or flow? Did natural qualifications make him quietly submit to fortune, and shall not theological considerations make you acquiesce in a providence? Did the spring-head of mere reason rise so high as contentation? And shall not religion, like the waters of the sanctuary, rise as high? O Christians, lie down at the foot of God's mercy, saying, Thy will be done.

1. Otherwise you will grieve God.
2. And you will gratify the devil.
3. And lastly, you will no way advantage yourselves.

Reason 1. First, I say you will grieve God. * See Heb. iii. 10. " Wherefore I was grieved with that generation," saith God. What generation was that, which God was thus grieved with? Look but into Exod. xvi. 8. and you will find it was a murmuring generation, a dissatisfied, and discontented generation.

It is a grief no doubt to a godly parent, to see his child discontented with his allowance, and Esau like, slight his birth-right. Ah! God is not pleased to see his children displeased; nor contented, to see them discontented. I read in Psal. xxxv. 27. "That God takes pleasure in the prosperity of his people." But I no where read, that he takes pleasure in the discontent of his people. No, no, this passion made God himself angry with the Jews of old, " because," saith he, " you have not walked thankfully before me in the use of my blessings, therefore you shall serve your enemies in hunger and nakedness." Whereas on the other hand, it pleaseth God to see his people truckle under the cross, and yet content; to be ground betwixt the teeth, and wounded with the tongues of malicious neighbours, and yet content; to see and hear the delicious accents of his dying martyrs, when in their extremest tortures, they cried out nothing but Holy Jesus, Holy Jesus.

To see and hear patient Job sitting on his dunghill, and bearing his burthen bravely, mingling his groans with praises, and justifications of God; this, this pleased God like an anthem sung by angels, in the morning of the resurrection, and therefore he hath crowned him with the wreath of glory. In all this Job sinned not.

II. Secondly, By discontent, you gratify the devil. When Nero (that he might the better conceive the flames of Troy) had set Rome on fire, he sat down and

---

* This expression is not to be taken properly, but theologically.

sang songs unto it. Oh, the devil is never so merry, as when he sets us on fire with contention; consuming and smudging our lives away in the smoke of discontent. Such a fire makes the devil a bonfire. And this was his aim in afflicting Job, not to make him a poor man, but an impatient man. But he was basely mistaken, for when he expected that Job should have fallen down to blaspheme God, Job on the contrary falls down and blesseth God. "The Lord hath freely given and justly taken away, blessed be the name of the Lord."

Ah! how black looked Satan at the fall of that expression from Job's lips! How did this gall and gravel a malicious devil! Certainly this one word of Job's did wound Satan more than all the afflictions wounded Job.

Ah, friends, get but your wills to buckle under the will of God; and in all overture of condition to acquiesce in a providence, and this double advantage will come of it, God will have his end, and Satan will miss of his.

3. Thirdly and lastly, you can no way advantage yourselves by discontent, but may disturb your conscience, and hugely prejudice your own peace. As the prisoner in irons hurts himself more by striving to shake them off, than the fetters would do by being on: so many a man, by fretting and discontent, makes the cross bigger to himself, than ever God made it. His discontent being a greater affliction to him, than the affliction itself. Greater, I say, by how much it sits nearer to the spirit, than any outward crosses do, or can do. I remember what Seneca writes of Cæsar, who having appointed a great feast for his nobles and friends, and it falling out that the day proved exceeding foul, even so as nothing could be done, and being extremely displeased at it, in the height of madness took their bows, and shot at Jupiter, in defiance of him; but it happened that their arrows lighting short of Jupiter, fell down upon their own heads, and wounded them mortally. Thus is it in the point in hand, our murmuring,

and impatience are as arrows shot, not at Jupiter, but at Jehovah, at God himself. Hence, said Moses, Exod. xvi. 8. to that murmuring generation, " your murmurings are not against us, but against God;" which arrows may wound yourselves deeply, but they never hurt God at all. They wound your consciences with guilt, and your hearts with disquiet, and ofttimes causeth God to wound you too with punishment, which if it had not been for your murmurings he would never have brought upon you.

Miriam murmured, and God smote her with leprosy. The Israelites murmured, and God sent serpents among them. They stung God with fierce tongues, and God stung them with fiery serpents. Never then let a people murmur against their Maker more, but quietly submit to his providential proceedings, lest otherwise by struggling and striving against God they do but make their bands stronger, and their condition worse; like the silly partridge, which by her fluttering breaks her wings, but not the net. My advice then, friends, is this, whenever God binds the cross upon your backs, or ties or stakes you down to a sick bed, or any other sad or uneasy condition; since these cords of his you cannot break, lie down gently, and suffer the hand of the Lord to do what he pleaseth, swallowing down this bitter pill which he forceth down your throats for the health of your souls.

I come now to the second thing; viz. The

USES OF THE DOCTRINE.

And upon enquiry I find two sorts of men reproveable
1. Those that do their own will.
2. Those that do the devil's will.

First, then, it speaks terror to those that do their own will. Such were the Israelites, 2 Sam. viii. 5. They would needs have a king to rule over them; this was their will, and their will they would have, although they knew it jarred, and extremely interfered both with the will of God, and his prophets; yet still the cry of the rabble, and the vote of the multitude was this, "nay but we will have a king," ver. 19.

The like you see in Rachel, Gen. xxx. 1. " give me children, or I die." Albeit she saw that her husband could not, and that God would not humour her, yet still she cries, give me children, or I die. Wilful woman! If thou canst not live in pleasure, wilt thou needs die in a pit? Chusing rather to have thy body killed, than thy will crossed?

This is the case of all mankind, till grace work a change, and till God of an unwilling, make us a willing people in the day of his power. Till then, we have a will, which is not only blemished with an indisposition, but also biassed with an opposition to God's; for saith Paul, that doctor of the Gentiles, Rom. viii. " It is not subject to the will of God, neither indeed can be." Mark, it is not subject, nor can be subject. What more can be said to abase the natural pride of man? As he hath such a mind as neither understands nor can understand the things of God, 1 Cor. ii. 14. So he hath such a will as neither is subject, nor can be subject, Rom. viii. Thus lies fallen man, lost man, forlorn man, degenerated man. Thus lies he locked up in obstinacy, darkness, and unbelief, minding his own things, doing his own will, and damning his own soul, until God spring in, as the angel did to Peter in prison, and bring him news of his spiritual enlargement out of that dead and damning estate, to which he had thrown, and enthralled himself, body and soul for ever.

O thou heavenly Samaritan, that once poured wine into the half dead traveller, draw near, draw near! Here is a church full of souls, not half dead, but wholly dead, their eyes closed; they cannot, they cannot see thee; their hearts grown stiff, and cold, and hard, and have no feeling of thee, unless in mercy thou speak a resurrection word, and make them live again to praise thee! Oh let this be the time of life! Oh let it be a time of love! Apply unto their festered sores this saving salve of Christ's blood, that they putrify not to death, nor languish in despair! Drop into their wounded souls the sharp wine of thy wrath, search them, and pour in also the supplying oil of thy tender mercy to heal them, that so both them and their wills (which further than they are driven will not go) may be brought into a conformity to thee and thy will!

Secondly, It speaks terror to those that do the devil's will. It was an indictment which Christ preferred against the Jews, and may, I fear, too truly be laid to the charge of many nominal Christians, John viii. 44. "Ye are of your father the devil, and the works of the devil you will do."

Adam, when the will of God, and the will of the devil hung in equal balance before him, we know how ready he was to chuse the wrong scale. God said, "touch not the forbidden fruit." Satan said, "take, and eat the forbidden fruit." And you know the sad event of that affair. Now if Adam was at the devil's beck in the state of creation, when his nature was not depraved with sin, nor his soul debauched with lust; who in the state of corruption can say, my heart is clean?

Obj. It may be some will object, none is so devoid of grace sure, none gone so far in the stupification of their conscience, as to do the will of the devil.

Answer. Ah, poor soul! I could wish that the party here concerned be not nearer than thou art aware of. Put thy hand into thy bosom, and it may be, thou mayest resolve the objection thyself. Thou wouldest possibly take it ill, should I come to thee (as Nathan did to David) and clap thee on the shoulder with this arrest, thou art the man. I confess this would be more than my commission warrants me to do, yet give me leave to whisper one word or two in thine ear.

When thou makest a lie, whose will dost thou? God's, or the devil's? Not God's, for God saith, put away lying. Surely lying is the work and will of Satan, whom the scripture records for a liar from the beginning. Again, when with Jezebel thou paintest thyself with pride, and standest sacrificing many a precious morn to the idol in the looking-glass, whose will art thou doing at such a time? Sure not God's; for in Isa. xxviii. 1. you have him declaiming against such practices, "woe to the crown of pride, to the crown of pride." When thou art acting the good-fellow upon the ale-bench, and with thy drivelling oaths damning all that are wedded to the rules of sobriety, and dares not break off thy drunken fraternity, whose will art thou doing—in whose work art thou employed at such a time? Certainly not God's, he calls no such conventicles, nor allows no such societies. Witness that alarum, which he sounds under the window where such swaggerers sit, Joel i. 5. "Awake, awake, ye drunkards, weep and howl all ye drinkers of wine; for the time is at hand when your sweet draught shall be cut off from your mouth." In a word, when thou art sinning, whose will art thou doing? Not God's; for he saith, "cease to do evil, and learn to do well." Certainly while it is thus with thee, the words of Christ are applicable to thee, "thou art of thy father the devil, and the work or will of the devil thou wilt do," John viii. 44.

Thirdly, Is it so? then ever make God's will the standard of yours, and think not to bring down his will to yours, but resign up your will to his. That epitaph would not become a Christian tomb-stone, which was found engraven on a miser's monument, "Here lies one against his will." The blessed apostle was of another mind, when he said, "I have learnt in whatever state I am, therewith to be content." Many can be content in an honourable estate, or in a wealthy estate, or in a plentiful or prosperous estate; but to be reproached and yet content, to be belied, and yet content, to be affronted, and wronged, and yet content, in such estates as these to be content, is far above nature, and none can do it, but he that hath learnt it. "I have learnt," saith Paul.

But alas! How few scholars hath this great doctor St. Paul in his heavenly academy! Children can learn to be proud, can learn to be covetous, can learn to be undutiful to their parents, can learn to lie and swear, before they have well learnt to speak. But he must be a man, nay more than a man, that can learn to love an enemy, to forgive an injury, and with Paul, to be content with every contingency.

For the Lord's sake ply this lesson well. If thine enemy lay thy honour low, entreat the Lord to lay thy heart as low, and be content. If authority bring thy estate down, beseech God to bring thy spirit down, and be content. When thy comforts run a tilt, and thy blessings run dregs, then let patience have her perfect work, and be content; feast upon thy own lentiles, quash thy penitential tears instead of luscious wine, and count thy sins instead of pounds; keep thy heart at home, and suffer not thy ambition to climb up beyond thy Maker's pleasure.

Mahomet, when he could not make the mountain come down to it, he went up to the mountain. So when thou canst not enlarge thy dominions to thy mind, then confine thy mind to thy dominions; and when thou hast more, be the more thankful, and when thou hast less, be content. This is the third use, make God's will the standard of yours.

Now if you put Paul's query, "Lord, what wilt thou have me to do?"

I will answer the question, and tell you, what God would have you to do.

1. God would have you obey his command, and live piously.

2. God would have you bear his cross, and suffer patiently.

First, It is God's will you should live piously. For the proof of this you may read, 1 Thes. iv. 3, 4. This is the will of God. What is? even this, saith Paul; your sanctification, that every one of you should possess your vessel in holiness. Mark this, in holiness; and if so, what will become of all those befooled and abused souls, who debauch their vessel with uncleanness, and defile themselves with drunkenness? If Belshazzar was so severely punished for desecrating and profaning the vessels of the temple dedicated unto God, of how much sorer punishment shall these wretches be thought worthy, who have adulterated and defiled the temple of the Holy Ghost! He drank intemperately to the honour of his idol, only in dead vessels of gold and silver. But these in doing thus, abuse living vessels, living bodies, and living souls; such vessels as by baptism were marked out for God, and separated and sealed to his holy service, they abuse and prostitute to a lust, to a harlot, to the devil. Ah! who can but weep, and weep again to see how much of our English blood is poisoned with these beastly enormities at this day; and how many of our otherwise hopeful gentlemen, who might do God and their country much service, and be a great help to the public good, and peculiar blessing to the place where they live, do basely and unworthily melt away their youth, and emasculate their spirits in drunken societies and effeminate embraces!

Alas, that so many noble births, so many sparkling wits should be prostituted to Satan's service, and employed in carrying on Satan's cause, while they know it not! If they had found a golden chalice (as Augustine observes of Lucinus) they would have given it to the church. But God hath given them a golden wit, a golden head, and golden parts, and in these golden cups, and chalices, they drink themselves to the devil, both body and soul for evermore.

Ah, deluded and degenerated gentlemen! Think with yourselves seriously, what answer you will make to your Judge at the general audit-day, for taking the members of Christ, and making them members of an harlot.

Never see my face more, said Joseph, unless you bring your brother Benjamin with you. Oh friends, never think to see God's face to your comfort in glory, if you carry not holy bodies, and holy souls, and holy affections with you; God tells you his mind in Hebrews.

"Follow peace and holiness, without which you shall never see the Lord." You may go to heaven without a penny in your purse, but you shall never come there without holiness in your heart. Heaven is a city where righteousness dwells, and therefore though God in his wonderful patience to poor lost man, suffer the earth to give the ungodly a little house-room a while, yet sure I am, he will never cumber heaven with such a crew.

Before Enoch was translated to heaven, he walked holily upon earth, else God had never desired his company so soon as he did. And before the saints departed, commenced, and took their degree of glory, they kept their acts, and performed the exercises of grace, and so must you: the scripture is plain, without holiness, none shall see the Lord. It is true, none go to heaven for his holiness, and this shews the insufficiency of holiness. But it is as true, that none go to heaven without holiness, and this argues the necessity of holiness. And therefore though it be no plea for heaven, yet it will be your best evidence, and will you have your evidences to seek, when you should have them to shew? Ah then! as you value a portion among the saints in light, and hope to live in heaven, when you can live no longer upon earth, "be holy, as your Father which is in heaven is holy."

Cæsar's money must be known by Cæsar's image and superscription, and so must the Christian at the reckoning day, by the terror of his conversation. "Not every one that saith Lord, Lord, but he that doth the will of the Lord shall be saved," saith Christ. Your works must be your witnesses, and your deeds must declare whose you are, and to whom you belong. And therefore begin to live that life now, which you intend and hope to live for ever; and continue not one day longer in that condition, in which you would not die, and appear at judgment in. Therefore go home and dress yourselves, not with good clothes, but with good works; and while others are querying "what they shall eat, and what they shall drink, and what they shall put on," study you how to live, and how to die, and to put on the Lord Jesus Christ, making no provision for the flesh, to fulfil the lust thereof. And when others are projecting how to improve a barren piece of ground, let your contrivance be how to improve a barren mind; and as their care is, that their fields should not lie fallow, so let it be your study, not to let your hearts lie fallow; and the rather because you see that this is the will of God, even your sanctification, that every one of you should possess his vessel in holiness, 1 Thes. iv. 3, 4.

Now, that this is the will of God, will appear upon a twofold account.

1. First, from the price with which he hath redeemed us to it.

2. And, secondly, from the promise which he hath made to reward us for it.

I. The price he paid down upon the nail, was his own blood, Tit. ii. 14. "He gave himself for us, that he might redeem us from all iniquity, and purify unto himself a peculiar people." Had man kept his primitive holiness, Christ might have kept his life, and have spared his pains. It was man's lost righteousness, lost holiness, that Christ came to recover. But this is a point that needs pressing rather than proving, which I shall undertake to effect by these ensuing obtestations and entreaties. I beseech you, upon the account of these three considerations, that you would approve yourselves a holy nation, a seed which the Lord hath blessed.

I beseech you, 1. For my sake.—2. For your sakes.—3. For Christ's sake.

First, for my sake, who am to come to you as a petitioner and messenger from the Lord, and the sum of my desires is this, I beseech you in Christ's stead, that you would be reconciled to God. I am not courting you for your silver, but for your souls; and what will you grant me, if this be denied me? "O the Lord make you a willing people in the day of his power."

God hath sent me to you (as Jesse to David) with this present in mine hands, and these breathings in my heart, after your salvation. O may they but prove serviceable and successful to your souls, and I shall bless God that hath put it into mine heart thus to visit you. But if you will not hear, nor fear to do no more so wickedly, " My soul shall weep in secret for you."

Is it not sad to a tender physician, to see his patients to die under his hands? Much sadder sure to a poor minister, to see souls drop to hell, one by one, under his pulpit, and cannot help them, cannot save them. This must needs be a heart-sadding sight to one that is sensible of the worth of souls. It costeth the mother no small pains to bring forth a living child. But ah the bitter throes of that minister that travels all the year long, nay all his life long, with a dead child, a dead-hearted people. That spends his strength, and like a candle, swails out his life amongst his parish, and is forced at last, to take up the prophet's complaint : " Who hath believed our report, and to whom is the arm of the Lord revealed ?"

O my dear friends, think solemnly, and seriously, what answer you intend to give me, before I leave you. Christ will not always cry, Come. The spirit will not always cry, Come ; neither must I. The time is at hand, when you will say one to another, We had a preacher, we had a teacher, we had a well-wisher, and a lover of our souls amongst us ; but we did not improve and profit under him as we might, and therefore God hath sent him away from us, as he did Jonah to Nineveh, when Jerusalem despised him. O hear me then while you may, and pray with me while you may, and accept of the tender of salvation from me, while you may. " Yet a little while, and you that have seen me, shall see me no more." And you that have heard me, (as Job saith) shall say, Where is he ? It is but a little, and those seats shall have other hearers, and this pulpit have another preacher. It is but a little that you have to hear, and I have to speak in this place; and shall not my dying words be living words to you? Shall my farewell-sermon be a forgotten sermon? and the last request I am like to make to you, be repulsed and slighted by you? O my dear neighbours and friends, of whom I travel till Christ be formed in you, awake, and live! Seek the Lord before the grave and hell shut their mouths upon you, and before the servant of the Lord, sent now to warn you, takes his last leave of you, and sees your faces no more.

I am wounded, I am wounded to think this sermon should be concluded, before all your souls be converted, and to leave any of this congregation, walking on in hell road, when I am gone. Oh that I knew but what to do, to get you to do that to-day, which must be done, or you may be undone to-morrow!

If it were to follow you home, and there to beg your conversion on my bare knees, as a child begs his father's blessing, if it were to go to my closet when sermon is done, and there to wrestle with God, as Jacob did, for a blessing upon you, my loving parishioners, till I get this answer from God, " I have blessed them, and they shall be blessed"—nay, though I were sure to go to prison as soon as I come forth of the pulpit, yet I should think all well bestowed, could I but see you begin to turn this sermon into practice, and to follow peace and holiness, without which you cannot see the Lord.

Oh what a joyful hour's work would I esteem this, and how heartily would I bless your God and my God, that prospered his word in the mouth of his servant, making it a salvation word to as many as are ear-witnesses of it this day!

This is the first argument, I beseech you for my sake. Little do you think what a joy it is to your minister to see his children (as St. John speaks) walking in the truth. And on the contrary, what an affliction, to see you walk in error, and sin. Little do you think what a comfort it is to me to think of making this account to God at the judgment day, " Here are the children which thou gavest me, and I have lost none." And on the other hand, what an aching it is to my heart, to think of bespeaking God at that time, on this manner, " Here are none of the children, O Lord, none of the souls that thou didst commit to my trust, for I have lost them all." But I hope better things of you, though I thus speak.

II. Secondly, I beseech you for your own sakes. Who will have the worse of it, if this advice be not followed, you or I ? Alas, though it may be matter of grief to me, yet not of guilt. God will reward me according to my labour, not according to my success. We are, said the apostle, a sweet savour of Christ in them that perish, mark, in them that perish, as well as in them that be saved. Though the patient die, yet the physician must be paid. So albeit the people die in their sins, yet God's ministers may comfortably conclude with the prophet, Isa. xlix. 4. " Though I have laboured in vain, and spent my strength for nought, yet surely my judgment is with the Lord, and my work (namely, the reward of my work) with my God."

Ah, my friends, it is you that will have the worst of it one day, if this sermon be not faithfully followed, and obeyed. Read at your leisure, Ezek. iii. 16, 17, 18. and see whether I speak truth or a lie. It is you that must have the reward of punishment. It is you that must stand or fall, that must be the subjects of the pleasures of heaven, or the objects of all the pains in hell ; and should not you then be as much concerned for yourselves, as I am for you ? Now you enjoy your health, and the sad accents of a dying sinner are not heard in your habitations, but will it be always thus ? Now each of you sits under his vine with delight, and there is no carrying into captivity, no crying in your streets; but will such times last always ? Now you can hawk, hunt, swear, and drink, and then you think you are qualified like gentlemen ; but will this last always ? Suppose thou hadst a crown on thy head, how long wouldst thou wear it ? Suppose thou hadst a sceptre in thy hand, how long wouldst thou hold it? They are sick at Rome, and die in princes' courts, as well as at the spital; yea, kings themselves cannot keep their crowns on their heads, nor their heads on their shoulders, but must stoop when death strikes, and goas naked to their beds of dust, as other men; and in that day all their thoughts, their projects and their pleasures perish with them; only their guilt of their sins, which were the ladders, by which they did climb up to the top of their pleasures, the top of their honors, and preferments will dog them into another world. Hence said Abner to Joash, 2 Sam.ii. 26. " Knowest thou not that these things will be bitterness in the end?" You will now have your sweet meats, and your sweet drinks, your sweet pleasures and pastimes, let the minister say what he will, but do not you know that this will be bitterness in the end? In hell all the sugar will be melted off, wherein the pill of your sins and temptations is wrapt, and then the note you will sing will be that of the emperor, *O quantum ob quantillum!* O what an eternity of pain have I for an inch of pleasure, or an ell of sinful delight! As the malefactor said to his neighbour, dost thou envy me my grapes that I have stolen? Alas, they cost me dear, I must die for them! Ah envy not at the pleasures of a poor sinner, they will cost his soul dear one day. What doth Dives's wine-cellar advantage him now in hell, while he cries out for a cup of cold water, and cannot have it? O, Sirs, you cannot now conceive while you sit in health and ease, what different thoughts you will then have of a holy, and unholy life, and with what gripes of conscience will your undone souls look back on a life of mercy, thus basely, and blockishly slept away, dreamed and sinned away. I beseech you then, and that for your own sakes, that you would not for a few fleshly pleasures, which are passing away, incur the torments of hell, which shall never pass away.

III. Thirdly, I beseech you for Christ's sake. And methinks when I beg of you in Christ's name, and for Christ's sake, you should not say nay. " If you love me," saith

Christ keep my commandments," John xiv. 15. See with what persuasive rhetoric he presseth this duty. "If ye love me (saith he) do it." O Christians! what may not the love of Christ command you? If it were to lay down your blood for him, would you not do it? and will you not be persuaded to lay down your strifes and divisions, your animosities and corruptions for his sake?

As Absalom said to Husnai, 2 Sam. xvi. 17. "Is this thy kindness to thy friend?" Such a friend as Christ hath been, is, and ever will be? Certainly that indictment will one day be preferred against you, which the apostle pronounceth with tears in his eyes, Phil. iii. 18. "You are enemies to the cross of Christ;" as if he had said, Christ came to destroy the works of the devil, and you by your loose walkings destroy the works of Christ, the image of Christ, and the interest of Christ in the soul. Christ laid down his blood to purge you, and you unworthily lay down yourselves in sin to pollute you, and so become guilty of denying the Lord that brought you, and trampling under foot the blood of the covenant. What ear doth not tingle, and what heart doth not tremble at such a horrid and flagitious act? I beseech you then be tender of Christ's honour, and be holy for Christ's sake,* whose heart you see, or may see by what follows, is engaged and concerned to promote holiness among you.

Consider, 1. His strict command calls for it. 2. His fervent prayer implies it. 3. His holy example teacheth it.

First, I say his command calls for it, Mat. v. 16. "Let your light shine before men, that they may see your good works;" that is, lead such convincing lives, that the world may witness and certify with you, that you are certainly a choice generation; a seed which the Lord hath blessed. Here is a command, you see; now where is your obedience? Will you make conscience of it, or will you not? Will you swear allegiance to it, or will you

* Quod vos divites relinquam.

not? Shall it pass for an irrefragable rule of life, or shall it not?

It was Pompey's boast, that with a word or a nod, he could awe his soldiers to any thing; and shall God command, and go without? Shall God's word have less authority than Pompey's?

I read much of the blind obedience of the papists to their rulers, even in things scarce credible, but that themselves have published them.

One Messeus, a Franciscan, tumbled himself in the dirt, and crawled like a child, because that St. Francis told him, "that unless he became as a little child, he could not enter into the kingdom of heaven."

The Jesuits are so framed to obedience, that whatever service they are enjoined by their superiors, though never so abominable, they must accomplish it. Yea, if the blessed Virgin vouchsafe her presence to one of the brethren, if his superior call him, he must presently break from her, and go at his bidding; although it be on a bloody errand, and wondrous design, with a hundred more fopperies of his nature.

What do I reckon these for, but to assure you, that those who have paid such homage to man, will rise up one day out of their graves to condemn us, who are less careful in our obedience to God Almighty. They shut the eyes of reason to obey their earthly superiors, and we dispute, if not deny our allegiance to our heavenly Lawgiver.

God bids us believe, and we distrust. God bids us obey, and we dispute; God bids us "remember our Creator in the days of youth," and we forget him in our age. God bids us learn of him, to be meek and lowly, and we learn of the devil to be proud and haughty. God bids us be sober and watch unto prayer, and we surfeit with excess, and sleep at prayer. God bids us forbear, and forgive one another in love, and we reproach and persecute one another with much opposition and hatred. In a word, God bids us be content with what we have, and we unthankfully murmur for what we want.

Ah, sinners, God sees and hears you all this while, and his hand is setting down in the table book of his remembrance all your undutifulness and disobedience, and when the book shall be opened, how think you will these indictments be answered?

II. Secondly, Christ's fervent prayers call for holiness, John xxvii. 17. "Sanctify them through thy truth," saith he. Should you hear a minister with abundance of zeal press a duty upon his people in the pulpit, and as soon as he gets home, you should go under his closet window, and hear him hard at prayer, begging of God a blessing upon his labours that day, you would easily believe the minister was in earnest. So here, our Saviour hath no sooner done his sermon, but you find him at prayer. John xvii. 17. And what he most insisted on in the pulpit, that he enlargeth most on in his closet; "Father," saith he, " sanctify them."

III. Thirdly, as Christ's prayer, so his pattern and example shews his desire to have his people a holy people. Was not he a lover of holiness in others, and a true practiser of holiness himself? Was not he the Israelite indeed, in whom there was no guile, no sin, no spot? And why was he so? Doth he not tell you, John xiii. 15. "I have given you an example," saith he, " that you should do as I have done." He was content to have his honour laid in the dust, his credit or blood laid in the dust, but it was for an example of all self-denial to you. Again, he was content to take a towel and a bason in his hand to wash his disciples' feet, John iii.14. but it was for an example of humility to you. In a word, he was so heavenly upon earth, so mortified to all worldly interests, and lived so convincingly before men, that his very enemies were forced to own his divinity, and to say, that he could not possibly do such things, unless God were with him; now all this was for an example of holiness to you. "I have given you," saith he, " an example, that you should do as I have done."

O then set Christ in his holy example before you, (as one would set the person whose picture he intends to draw) and labour to draw every line in your life, according to your copy. O, this would be a sweet way indeed to maintain the power of holiness. When you are tempted to any vanity, or extravagancy, then set Christ before you in his holy walking, and ask thy soul, Am I in this speech like Christ? Do I in this action write after my copy? Did Christ, or would Christ, if he were to live again upon earth, do as I do, and live as I live? Would not he be more choice of his company? more watchful over his words than I am? Were ever cards and dice seen so frequently in his hands as in mine? Did he ever ruin his debtors by extracting his right, or defraud his creditors by detaining their rights? O friends, study Christ's life more, and you will sooner learn to amend your own.

Well, I will conclude this discourse with one word of counsel. Is it God's will that you should be a holy people? then let your wills be so too, and be holy in all manner of conversation.

The last words that Mr. Bolton spoke to his children on his death-bed, were these: " I charge you, my dear ones, as you will answer it at the day of judgment, that you live so, as that you meet me not at that time in a state of unregeneracy."

Beloved, I have not many words to speak to you, for the hour of my departure hasteneth; therefore, I will compose what I have to say, in this dying request. You and I like Elijah and Elisha, are at the point of parting; I do, therefore, require of you, and in the name of God conjure you, so to improve this sermon, this opportunity, this hour's discourse, that we may take comfort at our next meeting, and rejoice to see one another's face at the judgment day, which we shall never do, if we appear there in a sinful and unsanctified estate.

Oh that the Lord would make me a happy instrument to convey converting grace into your souls this day; so that as Samson slew more at his death, than he did all his life before, so I may save more with this dying speech, than ever I did with all that is gone before. I have read of a rich Florentine, who being to die, called his sons together, and thus bespoke them. " It much rejoiceth me, now upon my death-bed, to think that I shall leave you all wealthy. But oh, my friends, it would rejoice me more if now at my departure, I could leave you all gracious, and if before I die, I could see Jesus Christ to live in you."

Awake, awake, ye sons of sleep, and hear what concerns your peace, before the time come when you shall hear no more. Let not your hearts run after fields, and vineyards, houses and orchards, for before thy fruit be ripe, thy flesh may be rotten: before thy next harvest be ready for the sickle, thy soul may be ripe for judgment.

Up then and be doing! Thou knowest not what a punctilio thy time is reduced unto. Thou hast gone over some men's graves to-day, and it may be, others may go over thine to-morrow. Or, if God spare thee with life and health, yet if thou neglectest God's call this sabbath, God may neglect to call thee the next. It is well known how many merciful messages Pharaoh had brought him by Moses, and what fair and frequent warnings he had to amend his life; but when all this would not do, Moses took his leave, and he saw his face no more.

Beloved, I have appeared many a sabbath amongst you, and once again am I come as a collector, to gather souls for God, and to try how many hearts I can hug to heaven with me. Oh consider now in time, what you resolve on! Stand out against the offers of mercy this day, and God knows whether ever you may hear him again knocking at your doors upon the like errand. God makes short work with some in his judiciary proceedings. If he finds a repulse once, sometimes he departs and leaves that dismal curse behind him, Luke xiv. 24. " Not one of those that were bidden, and would not come shall ever taste of my supper." They were but once bid den, and for their very first denial, this curse is clapped upon their heads, " Not one of them shall taste of my supper." It is not said, they shall never come where the supper stands on the table; but they shall never taste it. Poor souls, you may sit under the ordinances, and you may come to sacraments, and sermons, where Christ is brought in, both as first and second course; but through the efficacy of this curse, never taste; why? because, " when I called (saith God) you refused, and when I stretched forth my hands, none regarded, therefore I will now give you to eat of the fruit of your own doings, and fill you with your own devices, Prov. i. 24, 31.

Therefore consider of it, and give up your names to God to-day, lest to-morrow be too late. His manna is ready if you come in time to gather it; but if you linger, he hath his sun to melt it away, and it is gone.

Thus have you had the first particular opened to you, and urged upon you, namely, " That it is God's will you should obey the command and live holy."

The next follows, which is this:

I. It is God's will you should bear the cross, and suffer patiently, 1 Pet. iii. 17. It is better, saith Peter, if the will of God be so, that ye suffer for well-doing, than for ill. Now, if the will of God be so some time, that you should suffer, albeit for well doing, then let your wills be so too, and quietly compose yourselves to a suffering condition.

It is said of the Israelites, that at the commandment of the Lord they journeyed, and at the commandment they pitched; whence it may be inferred, " that it is God that assigneth to us, and ordereth for us the several vicissitudes of fortune, and changes of condition." Our pitching here or there, is from a Providence, whether in a fair house, or a foul, in a great living, or a small, in a barren soil, or a fruitful, and wherever, or whatever it be, it is above our desert, and therefore should not fall below our thanks.

I read of one who was never the more proud when dignified with honour, nor never the less patient, when disgraced with slander. Oh this even temper, is an excellent temper, when a man can so eye his wants, as not to be puffed up with his receipts, and so eye his receipts, as not to be cast too much down in the sense of his wants. And this is that frame of spirit, which I would fain have both myself and you to come up to; and therefore if God please hereafter to make a gap in thy estate, let not that open a gap to discontent, but remember Job's carriage in the like case, and join with him in that penitential prostration of his, "I will bear the indignation of the Lord, for I have sinned against him." If God strike thee with dumbness, strike not thou God again with thy discontentedness, but remember speechless Zachary, and be content. If God open the mouths of thy enemies, or wicked neighbours against thee, do not thou open thy mouth against them, but think oft on David's words, " I opened not my mouth, said he, because thou didst it." Yet David opened not his mouth to recriminate them, nor vindicate himself, but took all in good part, because he knew that God did it. I shall now propound some considerations to contentment under the cross; I can only propound them, it is God that must prosper them to you.

1. Consider for your comfort, God will be with you in your troubles.

2. Consider, you shall be with God after your troubles.

First, God will be with you, Isa. xliii. 2. "When thou passest through the water, I will be with thee." Mind, I will be with thee; fear not drowning so long as God is in the ship.

Thou carriest Cæsar in thy bark, said the emperor to the trembling mariner, and therefore be not afraid. O Christian, thy God is with thee in a suffering time, and how canst thou be afraid of that condition wherein thou hast God's company? I will be with thee in six troubles, and in seven, saith the Lord, and surely it cannot be ill with that man, with whom God is. It is infinitely better to be able to say, God is with thee, than to say, peace is with thee, or health is with thee, or honour is with thee, or credit, or friends are with thee, for in these you have but some particular good, but in God you have all good; and this is the first, you have an excellent scripture for it, Heb. xiii. 5. "Be content with such things as you have, why? For I will never leave you, nor forsake you. Though your riches may leave you, and health may leave you; yet will not I.

Oh what an argument is this to force contentment in every condition, to consider that he will not leave us comfortless, but will come unto us! Cheer up then my drooping soul, thou shalt never want, so long as thy God hath it; for by the promise thou hast command of God's purse, and mayest be sure of his presence!

Let others repine, do thou rejoice, and let such as be without God in the world, shark and shift, live by their wits, but in all straits do thou live by faith.

O beloved, you know not how soon God may call for your comforts one after another, and bring you as he did his people Israel, out of a fat land, into a famishing wilderness, where no water is, no comfort is; what will you do in such a case as this? If you please, I will tell you: when your hearts fail you, and your friends thus fail you, let not your hearts fail you, nor your faith fail you, for you have a faithful God which will never fail you, but will be instead of all things to you, from himself alone.

As Joseph said to Pharaoh, "Without me God will provide an answer for Pharaoh." So may I say in this case; without silver, without gold, without fair houses and rich furniture, "God can provide for the welfare of his people." Though your means be gone, yet your God is not gone; and if you cannot be contented now, it will argue that it was not God, but your means that did content you then.

Well, this is the first. Consider God will be with thee in thy troubles, and that upon a two-fold account.

1. To behold thee.—2. To uphold thee.

I. First, to behold thee. God sees the wrongs, and hears the grievances you undergo from men; though your friends look off you, yet your God looks on you, Exod. iii. 17. I have seen, I have seen, saith God, the heavy burthens and taxations that my people undergo in Egypt. As if God had said thus, I have seen, and so seen as that my bowels are turned within me, and I can no longer hold my peace.

What a gracious God have we, that owns his people in such a low condition, wherein none will own them; for, saith God, " I have seen, I have surely seen the troubles of my people that be in Egypt." Fear not afflictions then, for they cannot chase God from us, nay, they are rather advantages, wherein God doth ordinarily discover himself most comfortably to us; which brings me to the second particular.

II. As God will be with you in your troubles to behold you, so, secondly, to uphold you. Cham looked on his father's nakedness and laughed, but God looks on a christian's trouble, and helps. The eyes of the Lord run to and fro, saith the prophet; what to do? To shew himself strong in the behalf of his people. Where God hath a seeing eye, there he hath a helping hand too, if man can but find a believing heart to lay hold upon it.

David is a witness of this truth, when he saith, in the day that I cried thou answeredst me, and gavest me strength in my soul; as if David had said, it is true, O Lord, thou assaultest me, and that is my trouble; but it is as true, that thou assistest me, and this is my comfort. " In the day that I cried unto thee, thou answeredst me, and gavest me strength in my soul."

Object. Aye, saith the scrupulous christian, would God do this for me? If he would put strength into my soul, strength of faith, strength of patience, strength of grace, then I should bid a freer welcome to the cross when it comes; but, alas! Instead of this strength you speak of I find nothing but weakness, a weak faith, a weak assurance, weak patience; all weak.

Answ. I answer briefly, hast thou not strong grace? And doth that discourage thee? It may be thou art not tried with strong afflictions, let this quiet thee. Hast thou not as much patience as another? It may be thou hast not yet as much need of it as others. Their patience is greater than thine, because their troubles are greater than thine. In a word, thou saidst thou hast not a martyr's faith; it may be thou needest it not yet, because thou hast not a martyr's fire. A weak faith may serve for a light cross. When God calls thee to hotter services of christianity, fear not but he will be at thy back, not only to behold thee, but as you have heard, to uphold thee, 2 Cor. xv. As the sufferings of Christ abound in us (saith Paul) so also our consolations abound in Christ. See here, as men lay on troubles, so God lays in comforts. Hence it was that David's heart did not fail him, when all his friends forsook him, 1 Sam. xxx. And David encouraged himself in his God, saith the text. It was sad with him at this time, Ziklag was burnt, his wives taken captive, he lost all, and like to have lost the hearts of his soldiers too, (for they speak of stoning him.) In this condition that David was now in, he turned his face from the creature, looked up to heaven, and encouraged himself in his God. When all other visible helps shrunk from him, then his God clave to him, and he to his God.

Oh christian, live upon the comforter himself, in the want of other comforts. If thou canst not say, that God is thy God, it is thy sin; but if thou canst say, he is thy God, and yet not content, it is thy shame; for if God, an all-sufficient God, will not suffice thee, will not content thee, sure nothing will.

II. Secondly, you shall be with God after your troubles. This day shalt thou be in Paradise, said Christ to the present thief. As if he should have said, I am with thee, bearing the cross, and thou shalt be anon with me wearing the crown, and therefore be satisfied. A parallel scripture to this you have in Rom. viii. 17. "If we suffer with him, we shall reign with him," said Paul. Who will not now willingly act a sufferer's part awhile, when he remembers what a blessed exit his sufferings shall have at last. Daniel was brought out of the dungeon, and immediately preferred at court. Joseph, of a slave, became the chief man of the kingdom. Ah, what a banquet did God provide for Paul and Silas in prison; and Jacob being banished from his father's house, what a comfortable vision saw he at Bethel! Better provision sure, than if he had been sitting at home at his plentiful table.

But albeit the Lord treats not all his children as he did these; yet are they all sure of his comfort. Glory shall be the end of their sufferings, and heaven their habitation for evermore. They have Christ's certificate under his own hand, Rom. i. " If you suffer with me, ye shall reign with me.

Oh that so much of heaven were revealed and unveiled to you, as to see something of those eternal joys, which they that be dead in the Lord, have received for a few momentary sufferings in their life-time; hungry Lazarus feasting, lame Mephibosheth dancing, and all the college of martyrs and confessors striking up their harps, and chaunting forth that epiphanema of praise, Rev. vii. 10. "Salvation, salvation unto our God, which sits upon the throne, and to the Lamb for ever!"

Oh who would not rejoice in their sufferings, with such music in their ears, and such a sight as this in their eye!

Let this then beget contentment, it is ill with such at present, but good news will be next. God's rod, like Jonathan's rod, hath honey, nay, heaven at the end. Look up, christians, and see, that the cloud, while dropping on you, is rolling over you; stand but in the shower awhile, and fair weather will be next, even an everlasting sunshine of glory. " When you have suffered awhile, saith Peter, 1 Pet. v. 10. the Lord will make you perfect; that is, your sufferings are not a killing you, but a perfecting you. Poets tell us that the hill of Olympus is so high, that on the top of it is always a calm. Beloved, it is hard climbing up the rocky and rugged hill of the cross, but when you are once come up to the top, you shall be in a calm, and say as Peter did on the mount, " It is good to be here," good to get heaven at any rate.

And this is the second argument to work contentment under the cross. God will not only come to you in your troubles, but you shall go to God after your troubles. God will make your afflictions to be inlets into glory, and your cross a ladder to climb up to heaven; and, therefore, fear not afflictions; they are not such bugbears as the flesh fancieth them to be. Which seriously thought on, would be enough to make thy soul ambitious of suffering, saying as one did once, I am afflicted, till I be afflicted.

A child that is going home will never complain of bad way. O Christian, thou art going home to heaven in a way of suffering; every affliction, every cross, sets thee one step forward to thy Father's house, and wilt thou complain of bad way? One beam of God's face in heaven, will dry up all thy tears. Hence saith the holy prophet, Rev. xxi. "There shall be no more death, nor sorrow, nor crying, neither shall there be any more pain, for all these things are passed away."

Thus have I given you two helping considerations to melt your wills into obedience to God's will, and to run the race that is set before you with patience. Therefore I shall be at the pains to help you a little further.

Consider, 1. The cross is necessary, and must be born. —2. Your cross is easy, and may be born.

I, First, I say it is necessary. God hath laid it on, and who can take it off? As Balaam said, " God hath blessed, and I cannot reverse it." So may I say, God hath crossed, and thou canst not repeal it; and, therefore, let it be

borne bravely. Now it is unavoidably necessary upon a double account.
1. In regard of the precept.
2. In regard of the means.

First, You have a precept for it, Luke ix. 35. " He that will be my disciple, let him take up his cross and follow me."

Secondly, It is necessary as a means to the obtaining the end. Christ, the Captain of our salvation, was made perfect through sufferings, and so must we. Heb. ii. 10, " Ought not Christ first to have suffered, and then to have entered into his rest?" Saith Luke xxiv. 26. yes he ought, and so ought christians. For, " through many tribulations we must enter into the kingdom of heaven."

A hot burning furnace was a pleasant path, in which the three children walked to their celestial country, while Belshazzar's coaches like a sedan, conveyed quickly into the dwellings of furies, and habitations of devils. A fiery chariot hoisted up Elijah to heaven, whereas a feather-bed ushered Dives to hell. Therefore be not afraid of suffering for God, for he can give a happy issue when he pleaseth.

II. Again, as the cross is necessary, and must be borne, so it is easy and may be borne. And that
1. Absolutely.
2. Comparatively.

First, Absolutely, and in itself. Hence said Christ, " Take my yoke upon you, for my yoke is easy, and my burden is light." Never then call that cross heavy, which Christ hath called easy and light.

Art thou pained with the gout or colic? That is a light burthen; and the boys of Spain bore so much, and more without complaining that their cross was heavy; for I read that they would at their altars, endure whipping and scourging till their very entrails saw the light through their torn flesh without crying.

These children rejoiced in their sufferings like men, and this was their glory. But you that are men, you weep in your sufferings like children, surely this is your shame.

Again, are you sick? This is a light burthen, and so light, that the least child in the town can bear it. In a word, whatever thy cross be, if it be Christ's cross, it is a light one, and, therefore, not to be complained of. "Take my yoke upon you (saith he) for my yoke is easy, and my burden is light." And, indeed, there is no burthen can truly be called, or by christians can be counted heavy but sin; and this is a burthen which makes the whole creation groan under it. Take away sin, and a man's life will be no longer a burthen to him. This is the heavy burthen; as for other burthens, they are light. And that first, absolutely. Secondly, they are light comparatively.

1. If you compare them with the pains which Christ endured;

Or, secondly, with the pains of hell which you deserved.

First, If you compare them with the pains that Christ endured, look but into Isa. liii. and you shall see that whole chapter spent in relating that bloody tragedy which Christ acted for the salvation of the world. "He was despised and rejected of men (saith the prophet). He hath borne our griefs, and carried our sorrows," verse 4. "He was wounded for our transgressions, and bruised for our iniquities." And thus the text runs on in tears. O what a suffering race did he run, that he might overtake us before we got to hell!

Methinks I see what haste he makes on this suffering errand, and hear him cry to his Father while yet afar off, "Lo, I come to do thy will, O my God." See here how the heart of Christ, like an echo, rebounds to his Father's call.

When his Father spoke to him to undertake the redemption work of saving a lost and undone world, he did not reluct nor answer with Moses, Exod. iv. 3. "I pray thee send some other on this message; but, lo, I come (saith Christ) to do thy will, O my God."

And now, christians, tell me, doth not thy dear Lord deserve thus much from thee, to endure a little for his sake, who hath endured so much for thine? What though thy afflictions cost thee tears? Christ's afflictions cost him blood; and though thou losest the comforts of this life, this is nothing comparable to Christ's loss, who lost life itself.

Ah! what loss can match this loss? and whose sufferings like his sufferings? Dost thou sigh under the sense of thy grievance thus, my soul is sorrowful? But Christ went further, and said, my soul is sorrowful to death. Mat. xxvi. 38. Dost thou cry, "My God, my God, why hast thou *afflicted* me?" But Christ said more, " My God, my God, why hast thou *forsaken* me?" Consider this, and leave complaining.

Secondly, Your cross is easy, if you compare it with the pains of hell, which you have deserved. Ah! there is not one of you but would be in hell before to-morrow, if God should give you your due. There are many there, for those very sins which you live in. Dives is in hell for making an idol of his wealth; have none of you done so? Haman is in hell for pride; and are you not proud? Sodom is in hell for contempt of the prophets of the Lord, and for neglecting the day of peace, and the day of grace; the day of God's patience and striving with them; and is not this England's sin at this very day? The old world is burning in hell, for burning in lust on earth; and was this sin ever more predominant than in this juncture of time? Herod hath been lying in hell a thousand and six hundred years, for taking John Baptist's head from him.

Ah, England! England! Is not this thy charge? Hath not this been thy practice these late years? And art thou not plunged deep in thy own blood-guiltiness? Herod did but cut one man's head off, and he is gone to hell for it. Oh what a hell mayest thou look for, who hast got so many heads, and drunk the blood of thousands of the saints, and faithful servants of the Most High? What city is there wherein there is not some noble births, some of England's worthies sacrificed to the bloody itch, and Bedlam surges of a civil war? (I had almost said of an uncivil peace.) What town is there wherein there are not some families repeating over the lamentations of Jeremiah, and saying, "I am the man that hath seen affliction by the rod of his wrath." Sion doth mourn, Judah is gone into captivity, the prophets sigh, the sheep are scattered, and woe is my soul because of murderers!

How many of the dear children of God are crying for bread? (for the powerful preaching of the word amongst them) and there is no bread to be given them, nor the pleasant voice of their faithful ministers to be heard amongst them; and they are left to lament over their silenced ministers, as King Joash wept over the dying prophet, 2 Kings xiii. 14. "O my father, my father, the chariot of Israel, and the horsemen thereof! Will not God visit for these? Will he not be avenged on such a nation as this? Yes, yes, he will; Israel's woe may be England's warning, Amos iv. "Thus will I do unto thee; and because I will do thus unto thee, therefore prepare thy heart to meet thy God, O England!" But this is a digression.

That which I am to speak to is this, you are to bear the cross contentedly, because whatever you do endure, it is nothing to what you deserve, or to what the damned in hell endure.

In hell there is a variety of torments, and extremity of torments, and eternity of torments; not one way, but a thousand ways to make a poor soul miserable, everlastingly miserable? And who can bear variety? Who can bear eternity? Who can bear eternity of torments? Yet all this you must bear, if ever it be your lot to lie in hell.

Here it may be you want one mercy, but blessed be God you have another in lieu of it; you want health, but you want not friends; you want money, but you want not a Christ; you want an estate, but you want not a contented mind. Though your life be not absolutely made up of comforts, which is your misery; yet it is not altogether composed of crosses; and is not this a mercy?

And thus is your life checquered with blacks and whites, so that you have never such cause of mourning, but withal you have some just ground of rejoicing; but in hell there is nothing to be seen, but objects of sorrow; and nothing to be heard except inducements to grief; not one merry day, and one sad; not one hour of pain, and another of ease; not one cross, and one comfort; but all crosses and curses do meet there like lines in their proper centre. Compare now your sufferings with the sufferings of hell, and let this quiet you.

That school-boy thinks he gets well off, when deserving a rod, he escapes with a reproof. What a mercy then may you count it, that when you deserve a curse from Christ, you escape with the cross of Christ; afflicted on earth, when you might justly be tormented in hell.

Think of it then, are you corrected? "It is the Lord's mercy that you are not consumed." Hath God taken away your health from you? It is well you escape so, he might have taken away your life from you, and your Christ from you, and where had you been then?

In a word, how much soever God takes from you, it is less than you owe him; and how little soever he leaves you, it is more than he owes you. Therefore instead of murmuring that your condition is so ill, bless God that it is no worse, saying with Ezra, Ez. ix. 13. "Thou, O Lord, hast punished us less than our iniquities have deserved."

THE END.

www.ingramcontent.com/pod-product-compliance
Lightning Source LLC
Chambersburg PA
CBHW050425240426
43661CB00055B/2272